DANCING REVELATIONS

Alvin Ailey's

Embodiment

of African

American

Culture

OXFORD
UNIVERSITY PRESS

DANCING REVELATIONS

T H O M A S   F.   D E F R A N T Z

OXFORD
UNIVERSITY PRESS

Oxford University Press, Inc., publishes works that further
Oxford University's objective of excellence
in research, scholarship, and education.

Oxford   New York
Auckland   Cape Town   Dar es Salaam   Hong Kong   Karachi
Kuala Lumpur   Madrid   Melbourne   Mexico City   Nairobi
New Delhi   Shanghai   Taipei   Toronto

With offices in
Argentina   Austria   Brazil   Chile   Czech Republic   France   Greece
Guatemala   Hungary   Italy   Japan   Poland   Portugal   Singapore
South Korea   Switzerland   Thailand   Turkey   Ukraine   Vietnam

Copyright © 2004 by Oxford University Press

First published in 2004 by Oxford University Press, Inc.
First published as an Oxford University Press paperback, 2006

www.oup.com

Oxford is a registered trademark of Oxford University Press

Library of Congress Cataloging-in-Publication Data
DeFrantz, Thomas
Dancing revelations : Alvin Ailey's embodiment of African American
culture / Thomas F. DeFrantz.
    p. cm.
Includes bibliographical references and index.
ISBN-13 978-0-19-530171-4 (pbk.)
ISBN 0-19-515419-3; 0-19-530171-4 (pbk.)
1. Ailey, Alivn.   2. Dancers—United States—Biography.   3. Choreographers—
United States—Biography.   4. Alvin Ailey American Dance Theater.
5. African American dance.   I. Title.
GV1785.A38 D44   2003
792.8'028'092—dc21   2002156670

Credits:
Photographs: frontispiece and pages 5, 8, 19, 47, 63, 95, 101 courtesy and copyright by
Jack Mitchell; cover illustration and pages 11, 12, courtesy and copyright by J. Peter
Happel; page 43 courtesy Harvard Theater Collection, The Houghton Library,
copyright by Alix Jeffry; page 55 courtesy and copyright by Howard Morehead; pages
123, 145, 149, 175, courtesy Time-Life, copyright by Martha Swope; pages 126, 129, 183
courtesy and copyright by Rosemary Winckley; pages 139, 207 courtesy of the Dance
Collection, New York Public Library; page 158 courtesy and copyright by Judy
Cameron; pages 165, 167, 194, 215, 224 courtesy and copyright by Johan Elbers; page 186
courtesy and copyright by Fred Fehl; page 210 courtesy and copyright by Jack
Vartoogian; page 237 courtesy and copyright by Josef Astor. All other photographs
author's collection and courtesy of Alvin Ailey American Dance Theater archives.
Lyrics: "He Ain't Heavy," copyright 1969, renewed 1997, Harrison Music Corp. and
Jenny Music, all rights reserved, used by permission; "A Song For You," copyright
1970, Irving Music, Inc., all rights reserved, used by permission.

9   8   7   6   5   4   3   2   1

Printed in the United States of America
on acid-free paper

*To **Alvin Ailey**, who speaks to us all, still.*

A friend asked me if I liked Ailey's work; I blanched at the question. I could not have spent years thinking through Ailey's achievement, hunkered over newspaper clippings and programs in an airless room at the Alvin Ailey Dance Foundation offices, viewing this work repeatedly on videotape and, thankfully, in live performances, without an enormous admiration and respect for his accomplishment. This study is a testament to that respect.

This study also provides a stabilizing narrative of Ailey's creative work, one that places him at the center of a consideration of concert dance practice in the United States. Since he showed his first choreography in the 1950s, professional dance critics have consistently found fault with Ailey's process and product. My project does not involve rehearsing the "problems" in Ailey's work as a choreographer, nor am I looking for chinks in the armor of a widely celebrated African American cultural institution. Rather, following art historian Richard J. Powell's summation, I hope to provide an interpretation of Ailey's work that acknowledges its particular aesthetics and cultural processes in formation "from an *a priori* position of cultural wholeness, conscious historicity, and an inherent and unapologetic humanity."[1] This study follows a lead set by Ailey himself in its variety of approaches and propositions about the place of concert dance in contemporary African American life.

Above all, Ailey was aware of his position and potential as an African American man born in working-class, segregated, Depression-era Texas. To understand Ailey's achievement, we must look to the world he inherited and the degrees to which he transformed that world through his work. I do not compare Ailey's work to that of Martha Graham, George Balanchine, or Merce Cunningham as if Ailey, like them, had been born into an educated, middle-class white milieu. If Ailey made dances that were important to him, we must be willing to look to the particular cultural processes and social realities that inspired him. Ailey's dances may speak *to* a wide, global audience, but they speak *from* an African American ethos that remains insubstantially documented.

Ailey choreographed more than seventy-five works, most of which exist in the repertories of one or more dance companies or have been videotaped and archived at the New York Public Library at Lincoln Center. I consider underlying compositional structures in relation to the overall dance event. To better understand the role of interaction between Ailey and his dancers, I have paid close attention to published interviews, oral histories, and televised accounts given by dancers who have both worked with Ailey and danced his choreographies. In addition, I conducted several interviews with former Ailey company dancers.

The study is organized according to the parallel development of Ailey's choreographic themes and his company. Theoretical concerns are developed in reference to particular dance works or performances. Of special significance to this study are modifications Ailey effected to his own choreography. For example, *Revelations*, his signature work, has endured three distinct guises in its nearly forty-year history. An analysis of changes in its appearance points to changes in Ailey's conception of his company and its purpose as a bearer of African American culture.

I take the time to describe several of Ailey's works so that the reader might sense what I see as I appreciate these compositions. The limits of movement description may become readily apparent, but I find this technique useful, especially to discussions of work long gone or not easily accessible to a general audience. The descriptions also intend to give the impression of how these dances "feel" to a dance researcher at the beginning of the twenty-first century.

I rely on critical accounts contemporary to the premieres of Ailey's choreography for at least two reasons: to provide the reader with a sense of what writers present at performances chose to document of their immediate opinions of Ailey's work, and to offer a sense of the strangely consistent degradation Ailey suffered at the pens of some of those critics. This study does not concern itself primarily with the divide between the largely white New York dance critics cohort and Ailey's largely African American company and aesthetic interest. But that divide surely did exist, and according to Ailey's allies, the virulent attacks writers routinely launched against his enterprise troubled him deeply. Certainly, negative critical opinions of Ailey's choreography or company are not intentionally racist simply because they come from white writers; at times, negative opinions from any quarter are helpful to the process of improving performance. But, as the several examples of negative criticism in the manuscript that follow bear out, many of Ailey's (white) critics engaged a purposefully dismissive and derisive tone that deserves more explication than this text allows.

In addition to historical analysis, the manuscript includes a series of short, self-contained essays that constitute a counternarrative to the main body of writing. I intend for these breaks to resonate with black musical practice, in which an insistent beat is interrupted by a flash of contradictory rhythmic ideas. For me, the break is the most significant gesture of African American performance, as it contains both the tie to a ubiquitous rhythmic flow and the potential for complete anarchy and disruption. The break creates a liminoid space that allows listeners a place to enter the musical dance. I hope that the manuscript's literary breaks will function similarly to periodically revive the interests of readers who become bored with the cataloguing of Ailey's life work.

This manuscript veers toward academic language at times, but attempts to resist staying there for long. Following Ailey's lead, my effort questions the nature of the political and aesthetic in dance performance, but in language that might be widely understood. My hope is that this manuscript might reach anyone who has enjoyed a performance by the Alvin Ailey American Dance Theater and inspire that reader to think more deeply about the ways that performance has grown from a rich and fertile African American ground.

This manuscript has benefited from numerable influences, direct and indirect. I thank everyone who offered encouragement and criticism along the way. I thank the faculty of the Department of Performance Studies at New York University, especially Professor James N. Amankulor, who constantly reminded me to write within the African American grain and to honor all the deities—plus one more. Marcia B. Siegel shared of herself again and again to push me toward thinking critically and carefully about dance and its affect. Simply put, she is without peer as a critic and mentor.

The dissertation that gave rise to this book was funded by a Ford Foundation Fellowship for Dissertation Writing. Additional support to revise the manuscript came from a Provost's Junior Faculty leave and an Old Dominion leave from the Massachusetts Institute of Technology. This project was also supported by an unspeakably opulent residency at the Rockefeller Foundation's Bellagio Study and Conference Center; thanks to Gianna Celli and her staff for their superb efforts. I also thank my fellow residents from the summer of 1999, whose ideas added much to the structure of the present volume, including Neelan and Sithi Tiruchelvam, Ella Shohat and Robert Stam, Sissela Bok, and especially Nancy Hicks Maynard. Many thanks to James Gibson for referring me to the Rockefeller Study Center in the first place.

I thank everyone at the Ailey organization who helped this project along over the years, including the many students and guest faculty in the various dance history courses I've taught there. I especially thank Denise Jefferson, who first unlocked the door to the Ailey archive for me and ignited a passion that led to this book; Sylvia Waters, who shared stories and supportive energy at every juncture; and several individuals in the Ailey Press and Public Relations Office, including Molly Browning, Donna Wood Sanders, Cynthia Martin, and Jodi Krizer and their many unflappable associates: Vanessa Jordan, Minda Logan, Delva Haynes, Rubeny Hoyne, Lynette Rizzo, Sergey Gordeev, and Tara Wasserman. Thanks also to Anna Marie Forsythe, James Paulson, Karen Arceneau, Sathi Pillai, Stephen Brown, Samuel Coleman, and Amadea Edwards. And, of course, many, many thanks to Sharon Luckman, executive director of Dance Theater Foundation, Inc., and to Judith Jamison, artistic director of the Alvin Ailey American Dance Theater, for their support of this project.

Among American dance history and theory scholars, I thank my colleagues Constance Valis Hill, Susan Manning, Gay Morris, David Gere, Robert Tracy, Anne Cooper Albright, Ananya Chatterjea, Anna Scott, and especially Richard C. Green III, John O. Perpener III, and Veta Goler for their responses and prodding. Brenda Dixon Gottschild is a divine inspiration in person and in her writing; thank you for taking an interest in this work. C. S'thembile West graciously read portions of this manuscript in its earliest form and commented with clarity and enthusiasm that is very much appreciated. Richard Long, Beth Genne, and Lynn Garafola each allowed me to present sections of this manuscript in public lectures; I thank them as well as the staff and students at Emory University, the University of Michigan, and Barnard College for those opportunities.

Several librarians and archives contributed time and effort to answer my queries. At the Mid-Atlantic Black Archives, I extend warm thanks to Cynthia Hardy and especially Bill Livingston, who aided in crucial research for this project. The staff at the New York Public Library for the Performing Arts and the Schomburg Center for Research on Black Culture also provided invaluable research assistance.

Among many dance artists who shaped this manuscript directly and indirectly, I thank Sarita Allen, April Berry, Delores Browne, Donald Byrd, and especially Louis Johnson, whose comments pushed my thinking about Ailey's achievement. James Truitte and Marilyn Borde gave rounded depictions of Ailey's life and motivations to me, and each became friends along the way. Jimmy, we all miss you. Mickey, you're the best!

My colleagues at MIT, Stanford, and NYU have provided great support to me and, by extension, this project; I offer many thanks to Mary Cabral, John Lyons, Anne Richards, Pamela Hamada, and Priscilla Cobb, as well as to Alan Brody, Peter Child, Ellen Harris, Janet Sonenberg, and Brenda Cotto-Escalera, who have been especially supportive of this project. Dean Philip Khoury of MIT's School of Humanities, Arts, and Social Sciences is a tremendous ally to any junior faculty member; thank you for your sustained support.

Portions of this manuscript have appeared elsewhere. Sections of "Black Atlantic Dance" in chapter 10 originally appeared as "Foreword: Black Bodies Dancing Black Culture—Black Atlantic Transformations," in *Embodying Liberation: The Black Body in American Dance,* edited by Dorothea Fischer-Hornung and Alison D. Goeller (Hamburg: Lit Verlag, 2001 Forecaast 4). Discussions of official African American culture in chapter 3 originally appeared in "Stoned Soul Picnic: Alvin Ailey and the Struggle to Define Official Black Culture," in *Soul: Black Power, Politics, and Pleasure,* edited by Monique Guillory and Richard C. Green (New York: New York University Press, 1998). A discussion of early African American male presence in concert dance in chapter 3 appeared in "Simmering Passivity: The Black Male Body in Concert Dance," in *Moving Words: New Directions in Dance Criticism,* edited by Gay Morris (New York: Routledge, 1996). I also thank the many photographers whose work greatly enhances this volume.

Finally, I extend profound gratitude to my parents and family, who first encouraged my interests in the performing arts. To my partner, Christopher Pierce, who alternately calmed and cajoled when necessary, what dance could be of more interest than one we enjoy together? I think, none.

C O N T E N T S

Introduction

Alvin Ailey (1931–89) is arguably the most important black American choreographer in the short history of modern dance. He created a body of dance works that shaped African American participation in American modern dance during the thirty-year period before his death. The company he founded in 1958, the Alvin Ailey American Dance Theater, has grown from a small pick-up company of seven or eight dancers to a large, carefully managed, internationally renowned enterprise including several ensembles of dancers and a thriving school. This study of Ailey's dances illuminates the dual achievement of Ailey as an artist and as an arts activist committed to developing an African American presence in concert dance.

As my title suggests, I propose that Ailey encoded aspects of African American life and culture in concert dance. These "aspects"—aesthetic imperatives termed "Africanisms" by cultural theorists[1]—flourish in the movements of dancers Ailey worked with; they are also embedded within the very choreography Ailey made. They emerge in compositional strategies, choices of music, structuring of performance, casting, and approach to company operations. This study explores particular examples of how Ailey captured black experience in terms of concert dance.

Ailey's choreographic work and company outreach operations, however, do not encompass a universal "whole" of black experience. As cultural theorist Paul Gilroy has argued, there are no "homogenous and unchanging" black communities whose political and economic interests are "readily knowable and easily transferred from everyday life into their expressive cultures."[2] Ailey's work does not substitute itself for African American cultural processes, nor does his company's success offer a peremptory model for the creation and dissemination of performing arts in the African American grain. This volume considers how Alvin Ailey achieved his particular status as an icon in dance, and how he managed to link that status to his cultural motivations and interests.

Ailey's formal training began at Lester Horton's Hollywood studio in 1949. Horton had created a theater and school committed to dances performed by his own multiracial company, which included later Ailey associates Carmen de Lavallade, Don Martin, Joyce Trisler, and James Truitte. Horton's brand of modern dance was based on his personal interpretation of techniques he researched from traditions of Asian, Native American, and African diaspora cultures. Horton stressed the essentials of stage design, music awareness, costuming, and storytelling in his choreography, and the performance style he taught at the school was strictly theatrical.

Ailey began his dance career in the incredibly optimistic New York dance world of the 1950s, an era marked by a seemingly contradictory modern dance mandate of personalized dance expression within an accessible, theatrical style. A background in explicitly theatrical dance allowed him the latitude to explore the expressive potential of several choreographic techniques. His output includes ballets on pointe, modern dance works, and staging for musical theater pieces.[3] His dances privilege no form over another, stressing instead a facile interplay among genres. His theatrical tastes, combined with a variety of technique training undertaken at the Horton School, the Dunham School, and in classes taught by Hanya Holm, Doris Humphrey, Anna Sokolow, and Charles Weidman, contributed to a playful sense of movement-style juxtaposition in several works. *Blues Suite* (1958), for example, contains sections of early twentieth-century social dances, Horton dance technique, Jack Cole–inspired jazz dance, and ballet partnering. This study assumes, above all, that the fluidity Ailey indulged in his artistry and company practices stem from African diaspora aesthetic practices brought to bear on the enterprise of professional American concert dance.

Long before Ailey's work could be interpreted as an embodiment of African American culture, modern dance had been an expressive form nurtured by individuals for the collective soul of a gathered audience. In the 1930s and 1940s dancers and choreographers Pearl Primus, Asadata Dafora, and Katherine Dunham realized that African American cultural values emphasize the participatory nature of performance. For them, theatrical dance offered a way into the artistic imagination of black people grappling with the legacy of colonialist encounter. The concert stage provided a point of entry to a dialogue about dual processes of entertainment and enlightenment, expressed in terms of modern dance.

Building on the work of these black choreographers and company directors,

Alvin Ailey's company stretched the boundaries of the audience that can effectively share in the experience of modern dance. According to one estimate, the Alvin Ailey American Dance Theater has been seen by some 15 million people worldwide.[4] Still, the company draws from an African American wellspring through strategies of personnel recruitment and base operations in New York, Baltimore, and Kansas City. This feat of vast appeal, sustained across two generations of American modern dance, is discussed here in terms of its relationship to Ailey's choreography and its performance.

This study also examines how concert dance performance conveys meaning to its audience, considering bodily communication and the expressivity of gesture. Ailey's choreographic success stems from his ability to communicate effectively with a broad audience. His dances confirm the durability of particular Africanist aesthetics, including a reliance on individual invention in the moment—the "flash of the spirit"—and call-and-response connection to the gathered audience. Ailey's dances also offer vibrant examples of a choreographic method concerned with structure and style. Although he never repeated himself in terms of musical selection, costuming, or mise-en-scène, the whole of his output holds pronounced structural similarities. A careful look at Ailey's range of choreography illuminates how he intended to speak to his audiences and what sorts of stories he felt compelled to tell.

As a financially solvent arts organization cited repeatedly for its artistic excellence, the Ailey company holds special importance for concert dance worldwide. Continuing vigorously into the twenty-first century as a healthy multi-million-dollar operation inflected as incontrovertibly "black," the company offers a valuable model for the consideration of expressive commerce and creativity in black American life. Shrewd business management combined with an extraordinary artistic product have allowed the operation to achieve unprecedented celebrity as dance ambassadors steeped in African American cultural processes and available to a world audience. The company holds an even greater iconic status among portions of its black audiences, enacting "the custodianship of the racial group's most intimate self-identity." As in cultural theorist Paul Gilroy's formulation of the Black Atlantic, Ailey company performances make explicit "hidden links between blacks" even as they ground "an oppositional aesthetic constituted around our phenotypical difference from 'white' ideals of beauty and a concept of the body in motion which is the residue of our African cultures."[5] Ailey's choreography reveals beauty as a structural component of African American creative expression in dance gestures recognized and supported by both an international black audience and others.

Ailey's choreography offers vibrant examples of black subjectivity on public stages. His dances and dancers repeatedly engage the "act of being black" as they enact Africanist performance imperatives outlined in 1966 by Robert Farris Thompson, including percussive attack, apart-playing, call-and-response, multiple meter, and an overall "cool" demeanor.[6] Looking at Ailey's choreography, I am mindful of dance theorist Susan Foster's observation that "traditional dance studies . . . have privileged the thrill of the vanished performance over the

enduring impact of the choreographic intent."[7] Although this volume documents the whole of Ailey's choreographic output, it does not intend to whet an
appetite for performances long gone. Instead, it considers the overall impact of
Ailey's method to stage a black body as "capable of generating ideas . . . a body
that initiates as well as responds,"[8] to stage African American culture as a paradigm capable of representing high modernity. Indeed, Ailey's choreography and
company operations offer a sweeping variety of roles and personas for black
bodies and African American culture onstage, in the audience, in the classroom,
and behind the scenes.

Performance theory invites an evaluation of Ailey's choreography not simply as dance artifact, but as the focus of a larger experience. For instance, Ailey's
dances infuse the Western-defined concert dance event with African-inspired
participation. Different audiences experience Ailey's work in substantially different ways, and in much of his choreography Ailey exploited the tension between his audience's expectations and his dancers' abilities. This compositional
strategy emerged as a cornerstone of a system of performance that challenged
both a core African American audience and cultural outsiders. Ailey's choreographic themes, phrase structuring, uses of music, character, and narrative can
be understood in terms of their efforts to create a multifaceted representation of
African American experience.

Beyond choreographic analysis, this volume employs a number of analyti-
cal prisms through which to consider Ailey's achievement. I propose that these
several perspectives interweave in practice, that it is pointless to consider Ailey's
choreography *solely* as an arrangement of physical motion, or as a representation of gender or sexuality, or as a depiction of beauty or class mobility, or as
an arrangement of popular youth narratives. Ailey's choreography and company
operations offer an unusual nodule of everyday American politics in internationally recognized aesthetic action. No single, or indeed double way of looking at performances by the Alvin Ailey American Dance Theater sustains pri-
macy for long. For example, just when *Revelations* seems to be telling a story of
ethnic faith as movement abstraction in its first section, the work shifts to physically enact a waterside baptism, explicitly Christian in principle but Afro-
Caribbean in practice. At this point, gender emerges as a sure organizing feature
of the dance, as a female devotional leader with an umbrella orchestrates the
baptism, but the theatricality of expansive blue silk "waterways" intrudes on the
reading of the sexes. For a time, the audience is asked to consider the global cir-
culation of theatrical convention, as the silk streams, clearly borrowed from certain Asian theater traditions, reflect Ailey's initial theater training in California.
And surely the musical choices in this dance alone offer a methodology for map-
ping African American culture through time, in their various vocal arrangements and instrumental accompaniments. *Revelations* must also be considered
in terms of its material performance, that is, how audiences witnessing the work
imagine it to embody African American experience, and how that impression
forecloses its expressive possibilities.

This analysis places Ailey's work at the center of an Africanist aesthetic of dance making that emerged with the civil rights movement in the 1960s, an aesthetic that has defined "blackness" as surely as it has reflected its qualities and encouraged others to consider them. The financially solvent Ailey company stands as testament to the commercial viability of an African American aesthetic in the performing arts. This study lays out how the Ailey legacy contains cultural signposts that consistently renew performance.

This suite explores motivations and emotions of Negro religious

music which, like its heir, the Blues, takes many forms —"true

spirituals" with their sustained melodies, ring-shouts,

song-sermons, gospel songs, and holy blues — songs of trouble,

of love, of deliverance.

— Ailey program note, Kaufmann Concert Hall YM-YWHA,

    31 January 1960

Revelations 1962

Alvin Ailey intended for *Revelations* (31 January 1960) to be the second part of a larger, evening-length survey of African American music that would "show the coming and the growth and reach of black culture."[1] Designed to suggest a chronological spectrum of black religious music from the sorrow songs to gospel rock, *Revelations* mapped rural southern spirituality onto the concert dance stage.

For years American modern dance had searched for ways to connect with an expanded general audience. Ailey's dance confirmed that folk materials, carefully mediated by principles of modern dance composition, could retain the immediacy of their sources in the transformation to concert dance. The largest implications of Ailey's success for concert dance lay in the expansion of the audience that could enjoy its performance and the expansion of themes available to choreographers working in this idiom.

Determined to draw a lasting portrait of certain historical markers of African American culture, Ailey chose for *Revelations* the spirituals, or sorrow songs. Among the most prominent creations of nineteenth-century African American folk and the "prototype music of black religion" that evolved from black rebellion, spirituals release a central passion for freedom subversively contained in simple texts of Bible stories.[2] Rampant with intimations of "liberation

—spiritual liberation in most, physical liberation in the rest,"[3] the texts of spirituals typically align body control with power, escape, and liturgical rhetoric. For example, "Didn't My Lord Deliver Daniel?" poses a rhetorical question of impending salvation: If God delivered Daniel from the lion's den, won't He deliver me from slavery? Performances of "Wade in the Water" in slave society commonly signaled an impending escape by way of a nearby riverbank, the water "troubled" by the Underground Railroad for safe passage. Discussed by scholars as the unquestionable "archetype of protest seen later in antislavery, social gospel, and civil rights hymnody," spirituals approach a fundamental theme of "the need for a change in the existing order."[4]

Ailey certainly perceived this "need for a change" in terms of concert dance practice in New York City at the time he made *Revelations*. Few options existed for trained dancers of African descent who wanted to express musicality and corporeal memories of dance as a shared communal process. The one-night-only performance "seasons" of artists such as Talley Beatty, Geoffrey Holder, and Donald McKayle in New York City provided precious opportunities cherished by artists and audiences alike, but no institution existed to nurture a dance tradition that could effectively honor the musical stature of the spirituals. Ailey, in making *Revelations*, hoped to fill this void.

At its premiere, *Revelations* included sixteen selections, a live chorus of singers including two onstage soloists, and a running time of over an hour. Sections later excised were "Weeping Mary" and "Poor Pilgrim," both solos for singer Nancy Redi; "Round about the Mountain," a woman's trio; "Wonder Where," a solo for dancer Merle Derby; "Morning Star," a women's quartet; "My Lord What a Morning," sung by the chorus; and gospel versions of "Precious Lord," "God a Mighty," and the finale "Elijah Rock!"[5]

Ailey pared *Revelations* down to a half hour running time to travel to Jacob's Pillow dance festival in Lenox, Massachusetts, in the summer of 1961. Filmed for the WCBS-TV television program *Lamp Unto My Feet* just before the trip to Massachusetts, the dance assumed a fixed form of ten selections in three sections titled "Pilgrim of Sorrow," "Take Me to the Water," and "Move, Members, Move!" The following description of the television program broadcast on 4 March 1962 offers a sense of how the dance looked in its first complete form, performed by a trim complement of eight dancers, including Ailey himself.[6] After the detailed description, I look at why *Revelations* worked and situate it in contemporary African American cultural life.

Described by an off-camera television announcer as a presentation "for those unnamed preachers and anonymous choirs who, from generation to generation, evolve the unique expressions of Christian worship," the dance begins as a staged enactment of the choral singing of spirituals. A small group of four women and three men stand close in tight choral formation, their heads and bodies bent forward toward the ground. As the tape-recorded choir repeatedly chants "Praise Him" in short, percussive bursts, the dancers raise their heads and sway nervously. They spread their arms wide, palms facing upward, and tilt their heads

Alvin Ailey, James Truitte, Don Martin, Myrna White,
Ella Thompson, and Minnie Marshall in "I've Been 'Buked"
from Alvin Ailey's *Revelations*, 1961. Photograph by Jack
Mitchell

back, eyes toward the heavens. Some seem to look for a sign from God, while
others search with their eyes closed. They teeter pensively at the waist, with
knees bent deep and upper bodies stiff with anticipation. The dancers seem to
offer their low-to-the-ground stance as a conduit, to call God down to the earth.

The group disperses as a simple, introductory drumming pattern sounds,
and the camera captures four short solos, phrases added, according to dancer
James Truitte, for the benefit of the television producer, who needed to fill out
the half-hour program.[7] Set to a sorrowful, minor mode hummed figure, these
brief excursions are fraught with tension, with angry contractions of the torso
suggesting dilemmas of physical oppression and submerged strength. As off-
camera voices announce "I'm too tired; I need help; It's too heavy, Lord; I need
so much," the solo bodies describe spaces of angst.

Finally, the humming is transformed into a cappella singing and the spiritual proper, "I've Been 'Buked," begins. The group reforms its original tight
wedge formation to perform a creaky sway and dip to each side connected by a
lifting of focus upward. Holding their feet firmly planted in a wide stance, the
dancers push their weight downward even as they search the heavens with up-

turned faces. This image of bodies rooted to the floor while faces are directed upward confirms a choreographic motif of split focus that permeates the dance. These are people in physical bondage invoking, through their movements, spiritual deliverance.

Choreographically, the dance develops in tandem with the spiritual. Movement phrases begin and end with the musical breaths of the choir; as a whole, the staging offers a strict visual correlative to the sung lyrics. While the first verse lyrics tell the story of an individual's experiences—"I've been 'buked, an' I've been scorned, Children. I've been talked about sho's you' born"[8]—its musical setting for mixed chorus suggests a common experience within the large group. The dancers amplify this impression of shared individual experiences through unison passages and sculptural poses suggesting physical exhaustion mirrored by dancers on opposite sides of the stage.

After several brief excursions into the space, the dancers reconvene in the original wedge formation to recover the opening movement phrase, a formal repetition that underscores the cyclical pattern of "'buking and scorning" historically endured by African Americans. The repetition suggests that no matter how far apart the dancers travel, they must come together physically, as pieces of a larger sculptured mosaic, to complete the communal expression of spirituality. A single variation in staging distinguishes this verse from the opening passage. On the final lyric, "sho's you' born," the dancers perform a brittle and fragmented opening of the arms from overhead, moving downward in random, percussive accents. This striking, jagged motion, unlike any preceding it, suggests the piercing arrival of the Holy Spirit in a sudden, collective gasp for breath. The arms move in abrupt lurches, an outward, limb-driven manifestation of the inward-directed torso contraction featured earlier in the piece. The motion captures the overarching movement theme of split focus: as the arms break through space falling downward, tautly held bodies reach up, with powerfully lifted chests and pained faces focused on the heavens.

The group disperses as the spiritual ends, leaving a man and two women to dance a rhythmic song of deliverance, "Daniel (Didn't My Lord Deliver Daniel)." Arranged for choir accompanied by conga drumming, the song alludes to the story of a slave oppressed beyond reason whose salvation confirms the healing powers of faith. Like "I've Been 'Buked," the dance develops as a physical invocation for deliverance, tied equally to the overarching sensibility and substance of the spiritual's lyric.

Ailey's choreography is structured as a series of short solos set in counterpoint against a background "base" danced by the two-person ensemble. The solos, roughly one for each dancer, present short vignettes of anguish marked by slow, taut contractions of the torso, urgent head rolls, and restorative leaps through space. The choreography features recurrent imagery of enslavement, as in a gesture with arms brandished overhead and hands held together as if bound at the wrists, while the torso ripples percussively in a physical exaggeration of beating a drum or being flogged at a whipping post. The dance ends with a dramatic unison flourish: lying on their backs, the dancers all stretch one hand up just as the singers cut off on the last beat of drums. This punchy, off-the-beat ending amplifies an emotional urgency common to the dances of "Pilgrim of Sorrow."

"Daniel" clarifies a compositional strategy consistent with several sections of *Revelations*: movement is performed in unison at the beginning of the piece, followed by solo excursions set contrapuntally against movement of a background group, and ended with a unison group effort and a strongly accented pose. This A-B-C-D-A choreographic structure visually enhances the strophic form of the accompanying spirituals. The structure also suggests a call-and-response format, in which the featured soloist's movement "calls" are "answered" by the group members, who work in a contrasting but interlocking rhythmic pattern. In "Daniel," for example, slow-motion leaning gestures performed by the background duo provide the rhythmic base for the soloist's urgent jumps and turns.

"Daniel" is followed by "Fix Me, Jesus," the central pas de deux of *Revelations*. A slow, moaning spiritual of supplication, "Fix Me, Jesus" offers extreme musical contrast to "Daniel" in sustained notes, extended out-of-rhythm musical phrases, and a soaring soprano solo. The vocal solo is embodied by the female dancer onstage, depicted in a private and emotional moment of prayer. The male dancer acts as a guardian angel waiting to assist the praying woman. The paternal configuration—female supplicant aided by male angel—fits neatly with traditional techniques of dance composition in which the woman is physically supported by a male partner.

The dance begins with the woman center stage with arms overhead and eyes closed, swaying in troubled circles from her waist like a tree bending in the wind. Off-camera voices call out over a chorus of humming: "Help me, Lord," "Need help," and "Make me ready, Lord." Repeating motions of searching and blindness from "I've Been 'Buked," the woman is suddenly lifted upward by the man, who had been awaiting her quietly in the shadows. She does not see him and seems unaware of his presence here and throughout the duet. Her trust and his authority are each depicted as absolute.

The woman composes her prayer in reaching and searching gestures, allowing the guardian angel to catch her gently in a variety of yielding positions. Her physical focus remains soft and hopeful, marked by an easy swing of the torso over strong, often straight, supporting legs. At one point she is supported precariously only by his hand on her neck, inches from the ground. Her hushed, unassuming confidence reflects the directness of the spiritual's vocal soloist.

The staging builds through a series of dramatic, extended balances in unlikely sculptural positions executed by the woman. At first, her dance tasks seem physically simple: she is a devout woman physically expressing her faith. The exaggerated balances and "superhuman" feats of daring in later sections—falling toward the ground without hitting it, unfolding her limbs to extraordinary heights—demonstrate her strength and resilience in the world. The mood climaxes as she is lifted, held at the waist and knees by the angel lying on his back, in an extremely vulnerable, arched-back position. Reaching her arms upward,

James Truitte and Minnie Marshall in "Fix Me, Jesus" from Alvin Ailey's *Revelations*, 1961. Photograph by Jack Mitchell

she dances in the spirit without seeing the angel; she performs her faith without reference to her physical surroundings.

As in "I've Been 'Buked," the final chorus of "Fix Me, Jesus" reprises movements from earlier sections of the dance, formally closing the woman's ritual of prayer through the structured repetition. The dance ends with a surprising theatrical variation: the woman balances standing on the man's leg, arched in a remarkably full arabesque position. Suspended in the air and reaching upward toward God, she stretches her back and arms into spiritual ascension. This supple, curving gesture arrives in stark contrast to the brittle and contracted, turned-in impulses of *Revelations*' preceding dances. The ending suggests spiritual fulfillment achieved in the balance of an open, arching back and a complete exhalation of breath released upward.

The next selection, "Sinner Man," begins with contrasting textures: the angelic voice of a solo soprano juxtaposed with the earthy running of three male dancers. Dressed in simple black tank tops and pants and wearing no shoes, the men portray sinners desperate to escape purgatory. Their dance explores a generalized emotion of fear through movement passages arranged in bold, dynamic strokes.

Like "Daniel," the dance follows an A-B-C-D-A design of a short, out-of-rhythm introduction; three solos set to three sung verses, one for each man; and a final unison group segment for all three dancers. Here, the solos are not set against contrapuntal movements of a background group; the dancers work alone on stage. The formal structure obliges each man to convey fearful distress with contrasting movement ideas: the first solo features reaching gestures, with long, slow extensions of the arms and hands; the second solo is concerned mostly with spiraling turns and slides across the floor on the knees; the third solo contains a challenging array of forceful jumps, turns, and kicks. All three solos use running to connect dance movements.

"Sinner Man" reveals the dramatic and technical facility of each dancer in a format reminiscent of challenge dancing. Each man elaborates on the theme of fear, displaying his particular version of emotional distress in a sequence of ever-rising intensity. As each soloist builds on ideas offered by his predecessor, then adds his own variation, a structured one-upmanship emerges, resolved when the men appear together for the ending unison chorus. Moving through a final flourish, they travel with a gasping, turning leap, then slide on the floor and turn onto their knees to drop their heads backward with the last beat of the drum. The flamboyantly dramatic, punchy ending presents irreconcilable anguish as the sole accomplishment of the sinner man's pursuit.

"I Wanna Be Ready," the male solo Ailey and dancer James Truitte created quickly to satisfy the strict timing needs of the television taping,[9] offers *Revelations'* climactic spiritual of sorrow and desolation. Built on Lester Horton–inspired floor exercises, the dance demonstrates both a man's private wish for redemption and his physical preparation in a ritualistic test of control as he prepares to meet God. As if performing an act of penance, the man alternates holding his body with fearful tension and releasing that tension in controlled breaths of resignation. Moving in tandem with the baritone soloist's musical phrasing, the dancer performs short, repetitive actions phrased to visualize the music: reaching and pulling, pleading and praying, balancing and meditating. Several movements pass through the shape of the cross.

The song lyric casts the singer and, by extension, the dancer as a sinner seeking penance: "I wanna be ready, Lord, ready to put on my long white robe."[10] Staying low to the ground for a remarkably demanding series of floor-bound movement, including an exacting passage of coccyx balances, the man describes his intertwined trepidation and piety. The solo ends inconclusively, with the man collapsed in a heap with his head to the ground on the final beat of the music, one hand subtly shielding his body from the premature arrival of the Lord.

After "I Wanna Be Ready," *Revelations* shifts from the mournful solemnity of private supplication to the communal enactment of a waterside baptism. A large processional of eight dancers bursts onto the scene, swirling in bright white costumes and bearing mysterious, all-white props: an umbrella, a tree branch, and long swatches of gauzy white fabric. The off-camera voices return, and two young women discuss an impending baptism, speaking over a sung, syncopated walking bass figure. Their dialogue stresses the importance of the ceremony, their discomfort at the prospect of entering a cold, muddy river, and general anxiety surrounding a rite of passage after which they "Ain't gonna be a little girl no more."

Turning in easy, loosely phrased patterns that move the group forward, the erect bodies and joyful fellowship of the dancers provide sharp contrast to the angst-ridden, contorted shapes of the preceding spirituals. The dancers form a column to move with steady determination toward the offstage riverside site of the impending baptism. Two initiates, a man and a woman in the center of the group, are distinguished by their lack of ceremonial props; the other dancers bear baptismal agents—the branch to sweep the earth, cloths to cleanse the sky, an umbrella for protection—to be used in the ceremony. The dancers move in confident, inexorable slow motion, directing their weight downward into the floor, holding their upper bodies still as their hips sway gently below.

At times, some dancers break the slow rhythm of the processional to run ahead, clearing a path for the celebrants with sweeping turns and tilted layout extensions. At one point, the group stops suddenly to bow their heads toward the ground in a tableau of genuflection. Arranged in a wedge formation reminiscent of the recurrent design of "I've Been 'Buked," the tableau suggests coherence between this ceremony and the group prayer that began *Revelations*.

"Honor, Honor" follows the chanted processional with upbeat music of preparation to precede the act of baptism. The acolytes and deaconess bearing the umbrella sweep through the space, running in joyful, measured steps and turns, enacting the lyrics' exhortation: "Run along children, be baptize[d], mighty pretty meeting by the waterside. Honor, honor unto the dying lamb." As the music slows for a short, out-of-rhythm interlude of prayer, the initiates are blessed by the deaconess in simple mimetic gestures. Two acolytes writhe on the ground in front of the initiates, physically preparing the ritual space with ecstatic movements suggesting spirit possession. As the music resumes a joyful rhythmic urgency, the initiates and their sponsors stride toward the imaginary riverbank in sober, half-time steps while the two possession dancers buzz around the periphery of the space performing fast, swirling turns. The sequence employs a layering of rhythmic activity to suggest an assembly of individuals fulfilling discrete but interconnected tasks of preparation.

"Wade in the Water," the most commonly known of all the spirituals selected by Ailey, accompanies the centerpiece dance of *Revelations*. A continuation of the baptismal ceremony, the dance begins simply, with the deaconess leading the two initiates into a river, represented by two long pieces of silk-like cloth stretched across the stage. With focused seriousness of intention, the initiates step into the water to begin a rippling motion of the torso which builds over the course of the song into full-bodied ecstatic dancing.

Ella Thompson, the deaconess with the umbrella here, guides the initiates into the dance, beckoning them forward while physically suggesting complex patterns of shoulder, arm, and torso isolations which they echo. Remaining in-

"Wade in the Water" from Alvin Ailey's *Revelations*
from the television program *Lamp Unto My Feet,* 1962.
Photograph by J. Peter Happel

tent on facilitating the ceremony, her dutiful presence inspires, calms, and ar-
bitrates as she moves between the initiates, directing and judging them, all the
while holding her oversized white umbrella high in the air. Satisfied at their
progress, she leaves the riverbank and allows the initiates to dance out their passion together.

The two initiates continue with serious, focused intention, dancing to complete the ceremony for themselves and the offstage congregation. Depicted as
two individuals rather than a couple, they do not dance for, or see, each other.
Moving in unison, their dance suggests spiritual commonality between man and
woman, framed by the ceremony's ritual purpose, without any reference to gender difference. Their costuming, however, underscores their sex: the woman
wears a full white dress that leaves her arms and neck exposed, and the man
wears only tightly fitted white slacks that bare his torso to the riverbank.

The final three dances of *Revelations* enact a rural southern gospel church
service. Set inside a wood-framed church designed specially for the television
presentation, the sequence is introduced with a brief piano interlude as two off-
camera voices banter about gospel church service. "We don't sing dead songs,"

"Rocka My Soul" from Alvin Ailey's *Revelations*
from the television program *Lamp Unto My Feet*, 1962.
Photograph by J. Peter Happel

says one man, as another offers, "Make a noise unto the Lord, and jump up into the dance!" to which the first man agrees, "Praise the Lord with Dance!" The narrations here and throughout the television program underscore the theatricality of *Revelations* as dance theater; they provide an enhanced context for the choreographic coordination of religious music and concert dance.

The camera pans across the stage set to center on a preacher, the singer Brother John Sellers, singing the invocation to service, "The Day Is Past and Gone." Seated on stools and chairs, the eight dancers face the preacher and rock in assent to the sermon with deflected-focus cool, their eyes barely open, the women fanning themselves gently with straw hand fans. As the invocation segues to an up-beat, gospel-style preaching spiritual, "You May Run On (God a-Mighty)," the dancers become animated, swaying and turning on their stools, until the women eventually rise to dance in unison. The progression from seated to dancing congregation is accomplished slowly, over an entire sung verse, as the women respond naturalistically to the lyrics. The dance builds seamlessly from simple swaying gestures through full-bodied leans and circles of the feet on the floor, into animated gestures of pantomimed conversation to each other and finally stylized, character dance movements incorporating the whole body.

The men rise from their chairs to join in the dancing, skipping transitional states of everyday gesture to launch into a flowing, tightly syncopated phrase of bounding jazz dance. The choreography here is mostly defined by the feet, building on small hopping bounces, catch steps, and occasional lurching contractions of the torso. The men dance in unison, without seeing each other, and beyond the purview of the women, who sit down and turn away from them. Later, the women stand on their stools to point at the men, chastising them in gesture as singer Sellers admonishes: "Some folks go to church for to signify, tryin' to make a date with the neighbor's wife. But neighbor, let me tell you, just as sure as you're born, you better leave that woman, better leave her alone!"[11] The layering of chanted text and naturalistic gesture allows the sequence a relaxed playfulness in sharp contrast to preceding sections of *Revelations*.

The final gospel exclamation, "Rocka My Soul in the Bosom of Abraham," ends the service on a celebratory high. Again the staging follows the musical structure closely, with choreographic changes mirroring transitions from chorus to verse, tonal modulations, and the rising intensity of the singing ensemble. The dance begins as the small congregation looks about, fanning themselves, allowing the spirit to descend in waves and hit individuals separately. When touched by the spirit, the dancers stop fanning and swaying to suddenly jerk an arm or head percussively upward, a movement that effectively breaks the underlying flow of rhythmic pulse. The dancers pair up, men to women, and in a staging detail reminiscent of ring-shout performance in the rural South, clear out the central area of the sanctuary for dance. Moving stools and chairs to the edges of the space, they emulate rural parishioners, walking with a stooped-over, lurching stride, holding their weight low to the ground as they test the floor's strength. The women break out to dance first, in a flowing, rhythmic stepping passage that rises in urgency as a female soloist sings improvisatory riffs against a repeating choral background. They dance simple combinations of eight-count duration, first in a loose group, then, at the beginning of a new chorus, in a formal, diagonal line.

The song modulates upward again and again—like Jacob's ladder, every round goes higher, higher!—and the entire company spreads out across the sanctuary to dance in unison. Their movement is all earthbound, but as the dance progresses, they pull their center of weight higher and higher into the upper body, away from the floor. Their dance explores a counterpoint of men against women, add-on steps begun by a single dancer and completed by the entire group, and the kaleidoscopic fanning out of dancers across the sanctuary space. By its end, the dancers hold their bodies proudly erect, no longer impersonating rural churchgoers, but now displaying facility in concert dance technique. Moving in unison, they turn and drop to the floor, ending on their knees in a frozen pose timed to the last beat of music, their arms stretched toward the heavens and heads thrown back in ecstasy.

The movement vocabulary here draws on classic jazz dance steps: struts, rhythmic floor patting by bare feet, shaking of the shoulders and torso, and movement phrasing in blocks of insistent eight. The alignment of jazz dance with gospel music reveals similar ecstatic intentions motivating both forms. In "Rocka My Soul," Ailey confirms the fundamental connection between worship, a feature of daily life for many rural southern African Americans, and exuberant social dance, the root form of the codified jazz dance movements performed here.

▌ Why *Revelations* Worked

Dancing to spirituals allowed Ailey to suggest a political collaboration between his performance and the music's historical legacy. Writing about the figurative power of spirituals in African American literature, Henry Louis Gates Jr. called them of "such import to black poetic language that when they surface as referents in the poetry—spoken, sung, or danced speech—they cannot but bear the full emotional and structural import of another lurking but not lost hermetic universe."[12] Ailey's choreography embodied that "lost hermetic universe," as it physically represented what composer Hall Johnson termed the "musical alchemy" of African American history crystallized in the choral singing of the spirituals: conscious and intentional alterations of pitch, bewildering counterpoint, and an insistent overall rhythmic base.[13] These aspects are most obviously embodied in the extended, off-center balances of "Fix Me, Jesus," the bursts of chaotic motion of "I've Been 'Buked," and the rhythmic interplay of "Rocka My Soul," respectively.

In all, Ailey's choreography complements the vocal production of its singers in terms of performance technique and style as much as lyrical and musical content. The choreography "breathes" along with the vocal arrangements, in effect amplifying the communal production of performance that the spirituals require. At times, the staging physically represents an extended vocal line melisma, as in "Fix Me, Jesus." When the vocal soloist leans against the tonal center offered by the group as she exclaims "O! Fix Me!" Ailey's prayerful dancing woman balances precariously on one leg, then leans even further into the difficult, off-center stance in response to the singer's call. In this moment, the audience is invited to visualize, hear, and feel the human effort of resistance performed simultaneously by the vocal soloist and the dancer.

In the final "Rocka My Soul" selection, Ailey's choreography makes visible underlying rhythmic structures of the music's transformed drumming patterns. As the steady and simple, four-beat rhythmic base proceeds, the vocal arrangement develops syncopated phrasing executed in three- and four-part harmony, rising through several tonal key centers. Ailey's choreographed stepping patterns here offer visual counterrhythms to the basic beat as well as the choir's increasingly complex patterns. As the work drives toward its finish and the choir settles into a single rhythmic gesture sung in all vocal registers, the dancers perform a unison phrase of strongly accented rhythmic ideas that amplify the overarching sensations of rhythm that ends the work. These rhythms are made visual, aural, and kinetic. The performing artists—singers, dancers, and musicians as well as the affiliated designers—embody and propel the rhythmic ideas to fill the performance space in several dimensions.

The vocal choirs Ailey worked with in early performances of *Revelations* followed the tradition of heavily embellished, technically demanding Western-style choral singing honed by the Fisk Jubilee Singers in the late 1800s. The Fisk singers, who toured extensively after the Civil War, tied the singing of spirituals to what was then a revisionist view of the Negro as skillful, capable, and artistic. The Fisk tradition of choral singing demonstrated what literary critic Houston A. Baker calls "mastery of form," a politically motivated accomplishment of precision designed to subvert essentialist critiques of black performance.[14] As the Fisk singers, and their primary rivals, the Hampton Institute singers, achieved inordinately modern arrangements of the sorrow songs, they challenged "the essentialist idea that there is a 'real' Negro."[15] The Fisk and Hampton traditions, ably continued by the tape-recorded Howard Roberts Chorale in the television performance of *Revelations*, suggest the radical revision of folk materials to enact mastery of form for disbelieving audiences.

In a like manner, the 1962 national television broadcast of *Revelations* demonstrated the ability of black dancers to inhabit concert dance technique. From its opening phrases, which aligned the dance movements closely with their musical accompaniment, *Revelations* displayed its dancers as "masters of form," able to perform movements culled from Martha Graham, Lester Horton, and Doris Humphrey techniques. In all, the dance requires a strong technique and agility in several movement idioms to be performed successfully; its contents pointedly display the mastery of its performers as dance artists in, at least, the blank modernist gestures of the spirituals section, the ecstatic improvisations of the baptismal scene, and the rhythmic precision amid character-based dramatic overlay of the sanctuary sequence. In this, the corporeal fact of dancers demonstrating physical mastery offers unimpeachable evidence of embodied knowledge. Working with the excellent musical accompaniment of various vocal choirs, Ailey's dancers effectively trumped derisive speculation about the possibilities of African American concert dance. They transformed complex encodings of political resistance, musical ability, and religious narrative onto their bodies to imply a historical reach of black culture, continued here by the act of concert dance.

In interviews conducted around the time of its premiere, Ailey called *Revelations* a "blood memory" piece, born of fragments from his Texas childhood: "These are dances and songs I feel very personally about—they are intimately connected with my memories of the Baptist Church when I was a child in Texas —baptismals by tree-shrouded lakes, in a lake where an ancient alligator was supposed to have lived—the holy-rollers' tambourines shrieking in the Texas night."[16]

As exotic as Ailey made rural black life sound to his largely urban, white audiences in 1960, concert dancing to spirituals was nothing new. Dances to a variety of "Negro Spirituals" became a staple of concert dance in the late 1920s and early 1930s, when Helen Tamiris, Hemsley Winfield, and Edna Guy all made dances with this title. Later in the 1930s, Ted Shawn and Charles Williams both staged suites of spirituals; Wilson Williams and Janet Collins offered separate versions in the 1940s; and Pearl Primus staged at least one in 1950.[17] By the 1960s, the danced spiritual had established a successful, perennial niche as concert fare.

Ailey's version differed from its predecessors in its grand sweep and variety, its sure use of a large group of dancers, and its careful coordination of contrasting musical selections. *Revelations* created an optimistic, chronological narrative of African American release from physical slavery in its ordering of spirituals from the dark, somber-themed lyrics of "I've Been 'Buked" and "Daniel," through the up-beat songs of ritual ceremony in "Honor, Honor" and "Wade in the Water," to the gospel exclamations of "good news," "Rocka My Soul." The musical sequence suggests a historical triumph, a movement toward freedom. This narrative optimism, encompassed by the actual structure of the dance, confidently reflected Ailey's effort to create an American dance theater born of African American expressive practice. This optimism, in combination with Ailey's unflagging willingness to work within the existing exclusionist and racist structures of American concert dance practice, consistently placed Ailey's enterprise apart from other, similar efforts.

Ailey premiered *Revelations* at the 92nd Street YM-YWHA. Under the direction of William Kolodney, the YM-YWHA offered one of the few dependable outlets for African American concert dance artists in New York. Between 1957 and 1960, the Y produced one-night-only "season" concerts by African American choreographers Talley Beatty, Geoffrey Holder, Louis Johnson, Donald McKayle, Ernest Parham, and Eleo Pomare, as well as Jean-Léon Destiné's concert presentation of Haitian dance. Varied programming at the Y encouraged an interracial audience interested in African diaspora culture that included large numbers of African American students who rarely attended other dance events. Bolstered by the headlining guest artist presence of Martha Graham company soloist Matt Turney, Ailey's all-black company packed the small auditorium for its 31 January 1960 appearance.

Creating a dance to be performed by African American dancers that dealt explicitly with Afro-American folk materials allowed Ailey to appeal to several audiences simultaneously. African Americans familiar with the historical legacy of spirituals understood *Revelations* as an aesthetic reclaiming of the music in terms of concert dance. Audiences comfortable with traditional configurations of black performance recognized the passionate display of spirituality and a familiar convergence of despair, ritual, and rural black life. Dance critics recognized the versatility and striking original vision of Ailey's choreography, built on a vibrant theatricality typically missing from presentations at the YM-YWHA.

Indeed, Ailey's dances seldom resembled work made by his contemporaries for presentation at the YM-YWHA. Dancers from the original *Revelations* recalled Ailey's strong "sense of total theater—the decor, the costumes, the lighting" that underscored an extravagant theatricality in his early work.[18] Ailey collaborated with dancers and designers familiar with both the demands of commercial theater and the techniques of concert dance expression to create a punchy mixture of personality and abstraction in his works. He gathered his dancers from the expansive ranks of talented African Americans he met working on Broadway, dancing in other companies, and taking daily technique class. The eclectic group involved in the television taping for *Lamp Unto My Feet* in 1961 included two men from Ailey's days at the Lester Horton studio in Los Angeles, James Truitte and Don Martin; Herman Howell; Thelma Hill, who had danced in the New York Negro Ballet; Minnie Marshall, who studied Graham technique and danced in the Broadway musical *Kwamina*; Ella Thompson, daughter of a minister, ballet student of Karel Shook, and cast member of the Broadway musical *Jamaica*; and Myrna White, Broadway dancer from *West Side Story* and *A Funny Thing Happened on the Way to the Forum*.

Working together, the affiliated artists distinguished Ailey's theatrical vision significantly from other contemporary African American choreographers. *Revelations* offered a fuller scenic schema than many presentations by Beatty or Johnson, while it explored a more expansive range of dance techniques than work by Holder or Destiné. Significantly, Ailey's work in general, and *Revelations* in particular, landed somewhere between the political aspirations of usually radical Pomare and often universalist McKayle. *Revelations* offered an optimistic chronology that allowed all of its audiences to imagine a future brighter than the past; at the same time, it presented specific aspects of southern African American experience as significant and suitable for the concert dance stage. Working somewhere in the political middle, Ailey created a dance experience that honored the past while it gestured emphatically toward a future of African American creativity in concert dance.

Dancers were not paid at all for rehearsals and were paid only nominal fees for major performances.[19] Ailey galvanized his company through his grand vision and persuasive charisma. In a 1964 interview, Myrna White explained why dancers worked for Ailey whenever possible: "Alvin's great ability is that he reaches everyone in his audience, professional dancers and laymen attending their first concert. It isn't only his own dancing, it's the sense of theater in his choreography, the sense of drama he gets into the performance of every dancer he trains. . . . The reason dancers look forward to performing with Alvin Ailey and Company is that they know they will reach their audience, and their audience will reach them."[20] In this, White confirms the importance of a reciprocity between dancer and audience that *Revelations* perennially inspired.

Critical reaction to the hour-long 1960 version of *Revelations* ranged from subdued praise to bald enthusiasm. Writing for *Dance Magazine*, Selma Jeanne Cohen praised the "exciting stage designs, suddenly broken by huge surges of movement and resolved into mourning masses of stillness" of the opening, but found the suite "much too long for sustained effectiveness," burdened at times by "an almost literal reiteration of the musical phrase."[21] Walter Terry noted the thematic range of the musical selections contained by this "marvelous" work: "The movement invention, though rich in novelty, is always in accord with the thematic material and the choreographer has done a superb job of contrasting sorrow with joy, serious intent with innocent comedy, formality of design with freedom of expression."[22]

Other critics recognized the lingering minstrel show personae suggested by Ailey's oppressed slave archetypes. Writing for the *Village Voice*, Jill Johnston played up the exotic-primitive appeal of *Revelations* for her readers: "It's a swinging dance that could drive you easily out of your mind, or back to sanity. . . . You can't resist it; you can't resist the rushing rolling sinuous movement (pure uncontaminated movement) that involves the entire body in rippling waves of mutually activated segments; you can't resist the ecstatic extensions which throw the body into bursting arcs of mad abandon; you can't resist that music, that DRUM! The drum will never let you go. Ailey has made a theatre piece with the inspired drunken compulsion of a fertility rite."[23] Ostensibly a rave review, Johnston's hints at a limiting, essentialist racial scheme perceptible in *Revelations*.

Alvin Ailey, James Truitte, Don Martin, Myrna White, Ella
Thompson, and Minnie Marshall in "I've Been 'Buked" from
Alvin Ailey's *Revelations*, 1961. Photograph by Jack Mitchell

▌ Black Modernism

As object, the back body epitomizes modernism.
As subject, the black body offers a failed site of modernism.
It must be abject.

Music theorist Craig Werner points out that neoclassical discourse focuses largely on
the concept of universalism, in which "certain themes, images, and techniques express fundamentally 'human' concerns that transcend the limitations of any particular set of circumstances."[24] Although the actions and artistry of African Americans
may indeed express "universal" truths, the black body itself never achieves this transcendence in any discourse of the West. Marked even before it can be seen, before
it can even exist, the black body carries its tangled web of work and sexual potentials,
athletic and creative resources, and stratified social locations onto the stages of the
modern.

19

Black bodies offered a cipher of "not-ness" that enabled whites to articulate modernity in the first part of the twentieth century. Toni Morrison writes persuasively about blackness in literature, to remind us that the white American modern could not exist without its opposite of the black African primitive, and for American writers engaged in the construction of modernist literature, "a real or fabricated Africanist presence was crucial to their sense of Americanness."[25] Morrison's examples encompass a century of authors who encountered blackness as an oppositional presence, by design or default, and in the process imbricated blackness and the primitive in the conception of the modern.

In concert dance, the most celebrated first-generation modern choreographers—Martha Graham, Hanya Holm, Doris Humphrey, and Charles Weidman—struggled with the figuration of dancing black bodies in their work.[26] These artists could not—and did not—ignore black bodies altogether, but by and large they imagined blackness as an alternative to monotonous, everyday whiteness, as a site of ecstatic release to be summoned when needed. As dance theorist Brenda Dixon Gottschild reminds us, in 1930 Martha Graham quipped: "We have two primitive sources, dangerous and hard to handle in the arts, but of intense psychic significance—the Indian and the Negro."[27] The "psychic significance" of the Negro and the Indian refer, of course, to the formation of white subjectivity within modernity, but Graham's recognition of "danger" and "intensity" in Africanist expression predicts an enormous potential for black bodies on public stages in any expressive idiom.

In 1961, Graham's teacher, Louis Horst, published a small composition and analysis primer, *Modern Dance Forms*, which included reference to "primitive" shapes that look remarkably like the preferred angular stances and impulses of then contemporary African American social dances.[28] Black dance gestures arrived in modern dance works through compositional techniques like those set forth by Horst as referents of primitive movement. Some white artists, such as choreographer Helen Tamiris, attempted to choreograph the outward shapes and ecstatic release of black dance in works like *Negro Spirituals* (1937), but of course, these dances avoided actual dancing black bodies.[29] Black movements may have been untidy and dangerous to some white viewers because their aesthetic imperatives were largely inscrutable. How black dance gesture conveyed more than its iconography mystified even those who recognized its power; in her autobiography, Isadora Duncan suggests avoiding all African impulses because of their potent modernist appeal.[30]

For example, consider the critical response when Agnes de Mille created "Black Ritual" for the New York Ballet Theater, the precursor to American Ballet Theatre, in 1940. Performed by a cast of sixteen women to a score by Darius Milhaud, the piece intended to "project the psychological atmosphere of a primitive community during the performance of austere and vital ceremonies."[31] This was not a classically shaped ballet, but its cast had received dance training in a specially established, segregated "Negro Wing" of the Ballet Theatre school. Critical reaction to the piece was muted, and the dance was considered unsuccessful, at least because, under de Mille's choreographic direction, the Negro dancers were not performing authentic Negro material. After viewing the work, dance writer Walter Terry called for "a Negro vocabulary of movement . . . composed of modern dance movements, ballet steps, tap and others

. . . [which] should enable the Negro to express himself artistically and not merely display his muscular prowess."[32] By 1940, black dance movements and aesthetic principles, seldom viewed on concert dance stages, were considered in and of themselves "antimodern."

Eventually, some white artists moved beyond the outward shapes of the "black dance" to try to get at the impulses that drive it. Among neoclassical and postmodern choreographers, George Balanchine and Twyla Tharp absorbed Africanist aesthetic devices of downward-directed energy, insistent rhythmicity, angularity of line, percussive rupture of underlying flow, individualism within a group dynamic, and access to a dynamic "flash of the spirit" that confirms simultaneously temporal presence and ubiquitous spirituality.[33] But again, these choreographers often worked without the dancing black bodies that first explored these dimensions. Overwhelmingly, black presence in the construction of modern dance has been positioned implicitly as an antidote to (premodern) classicism, but explicitly as an afterthought or footnote. Paraphrasing Morrison, modern dance in the United States has, for the most part, taken as its concern the architecture of a *new white woman*.[34]

If the modern dance emerged to explore white female subjectivity, there was likely little space for black innovation in its early years. The critical record for early concert dance is largely white, and few artists or authors paid attention to the permutations of form that black artists inspired.[35] The audience, too, for concert dance mirrored the readers of American literature, and, as Morrison reminds us, "until very recently, and regardless of the race of the author, the readers of virtually all of American fiction have been positioned as white."[36] For white audiences and critics to understand African American excellence in modern dance, their work had to be read as "universal" in theme.

Ailey positioned his work among the Afro-modernists of the 1950s, both writers and choreographers, who explored "universal" aspects of human experience. Werner notes that "only those black writers whose work can be presented in terms of the 'universals'—[Ralph] Ellison is perhaps the most obvious example—receive 'serious' (if extraordinarily narrow) attention and financial rewards."[37] Ailey, like Ellison and choreographer Donald McKayle, sought a broad audience for his work, and he sought a committed African American audience for modern dance as well. For Ailey, dance had to be "modern" in that it had to offer a unique synthesis of similar choreographic ideas that preceded it, but it also had to satisfy an impulse to honor ancestral legacies of performance. *Revelations* managed to achieve both of these tasks.

Ailey's goal and achievement was to make black bodies visible, if not dominant, in the discourse of modernist American dance. He did this in selecting his company of mostly black artists, but also in the very real establishment of a solid, African diaspora concert dance–going public. This accomplishment of visibility carries mixed fortunes because, as performance theorist Peggy Phelan points out, "there is real power in remaining unmarked; and there are serious limitations to visual representation as a political goal."[38] Ailey did identify a community of black dancers and allowed his work to address black audiences and, through this increased visibility, set in motion increased opportunities—social and political power—for African diaspora dance artists. But the overexposure of visible black bodies Ailey engendered in works, including *Revelations*, collapsed representation and identity to such a linear and mimetic extent that stereotypes of pious and exuberant black bodies threatened to emerge from the black churches of Ailey's "blood memories." For generations, any African American concert dance artist might have been expected to make a *Revelations*-style dance.

Still, *Revelations* fits into the project of the modern because, in its first gestures of oppression encoded in the opening stance of immobile tension, it highlights freedom. As music historian John Lovell notes, "The I of the spiritual is not a single person. It is every person who sings, everyone who has been oppressed and, therefore, every slave anywhere."[39] The opening posture of the dance implies physical bondage and slavery, and, as Morrison writes, "Black slavery enriched the country's creative possibilities. For in that construction of blackness *and* enslavement could be found not only the not-free but also, with the dramatic polarity created by skin color, the projection of the not-me."[40] This is what audiences—all audiences, by 1960—are invited to contemplate. The not-me-ness of the dancers highlights difference. Not-me as black dancing body; not-me as slave archetype; not-me as rural worshiper. Not-me as abstract expression of the spiritual, because I am, in fact, religious and spiritual; not-me as enclosed within a hermetically sealed community, because I am seated in an integrated concert hall witnessing modern dance. I am made visible by the dance; strikingly, its gestures provide corporeal narrative of my memory of pain.

This memory of pain is actually what I feel as I witness the dance. How the world of "I've Been 'Buked" *hurt*: its subjects imprisoned by an essential subjugation reflected here in attitudes of deflected focus and a lack of visual connection. Here, dancers rarely look toward each other or the audience. They are sorrowful, beaten, without individual agency. The modern enervates them, saps their bodies of dynamic potential. Significantly, as *Revelations* becomes more jubilant, its movements migrate from (white) modernist abstraction to (black) vernacular dance structures. The dancers escape the dead confines of abstract dance that expresses inner turmoil to inhabit the living representation of people dancing for and with each other.

If modernism fails on black dancing bodies, it is because the act of performance supersedes its implications in the Africanist paradigm. Or, what the black body *means* in stillness on a Western stage is transformed by its motion through what it *does*. When dancing black bodies connect to their audience, they are never abject. They are the initiators of vital communication that is ancient and traditional, ephemeral, and, in some paradigms, *modern*.

Situating *Revelations* in African American Cultural Life

For many African American audiences, Ailey's work gained special significance as modern art through its powerful, referential treatment of familiar spiritual texts. According to Henry Louis Gates Jr., whose writings about black poetry are applicable to modern dance and especially *Revelations*, spirituals as referents "give black poetry an opulence of meaning—one translated through time and space by an oral tradition of over three and a half centuries—not readily available to exterior exploration." For Gates, this "assumption of especial meaning to the initiated becomes more than simply knowing the lines," because "the best of poetic expression is essentially untranslatable." African American audiences, then, could experience *Revelations* in marked variance to others, because they could acknowledge Ailey's competence as a black poet of dance able to create mythopoesis that could "predict our future through his . . . sensitivity to our past coupled with an acute, almost intuitive awareness of the present."[41]

Revelations quickly became a defining dance document of African American culture for all of its audiences. With its ending staged to familiar gospel selections that could then be heard on radio hit parades, the dance confirmed an easy continuity of African American social dance, spirituality, and accomplishment in modern dance. By 1964 critic P. W. Manchester referred to it as "one of the great dance works of the day,"[42] its staying power tied to the choral grandeur of Ailey's staging for ensemble. Ailey captured the essential choral form of black hymnody, "where[in] large crowds sang freely"[43] and created choreographic guideposts within which his dancers could flourish, confident of their connection to the material and its cultural importance. Fully aware that the dance represented the history of a people's faith, the dancers filled out the movement patterns with a sense of drama, with passion and zeal, and what Ailey later recalled as "menace and funk."[44]

Revelations recalled a segregated era when African Americans had little access to mainstream American life. In the opening section of the dance, shoeless, drab costuming evoked a rural, antebellum setting fitting both a historical conception of slave clothing *and* the barefoot modern dance. Ironically, the appropriate barefoot "modern" costuming accurately linked the dancing black bodies with poverty, paucity of means, and an affinity for powerful physical expression. But if the work proposed anything "dangerous" or "messy" in its opening gestures—perhaps in the staged reenactment of physical bondage, a sticking point for most Americans—those edges were quickly smoothed by the economy of its dance motion, the brevity of its musical selections, and the confident dispatch of its staging.

But the summary nature of the suite form threatens to collapse its structure into neat boxes, and surely part of the success of *Revelations* stems from its reliance on "traditional" roles for men and women. Indeed, black feminists looking to *Revelations* for a visionary depiction of gender equity found little of modern comfort in Ailey's choreographic scheme. Though the dance had several sections featuring women in its original 1960 form and was designed around onstage soloist Nancy Redi, according to Ailey's notes, the 1962 television version relied heavily on male presence for momentum and dynamism. The ordering of "Fix Me, Jesus," with its dominating male angel, followed by the male trio of "Sinner Man" and the solo "I Wanna Be Ready" focused attention on the four men of the eight-member ensemble. Ailey's electrifying rhythmic abandon, his superbly developed athletic body, and his confident, seething dramatic presence command the viewer's attention in "Daniel," "Sinner Man," and the baptismal sequence of "Wade in the Water." Costuming by Ves Harper amplified the men's visual dominance: always dressed in form-fitting trousers, the men dance bare-chested or with loose mesh tank tops through the first two sections of the dance. In contrast, the women's bodies are consistently concealed by voluminous skirts in the first two sections and loose-fitting go-to-meeting dresses for the final gospel section. The strict gender coding confirms traditional roles for men and women in the world of the dance, even if those roles do allow for female leadership in some scenes, as in the waterside baptism.

Certainly Ailey's reliance on masculine domination as a component of choreographic structure allowed his work to appeal to a vast audience conditioned to welcome this representation. In all, *Revelations* explored coherent visions of class, gender, and sexuality. The dance concerned itself largely with issues of cultural representation and structures of feeling as if they could be either detached from other social paradigms or evacuated in service of the work's well-being. Like other works of its era, it offered a rare representation of black subjectivity without questioning the social foundations of gender, class, or sexuality implicit in its portrayals. The rural southern worshipers are depicted as black men and women; their shared cultural values mitigate other social differences they may experience. Significantly, however, the work contained several scenes of private, or solo, supplication, sequences such as "Fix Me, Jesus" and "I Wanna Be Ready" that presented inscrutable personal questioning. In these sequences, audiences were invited to project their own personal concerns about African American social structures onto the meaning of the modern dance.

Ailey's choreographic notes indicate that he originally conceived the dance's three-part form to draw a "story line connection for spirituals," to suggest an extended single-day church service moving from an opening indoor service to the banks of a nearby river for a baptism and then back into the church for a "celebration of [the] baptismal in ecstatic dances."[45] To choose musical material, Ailey "did extensive research . . . listened to a lot of music," and consulted music historian Hall Johnson.[46] Johnson probably directed Ailey to Marc Connelly's drama *The Green Pastures*, which included three selections found in *Revelations*: "I Wanna Be Ready," "Sinner Man," and "You Better Mind."[47] For the baptismal sequence, in which he intended to suggest "the Afro-Brazilian fetishist rituals and their influence on the Church," Ailey remembered waterside rituals from his Texas childhood.[48] He recalled the vibrantly theatrical vision of ethnographic dance that Katherine Dunham had presented in the 1940s, even as he also drew on his extensive Broadway and film performing experiences, which included several ritualistic processionals and "voodoo" numbers.

For Ailey, *Revelations* realized the largely untapped potential of black dancers to inform concert dance with the profound cultural heritage of African American experience. The original hour-long version of the dance depended heavily on its dancers to fill in the dramatic specificity of its setting. At a 1993 symposium devoted to *Revelations*, dancer Ella Thompson recalled that Ailey gave insight into the quality of certain movements through descriptions of people he had known—qualities of personality familiar to dancers raised in similar cultural environments. Dorene Richardson, who danced in *Revelations*' world premiere, recalled that each rehearsal for the dance began with a gesture of the hands moving in circles as the torso undulated in its own rhythm, a movement sequence common to many ecstatic dances of the African diaspora. Judith Jamison spoke of the space between the steps that "allow the dancer to reveal himself—it is up to the dancer to give the steps meaning."[49] As this discussion suggests, however, the "meaning" Jamison alludes to is embedded in a variety of explicitly African American expressive and interpretive paradigms.

Revelations challenged its dancers to pull together abstract dance technique and cultural memory to create archetypal black personae. The huge, sweeping variety of the dance offered "something for everyone," providing its dancers and audience a constantly shifting range of emotional material. Ailey employed an expansive range of dance technique in *Revelations*: jazz dancing, balletic positions, Graham, Horton, Humphrey, Brazilian stance, West African isolations and complex rhythmic meter, and a fundamental African American musicality all find their way into the choreography to form a seamless whole, an unprecedented site of entry for black dancers to concert performance. In *Revelations* Ailey embodied the spiritual's "naturally veiled and half articulate" message of faith, to physically re/present W. E. B. Du Bois's classic trilogy of the African American legacy: a gift of story and song, a gift of sweat and brawn, and a gift of the Spirit.[50]

Early Dances

Ailey created his company with three goals in mind: he wanted to employ the scores of excellent black dancers in New York who had no performing homes; he wanted to create a racially integrated repertory company that could perform both modern dance classics and new works by himself and other young choreographers; and he wanted to give artistic voice to African American experience in terms of concert dance. His most obvious success came in this last, as early performances of *Blues Suite* and *Revelations* established Ailey's company as the foremost dance interpreter of African American experience.

But of the first dozen dances Ailey made, only these two dealt with African American cultural history. Still, Ailey was consistently reviewed as a Negro dancer and, by extension, someone suited to make dances only on Negro themes. Jill Johnston, writing for the usually progressive *Village Voice* in 1961, praised *Blues Suite* and *Revelations* at the expense of Ailey's other dances: "I would have been happy if the program had consisted of those two dances and nothing else. . . . In those serious 'concert' pieces he moves constantly, in high gear, as though in a panic, and like a synthetic composite figure of a smattering of contemporary influences. . . . And Modern Dance be damned too if it means the prevention of what comes naturally. On with the business of nature and excitement."[1] However tongue-in-cheek Johnston's comments, critical traditions that aligned black bodies with things "naturally exciting" stretch back from the days of minstrelsy and the myth of "untrained" professional black performance.

During the 1950s and 1960s, as he rose to prominence, Ailey rarely discussed his hardscrabble childhood with white journalists. The outlines of that existence would have been familiar to his African American contemporaries; like other integration-minded African Americans of his generation, Ailey typically stressed childhood experiences he assumed to be similar to those in the white mainstream. Until African American doctoral candidate Jacqueline Latham conducted biographical interviews with Ailey in 1971, the rough contours of his early life escaped note.

▌ Ailey's Childhood: Race Matters

Born 5 January 1931 into the abject poverty of rural Texas, Ailey was raised by his mother after his parents separated when he was an infant. He suffered a difficult, transient childhood in Depression-era Texas, moving often as his mother struggled to find work. Strictly segregated life in southeast Texas offered a hostile environment for African Americans and nurtured a fear and mistrust of whites Ailey often recalled in interviews: "I heard about lynchings. Having that kind of experience as a child left a feeling of rage in me that I think pervades my work."[2] This background also created a fierce pride in black social institutions, including the church and jook joints, which figure prominently in his later work.[3]

Racial division played a significant role in Ailey's childhood and adolescent self-awareness. An atmosphere of fear "which seemed to prevail among the blacks in Southeast Texas"[4] emerged in Ailey's "blood memory" pieces, dances that traced remembered fragments of his Texas childhood, specifically *Blues Suite* and *Revelations*. Among these blood memories loomed Ailey's shadowy memory of his mother's rape by a white man when he was five.[5] Like many African Americans of his generation, Ailey came to understand black life as the result of political domination by anonymous bands of whites.

Ailey's mother moved to Los Angeles in January 1942, and Ailey joined her there later that year. They first lived in a mostly white school district, but Ailey protested to his mother, feeling "they did not know exactly what to do with me" as one of the only black students at the school. The Aileys moved so that he could attend the predominantly black George Washington Carver Junior High School and later, Thomas Jefferson High School. These schools, and the expanded cultural vistas of the entertainment districts of Central Avenue and downtown Los Angeles, offered Ailey vibrant models of African American performance in the integrationist mold prevalent during the Second World War. He frequented the Lincoln Theatre on Central Avenue, where he saw Pearl Bailey, Fletcher Henderson, Billie Holiday, Lena Horne, and Pigmeat Markham. At the downtown Orpheum Theater, he first witnessed performances by Count Basie and Duke Ellington.[6] Ailey's interest in concert dance was eventually sparked by a high school–sponsored excursion to an all-white company, the Ballet Russe de

Monte Carlo, and Ailey's solitary visits to Katherine Dunham's all-black 1943 "Tropical Revue."[7]

Ailey arrived in California shy, lonely, and particularly sensitive from his itinerant childhood. He found solace in the fantasy world of theater and the movies: "I first became aware of dance by going to the movies . . . I became very, very impressed with Fred Astaire and Gene Kelly—the glamour of it all."[8] During this period he spent much time alone, responsible for the maintenance of the apartment he shared with his mother and making his own meals. He indulged his artistic interests at school, where he sang spirituals in the glee club, wrote poetry, and proved proficient in foreign languages. He discovered his homosexuality during this period, adding a layer of difference and isolation to his adolescent self-awareness,[9] and, like many young gay men eager to corral the sensual impulses of the body, he turned to dance study. He briefly studied tap dancing and, encouraged by classmate Ted Crumb, tried 1940s style "primitive dance" as taught by Dunham dancer Thelma Robinson in a dank night club.[10] That experience proved unpleasant, no doubt because of its physical location and old-fashioned sensibility, and Ailey turned to "modern dance" only when Crumb introduced him to Lester Horton's flamboyantly theatrical Hollywood studio in 1949.

Modern dance was still in formation as a local art in California, and dance technique taught at the Horton school was idiosyncratic and experimental. The types of dances Ailey rehearsed there were tinged with a theatrical exoticism common to postwar America, including heroic enactments of Bible stories, dance portrayals of "folk" warriors, and Horton's personal and impressionistic renderings of non-Western dance forms. Horton's work stressed the overall sensory effect dance could have on its audience. In following Horton, Ailey conceived theatrical dance as the formalized display of movement narrative tempered by lighting, costuming, and the emotional presence of the dancer.

Horton, a gay white man from Indianapolis, also enticed Ailey with his utopian vision of a multicultural dance melting pot. Horton's dancers included African Americans James Truitte and Carmen de Lavallade, white dancers Bella Lewitzky and Joyce Trisler, and Japanese dancer Misaye Kawasumi; in later years, the Chinese American critic Frank Eng was Horton's lover. Horton encouraged his company to see beyond common constructions of race and sexuality. Ailey gravitated to this vision of personal and sexual liberation and poured himself into study to develop a weighty, smoldering performance style that suited his athletic body and his concern with the representation of masculinity: "I didn't really see myself as a dancer. I mean, what would I dance? It was 1949. A man didn't just become a dancer. Especially a black man."[11]

If Ailey enjoyed the prospect of creating art with his body, he also realized that few established venues for black male dancers existed. He acted on this ambivalence toward dance as he would many times during his professional career: he stayed at the studio for only a month before quitting to go to college. Over the next four years Ailey worked sporadically at the Horton school, dropping in between coursework at the University of California at Los Angeles in 1949, Los Angeles City College in 1950–51, and San Francisco State College in 1952. He was a grown man of twenty-two when he finally immersed himself in serious study at the Horton school in 1953. His training included daily technique classes, informal studies of art and music prescribed by Horton, teaching children's classes, and performing as a full-fledged company member in the 1953 Horton revue *Le Bal Caribe.*

Ailey made *Afternoon Blues* (summer 1953), his first dance composition, in a workshop during the summer of 1953. Three minutes in length, the solo was a "blues adaptation" of *L'Après Midi d'un Faune* he had seen presented by the Ballet Russe de Monte Carlo. Working with a musical selection from Leonard Bernstein's *On the Town*, Ailey danced the hypersensual, animalistic role of the Faun.[12] Thus, in this first work of structured choreography, he imagined dance as a release from heterosexual white hegemony, a safe place where he could explore himself as a fully sensual being exempt from everyday constructions of race and sexuality.

Horton died suddenly in November 1953. The Horton company, which had been run like a family unit with Horton as the father figure, made an effort to continue without its namesake. Ailey enthusiastically offered choreographic scenarios and, because no one else stepped forward, assumed the role of artistic director.[13] Several engagements had already been contracted for the coming months, including a performance at the famed Jacob's Pillow dance festival in the summer of 1954. Ailey began devising his own choreography, directing scenery and costume designs, and running rehearsals. He was twenty-two years old, had been dancing seriously for a total of two nonconsecutive years, and had choreographed only one dance piece for a composition workshop.

Ailey's creative reaction to Horton's death was to make dances about people he knew. He designed his first choreographic scenarios to "pay tribute to Lester Horton, to demonstrate the strength of James Truitte, and to emphasize the beauty and dramatic ability of Carmen de Lavallade."[14] Significantly, these dances were not created to investigate methods of dance composition. Just as significant was the necessity of Ailey's choreographic output to the financial well-being of the Horton company. The company needed new works to fulfill the spring performance contracts.

Ailey threw himself into the persona of Horton's creative heir: "I knew nothing about making dances for a group so I put everything about modern dance which I had read or seen into the work. In addition, I did everything the way that I thought Lester would have done it. . . . I was just trying to be like Lester because I thought that was the way to be creative."[15] The strategy also secured the support of the Horton company dancers, each of whom possessed substantial experience beyond Ailey's. Working collaboratively, Ailey found choreographic inspiration in dances that expressed his feelings toward the Horton studio family.

Ailey conceived *According to St. Francis* (4 June 1954) as a tribute to Horton, as "kind of an allusion to Lester's life." He cast Truitte as St. Francis of Assisi, founder of the Franciscans and prophet of joy and man's harmony with nature.

James Truitte, Don Martin, Alvin Ailey, and Roland
Goldwater of the Lester Horton Dancers in Alvin Ailey's
According to St. Francis, 1954. Photographer unknown

He designed the dance to demonstrate Truitte's control and stamina: "It was all so technical—there were slow hinges, fast whirls and any movement that I could think of which was extremely difficult to perform."[16] In a conceptual gesture he followed throughout his career when choreographing for men, Ailey imagined the dance as a challenge to Truitte's ability, a site in which to publicly contest the dancer's mastery of dance technique. Set to a commissioned score from Gershon Kingsley, the dance originally lasted some forty-five minutes, though it was finally cut to thirty-seven minutes before its premiere.[17] A rare photograph of the dance shows Truitte posed with an oversized prop cross, balanced on his toes, his body hinged from the knees, holding a cross with a sense of familiar care.[18]

Morning Mourning (4 June 1954) featured Carmen de Lavallade as the dramatic heroine of "three continuous dance episodes after themes explored by Tennessee Williams."[19] Ailey designed the dance to present de Lavallade's body in its most graceful states: "Carmen was the star and I had her doing everything which I thought would exemplify her dramatic ability and enhance her beauty."[20] Divided into three parts, the dance followed de Lavallade through episodes of frustration, despair, and regret. "Morning" began the piece with a girl returning home from a night "in the world," fighting with her parents, dissolving her family ties, and mourning her lost sense of family. "Afternoon" followed de Lavallade through the "the love world of womanhood," an episode of lost love involving a young man and another woman. "Evening" presented a "dark, lightning-lit bacchanale" in which a mature woman mourned missed opportunities and indulged her deep anger. Ailey and Truitte alternated as the men in de Lavallade's life and Lelia Goldoni played all the other roles.[21]

Following the example set by Horton, Ailey designed the sets and costumes for *Morning Mourning* himself and collaborated with Diane Kadden on lighting effects. Suzanne Jonson performed the original score by Gertrude Rivers Robinson on a solo piano. In Ailey's recollection, the dance premiered slightly overblown: "I took everything Tennessee Williams had ever written and put it onstage. And I did this with a cast of three people. It was so confusing that I'm sure nobody knew what was going on."[22] As a depiction of de Lavallade's beauty, *Morning Mourning* established a model of glamorization Ailey followed throughout his career when choreographing for women. De Lavallade's role confirmed a woman's heroic ability to command the stage in an emotionally wrought portrait of her femininity, defined here by her relationship to, and rejection of, various men.

Unlike his contemporaries, who might develop choreographic technique over months of private study and experimentation, Ailey thus began his dance-making career as the resident choreographer of a nationally recognized ensemble. In addition to these two inaugural works, he made his first large group piece for the Horton company. He set *Creation of the World* (13 July 1954) to Darius Milhaud's score for a single summer performance by the Horton company with the San Diego Symphony. All of these dances were presented to a wide general public that included critics.

Of Ailey's entire choreographic output, only two or three short dances escaped serious scrutiny by professional dance critics. He also began making dances with the guarantee of public performance, to fulfill contracts the Horton company had already made. He thus placed the business of turning out finished dances on a level with the act of expression through choreography. This parity of function and form followed him throughout his career, manifesting a consistent professional veneer in his work and a respect for the serendipitous discoveries of the choreographic process. Ailey learned early on how far, or near, he had to reach to create a presentable dance.

As a dancer, Ailey learned to capitalize on the simmering, hypermasculine persona he developed at the Horton studio. Aware of his technical limitations, he relied on a stance that fortunately fit neatly with Horton's choreographic depictions of "ethnic" male-female duets still in the company repertory. Often partner to willowy and lithe Carmen de Lavallade, Ailey brought brutish muscular force to Horton's erotic "Cumbia" and the dedication "To José Clemente Orozco," both of 1953. Dancing engagements picked up through 1954: with partner de Lavallade, Ailey appeared in a segment of the film *Carmen Jones* choreographed by Herbert Ross, and the Horton company performed Ailey's commercial choreography on the television programs *Party at Ciro's*, the *Red Skelton Show*, and the *Jack Benny Show*.[23]

At Herbert Ross's request, Ailey moved to New York in December 1954 to appear with de Lavallade in the Broadway musical *House of Flowers*.[24] Their appearance featured "a very sexy pas de deux" designed to titillate the mostly white audience.[25] Among the last-gasp attempts at exoticized, "mostly black" Broadway musicals set in foreign locales, *House of Flowers* boasted an extraordinary company of African American dance talent, including Leu Comacho, Geoffrey Holder, Louis Johnson, Audrey Mason, Arthur Mitchell, Albert Popwell, Glory Van Scott, Margot Small, and Walter Nicks. Truman Capote's libretto described two competing West Indian bordellos and offered African American actresses myriad "hooker" roles. According to Brooks Atkinson's *New York Times* review, the cast must have exuded a predictable exotic-primitive appeal: "Every Negro show includes wonderful dancing. *House of Flowers* is no exception in that respect. Tall and short Negroes, adults and youngsters, torrid maidens in flashy costumes and bare-chested bucks break out into a number of wild, grotesque, animalistic dances . . . [which] look and sound alike by the time of the second act."[26] Although Atkinson and the Broadway audience he represented, along with the performers, led by the sarcastic wit of Pearl Bailey, surely all took the show with a wink and a nod, its racial and sexual stereotyping persisted. By its authors' design or default, *House of Flowers* introduced Ailey to the New York dance scene as part of the wild, monotonous grotesquerie of black bodies performing for white audiences.

Ailey found the New York dance community remarkably fluid and available to handsome young men willing to "play black" in a limited range of ethnic roles. He danced in several Broadway musicals and fulfilled his aspirations to be recognized as a professional dancer, but he also wanted to continue the creative work he had begun at the Horton school. He found few mentors sensitive to his cultural background, and the concert dance techniques he encountered failed to engage him: "I went to watch Martha Graham, and her dance was finicky and strange. I went to Doris Humphrey and José Limón and I just hated it all. I suppose that I was looking for a technique which was similar to Lester's and I just did not find it."[27] Ailey focused on performing and teaching more than study, working at New Dance Group and teaching in rented studios around town.[28] While dancing in the Broadway musical *Jamaica*, he gathered a group of dancers to fill a shared afternoon concert slot at the 92nd Street YM-YWHA. Five years after Horton's death, Horton's legacy provided the conceptual and thematic underpinnings for each of Ailey's new works.

Ailey danced in two of his three world premieres: *Redonda* (30 March 1958), a curtain-raiser suite of five dances to a Latin theme, and *Ode and Homage* (30 March 1958), a solo dedicated to the memory of Horton. Ailey's stage presence captured most of the critical attention given the concert, and critics likened his passionately flamboyant style to the movements of wild animals. Doris Hering, reviewing for *Dance Magazine*, compared him to "a caged lion full of lashing power that he can contain or release at will," and John Martin noted his "rich, animal quality of movement and innate sense of theatrical projection." Ailey's machismo caused P. W. Manchester to resort to the cliché that he presented a stage world "in which the men are men and the women are frankly delighted about it."[29]

Redonda, later retitled *Cinco Latinos* (21 December 1958), strung together five short pieces of exotica described as "Latin Theme." Ailey's program note explained that the dances were "not intended as exact duplications of any ethnic form but creative interpretations of the mood, style, and rich variety of the Afro-Brazilian-Caribbean heritage.[30] Normand Maxon's costumes relied on feathers, plumed headdresses and wigs, an array of flower and bead necklaces, and "fetish masks" to suggest an exotic atmosphere, although posed photographs indicate that Ailey's choreography relied on postures from theatrical jazz dance styles.

Redonda looked a lot like dances Ailey had performed at the Horton Theater,[31] and on at least one occasion (27 January 1962) included several Horton-credited pieces among its number. Most successful of the suite was the bawdy "Rumba," alternately titled "El Cigaro," that Ailey conceived for Charles Moore

Jacqueline Walcott and Charles Moore in Alvin Ailey's *Cinco Latinos*, 1958. Photograph by James O. Mitchell

and Jacqueline Walcott as "the age-old fight between men and women stated in new terms."[32]

Redonda's thematic gambit blatantly aligned overt heterosexuality and primitivism with the dancing black body. Ailey acknowledged this regressive tension in program notes for the "Rite" which ended the suite: "The innate sense of melodrama of the primitive ritual is *exploited* in this interpretation of an Afro-Brazilian fetishistic ritual, with movements based on both the sensual and animalistic elements of these rites."[33] "Rite," alternately titled "Canto al Diablo," included roles of a Shaman, several Acolytes, and two Initiates, performing a ceremony framed by a processional danced in swirling white robes. Ailey danced the role of the male initiate bare-chested, costumed in form-fitting white pants adorned at the waist by a belt of feathers. Obviously an early draft of the "Wade in the Water" sequence of *Revelations*, "Rite" contained a theme Ailey recreated throughout his career: a ritualistic ceremony describing initiation into the larger group.

Ailey danced *Ode and Homage*, a solo "dance of faith, respectfully dedicated to the memory of Lester Horton, modern dance pioneer and innovator,"[34] to a recorded score by Peggy Glanville-Hicks. Essentially a choreographed demonstration of Horton classroom exercises,[35] *Ode* conveyed "moving dignity and a naively baroque air of poetry," although Ailey "revealed a lack of experience in the manipulation of his props."[36] A "tender, introspective piece," *Ode* allowed Ailey to demonstrate his lyrical abilities, to dance "with a kind of solemn mournfulness."[37]

The relative quiet of *Ode* stood in stark contrast to other material presented on the 30 March 1958 program. Twenty-eight African American dancers and a number of musicians participated in the concert Ailey shared with choreographer Ernest Parham, with headlining guest artist Talley Beatty performing the role of Icarus in Parham's *Trajectories*. The powerful roster and massive range of material Ailey and Parham presented confounded the *Dance News* columnist, who wrote, "There were too many dancers, too many compositions and too much going on, to carry away any definite impression of the performances as a whole."[38] The unprecedented scale and ambition of the program arranged by Ailey and Parham suggested a strategic takeover of the Kaufmann Concert Hall to confirm, in a single performance, the undeniable range of facility possessed by the black body in concert dance.

Harold Pearson, Nat Horne, and Alvin Ailey in Alvin Ailey's "Rite," 1958.
Photograph by Normand Maxon

■ Unquenchable Racial Desire

For the majority of white men the Negro represents the sexual
instinct (in its raw state). The Negro is the incarnation of a
genital potency beyond all moralities and prohibitions.
—*Frantz Fanon,* Black Skin, White Masks

Ailey's dances often confront their audience with the display of beautiful bodies, to be consumed at the willing viewer's leisure. Modern dance did not begin with an obsession with bodies, but Ailey's company always offered voracious (white) audiences a feast of physically elegant (black) bodies. Most audiences, including critics, enjoyed this allure, but some resisted the visibility of flesh as an unwelcome distraction, as an attraction beyond the tacitly agreed-on boundaries of psychological and emotional

35

landscapes to be explored in modern dance. Concert dance performance allows, often demands, a visual consumption of physical form in public spaces. The Ailey company leaned into its ability to feed an appetite for delectable black bodies; from its earliest performances, the company encouraged it. When critic P. W. Manchester wrote that Ailey's 1962 "Rite" "retained a strange delicacy in spite of its unashamedly sexual basis," she predicted a prominent strain of willing discomfort that hovered over the company's profile.[39]

Some of Ailey's dances seem to be about displaying the body and the dialectic of physical desire and intellectual abstraction enacted by the presence of beautiful black bodies engaged in concert dance. The brawny black men who "play" laborers in modern dance works such as Ailey's *Blues Suite* or Donald McKayle's *Rainbow 'round My Shoulder* (1959, revived by the Ailey company in 1972) revise conceptions of "work" through their presence on opera house stages. These men may look like laborers, but they are, in fact, artists; the pleasure their bodies in motion provide for them and us is the labor of their trade. As art, it is a self-referential, self-conscious labor that exists only by the force of its own volition. Surely this has something to do with why many of Ailey's critics felt compelled to record his work as "entertainment." To them, the work of Ailey's dances seemed concerned with satisfying the audience rather than exploring form. One distinction between art and entertainment focuses on its generative impulse. In dance, entertainment is created for the pleasure of the audience, whereas art emerges to explore the interests of the artist. Which was Ailey interested in pursuing?

If Ailey had been interested only in the drama of the black male body, he might have joined prominent ranks of visual artists including realist painter John Singer Sargent, whose African American model Thomas E. McKeller became the prototypical (white) male body in a series of frescoes completed at the Boston Museum in 1921,[40] and photographer Robert Mapplethorpe, whose 1986 *Black Book* inspired controversy in its depictions of black anatomy as aesthetic destiny.[41] Both of these visual artists explored black musculature as a source and solution to the "problem" of representing masculinity. For his part, Sargent erased McKeller's race in the completed frescoes; he attached more "classical" (European) heads to McKeller's physical form. Black male musculature on display embodies a history of racialized social relations in America; that politicized history pulsates from imagery that Mapplethorpe offered, as it does in some of Ailey's dances.

Even as Ailey framed his early dances in a theatrical milieu that allowed his dancers to be "everyday people," he consistently sexualized their stage personas. The "Preaching Spiritual" in *Revelations* details gender roles according to sexualized play; in *Blues Suite*, the black body is repeatedly represented as libidinous. In other early works, Ailey glorified the beauty of Carmen de Lavallade and Matt Turney in works that displayed their physiques, extravagantly, to the audience. If Ailey understood the political dimensions of a physical discourse of difference that his mostly black company held for his mostly white audiences, why did he consistently revisit sexually tinged depictions?

An answer to Ailey's strategy may be found in the theatrical frames he invented for the display of the body. The chaste monk of *Hermit Songs*, the work of respected (if risqué) American literary legend Tennessee Williams that provided the narrative for *Morning Mourning*, the biblical creation myth of *Creation of the World*, a religious ceremony in *Revelations*, and the frame of race- and class-based pathos of *Blues Suite* each offered a narrative frame that mitigated the directly erotic effect of bare bodies in public spaces. Even as Ailey subscribed to the trope of the (black) primitive in works like *Creation of the World* and *Redonda*, he underscored the revisionist reality that positioned him, a young black man, as the author of these explorations of mythic pasts circumscribed by physicality. Ailey may have "titillated" as a means to an end: to expand the possibilities for patronage and audience loyalty that black concert dance artists deserved.

Ailey offered his dancers an oversized construction of the dancing black body that glorified its resilience, its musculature, and its knowledge of embedded cultural practice. The dances he made before 1965, when he still performed regularly, encouraged an overtly physical, brawny style of male stage dancing that subscribed to traditional associations of black male bodies and their implicit potential for work. Eager to debunk public perceptions of male concert dancing as precious or fey, Ailey settled into his hypermasculine stance, and for some time snubbed classical ballet training for boys, which might "tend to make boys seem effete on stage."[42] His powerful projection attracted a strong ensemble of male dancers in the company's early years, including Glenn Brooks, Donato Capozzoli, Louis Falco, Miguel Godreau, Nathaniel Horne, William Louther, Charles Moore, Harold Pierson, Robert Powell, Kelvin Rotardier, and Morton Winston in the 1960s. In later years, Hector Mercado, Clive Thompson, and Peter Woodin in the 1970s; Kevin Brown, Gary DeLoatch, Dwight Rhoden, and Andre Tyson in the 1980s; and Michael Joy, Leonard Meek, Desmond Richardson, Uri Sands, and Glenn Sims in the 1990s all attracted audiences through their tangible bulk and powerful projection of recognizable masculinity.

The glamorous, sexualized black female presence Ailey constructed on concert dance stages fit stereotypical models familiar, at least, from the stage successes of Josephine Baker and Katherine Dunham. Both Baker and Dunham aligned their undeniable beauty with an erotic power expressed through dance motion. Although each of these artists was uniquely talented, their celebrity generated stereotypes of powerful black women as both manipulative—ironically, by virtue of their very eroticism—and sexually available. These "Jezebel" characters emerged purposefully in some Ailey dances, including *Blues Suite*.

In all, the sexualized "black buck" and "Jezebel" imagery that Ailey and his dancers inhabited, largely by their presence as muscular men and glamorous women on public stages, satisfied racialized desire even as it encouraged it. This double-edged effect allowed white audiences access to glamorous black bodies in heightened states of grace, whether those audiences viewed their efforts as aesthetic, erotic, or, more likely, a combination of the two. Black bodies on display seem to enact this duality by virtue of America's peculiar social history. As James Baldwin quipped in his essay "The Black Boy Looks at the White Boy," "To be an American Negro male is also to be a kind of walking phallic symbol, which means that one pays in one's own personality, for the sexual insecurity of others."[43] For Ailey and his male dancers, this often seemed an apt depiction of their effect on audiences.

▌ *Blues Suite*

Blues Suite (30 March 1958), the closing piece on the Ailey–Parham program, garnered immediate popular and critical acclaim. Drawing on fragments of his Texas childhood, Ailey set the dance in and about a "barrelhouse," a backwoods music hall/whorehouse for working-class African Americans. To a musical background of standard twelve-bar blues, ballads, slowdrags, and shams, archetypal Depression-era characters conveyed the fleeting pleasures of dance buried in an evening fraught with fighting, regret, and despair. Costumed with dazzling Broadway-style flair, the suite sizzled with rage and sorrow, at once highly theatrical and pointedly dramatic.

Ailey's original program note aligned his dance with cultural roots: "The musical heritage of the southern Negro remains a profound influence on the music of the world . . . during the dark days the blues sprang full-born from the docks and the fields, saloons and bawdy houses . . . indeed from the very souls of their creators."[44] The note served to validate the blues milieu for an uninitiated white audience by defining it as both personal (from the soul of their creator) and artful (part of a profoundly influential musical heritage). The reference to the dark days (of southern slavery) neatly telescoped cultural history into the premise for the dance: audiences were invited to view the dancing black bodies as authentic bearers of the blues. *Blues Suite* intended to map this southern musicality onto the concert dance stage.

The bawdy house setting played directly into traditional stereotyping of the black body as at once morally corrupt and titillating. As in *House of Flowers*, the women in *Blues Suite* portrayed hookers, and the men, their eager clients. But Ailey managed to explore the cultural basis of the stereotype, to locate the gender role playing within a larger frame of African American pathos. Here blues dancing stood explicitly for the ephemeral release from overwhelming social inequities suffered by African Americans. The frame allowed Ailey to implicate harsh political realities in the formation of intensely flamboyant and entertaining blues dance styles.

Blues Suite reached its final format in the fall of 1964. The dance was alternately titled *Jazz Piece, Roots of the Blues* (under both titles, 12 June 1961) and *The Blues Roll On* (6 September 1963) in slightly varied formats. Ailey's revisions were mostly the result of shifting company personnel. The scenic element of a large ladder, subtle changes of costume pieces from scene to scene, and an arching narrative suggesting cyclical and inevitable despair are common to its several versions. The dance became a classic example of the choreographer's early style and remains in the active repertoire of the Alvin Ailey American Dance Theater. The reading of the dance that follows is based on filmed performances made in the 1960s and 1970s, and live performances attended in the 1980s and 1990s.

The dance begins with two traditional calls to attention in African American folklore: the train whistle, which suggests movement away from the repressive conditions of the South, and church bells, which toll the arrival of news worthy of community attention. Fast conga drums beat incessantly as the curtain rises, echoing the talking drum sound that traditionally dispersed information in sub-Saharan cultures. The curtain reveals bodies strewn across the stage in posed attitudes of fitful despair: eyes closed, energy drained. Are they asleep or dead? To classic strains that acknowledge the capitulation to oppressive circumstances—"Good morning Blues, Blues how do you do?"—they rise, shake off the inertia that held them, and begin an angry ritual of fighting each other to stake out territory. The atmosphere is heavy with stifled rage and disappointment.

As simple gestures like a weighed-down walking motion take on rhythmic regularity, the fighting gradually evolves into dance movements. In this casual progression Ailey suggests that his dance occupies a cultural space similar to the blues themselves, as the transformation of social and political rage into art. The lexicon shift—from stasis, through the stylized drama of angry individuals, to a common ground represented in dance—draws the audience into concert dance without removing the markers that distinguish the characters as disenfranchised African Americans. These Blues People are black people, and the dance they do is defined by that unique political circumstance, whether it contains elements of social dance, ballet, Graham, or Horton technique.

Male roles in *Blues Suite* are largely defined by interaction with female characters, a libidinous virility underscoring most of the men's motion in the dance. The male solo "I Cried" includes a striking demonstration of public male vulnerability. Backed by contrapuntal motions from the group, a single man sits, center stage, his body racked with contractions of pain and anger. As he shakes and trembles, detailing the depths of his anguish, the group extends a hand toward him, bearing witness. He rises to gesture toward some unseen offstage goal while holding his body tense, elongated, and brittle. The group reaches after him to offer help, but he pushes them away defiantly, wrestling one man to the ground in the process. The group disperses to strike poses of studied indifference with their faces averted from him. He works out his frustration in a solo dance built from failed movements: turns that plummet out of control, interrupted by sharp rhythmic accents in briefly held frozen poses suggesting confusion; a sudden drop to the floor, from which he tries to rise by pushing feebly against the ground with splayed legs; and desperate running gestures, which get him nowhere.

"I Cried" emerges as a danced meditation on black masculinity, defined here in terms of its intense collaboration with, and rejection of, the larger group. The solo is typically danced by a mature member of the Ailey ensemble; among its prominent interpreters are James Truitte in the 1960s, Kelvin Rotardier and Clive Thompson in the 1970s and 1980s, and Michael Joy in the 1990s. Each of these dancers infuses the dance with authority, commanding the central focus through the projection of longing and regret. Their performances enact the possibility of public vulnerability in the dancing black male body, a potential routinely absent from the concert dance stage. In allowing his dancers this moment of private anguish, framed as a feature of daily life in the larger southern landscape of *Blues Suite*, Ailey began his career-long choreographic project of re-defining stage imagery and roles available to dancing black bodies.

The solo is complemented by the full-throated wailing of singer Brother John Sellers, who performed this piece with the Ailey company beginning in 1961 both live and on its taped accompaniment.[45] Sellers's wailing has a strident masculine urgency rarely heard outside the rural South. Musicologist Albert Murray associates the sound with itinerant folk-style guitar strummers.[46] His vocal style gives an intensely personal interpretation to what is essentially a common song, without author or copyright. The song lyric, "I cried, tears rolled down my cheek/Thinking about my baby, how sweet the woman used to be," is a simple, bare-bones couplet, practically devoid of character. Firmly rooted in the Afro-American vernacular, Sellers's aggressive sound resonates a masculine connection between the expression of sorrow and the male dancer: it validates concert dance as an extension of wailing the blues, an "authentic" mode of black male behavior.

A train whistle serves as the bridge to "Mean Ole Frisco," a dance for five men. Entering the space singly, each man looks toward an offstage train imagined to pass over the audience's head. Watching the train closely, they undulate in seething slow motion, sinking into asymmetrical stances with one hip thrust sideward. A swaying hip movement begins slowly and accelerates, finally matching the fast shuffle tempo of the song. Their dance emerges as an arrangement of stylized locomotion: fast walking with sharply swaying hips; running with a loping, downward-directed jump; and striding in circles with bold, purposeful steps. The men describe powerful accents at the ends of phrases: shooting an arm into space, stopping the flow of bubbling energy with a tightly clenched fist. They dance separately, in wide spatial formation, without ever seeing each other.

Although the dance is about the men's longing for a lover whom the train took away (the "Frisco" of the blues lyric), sexuality is buried deeply beneath a brawny veneer. Ailey's choreography studiously avoids intimations of homo-eroticism here through blockish movements arranged in square, eight-count phrases, constant explosive movement, and a fierce abstention from physical or emotional contact by the men. The result is a strangely harsh depiction of black men as unable to relate to each other. The exaggerated heterosexuality of the staging becomes more poignant in light of Ailey's own homosexuality. His hy-permasculine performance stance, readily apparent when he performed this dance in the 1960s, masked his offstage homosexuality through the enactment of libidinous bravado, a practice he reiterated throughout his career. In this dance, the desirous black male body is overtly heterosexual, single-mindedly in pursuit of an offstage woman.

"House of the Rising Sun," a moody character study for three women, de-scribes the private despair enacted in the safety of the hookers' boudoir. Three women are revealed in posed attitudes of introspection: looking into a hand mirror, combing their hair, and gazing pensively out of a window. In slow, reaching extensions of arms and legs, the women come to life as the musical ballad begins its tale of woe. Eventually, they run to the corners of the room, reaching and leaping in an effort to get out. In a choreographic structure later duplicated by "Daniel" of *Revelations*, "Rising Sun" follows the ballad's strophic musical form with an introductory chorus, solo verses for each of the three women, a verse for all three women in unison, and a final musical tag. In the same manner as the three celebrants of "Daniel," who collectively express a dramatic impulse of persuasion fed by emotional states such as anguish and obstinacy, the three women's solos are expressions of a single dramatic impulse of regret, fed by a string of emotional colors including anger, despair, and self-loathing.

"Rising Sun" offers feminine counterpoint to the men's "Frisco" dance. Ailey constructs the women's movement largely from lyrical, swirling phrases and supple, balletic postures. Unlike the men of "Frisco," the women here commiserate, holding their bodies close together as they comfort and witness each other's dances. Both "Rising Sun" and "Frisco" suggest a dramatic situation unaltered by the occurrence of the dance; the women here finish in a careful resumption of their opening tableau, apparently trapped in an unchanging cycle of despair.

"Backwater Blues," the central pas de deux of *Blues Suite*, features a man and a woman in a low-down, brutal lovers' battle. Drawn in broad strokes of gender role playing, the dance depicts several stages of a courtship ritual built from boasts, struts, and apache-style physical confrontation. The choreography depends heavily on a realistic acting approach Ailey derived from study at the Stella Adler acting studio.[47] A pervasive use of body language, stance, and gesture fills out details of the emotional life between the characters. Formal dance movements function as extensions of the dramatic narrative, making the rare motionless position stand out in sharp relief. In one instance, the woman, precariously balanced on the kneeling man's shoulder, throws back her head to pound her chest in angry defiance. The image resounds beyond this couple's dance encounter, speaking of the emotional outrage brought about by dysfunctional circumstance—in this case, life in a southern whorehouse.

While trading on the entertainment value of the age-old battle of the sexes, Ailey aligns black social dance styles with concert performance, framing the dances as the currency of sexual power negotiation. The black social dance structures evident here embody African retentions described by Robert Farris Thompson in his study of sub-Saharan art, including a percussive concept of performance; the use of complex rhythmic meter; apart playing, in which each musician/dancer remains "intent upon the production of his own contribution to a polymetric whole"; call and response; and dances of social derision.[48] These markers appear in flamboyant percussive breaks at the end of musical phrases, complex meter elaborated by isolations of body parts, and apart phrasing palpable in complementary rhythmic patterns executed simultaneously by both dancers. In the frame of Ailey's choreography, these markers are carefully embedded within a theatrically constructed tension between (black) man and woman. Here, blues dance is itself construed to be a marker of heterosexuality in which, as in the rhythm and blues music that inspired it, ritual conflict between man and woman becomes "a heavily encoded symbol of racial difference and racial distinctiveness."[49]

The brief solos of "In the Evening" render three men preparing for a night at the barrelhouse. Ailey uses formal dance vocabulary to describe three distinct personalities in movement terms. Arcing turns interrupted by slight hesitations for a methodical man, swooping balances cut off by full-bodied contractions for an impassioned man, and cool struts stopped by percussive attacks of static poses for a self-possessed gigolo all visualize the music's underlying rhythmic structures in terms of breaks and ruptures. These oppositional contrasts are obvious functions of lingering West African aesthetic principles of compositional balance, where breaks offer an expected and welcome intensification of rhythmic process. Ailey fashions movement phrasing here mostly in square blocks of four and eight counts, but sharp accents and strong rhythmic shifts from fast, sixteenth-note foot-tapping accents to slow, half-note balances separate the dance from the music: the dance is conceived both to and apart from the steady musical beat.

The dance solos end when the women reappear, beginning a long sequence of festive blues dancing by the group and two comic characters constantly out of step. The giddy playfulness of "Sham" contradicts the anger, despair, and fierce attitude of previous sections, exploring instead the entertainment aspects of blues music. The section ends with tightly focused unison phrases, with the dancers' smiling faces turned toward the audience in a gesture of communal celebration. Reminiscent of a scene from a Broadway musical, this false happy ending is followed by the repetition of "Good Morning Blues," signaling the return to the painful everyday life of labor and oppression. Faces are deflected and suddenly solemn; bodies carry an intense weightiness; speed and agility are buried in downward-directed motions and angry demeanors. In this "real" ending to the piece, the characters are again solitary, sprawled across the stage, separated by forces beyond their control, apprehensive, gloom-ridden, and tormented.

The violent juxtaposition of bald euphoria and deep despair that ends *Blues Suite* parallels the professional experiences of Ailey and other black dancers through the postwar era of concert dance. Smiling through a fleeting triumph, they were inevitably burdened by political circumstances rife with racism, homophobia, and disinterest. Forced to entertain audiences conditioned by broadly stereotyped personae, African American men danced savage, hypermasculine, and aggressively heterosexual roles that catered to traditional assumptions about the black male body, and African American women danced histrionic, sexually savvy, and submissive roles that demonstrated traditional correlations of exotic beauty and sexual availability.

Blues Suite possessed an ironic resemblance to the dances of *House of Flowers* and similar Broadway and Hollywood works that associated black bodies with rampant sexuality. In claiming stereotypical roles traditionally available to black bodies as his choreographic material, Ailey asked his dancers to question the assumptions surrounding the stereotypes. The black male bodies in *Blues Suite* tempered the overwhelming sensuality and impervious brawn of the whole

Barbara Alston, Merle Derby, Minnie Marshall, and
Alvin Ailey in Alvin Ailey's *Blues Suite*, 1958.
Photograph by Alix Jeffry

with "I Cried," a public display of vulnerability and regret. The black female bodies in *Blues Suite* mitigated the projection of hardened, glamorous sexual availability by the fiercely passionate and lyrical meditation of "House of the Rising Sun." Together, the dancing bodies filled the familiar scenario with an unprecedented attention to dramatic detail, investing the stereotypes with contradictory/complementary impulses of power and pathos, technical facility, and emotional abandon. *Blues Suite* veered closer than its predecessors to a layered depiction of the heightened, competitive cultural processes that give rise to blues music. In 1958, black bodies dancing Ailey's blues best fulfilled the music's "autobiographical chronicle of personal catastrophe expressed lyrically."[50]

With his two breakthrough choreographic successes, *Revelations* and its predecessor *Blues Suite*, Ailey arrived fully formed as a black creative artist of obvious importance. His early work echoed literary traditions of black autobiography, registering "the existence of a 'black self' that had transcended the limitations and restrictions that racism had placed on the personal development of the black individual." Echoing a distinctive African American tradition, in which "an author typically publishes as a *first* book her or his autobiography, establishing her or his presence and career as a writer through this autobiographical act,"[51] Ailey built his career on these two works and their cogent distillation of childhood memory into concert dance.

■ Ailey's Early Dances

Following the success of the 30 March 1958 concert, Ailey continued making dances for a constantly shifting roster of dancers available for concert dates at the 92nd Street YM-YWHA and the Clark Center. The range of thematic material and compositional strategies he employed expanded throughout this period. Common to all the dances was a heavy reliance on flamboyant costuming, properties, and decor designed by Normand Maxon and Ves Harper and extravagant shifts of mood created by the lighting designs of Nicola Cernovich.

Ariette Oubliée (21 December 1958), set to music from Debussy's song cycle of the same title, received a single performance. Ailey developed a choreographic fantasy from Debussy's impressionist settings of Verlaine's symbolist poetry. He portrayed a distracted youthful Wanderer who met a Clown (Don Price) and traded the flower of reality for the illusion of a beautiful Moon (Carmen de Lavallade).[52] Much of the action was conveyed in pantomime. The Clown's crescent moon, exchanged for a flower plucked from the brim of the Wanderer's hat, became first a large cardboard moon, and finally de Lavallade and her retinue of attendants bearing branches and sea shells. Lovestruck, the Wanderer caught the Moon in a net, only to find himself captured by her spell. The Moon left, and the cardboard moon followed her. The man found a sea shell beneath his hat.

Ailey certainly made the dance to display the beauty of de Lavallade, who, when "borne about the stage by her votaries in sweeping crescents, might have been an incarnation of Diana, chaste goddess of the moon." (Two years later, de Lavallade played the same role in Glen Tetley's version of the theme, titled *Pierrot Lunaire*.) The performance of Don Price as the Pierrot Lunaire figure in Ailey's dance seemed "not quite firm enough,"[53] although Ailey conveyed a "believable simple conviction" as the man.[54] *Ariette Oubliée* relied heavily on Maxon's sumptuous decor and costumes, though, as one critic quipped, "props are no substitute for meaningful dance."[55]

Sonera (31 January 1960) became Ailey's first effort at choreographing on pointe. These "three abstract dances after Cuban dance forms" were poorly received as a "far from satisfactory" mixture of ballet and free-style dancing.[56] Ailey unsuccessfully submitted the dance to audition for a choreographer's workshop sponsored by the New York City Ballet in the summer of 1960.[57]

Ailey reworked *Creation of the World* (second version, 31 January 1960) as a duet for himself and guest artist Matt Turney from the Martha Graham Dance Company. He enjoyed rapturous acclaim for this "fresh, inventive, and beguiling" depiction of the "oldest love story known to man," which "showed the emergence of man, his delight in the beauty of nature, his discovery of woman and their joy in living together. The plan could not have been simpler, but it had a marvelous quality of breathless, unquestioning wonder."[58] Walter Terry concurred in praising the general structure of the work, though he noted "some unmotivated (either formally or dramatically) bursts of virtuosity" at odds with the overall "taste and imaginativeness" of the action.[59]

Again relying heavily on stage decor, Ailey emerged from a prop cocoon to dance in front of projections of flowers and trees. According to one critic, he seemed "small, awed and apprehensive" as the first man in a world "absolutely new and completely wonderful. . . . But he is human, and therefore curious, and his fingers reach out to touch and experience. Then, out of his growing sense of loneliness, comes the creation of Eve, as innocent and wondering as himself."[60]

In 1962 Ailey again reworked *Creation of the World* (third version, 9 September 1962), adding roles for seven additional dancers to suggest the creation of the first man and woman "as it might have been envisioned by the primitive mind." The shift of frame added significant theatrical distance between Ailey and his "awestruck and innocent" role in the dance. Ailey's new program notes convey an increased theatrical-cultural awareness, if not specificity: "Among certain primitive tribes there is the belief that the creation of man was a whim of certain primitive gods, that the sun, moon, sky and stars rose from the mist summoned by the Great Shaman, that the first man and woman rose from the mud of the great dark river."[61]

Ailey commissioned designer Ves Harper to create masks and gilded props for the tribespeople and outlined a six-part sequence: "Overture," "Adam's Birth," "Eve's Birth," "First Tango," "Celebration," and "Final Adagio" for all, to end with huge branches suspended over the heads of the couples.[62] Critics found the new setting "over-produced" and "not up to Mr. Ailey's best standards,"[63] and the work disappeared after only two performances.

Ailey conceived *Knoxville: Summer of 1915* (27 November 1960) as a "dance visualization" of Samuel Barber's 1949 work for voice and orchestra.[64] The text, drawn from James Agee's *A Death in the Family*, expressed the estrangement remembered by an adult narrator "talking now of summer evenings in Knoxville Tennessee in the time that I lived there so successfully disguised to myself as a child."[65] Ailey first heard the score while working at the Horton studio in the early 1950s and professed deep personal affinities with the feelings of alienation expressed by a narrator "wandering among his family, he not knowing who he is and the family not recognizing him."[66]

Set on six dancers, *Knoxville* evoked a world of "long summer evenings with people sitting around, picnicking or walking in the fields."[67] Ailey used a scrim to suggest shifts of time: "The boy is first seen silhouetted in front of the stage, separated by a scrim from the people of his childhood, who sit quietly waiting for his thoughts to recall them to life. The scrim rises, and he moves among them until—with its fall—they return to their places, inanimate memories."[68]

Although Ailey's choreographic notes indicate that he wanted a child or young boy for the principal role, Kevin Carlisle, a European American dancer with a slight build, danced it at the premiere.[69] Ailey offered Carlisle movements suitable to "the particular gifts of this dancer which lie in the direction of large,

45

wheeling turns and soaring jumps."[70] The figures of memory moved with "softly swaying, fluid bodies" in visual contrast to the tenseness of the narrator, who yearned to join them.[71]

Ailey expanded *Knoxville* to include a company of ten dancers in 1968 (26 August 1968). The revised version clarified familial relationships of the Mother and Father to the principal character of the restless Son, to create "an unusually attractive and satisfying small work."[72] Effective, tailored costuming by Joop Stokvis provided a romanticized encounter with the idyllic dusk of a small-town summer evening. Ailey used a long piece of patterned silk as both a metaphoric and a physical barrier between the man and his memories, at times functioning as a scrim and at other times stretched taut as a harness about his torso. Reviewing for the *New York Times*, Don McDonagh focused on the successful atmospheric evocation, the accurate "mood of reverie without recrimination," and the "splendid" performances of principal dancers Judith Jamison, Kelvin Rotardier, and Dudley Williams.[73]

Modern Jazz Suite became a catch-all title for various line-ups of short curtain-raiser dances to jazz music alternately titled *Three for Now* (27 November 1960) and *Two for Now* (26 January 1962). The 1960 version, danced to recorded music by Jimmy Giuffre and John Lewis, disappeared after a single performance, as did "Trane in Three" (16 January 1962) to music by the John Coltrane Quintet.[74] "Gillespiana" (19 July 1961), danced to a recorded score by Lalo Schiffrin, remained in the *Jazz Suite* for several seasons. Ailey called this light dance for five "a 'music-visualization' of jazz music—the freedom—the interplay between dancers and instruments—the feeling of improvisation—a series of divertissements to introduce the Company to the audience."[75]

Hermit Songs

Ailey first conceived *Hermit Songs* (10 December 1961) as a group work to be set on "a company of male singers and dancers in the form of a journey." The dance premiered as a solo for Ailey, performed to Leontyne Price's recording of Samuel Barber's score. Ailey chose six of the ten anonymous Irish poems Price recorded and structured a character study of "a man like St. Francis of Assisi" engaged in "the journey thru life to death and fulfillment."[76]

Warmly received at its first performances, *Hermit Songs* provided Ailey an important solo vehicle to affirm his potent dramatic presence. Though his notes projected at least two changes of costumes and physical interaction with a setting of some sort, the dance premiered with a simple brown monk's robe and shifts of mood suggested only by lighting effects. Ailey excised two of the six sections, "The Heavenly Banquet" and "Church Bell at Night," when setting the dance on members of his company in 1965 and 1978, and *Hermit Songs* remained in the repertoire of the Alvin Ailey American Dance Theater through 1991. The reading of the dance that follows is based on film and videotape performances of the revised version made in the 1970s.

Alvin Ailey in Alvin Ailey's *Hermit Songs*, 1960.
Photograph by Jack Mitchell

The dance begins with a depiction of the monk's isolation on his pilgrimage ("At St. Patrick's Purgatory"). The monk strides onstage in a simple rhythmic pattern, holding his arms tautly across his body while carefully containing his physical energy through strictly measured steps. Brief excursions along a circular path interrupt his direct, linear course, and his outward releases of energy suggest an inner turmoil and confusion described in scooping turns and sweeping, spiral kicks. As the song shifts to a setting of direct prayer, he falls to his knees to appeal: "O only begotten Son by whom all men were made, who shunned not the death by three wounds, pity me on my pilgrimage to Loch Derg."[77] He prays in gestural accord with Barber's chiming clusters of bell tones, one sharp, emphatic gesture to each tone cluster. His petition apparently unanswered, the monk attempts to rise to his feet, only to fall backward and end crumpled on the ground.

The lyric of "St. Ita's Vision" tells of a woman who would not believe in the Lord unless He gave her His Son from Heaven in the form of a baby she may nurse. Ailey's setting describes the story as a portion of the monk's continued penance. Driven to the ground by four sharp contractions, the man mimes flogging his back as he skitters in a circle on his knees. As the music shifts to suggest the woman's prayer, the dancer's gestures soften. He rises to run in easy, gently shaped circles, stopping to cradle an imaginary baby, spinning to convey his joy at the baby's presence. He trumpets his pleasure in a series of high leg extensions, moving his weight upward toward the heavens in gleeful abandon. The section ends as he again cradles the baby, then with a gesture of his hands, releases it into the air. The monk watches the baby fly away, apparently transformed into a dove.

The short "Sea Snatch" presents the crashing of a ship in a storm. To suggest torrential catastrophe, the dancer fits frantic running phrases and quick jumps to Barber's surging score. Several times, he balances briefly in a posture of torment: holding one hand cupped to his forehead, he leans his body forward, one leg lifted backward, stretched beneath an extended arm. The dance ends with a quotation of the last movement idea of *Revelations*: the man turns several times, scooping his arms overhead, contracts at the torso, and falls to his knees, only to extend his arms on the final beat of the music in a triumphant reach toward the skies.

The final, "Crucifixion" segment contains the most theatrically effective imagery of *Hermit Songs*. Contracting his body sharply at three bell-like tones, the dancer suggests the piercing of Christ's body on the cross. Holding himself tightly at the stomach, in a gesture reminiscent of his first entrance to the dance, he revolves slowly, traveling away from the audience as if in pain. As he faces front and shoots his arms up toward the heavens, his robe opens and falls from his torso, exposing his chest.

"Crucifixion" continues with various suggestions of subjugation: rocking motions performed with the torso tightly held, walking on the knees, gestures of pleading and rolling on the ground, crawling along the floor, and harsh, spiraling falls to the ground. The dance ends with an unexpected floor-bound image of the cross. Moving after the music has ended, the man falls face first to the ground. As the lights dim, he slowly extends his arms to the sides, laying his body to rest in the position of the cross, a final gesture of submission.

Although *Hermit Songs* contains a loose narrative of a monk's pilgrimage and penance, as a whole, its theme derives more fully from imagery of the body in contemplation. The dancer performs with a meditative thoughtfulness, maintaining a strong internal focus throughout the dance. The mysterious logic of his gestures, often set to lyrics that are unintelligible to the casual listener, suggests a studied history but unknowable destiny; an indeterminate present moment rife with intense expectation. Brief moments of prayer offer the monk his only physical composure; overall, his motions describe an ambiguous spiritual transition left unresolved in his assumption of the cross position at the dance's end.

Hermit Songs also aligned religiosity with the display of the black male body. The monastic theme provided Ailey a morally chaste frame for the theatrical revelation of his torso. As the monk indulges his passion, casting off the costume of his office, he invites his audience to indulge in a voyeuristic devouring of his form.

Although no film of Ailey performing this dance exists, photographs taken in 1961 focus on the dynamic volume of his body, his thick musculature captured in sharp, sculptural relief.[78] Attention to the body is amplified by Ailey's expressionless face in the series of Jack Mitchell photographs, an attitude that forces the viewer's attention from the facial mask to the voluptuous torso extravagantly revealed during the "Crucifixion." In a 1965 *Dancing Times* photopictorial of William Louther performing *Hermit Songs*, Louther's exposed torso provides photographer Anthony Crickmay dramatic plays of chiaroscuro while ostensibly focusing on formal shapes achieved by the dancer.[79]

Reviewers of *Hermit Songs* commented positively on both Ailey's choreography and his body: "The dances, tender and ecstatic, have the exquisite simplicity and humility of the poems, and they are marvelously danced by Mr. Ailey, whose strong and supple body responds sensitively to his every command."[80] John Martin commented on Ailey's passionate performance of these trials of a tormented man "dedicated with single-minded intensity to his religious vocation. . . . Far from suggesting any cliches of monastic stillness, Mr. Ailey is almost continuously in motion, and with a superb quality of movement that is unselfconsciously beautiful in itself and altogether eloquent."[81] The "unselfconscious beauty" that Martin and other critics described surely emanated from their own desire, piqued by Ailey's sexual allure.

When Ailey revised *Hermit Songs* for Kelvin Rotardier, Clive Thompson, and Dudley Williams in 1971, he introduced technical demands absent from his original staging. Films of the three dancers reveal not only divergent portrayals of the role, but three distinct versions of the choreographic ground plan. Ailey allowed each dancer to come forward in a version presumably suited to his abilities. Rotardier, a bulky but remarkably gentle dancer with musculature reminiscent of Ailey's, performs the simplest version of the work, omitting most extended balances and several turning phrases. Thompson, perhaps the most technically proficient dancer of the trio and a then-recent member of Martha Graham's company, performs fully extended balances on one leg, multiple pirouettes, and dynamic barrel turns in his version of the dance, at times pausing in posed attitudes clearly inspired by the Graham technique. Williams creates an implosive, concentrated passion while deleting several turn combinations and moving quickly through balances on one leg.

The four distinct versions of *Hermit Songs* enlarge traditional conceptions of choreography and the dance document. Ailey provided his dancers a choreographic ground plan, then guided them toward performances best suited to their individual talents. Imperceptible to casual observation, the variations acquire profound significance for the dancers, as they allow intensely personal engagement with the music and Ailey's choreographic plan. Rather than assuming an ultimate, unbending formal construction for his work, Ailey assumes pliant dialogue between the dancers and dance figured in at the level of choreographic structure.[82]

This choreographic strategy contributed to the wide-ranging, all-encompassing emotional spectrum typically present in Ailey's work. Ailey often improvised his movements in performances of early works like "Sinner Man," *Creation of the World*, and *Hermit Songs*.[83] When later obliged to "set" these dances to teach them to subsequent interpreters, he pointed to the obvious emotional markers embedded at key musical transitions. For example, although the traveling phrases of "Sea Snatch" varied among the dancers Ailey coached in *Hermit Songs*, each version of the dance began and ended the same, passing, along the way, through specific gestural transitions. Unlike traditional modern dance choreographic practice, which attempted to distill theme into specific arrangements of movements bound by a preferred, predetermined emotional narrative, Ailey imagined choreography as an opportunity to indulge the dancer's unique impression of a general movement or musical theme. This creative technique had obvious resonance with long-established participatory standards of African American musical production, especially gospel music and small ensemble jazz.

The range of themes Ailey approached in these first dances suggests an awareness of the challenge critical stereotyping posed for an African American choreographer in the post–World War II era. Committed to the creation of stage imagery that reached beyond stereotypical presentations of "blackness" for white audiences, Ailey made ballets on pointe, created dance adaptations of Agee and Williams, and choreographed to Debussy and Milhaud. But as he attempted to expand the horizon of expressive material available to African American dancers, critics and audiences responded best to pieces that addressed obvious Afro-American themes.

Ailey was caught in a narrow cultural space available to African American choreographers, bound largely by lingering minstrel and jazz-era configurations of blackness, dance, and public performance. Racial segregation dictated the degree to which white audiences thought *Revelations* and *Blues Suite* to be autobiographical documents of Ailey and the "black race"; the choreographer shrewdly amplified that impression to enlarge the vistas available to himself and his dancers. In some ways, the characters and scenarios of *Blues Suite* and *Revelations* glamorized a separatist historical vision of black Americans oppressed by anonymous, offstage whites.

Ultimately, Ailey, who rarely claimed membership in the church as an adult, exploited religious themes in works like *Revelations*, *Hermit Songs*, and *Creation of the World* throughout his career for many of the same reasons visionary African American leaders turned to, and emerged from, the black church: to inspire hope and mask critique of mainstream social order. His success in these works aggressively confirmed the expressive potential of black dancers in the concert forum, effectively reproaching white producers and choreographers of the early 1960s who peremptorily dismissed black dancers because of their race.

Early Company

In notes outlining his plan for the formation of an American dance company, Ailey listed the following among his requirements: a home base that would include a school and center of operations; company teachers of jazz, ballet, and modern, supplemented by guest teachers of acting and related arts; an administrative staff, including an artistic director, a resident choreographer, and a ballet master; an office staff; and a company repertory of "at least 12 ballets of varying textures—[with a] main emphasis [on the] hist[ory] of [the] Negro in this country."[1] In a grant proposal dated June 1965, Ailey positioned himself as heir to a lineage from "Isadora Duncan, Ruth St. Dennis [sic], Ted Shawn, Charles Weidman, Doris Humphrey and, of course, Martha Graham," performing and creating "out of that background and an overlay of influences from film, ethnic dance, Broadway and Ballet." He suggested an alternative model to the "star dominated company" in his "group of top performers who as individuals are permitted equal opportunity to display their best." Stating that "the only way Modern Dance can survive is by a broad offering of its works in its best forms to a wide audience," Ailey offered a general purpose for his company: "to provide education in dance, to disseminate information with regard to the dance, to illuminate the history of American Modern Dance, and to entertain."[2]

Ballet companies had long acquired works by several choreographers to build a repertory and showcase their dancers, but Ailey's repertory plan had few precedents in American modern dance. In interviews, he trumpeted his ambition to "get together a repertory company—not just like a Martha Graham Company which is nothing without Martha Graham—but a company whose strength will be its repertory."[3] To achieve the technical demands of dances with varied themes, movement idiom, historical legacy, and artistic intention, Ailey predicted the necessity of ballet training: "I think . . . dancers have to be basically ballet trained. I think ideally they should have two-thirds ballet in their training for the sake of the discipline and line, and one-third modern for all those contractions and releases and, of course, the intensity."[4]

Ailey's repertory plan capitalized on the versatility that black dancers historically had achieved in order to work. Versatility long represented survival in core Afro-American culture; Ailey's company required dancers to demonstrate mastery of several forms to confirm a supreme resilience and fly in the face of racist critique. Following the example set by Lester Horton, he set out the high expectations he held for his developing company as early as 1959:

> What I will expect of dancers and myself now technically[:] proficiency in many dance areas. Dance and acting. The ability to create a dance role in movement texture as well as dramatic. Study acting. Learn to use things to induce words into oneself. Their imaginations. Physical *and* mental preparation. Makeup. Costume. We do not get to perform enough—we must do something to help our young artists. To encourage them. Make it easy for them to create. Guide them. *Care* about them. We must educate our audience.[5]

Ailey's intention to use concert dance performance as a tool of education had deep roots in African American discourse. Modern dance had been first conceived and enacted by white women, although two black women gained celebrity status as pioneers of African American modes of concert dance performance in careers that addressed issues of racial difference, cultural memory, and standards of beauty. Katherine Dunham (1909-) and Pearl Primus (1919–94) each engaged serious academic inquiry into the nature of Afro-American dance. Each surrounded her artistic innovations with graduate work in anthropology, a strategy that ensured attention respectful of the effort to catalogue deep structures of African American performance.

Painfully aware of both the need to develop a competent audience for concert dance and her limited economic and political resources, Dunham achieved her greatest performing success in the commercial arenas of Broadway and Hollywood. Much of her choreography perpetuated an exoticized Afro-Caribbean stage legacy, which linked public performances by black dancers to the stylized display of "primitive" movement. Dunham wrote and lectured widely and developed a technique built on aesthetic features of African movement retentions visible in the Americas. She worked to contextualize Afro-dance in an "effort to teach dance literacy to performers and audiences alike based on her anthropological research transformed for the stage."[6]

Primus synthesized extensive fieldwork to focus attention on dances from several African cultures. She understood dances to be compelling documents of culture in their own right: her 1952 concert of African dances was presented not in a traditional concert hall but at the American Museum of Natural History. In her remarkable essay "Primitive African Dance (and Its Influence on the Churches of the South)," written for the 1949 *Dance Encyclopedia*, Primus argued an unassailable aesthetic connection between African American dance practice and African musicality. Pointing out the absence of audience in African rituals and southern American black church ceremony, she suggested a continuity of performative intention among Africans in diaspora.[7]

The accomplishments of Dunham and Primus inspired Ailey's plan for a dance company steeped in African American cultural material. He later paid public homage to each of these dance pioneers with his company's revivals of their choreography: Primus's "Fanga" and "The Wedding" in 1974 and an evening-length tribute, *The Magic of Katherine Dunham*, in 1987. Ailey understood the difficulties Dunham and Primus surmounted to gain critical attention within the tiny public space allowed African American women in the 1930s and 1940s, a space permanently enlarged by their efforts in modern dance. Although Ailey's hypermasculine, heterosexual imagery garnered him a sizable audience from his first performances, he, too, faced obstacles as a black man in this field, including racism, public resistance to extended discussions of cultural diversity, and widespread ignorance of historical connections between African Americans and concert dance.

Black men entered the concert dance arena in the late 1920s, and the earliest dances they performed were aligned with emergent modernism in terms of theme, conception, and technique.[8] To give a few examples, in 1929 Hemsley Winfield caused a sensation dancing the role of Salomé at the Greenwich Village Cherry Lane Theater. Among Winfield's numerous concert works, "Life and Death," created for the theatrical pageant *De Promis Lan'* in May 1930, cast sixteen men as the inexorable force of Death which overcomes the singular being of Life, danced with charismatic vigor by the choreographer himself. Charles Williams formed the Creative Dance Group at Virginia's Hampton Institute in 1934 as an extension of that school's physical education activities. Heavily influenced by Ted Shawn's all-male company, which visited Hampton in 1933, Williams made dances that exploited the physical dynamism of Hampton's male dancers in traditionally masculine settings. "Men of Valor" (1934) featured movements derived from track and field events, and "Dis Ole Hammer" (1935) set a labor dance to traditional work songs. Williams also created African dance suites in collaboration with African students studying at the school, as well as dances with Afro-American themes, including a 1935 suite of "Negro Spirituals."[9]

The post–World War II era saw a number of dancers and choreographers working to redefine black male presence on the concert stage. West African aesthetic principles, persuasively outlined by African art scholar Robert Farris Thompson, emerged intact in the concert choreography of Talley Beatty, Louis Johnson, and Donald McKayle.[10] These principles, still prominent in black

American social dance forms, including the Lindy hop and the twist, arrived on the concert dance stage in the 1950s, signaling a shift in the political frame surrounding performance. Buoyed by the liberal optimism of the New York dance community of the postwar era, dancers explored ways to self-consciously align power and the black male body onstage.

▌ Early Years in New York

Ailey began his career in a commercial theatrical world that included Broadway performances, nightclub dancing, and television appearances. These circumstances appreciably influenced his aesthetic concerns, even as they brought him wide acclaim. For example, in 1955, during the year of his New York concert dance debut, Ailey posed for a series of photographs taken by prominent aesthete Carl Van Vechten, a distinction that confirmed his arrival as an artist of note.[11] Broadway appearances in plays and musicals that traded on "Negro themes" also shaped Ailey's impression of performance bound by explicitly racial concerns.

After enjoying the financial reward of a $150-per-week paycheck for dancing in *House of Flowers*, Ailey continued to work off-Broadway, playing the mysterious role of the "Purple [Chinese] Bandit" in the Phoenix Theatre production of *The Carefree Tree* (October 1955); partnering Graham dancer Mary Hinkson in a U.S. tour of the Harry Belafonte vehicle *Sing, Man, Sing* (March 1956); dancing in *Calypso Carnival*, a calypso revue staged by Geoffrey Holder (April 1957); and performing in a production of *Show Boat* that played summer stock at Jones Beach in 1957. Each of these roles made concessions to traditional American constructions of race, masculinity, and the presumption of a largely white audience. Speaking of *Show Boat*, Ailey later recalled that he "hated the whole scene" and danced only for the much-needed paychecks.[12]

Ailey cast himself as an outsider-rebel to the New York dance scene of African American artists, creating a persona that resisted established norms: "I hated everything which was the 'accepted' thing to do. I insulted everyone because I wore jeans and tee shirts and boots when we traveled; I also slept on the bus" rather than socialize with colleagues. Choreography for the musical shows offered him "a whole new way of dancing and I didn't try very hard to adjust to it." During this period he also began staking out territorial claims on black culture, arguing with West Indian specialist Harry Belafonte about the authentic roots of black music: "Ailey felt that he knew about 'real' black music and songs, and that Belafonte had no innate identification with American blacks and that he was not a serious artist."[13]

Throughout the late 1950s Ailey studied dance technique sporadically at the New Dance Group with Hanya Holm, Anna Sokolow, and Charles Weidman, and ballet master Karel Shook. His dance training was neither exhaustive nor broad. Still, his flamboyant and intensive performance style brought him offers to work with several choreographers, and he danced in the one-night-only sea-

Alvin Ailey and Red Skelton
backstage at the *Red Skelton
Show,* 1954. Photograph by
Howard Morehead

sons of Donald McKayle's company, in *Games* and *Her Name Was Harriet,* took over McKayle's role in Sokolow's *Rooms,* and appeared in Sophie Maslow's *Manhattan Transfer.* Sokolow's "poetic approach to choreography" made the strongest impression on Ailey in this period, and in interviews, he lauded her exaggerations of the everyday as a strong influence on his own work.[14]

In August 1957 Ailey began rehearsals for the Broadway production of *Jamaica,* choreographed by Jack Cole. Cole's magnetic presence and theatrically conceived staging reminded Ailey of Horton, and once again Ailey's attention turned to making dances. He identified with Cole's theatrical macho and Hollywood style: "I was impressed by his style, by the way he danced, by his manner, by the masculinity of his projection, by his fierceness, by his animal-like qualities."[15] Lena Horne, *Jamaica*'s headlining artist, was supportive of Ailey's dance-making ambitions and lobbied producers to allow him to use the stage between performances to develop movement ideas. It was during the extended run of this show that Ailey was able to rehearse the dancers who worked with him in the 1958 YM-YWHA concerts that began the Alvin Ailey American Dance Theater.

Even after the critical success of his 1958 and 1960 dance concerts, Ailey pursued work as a choreographer in the commercial theater. He restaged dances for *Carmen Jones* (August 1959) and *Jamaica* (1960) for summer stock. He staged dances for the theatrical revue *African Holiday* (February 1960), and the Equity

Library Theatre production of *Dark of the Moon* (May 1960), directed by Vinette Carroll at the Lenox Hill Playhouse. These commercial engagements remained decidedly segregated, with "all-Negro" casts hired to entertain mostly white audiences.

Ailey first integrated his own company roster when white dancer Don Price played the Clown in *Ariette Oubliée* in 1958, and his work outside of the commercial arena continued this trend in collaborations he created for his own company and others. He choreographed a successful version of Strindberg's *Miss Julie* titled "Mistress and Manservant" (1 February 1959) to a score by Ravel for the Shirley Broughton Dance Company. Reviewing for *Dance Magazine*, Selma Jeanne Cohen proclaimed Ailey's work the high point of the evening, in which "the stage came to life, the performers really danced, and the audience was caught up in the drama." As usual, Ailey created for his dancers' special abilities; Broughton danced "a role beautifully suited to her talents" and "the company shed their self-consciousness and moved with real conviction."[16]

Ailey undertook acting lessons with Stella Adler from 1960 to 1962. Non-dancing appearances in dramatic plays through the early 1960s included a leading role as a college student troubled by race in *Call Me by My Rightful Name* (January 1961) with costars Robert Duvall and Joan Hackett at the Sheridan Square Theatre, the role of a political leader in *Ding Dong Bell* (summer 1961) at the Westport Country Playhouse, a soft-hearted prize fighter in *Two by Saroyan* (October 1961) in New York, and the central role of a male hustler/gigolo in the Joshua Logan–directed Broadway run of *Tiger, Tiger Burning Bright* (December 1962), which also starred Roscoe Lee Browne, Al Freeman Jr., Claudia McNeil, Diana Sands, and Cicely Tyson. Each of these plays constructed race as a societal force, as the agent of division between the black minority and the white majority, and as the source of unimpeachable difference. Not surprisingly, these plays also presupposed the tragic difficulties of racial interaction in America. Writing for the *Morning Telegraph*, Whitney Bolton claimed that *Call Me by My Rightful Name* managed to "show the prickly, stabbing difficulties of completely easeful relations between whites and Negroes even when the protagonists have pretensions of advanced thought and feeling."[17]

Ailey easily adapted to acting, though the roles he played veered slightly from his everyday persona as a young African American arts activist, dancer, and student. Each of these stage roles capitalized on his physical presence, and he was often called on to display his physique. Ailey noted a distinction between acting and dancing in terms of the transformative power of dance: "Everything in dancing is style, allusion, the essence of many thoughts and feelings, the abstraction of many moments," whereas in acting, "you don't condense that way, you have to live every moment, you're there to make that moment a living reality." These dramatic experiences affirmed his basic sense of heightened theatrical scope and projection: "I've learned a great deal from method acting. I've learned to abstract what is real and to make it bigger than life."[18]

Ailey's experience in the commercial theater influenced his understanding of what appealed to audiences of the postwar era. Called on by writers and producers to repeat his earlier successes, Ailey learned to create work quickly that enhanced the particular gifts of his collaborators, often without regard for originality. For example, in 1964 he codirected a production of Langston Hughes's *Jerico-Jim Crow* (12 January 1964). A music travelogue performed in a Greenwich Village church, the production featured a gospel choir singing spirituals while several actors recited an "unabashedly sentimental and tuneful history of the Negro struggle up from slavery."[19] Having obvious structural resonances to Ailey's *Revelations*, *Jerico-Jim Crow* garnered good reviews but probably taught Ailey little, as he later claimed to have taken the assignment "only because of a direct request from Langston."[20]

These varied theater experiences contributed heavily to the amalgam of dramatic, theatrical, and pure dance technique that became Ailey's signature choreographic style. Playing angry young Negroes in dramatic works, performing happy-go-lucky or sensuous dance specialties in musical comedies, and staging exotic-primitive, "all-black" dances for musical revivals eventually lost their appeal for Ailey, who realized that concert dance offered him an expressive plane and committed audience missing from the commercial arena. If he had any later aspirations to the commercial, they were squelched with the quick failure of his single Broadway effort as choreographer, the musical *La Strada*, which opened and closed in one performance, 14 December 1969.[21]

Early Residencies

In 1960 Edele Holtz offered Ailey rehearsal and administrative space in what would become the Clark Center of the Performing Arts. Located in the West Side YWCA at 51st Street and Eighth Avenue, Clark Center became home for Ailey's extended family of performers, offering space for costume storage, classes, rehearsals, and performances. Clark Center opened officially in October 1960, and Ailey's pick-up company had its first concert there on 27 November of that year. Ailey used the occasion to present work by two other choreographers: Lester Horton's classic study of Puritan angst, *The Beloved* (1947), and John Butler's recent jazz duet, *Portrait of Billie* (1960), a study of the despair behind the public glamour of singer Billie Holiday. From this concert forward, Ailey made an effort to include the works of other choreographers in the repertory of his company.

The Alvin Ailey Dance Theater's arrival on the New York dance scene in the late 1950s coincided with a rise in government-sponsored cultural exportation. In 1962 the Ailey company undertook an unprecedented thirteen-week engagement in Southeast Asia and Australia sponsored by the President's Special International Program for Cultural Presentations under the Kennedy administration. Subsequent government-sponsored tours included an engagement at the World Festival of Negro Arts in Dakar, Senegal (1966), a nine-nation tour of Africa (1967), and performance at the Edinburgh Festival (1968). In 1970 the Ailey company became the first American modern dance company to perform in the Soviet Union.

Alvin Ailey, Loretta Abbott, James Truitte, and Joan Peters in
Australia, from *The Sydney Morning Herald*, 1965

Appearances of the Alvin Ailey American Dance Theater on international
tours and television widely advanced the reputation of Ailey's choreography and
the potential of African American concert dance performance as an American
cultural offering. Playing large European theaters brought Ailey before a wider
general public than he could have known in the United States. As Mary Clarke
ironically noted in 1964, "Probably more people saw the company in London
during this season than see it in New York in the course of a year!"[22] Sponsorship by the U.S. government offered Ailey a unique advantage from which to
present dancing black bodies to the world, an opportunity he honored and embraced in order to found his school and incorporate his company.

The Ailey company's unique status as the sole exponent of an emerging standard of African American concert dance during this period complicates an assessment of racial politics and the delineation of "official" black culture. As the U.S. government sanctioned the Ailey company, producing its tours, it took a covert hand in molding what became the signature style of Afro-American concert dance. In some cases, government sponsorship influenced choreographic and casting decisions. State Department propaganda also played a role in shaping the international celebrity accorded the Ailey company. For example, during the Far East tour of 1962, the State Department made much of two benefit performances it produced in Malaya, in which the proceeds of the company's performances in Penang on 28 February and 1 March 1962 were donated to the Jaycees Rural Community Service Projects Fund, a local charity. The colonial Malayan press praised the action generously: "It's a gesture as rare and noble as their programme is scintillating and without a moment's dullness and which won all-round appreciation."[23] To some extent, the company's success among foreign critics can be attributed to the political validation offered by the U.S. State Department.

The active relationship between government sponsorship and Ailey's choreographic creativity began in the fall of 1961, when the State Department invited the Alvin Ailey Dance Theater to tour Southeast Asia and Australia. The invitation prompted Ailey to assemble a repertory deemed appropriate by the State Department, as well as a company of ten dancers and four musicians available to embark on an extended, difficult string of performances. The tour began on 3 February in Sydney, Australia and ended on 12 May 1962 in Seoul, Korea.[24]

Ailey created a new dance expressly for the tour: *Been Here and Gone* (26 January 1962), a curtain-raising suite of folk songs and children's games inspired by his memories of Texas. Slightly reminiscent of Donald McKayle's 1951 dance *Games*, which Ailey had performed in 1956, *Been Here and Gone* embraced a comical musical theater tone that included singing, spoken dialogue, props, and onstage musicians.

Dedicated to the "anonymous" folk bards of the American South, including Hudie Ledbetter (Leadbelly), Blind Lemon Jefferson, Sonny Boy Williamson, and Big Bill Broonzy,[25] the dance began with a street scene in the Negro quarter of some southern city. Posed against a lighted cyclorama, the full company of eight dancers, two singers, and three musicians slid into motion as Ella Thompson belted an a cappella verse of "Jump Down, Spin Around/Pick a Bale of Cotton." The dancers enacted a series of vignettes, buoyed by song and dance, that presented a typical day for archetypal folk characters: vendors selling their wares, children at play, prisoners working on a chain gang, a woman mourning her lost love, and a final town square romp in couples for the entire cast.[26] Performed under the watchful eye of a traveling folk bard portrayed by Brother John Sellers, the suite imagined "a wandering singer entering a small town, stopping for a moment to rest and then moving on."[27] Music for the dance included the opening "Jump Down, Spin Around," danced in brightly colored outfits; the a cappella convict song "Working on a Chain Gang"; four women as children at play singing "Peter Piper Picked a Pepper"; an expressive woman's solo, "Dark Was the Night"; "I Wonder as I Wander," a vocal solo performed by Ailey; and the group finale "Big Boat up the River." In November 1964 Ailey dropped "I Wonder as I Wander" and added "Pretty Little Train," a solo for dancer William Louther. *Been Here and Gone* remained in the repertory of the Ailey company until 1965.

Ailey's notes suggest that he borrowed his original imagery for the dance from the familiar stock of Broadway musical scenarios or folklorica in the mold of Katherine Dunham: "Offstage the sound of Ella [Thompson] entering with an enormous basket of multicolored flowers on her head—she is a flower vendor and she sings of her wares—'Marigolds! Who will buy my Marigolds!' (That great song from *Free and Easy*)." He conceived the dance as a full theater piece, with oversized props of flower baskets to be held by the women and enormous fishnets on poles to be set up by the men and waved in varied swaying patterns. He also imagined *Been Here and Gone* as a program companion to *Roots of the Blues*, asking his designers if the "same ladders from *Roots* [could] be decorated with fabrics so as to be disguised for fishermen section—placed in different angles?"[29] *Been Here and Gone* intended to tell the story of a community, with the overarching story theater effect taking precedence over dance sequences.

Muted critical reaction to *Been Here and Gone* focused on its overt theatricality, seemingly produced at the expense of emotional depth. Allen Hughes of the *New York Times* noted that the piece "has a wandering blind singer, a children's play song, and other things, but it has little choreography of any kind, and such as there is seemed unworthy of Mr. Ailey's proved talents." Writing for the *London Spectator*, Clive Barnes termed the piece "little more than a blameless cabaret number" performed with "an air of almost pickaninny euphoria." Barnes took the time to note the high caliber of Ailey's dancers and the musicians' efforts to create an authentic "folk" sound: "Even here the dancing has a glow to it that digs deeper than polish, and the music . . . is not some synthetically whipped-up dollop of symphonic jazz, but the real article."[30] *Been Here and Gone* failed to rival *Blues Suite* or *Revelations* as a chronicle of an entire genre of southern African American musicality.

Southeast Asia Tour

For Ailey, the Southeast Asia tour continued patterns of dance making born of necessity and ingenuity. Again he reworked material to fit performance circumstances and the shifting roster of his collaborators. When dancers who sang left the company, Ailey rearranged sections of the suites. Eventually, *Blues Suite*, *Revelations*, and *Been Here and Gone* all lost their onstage musical personnel.

Carmen de Lavallade headlined the Southeast Asia tour along with Ailey, and her starring presence caused a series of drastic choreographic and billing negotiations. Ailey reworked the popular duet *Roots of the Blues*, restaged *Revelations* to include de Lavallade, and included three pieces in the tour repertory fea-

Charles Moore, Don Martin, Horace Arnold, Ella Thompson,
Bruce Langhorne, Alvin Ailey, and Les Grinage in Alvin Ailey's
Been Here and Gone, 1965. Photograph by David Hewison

turing de Lavallade in leading roles: Horton's *The Beloved*, performed with
James Truitte; John Butler's solo *Letter to a Lady* (1961), set to a score by Ravel;
and Glen Tetley's newly created *Mountainway Chant* (1962), a full-company cer-
emonial dance based on a Hopi legend starring de Lavallade as a sacrificial
maiden. Filling out the repertory with Ailey's *Gillespiana*, *Hermit Songs*, and
Been Here and Gone, the dancers toured under the unwieldy banner of the De
Lavallade–Ailey American Dance Company. Besides Ailey, de Lavallade, and
Truitte, other dancers on the tour were Minnie Marshall, Ella Thompson,
Charles Moore, Thelma Hill, Don Martin, and newcomer Georgia Collins, a former Dunham dancer who had also trained at the School of American Ballet. Determined to escape essentializing criticism as an all-Negro company, Ailey also
hired Connie Greco, a white dancer who had performed in the National Ballet
of Canada and several Broadway shows. Greco had worked previously for Ailey
in his 1959 "Mistress and Manservant." Brother John Sellers, bassist Les Grinage,
drummer Horace Arnold, and guitarist Bruce Langhorne filled out the musician
slots. Ves Harper traveled as lighting designer and assistant to veteran stage manager Keene Curtis, who had accompanied the Martha Graham Company on its

Far East tour. Dick Campbell, on the staff of producing agent American National Theater and Academy, managed the tour.

The company gave sixty performances in thirteen weeks, playing Australia, Burma, Vietnam, Malaya, Indonesia, the Philippines, China, Taiwan, Japan, and Korea. Ailey later recalled a grueling schedule, made harder by extensive official responsibilities: "When we weren't performing, we ate exotic meals, attended receptions, visited every music school in Southeast Asia, heard every children's chorus, met every head of a music school and every mayor in every village. . . . Because we were there under the auspices of the State Department, we were always going to parties and various government functions."[31] Critics and audiences consistently praised the company, and its success established a significant international reputation for Ailey as a choreographer and performer.

Even as he endured the physical and emotional demands of touring, performing, and officially representing the United States abroad, Ailey worked to expand the stage roles available to African American dancers. He discussed his work as an amalgam of his Negro heritage, personal feelings, and dance study with leading white teachers and Broadway choreographers: "I hope together with my natural feelings about what I do and the sophisticated act of imposing compositional form on my themes, something will come out that is both theatrical and communicative."[32] The repertory approved for the Asia tour consistently built on strongly defined tensions between men and women and traditional constructions of "hard" men as counterparts to "soft" women. The repertory also provided heavy doses of exoticized folklore, stylized and distilled through the idiom of American modern dance.

Japanese critics provided the most probing and racially influenced written responses to the tour. Reviewing *Roots of the Blues*, Akihiko Yamaki wrote in terms of a racial/cultural/gendered dialectic suggested by the pairing of dark-skinned Ailey and light-skinned de Lavallade: "Alvin, the most typically Negro, and Carmen, who has mastered the West European sense of grace and elegance, shaped two extremes; the songs of John Sellers connected the polarity; and the dancers deployed the world of Negroes around the wonderful axis." Shigeo Goda concurred that de Lavallade seemed "a dancer with utmost intellectual sensitivity," and Ailey was "favored with rich racial blood and emotions."[33]

Sumio Kambayashi, the compiler-translator of a file of reviews excerpted by the Press and Program Office of the Tokyo American Cultural Center, proclaimed that the Ailey company's visit "made an epoch in the history of dance in Japan (barring, of course, that of our traditional Kabuki dance)." Writing to the Press and Program Office itself, in his own addendum to a fat pile of positive translated reviews, he continued:

(1) For our classic ballet dancers, you showed how to make their ballet "modern." (2) To our old modern dancers who were trained at Wigman School and still German-Expressionistic, your example will serve as a new point of departure toward two-way communication between dancer and viewer. (3) To young modern dancers who are influenced

Carmen de Lavallade and Alvin Ailey in Alvin Ailey's *Roots of the Blues*, 1961. Photograph by Jack Mitchell

by *anti-theatre* and *anti-danse* and produce cerebral or sexual experiments, you pointed a way to a healthy total theater that includes [the] general public. All in all you taught us how a dance theater of tomorrow will be a theater which synthesizes arts and entertainments, traditional grace of ballet and contemporary tempo of jazz dance, fluid elegance in *legato* and jerky-percussive angularity in *staccato*—dance of a new world which unites our primeval memories of mythical protoexperience with the sensitivities of modern times."[34]

On tour, Ailey's mission to simultaneously enlighten and entertain apparently succeeded, clearing the way for an international wave of modern dance in the African American grain.

More than a year passed before Ailey again made dances for his own company. Buoyed by the prospect of a performance at the Brooklyn Academy of Music, he assembled a new company of dancers for a benefit performance on 28 April 1963. As if in recoil from his recent segregated Broadway experience in *Tiger, Tiger Burning Bright*, Ailey again integrated his company with several white American and Asian dancers. None of the three new works premiered dealt explicitly with Negro heritage.

"Reflections in D" (28 April 1963) combined with a slight new work, "Suspensions" (28 April 1963), and "Gillespiana" to make the latest version of *Three for Now*. "Suspensions," set to music by Giuffre, disappeared after a single performance. "Reflections in D," set to a recorded piano improvisation by Duke Ellington, fared better as a solo originally danced by Ailey, becoming a work that remained in the repertory of the Ailey company.

The dance begins with a downward pool of light encircling the posed dancer, who stands center stage with one leg crossed over the other, arms hanging to the sides in a relaxed attitude of ease. The piano completes a lazy, noodling introduction, then makes a slow statement of a simple, four-tone melodic theme. The dancer sways with this lolling music, lifting his arms in gentle, breathing alternation as the melody slides downward. He undulates his upper body easily, first initiating slight movements from his torso, then making abstract shapes with his entire body reaching and pulling through the space.

The man moves away from the center, easily walking, then running lightly toward the corners of the stage. The dance becomes an interplay of opposing tempos and releases of energy: slow, then fast openings of arms through space; turns performed with a widely opened upper back contrasted with tautly held positions and sharp contractions of the torso; quick, running motions followed by slow, extended balances on one leg.

The man spins downward to the floor at the song's bridge and remains there for a section of sliding, scooting, and crawling along the front edge of the stage. His focus remains detached but composed throughout this section, as he seems to look for something lost that can be found through the activity of his dance. He moves quickly but without an inner urgency, completing tasks of extended balances and multiple off-center turns with a sense of calm.

The song's final chorus repeats musical material from before, and the dancer performs a slightly altered version of his opening movement phrases. Positioned center stage, he undulates his arms and torso, this time adding sharp ticks of energy in the middle of the swaying phrases. Suddenly splaying his hands wide while holding his arms taut, his gestures break the smooth wavering patterns. These accents bring forward his balanced, cool motions as if in relief from underlying tensions and submerged postures of grief. The dance ends when he hinges backward to the floor, turns about on his knees, and finally lies down, face first, in a posture of sleep.

A dance of only five minutes duration, "Reflections in D" offered Ailey his first abstract solo vehicle danced without the benefit of dramatic narrative, setting, costume, or stage persona. Ailey's compositional structure confidently mirrors Ellington's musical organization, with phrasing joined to the song's repeating sections. Several movement passages are borrowed directly from *Revelations*: a staccato port de bras and a sweeping turn performed with an undulating rib cage and arms held overhead from "I've Been 'Buked"; a turning and kicking sequence from "Sinner Man"; and a spiral gesture to the floor recognizable from

"I Wanna Be Ready." The dance relies on Nicola Cernovich's subtle and effective lighting design, which casts the stage in shifting shades of blue that follow the dancer about the space. The dancer is costumed simply in a pair of blue tights.

By stripping certain movements of their original context as part of *Revelations*, Ailey engaged a deeper exploration of the actual movement qualities of his own choreography. "Reflections in D" enabled its dancer to explore the act of movement without reference to a predetermined character, the concerns of the audience, or broad theatrical projection. For Ailey, this piece represented a major departure from dances overtly concerned with dramatic narrative, to a plane of "dance for the sake of dancing."[35]

For his major premiere at the 1963 Brooklyn Academy of Music concert, Ailey turned further from African American themes to ancient Greek mythology. *Labyrinth* (28 April 1963) told the story of Theseus and the Minotaur, a theme Martha Graham had conquered in her 1947 *Errand into the Maze*. Ailey had planned the piece as early as 1961 with the working title "The Barricade," to be set on a "male soloist who is the Theseus figure and [a] chorus of 6 or 8 men who as a body comprise the Minotaur." Ailey imagined the piece to be "neo-realistically set as in a contemporary slum," with a labyrinth composed of a "barricade of boxes, barrels, broken chairs, [and] other refuse."[36] Apparently, his plans were not realized in the 1963 version, whose program credits no set designer and lists only three men as the Minotaur. Critical response to the piece was sparse and muted. Writing for the *New York Times*, Natalie Jaffe suggested Ailey's formidable thematic risk: "Dancers venture into Greek mythology in double jeopardy —the terror of the legends themselves and the ever-present image of Martha Graham. Unfortunately, Mr. Ailey neither encompassed the first nor banished the second."[37] *Labyrinth* disappeared after a single performance, to be reborn two years later as *Ariadne*, created for the Harkness Ballet (12 March 1965).

Ailey began a long and fruitful association with Duke Ellington in August 1963. Ellington invited Ailey and his company to perform in *My People (First Negro Centennial)*, a travelogue history of the Negro in America mounted in observance of the one hundredth anniversary of the Emancipation Proclamation. Ailey choreographed three pieces: "The Blues Ain't" (19 August 1963), a section of Ellington's sweeping orchestral work *Black, Brown and Beige*; "Light" (19 August 1963), and a short piece, "My Mother, My Father" (19 August 1963), quickly written to accompany a duet by Ailey and Minnie Marshall.[38] Only "Light" earned a life after the three-week run of *My People*, when Ailey included it as the closing number of *Modern Jazz Suite* in that dance's final and preferred lineup, following "Gillespiana" and "Reflections in D" (6 September 1963). A "breezy melange of popular dances such as the Big Apple and Suzy Q," "Light" featured "exuberant hip-swinging" in a facile arrangement, "sketching jazz dances of recent decades and the present."[39]

While working with Ellington in Chicago, Ailey received an invitation to present his company at the International Music Festival in Rio de Janeiro during the first week of September 1963. Ailey felt that he had to have a new ballet for the occasion, so he quickly rehearsed *Rivers, Streams, Doors* (6 September 1963), which he later described as "another version of *Been Here and Gone* with African singers and songs."[40] The work disappeared after four performances.

In August 1964, Ailey made a dance in honor of the golden wedding anniversary of Ruth St. Denis and Ted Shawn, celebrated at Jacob's Pillow dance festival. Performed for a single week, *The Twelve Gates* (11 August 1964) featured Carmen de Lavallade and James Truitte in a "small suite of songs and dances, inspired by the images of women in the Bible."[41] With costumes designed by de Lavallade's husband, Geoffrey Holder, and musical accompaniment led by Brother John Sellers, the dance again allowed Ailey to publicly laud the beauty of de Lavallade, here framed in a guise of feminine divinity and anchored by seven traditional Negro spirituals. This pièce d'occasion disappeared after its seven scheduled performances.

Ailey added the word "American" to the title of his company during a European tour begun in the fall of 1964. The Alvin Ailey American Dance Theater played Paris and London in a three-month engagement that further established the international renown accorded Ailey and his company. The change in title reflected an expansion of repertory to include dances by choreographers Talley Beatty, Louis Johnson, Anna Sokolow, Joyce Trisler, and James Truitte alongside those by Ailey, Butler, Horton, and Tetley. The title change and expansion of repertory also were intended to secure the company's appeal to the widest possible international audience, even as the actions positioned Ailey's company as "official" bearers of American modern dance to a growing world audience. Publicity during this period stressed the company's "we do it all" facility. For example, an Australian advertising guaranteed "wonderful entertainment for all tastes," proved in photographs captioned "Modern Dance! Folk Singing! Jazz! Blues!"[42]

As Ailey built his company's international reputation, largely through high-profile engagements secured by the U.S. State Department, he tried to exploit racial exoticism traditionally associated with dancing black bodies as his primary drawing card. By 1964, his program notes for a month-long London tour expressed the confident exploitation of African American materials, carefully arranged to educate and entertain:

> From his roots as a slave, the American Negro—sometimes sorrowing, sometimes jubilant, but always hopeful—has created a legacy of music and dance which have touched, illuminated and influenced the most remote preserves of world civilisation. I and my dance theatre celebrate in our programme, this trembling beauty. We bring you the exuberance of jazz, the ecstacy of his spirituals and the dark rapture of his blues.[43]

English critics sensed the tension between pleasing the audience and investigating form. Benny Green found the company's total effect to be "one of movement and gaiety rather than balletic subtlety" in work "coloured by the conventions of stylised showbiz." Clive Barnes noted how "the determination to be 'entertaining' at all costs perhaps led . . . to a programme, in effect, made up of nothing but *divertissements*." Writing for the *Sunday Times*, Richard Buckle explained his reaction to Ailey's facile ability to simultaneously entertain and enlighten in a single program: "I abandoned myself uncritically and with a kind of voluptuous delight. The dancers were so attractive and so well trained, the numbers they were given to do were so well calculated to bring out their good qualities and had so direct a message, and the lighting was so helpful, that I could not imagine a more agreeable combination of art and entertainment."[44]

Ailey and his company served the State Department well as ambassadors of culture. The carefully integrated roster of artists presented a liberal American philosophy of racial equity and harmony to an international audience. Government sponsorship implied an "official" U.S. policy of equal opportunity of expression. In Ailey's most successful works concerned with Negro heritage, the African American dancers physically represented burgeoning American art culture born of the peculiar institution of black slavery.

By 1964 Ailey settled into a preferred mode of heightened theatricality that relied heavily on lighting and costuming effects to produce glamorous and voluminous stage pictures. Critics noted the extent to which Ailey company performances hinged on the contributions of lighting designer Cernovich, who created varied, subtly shifting moods adaptable to the demands of both large and small performance spaces: "By his use of back projections and by a marvelous and exciting sense of colour he clothes the stage with magic yet scenically the only props in the whole show are a few chairs, stools, ladders and a hatstand. This combined with Ves Harper's simple yet stunningly effective costumes create some of the most beautiful stage pictures seen in London for a long time."[45] Besides Cernovich and Harper, over the years Ailey counted Timothy Hunter, Thomas Skelton, and Chenault Spence among an extraordinary roster of lighting designers, and Randy Barcelo, Carol Vollet Garner, A. Christina Giannini, Jane Greenwood, Geoffrey Holder, Toni Leslie James, Normand Maxon, and Rouben Ter-Arutunian among the gifted costume and setting designers with whom he worked.

The Ailey company and the State Department enlarged the symbiotic relationship they developed during the 1960s through the 1990s. Government sponsorship saved the company from dissolution on several occasions, typically by offering work as cultural ambassadors at various international festivals of the arts. In 1966 the company represented the United States at the First World Festival of Negro Arts held 1–24 April 1966 in Dakar, Senegal. This cultural assignment originally belonged to Arthur Mitchell, who rehearsed a large company of thirty-one African American dancers led by Carmen de Lavallade. Mitchell's pick-up company disbanded two weeks before the festival, when the government's Dance Committee announced a severe budget reduction for the event. Ailey's company, stranded for a month without work in Milan, accepted the government's reduced fee to perform successfully at the Dakar festival. Similar factors of last-minute government sponsorship surrounded the Ailey company's tours of North Africa and Russia in 1970.[46]

Ailey retired from his own dancing career in June 1965, in reaction to physical tensions and negative critical reviews he received at the Florentine Festival in Italy.[47] Given his slight and limited technical training, his early retirement from the stage did not surprise those around him.[48] Throughout his adult life, Ailey contended with a constantly expanding and contracting waistline. As he matured, his physique lost some of its youthful, sensual appeal, and his performance skills suffered. He had been performing only sporadically, taking a rare class and barely maintaining his technique. He hoped that retirement from the stage would afford him more time to aggressively attend to the business of choreographing and directing his company. These divergent tasks placed enormous demands on his time and energy.[49] Eager to continue developing his choreographic voice, Ailey made several dances for ballet and opera companies through the mid-1960s. Perhaps to ease personal frustrations he associated with maintaining his own company, he allowed four years to elapse between dances he made for the Alvin Ailey American Dance Theater, from 1963 to 1967.

"Official" African American Culture

The questions still stand: How did Ailey come to stand for black dance? How did his interracial company achieve status as the "official" bearer of black modern dance in the 1960s, a role it maintained into the new millennium? How does the company, following Ailey's mandate, remain in step with evolving African American culture? How does the company, securely positioned in the multicultural global arts economy we all share, stay "black"?

Some answers lie in the strategies Ailey enacted to bring dance to the widest possible public. In large part, his carefully groomed, nonconfrontational troupe presented work that represented black experience to cultural outsiders. Without the benefit of wealthy patrons who might have funded his early explorations of dance form,

Ailey built his company's success from the committed labor of his dancing collaborators, a "devoted band of friends, men and women whose professional lives were, in
effect, a work of hopeful activism,"[50] from his own affable, articulate persona, which
normalized American race relations for an international audience, and from a repertory chosen to showcase an accessible and glamorous vision of dancing black bodies
in several theatrical milieux.

Ailey's organizational gambit followed the lead of integration-minded black vi-
sionaries invested in "race progress," leaders who believed that "the improvement of
African Americans' material and moral condition through self-help would diminish
white racism" and who accordingly "sought to rehabilitate the race's image by embodying respectability, enacted through an ethos of service to the masses."[51] The sort
of cultural "rehabilitation" Ailey engaged in was not without cost: it obliged him to
minimize creative impulses of critique or protest. It also assumed a large audience of
cultural outsiders, unversed in the processes that gave rise to the work performed.
Still, Ailey positioned his company to "represent the race" at every turn.

According to literary and cultural historian Kevin K. Gaines, many artists willing
to stand for racial uplift "employed an assimilationist cultural aesthetic, hoping to refine Negro folk materials into a universalistic expression of high culture," a goal clearly
accomplished in Ailey's dances about black experience. But other artists "less be-
holden to 'positive' images and racial vindication played with white stereotypes of authentic blackness, manipulating minstrelsy, Negro folklore and dialect, and black vernacular forms in search of new forms of black cultural expression, including Negro
humor."[52] Ailey also sought to realize this revision of imagery in his company operations, which allowed a diverse group of choreographers access to both superb black
dance artists and the concert dance stages of the world.

Some dance aficionados found Ailey's mandate to represent black experience
limiting. Writing on the occasion of the company's engagement at the Edinburgh Festival in 1968, one critic noted, "What did most strongly emerge from the repertoire
was the consideration that dance-theater wholly preoccupied with the problems, joys,
triumphs and defeats of the Negro in a context of American contemporary living does
not encourage boldness of idea, width of vision or deep examination as to how much
can be done with stage dancing."[53] Not surprisingly, writers who disparaged black experience as narrow subject matter had little access to the daily experience of black life,
aesthetic imperatives of Africanist art making, or the necessity of art that provided a
healing balm for strained race relations in America.

Other writers intimated the importance of African American achievement in concert dance as a socializing force. Dance writer Arthur Todd termed Negro dance "a
national treasure" in his 1961 essay that began, "Check off a list of some of America's most noteworthy creative dancers and choreographers. . . . The fact that they
also happen to be Negro as well matters not a bit to their Caucasian brothers and sisters in the Northern States or across the world, where they have won a continuingly
wider following and acceptance during the past two decades." Todd's portrayal of
smooth race relations in the American dance community was certainly exaggerated,
but he noted with some satisfaction how black presence in the white-dominated field
advanced an ethic of racial uplift through accomplishment. He continued, "Martha

Graham, of all choreographers, stated this belief most eloquently when she recently said, 'I'm not interested in race, creed, colour or nationalty. I'm only interested in talent. I've said this over all the world on my tours and I *mean* it."[54] According to Todd, concert dance offered a site of racial collaboration worth promoting, as well as opportunities for artistic success too often denied black Americans.

The Ailey company's success was indeed of great political value to all Americans interested in soothing racial tensions. Through the company, black American bodies, which had historically been devalued and depersonalized, became valued as aesthetically intrinsic to the portrayal of American character on world stages. Because the early Ailey company avoided anything quirky or individualistic about modern dance, and anything that might have subscribed its operations to the whims of an individual artist, it ascended as an essential representative of black American experience at home and American experience abroad. In all, the Ailey company's arrival in opera houses around the world as an ambassador of black experience in dance proved that aspects of core black culture could be represented in concert dance and that representation could survive transference to extremely unfamiliar settings.

To feed its target African American audience, the Ailey company staged works that valorized a mythic African heritage. Geoffrey Holder's *The Prodigal Prince* (1967, revived 1998) and George Faison's *Gazelle* (1971, revived 1976 and 1997 as *Slaves*) offered explicitly black vistas that connected contemporary audiences through an idealized African diaspora. Each work featured recognizably regal imagery in a mixture of movement vocabularies, musical scores, and overall themes that spoke, in dramaturgy and kinesthetic approach, to the hybrid histories of black Americans.

The Prodigal Prince combined religious imagery with a crashing percussion score to tell the story of Haitian painter Hector Hyppolite. Costumed with extravagant flair by Holder, who also composed the score, the work mixed numerous processional patterns with theatricalized religious ceremony and acrobatics to describe a world influenced by Catholicism and Haitian vodoun, strict gender coding in explicit ritual roles for men and women, and combined West African and East Indian movement vocabularies. Overall, the work traded in a pageantry that confirmed black beauty in a coherent mythic environment.

Gazelle, originally created for the George Faison Universal Dance Experience but acquired by the Ailey company in 1976, offered a two-part scenario that actually depicted the horror of the Middle Passage. In its first section, members of a generic West African village, overseen by a griot figure who consecrates the stage space for the dance, engage in everyday tasks of hunting and gathering. Armed with prop spears, the men hunt a lithe gazelle in the forest as the women dance with straw baskets near their huts. In a stunning second section, the villagers are captured by unseen slave traders and chained together on a slave ship, imaginatively depicted through lighting effects. In an excruciatingly intense sequence, the dancers enact the terror of confinement onboard the ship, including the birth and death of a baby, an abortive reminiscence of village life, and the onset of psychological madness incited by the close physical confines. The work ends, curiously, with a dance of strength and protest, as the performers enact an illusory escape from slavery through the act of communal dance. Overall, *Gazelle* recalled the work of black arts movement literary artists like

LeRoi Jones (later Amiri Baraka) in its depiction of black history as contingent on the Middle Passage.[55]

Like *Revelations*, *The Prodigal Prince* and *Gazelle* offered histories of black American experience in terms of concert dance. Each work confirmed the Ailey company's ability to absorb and disseminate "official" histories of African Americans, using dance as a springboard to social action in the creation of a theatrical usable past.

For many African American audiences, the Ailey company operates as far more than a modern dance troupe. It represents the standard by which to gauge excellence in the performing arts. Because the company has taken on the mantle of responsibility as an ambassador of black experience, it serves as a totem of possibility; for young black dancers, it offers a place to aspire to; for general black audiences, it offers a hopeful confirmation of black presence and beauty on world stages. When black audiences attend performances by the Ailey company, we trust the vision and creativity cast before us; we revel in its truth, but, significantly, we also respect its appeal to others in the audience.

There is no performing arts institution like the Alvin Ailey American Dance Theater. It remains rare to see a large company of African American artists working together in opera houses or concert hall settings anywhere in the world. Several American regional dance companies modeled on the Ailey company's repertory plan thrive in their local communities, but no other American arts company committed to an exploration of black experience has survived the contemporary international arts marketplace. From the company's first season at the Met in 1984, this high visibility went grossly underexplored by arts promoters. Writing for the *New York Amsterdam News*, Zita Allen noted:

> The Met season is indicative of a career of mixed blessings. The City Center Spring season was canceled for financial reasons so now the Ailey company becomes the first Black cultural institution to hold sway in the mammoth Metropolitan Opera House. But, at the same time because the Met's staff is so inexperienced in reaching out to the company's tremendous Black audience it placed less than gigantic ads in *The Times* while overlooking major Black media outlets.[56]

Then, as now, the Ailey company offers its promoters a rare opportunity to galvanize broad-based interracial audiences for concert dance performance.

The company remains in step with evolving African American culture through its use of different generations of choreographers, by allowing its musical landscape to change over time, and by absorbing many points of view into its administrative structure. Ailey allowed this system to evolve not so much by executive fiat as by allowing his company to grow according to familial models of community-based ownership. As Ailey assessed on the occasion of his company's twentieth anniversary, "I don't make all the decisions around here, but I get a lot of help from people I trust, from people with a lot of good ideas and taste. So I can't say it's just an Alvin Ailey thing, because it isn't—and it shouldn't be that way either. We all have a lot to say about dance around here, and we say it freely. I think that more modern companies should be run that way; it would be healthier all around."[57]

Riedaiglia

The dance that brought Ailey out of choreographic hibernation for his own company fulfilled a lucrative commission from Swedish television. Quickly prepared in just ten days of rehearsal and five days of filming, *Riedaiglia* (June 1967) immediately won the Grand Prix Italia, a prestigious award for television production. Danced to a commissioned score by Swedish composer Georg Riedel, *Riedaiglia* depended heavily on the talents of television director Lars Egler, who collaborated with Ailey to determine its structure of images. Broadcast in the United States on a program entitled *Ambassadors of Dance* by New York City public television in 1971, *Riedaiglia* continued Ailey's habit of creating successful work on demand within the difficult scheduling needs of commercial production.

The program begins as a collection of decadent bohemian characters wander through an expansive, neutral, white space. The dancers approach the camera singly, making faces of anger and disdain toward the viewing audience as they parade by languidly. Costumed in colorful, wildly oversized garb, the dancers play at being the glamorous effete, caught by the camera at an obscure ritualistic party. James Truitte appears as a "Daddy Mack" character, clad in a pimp's suit with a porkpie hat and a large gold medallion around his neck. An off-camera announcer sets the scene in a warning: "There are seven deadly sins. This is a vision of what people undergo losing innocence. Hope reemerges in the cycle which returns to the beginning." The characters undulate listlessly, and the scene fades out.

Riedaiglia continues through surrealistic scenes describing decadence: nearly nude bodies emerge to undulate lasciviously from a large sheet with holes cut in it; four women in identical diaphanous dresses sway vacantly as a mass of prideful vanity; a trembling man is sacrificed to a cannibalistic woman; a leather-clad biker lustily lies down with a crowd of adoring women. In a scene demonstrating rage, the crowd of dancing bohemians taunt each other and the camera, then perform contemporary social dances with mounting fury, faster and faster, freezing abruptly when the music halts, then sinking slowly to the ground. In *Riedaiglia*'s final scene, the dancers awake as if from a dream, wearing only underwear, to form a line in search of hope. They find a flower and undulate mysteriously toward it. Daddy Mack Truitte gazes demonically first at the crowd, then at the camera as the lights fade to black.

Markedly distinct from anything Ailey made for the stage, *Riedaiglia* suggested the 1960s hippie scene, complete with flower child imagery, social dancing in outrageous, glamorous costumes, throbbing love-in sequences, and an overall mood of psychedelica. Ostensibly a danced meditation of the seven deadly sins, *Riedaiglia* brought Ailey his most contemporary material to date. Riedel's experimental, free jazz score combined with Egler's at once fuzzy and claustrophobic camera work to all but obscure Ailey's slight choreographic plan. Surprisingly, the movement vocabulary Ailey employed to tell these contemporary tales of lust, pride, anger, and envy differed little from movements used to

Members of the Alvin Ailey American Dance Theater
backstage during rehearsals of *Riedaiglia*, 1967.
Photographer unknown

detail Depression-era blues dancing in a southern barrelhouse. Ailey relied on music, costuming, and his dancers' sense of dramatic projection to suggest the mysterious rituals of a nefarious underground community.

Although the dance brought Ailey's company acclaim, as well as timely remuneration, it also predicted a pattern of creative apathy with which the choreographer regularly approached dance making occasioned only by paying commissions. In an effort to attain financial stability, managing agent Gil Shiva helped Ailey legally incorporate Dance Theater Foundation, Inc. as the umbrella organization for the Alvin Ailey American Dance Theater in 1967.[58] Incorporation afforded the company access to grants from the National Endowment for the Arts and subsequent tax-free corporate sponsorship. The official certificate of incorporation, dated 29 April 1967, set among its goals to "train the Young American Negro dancer and . . . provide a continuing source and outlet for the talented professional Negro dancers to the world of Dance."[59] This statement made explicit Ailey's political concern to broaden training venues available to African American dancers, a concern overlooked by many existing white-run dance academies. The statement also designated Ailey as an official guardian of professional Negro talent and its entrée to an imposing (white) world of dance, as it tacitly assumed a cultural and political gulf between African American dancers and concert dance, to be remedied by Ailey's growing enterprise.

Revelations II: 1969

By 1969, *Revelations* looked markedly different from its 1962 incarnation. Changes in the dance's performance reflected changes in Ailey's thinking about the importance of dance in American culture and the emergence of a new audience.

In May 1969 Boston public television station WGBH sponsored a week of performances by Ailey's company "to inaugurate its [WBGH's] new role as a 'cultural entrepreneur' for the community."[1] The station videotaped performances of Ailey's *Revelations* and Talley Beatty's *The Black Belt*, which were subsequently broadcast on the WGBH dramatic series *On Being Black* in June 1969. Ailey appeared briefly as the on-camera narrator for the program to remind his audience of his intention to "project the essential dignity and beauty of men" through concert dance.

Beatty's *The Black Belt* (1968) screens before *Revelations*. Ailey commissioned Beatty's piece in 1968 to explore "the realities of the black belt," or ghetto, its "ferment, paradox, conflict and dilemma," its "aspiration for mobility," and its "surge toward integration and assimilation into the mainstream of American Life."[2] Set to Duke Ellington's *Black, Brown and Beige*, *The Black Belt* offers a carnivalesque depiction of a day in the ghetto.

In its opening section, "On the Street," the dancers portray archetypal contemporary young adults, dressed in brightly colored, funky street clothes not unlike those worn in scenes of Ailey's *Riedaiglia*. Several of the dancers sport contemporary Afro hairstyles. One man, Dudley Williams in the taped performance, is cast as an outsider to the group, clad in plain trousers and a simple white shirt. The crowd remains wary and hostile toward Williams, who, in turn, seems bewildered at their seething sense of cool. The street scene proceeds with stylized strutting, relieved by slow-motion bends to the ground, snippets of contemporary social dances done in pairs, punctuated by balletic extensions of the legs, and extended unison phrases danced with unmasked antagonism toward Williams's character.

The second section, "In the Bedroom," renders a troubled woman in a short black nightgown, Judith Jamison here, engaged in a cryptic ritual of frustration. She is alternately antagonized by a group of haughty women dressed in high heels and short black teddies, and a brutish man, who partners her in a playful acrobatic dance of sensual foreplay. A third section, "In the Church," depicts a brutal encounter between worshipers in a storefront church and a gang of marauding male rapists in white-face masks. The scene returns to the streets for an extended sequence of fighting and confrontation, as the white-masked figures descend on Williams, strip him of his clothing, and carry him offstage in a modified crucifixion pose. After a short scene of mourning by a mysterious group of hooded women in black, a full-scale riot erupts in the streets, and the dancers enact frenzied looting, fighting, and mayhem. The dance ends when all of the rioters are shot by the machine guns of offstage (white) policemen. As the lights fade, the dancers are massed in a heap center stage, smothered by useless stolen merchandise.

In *The Black Belt*, Beatty draws a disturbingly violent portrait of contemporary ghetto life seemingly without purpose, hope, or apology. Its characters enact quirky rituals that collectively suggest a community unraveling at its seams. The dance employs blocks of hyperkinetic movement phrases built from impossibly fast sequences of turns, leg extensions, leaps, freezes, and shifts of direction, all executed with a suffocating rhythmic precision. A protest dance of anger and frustration with obvious references to civil rights activism and the contemporaneous black arts movement, *The Black Belt* depicts an explosive rage barely contained by daily life in the streets of an urban ghetto.

In an on-camera narration before *Revelations*, Ailey positions his dance as a lyrical counterpoint to Beatty's work: "I have myself composed a ballet to our own passionately beautiful spirituals." Ailey's dance, already a classic of the modern dance repertoire, here represents the strength and faith of mature African Americans involved in the struggle for sociopolitical equity. Notably, Ailey refers to the modern dance suite as a "ballet," effectively co-opting the language of "high" dance art for his own work. The shift in terminology speaks to his desire as well as the performance reality in which *Revelations* stood as a classically shaped exploration of American dance idioms for the concert stage.[3]

As the opening hummed chorus of "I've Been 'Buked" sounds, the camera pans across the stretched necks of ten motionless dancers grouped in a tight wedge formation, warmly lit in the center of a dark void. The women now wear long dresses of varying colors, including surprisingly vivid shades of green and orange. Afro hairdos and the presence of three white dancers, one woman and two men, mark the outward appearance of the dance as contemporary in terms of fashion and socially progressive.

While the basic movement sequences of the dance remain essentially unchanged from their 1962 manifestation, certain gestures and rhythmic accents pop out. The devotional leader figure in the center of the wedge now performs an accented extension of his arms over the down-turned backs of his parish. Timed in a break between musical phrases, this precise gesture amplifies his role. As performed by ten dancers, full-group excursions from the wedge fill a vast stage space, offering the audience a panoramic sampling of the dancers' individuality. A unison gesture of hinging backward to the floor without benefit of hands acquires a dramatic, daredevilish quality on this larger group. Tensely held hands, revealing open and expressive palms, provide striking visual "finish" to motion sequences in gestures timed in strict unison at the end of phrases. Extensions of the legs are higher and more secure in several balanced positions, and movement overall has a fuller quality of breath and suppleness.

The dancers in "I've Been 'Buked" convey a range of individual emotional foci. Some seem fearful, while others remain simply dutiful or solemn. Excepting the precise, accented ends of phrases, the dancers do not maintain a careful unison, even when the movement patterns require unity. Individual dancers press against the spiritual's slow rhythmic motion to expand the timing of their movements; the dancers do not always seem to be working together so much as working at the same time. Simple motions, such as the raising of stretched hands into the air overhead, now convey a weighty significance communicated by reverent gazes.

Although the lineup of spirituals Ailey used for *Revelations* remained constant after 1962, the recorded versions of the songs he used changed often during the 1960s. The recording of "Didn't My Lord Deliver Daniel" used for the 1969 videotaping sounds extravagantly different from the 1962 version. Performed here by the Robert Shaw Chorale, "Daniel" is sung a cappella, with no percussion accompaniment. The absence of drumming weakens the relationship between the spiritual and Ailey's dance. Sharply accented contractions of the torso, scooping jumps into space, and basic rhythmic step patterns seem to hold little relationship to the music, which coasts unhurriedly with a soothing, decorous warmth. Repetition of musical and movement phrases lose impact without the sensation of rhythmic layering, and the basic rhythmic organization of the dance becomes obscured. To compensate for the lack of drumming, the dancers employ a palpable vigor to convey a percussive rhythmic attack, wrenching the endings of phrases into unison by the sheer force of tightly held bodies.

Through their noticeable emotional connection, Consuelo Atlas and George Faison reconfigure the roles of praying woman and invisible male guardian angel Ailey originally choreographed in "Fix Me, Jesus." Dancing to a recorded vocal solo by soprano Inez Matthews with simple piano accompaniment, Atlas

The Alvin Ailey American Dance Theater in "I've Been
'Buked" from Alvin Ailey's *Revelations*, circa 1978.
Photograph by Bill Hilton

physically sees Faison guiding her motion and finishing her gestures of prayer.
She dances with a soft, yielding center of motion, giving her energy to her partner. At times, she visibly waits for his direction to continue her dance. Faison
also dances with a giving, conciliatory authority, watching his partner closely for
shifts of nuance. The dancers' contact blurs a sense of steadfast religious conviction, giving the duet instead an air of respectful, pliant passivity.

Throughout this version of *Revelations* dancers tend to dispel Ailey's original dramatic narrative to perform the movement patterns with newly minted
reverent care. The "Processional" leading to the "Wade in the Water" sequence
lacks dramatic specificity or urgency as a rural Texas religious ceremony. Instead,
the seven processional dancers surrounding the baptismal initiates and deaconess create a series of presentational tableaux directed toward the camera. Accompanied here by an a cappella choir with no drumming accents, the "Processional" seems long and unmotivated.

The unique abilities of individual dancers also profoundly revise the impact of *Revelations*. Dancer Judith Jamison transforms the sensibility of the "Wade in the Water" sequence from the enactment of a ritual to a showcase of her magnetic presence. Portraying the deaconess with the umbrella, Jamison gives a charismatic performance that all but erases the centrality of the two initiates, danced here by Michele Murray and Kelvin Rotardier. Jamison's long, expressive arms command attention in luxurious rolling motions that extend beyond the edges of the stage space. She projects energy outward, fervently pushing against the space around her, obviously reveling in the rhythmic layering of body part isolations. While ostensibly guiding the initiates into baptismal waters, she looks to them only on occasion. She focuses her attention on the process of her portion of the ritual more than the safe passage of her charges, and her exit from the stage produces a noticeable void.

As performed by Dudley Williams, "I Wanna Be Ready" becomes a quiet study of control performed with careful attention to gesture and body line. Williams makes his first appearance in *Revelations* in this solo; his unanticipated appearance in the dance grants him an aura of emotional authority. He moves with fluid hushed assurance, performing the dance's rituals of prayer and cleansing simply and without melodrama. He stretches unfolding and balancing actions out to the ends of musical phrases, so that extended, virtuosic balances surface during transitional movements.

Williams doesn't alter the choreographic plan of "I Want to Be Ready" so much as he fills in its physical possibilities. Controlled balances, fluid extensions of legs, and meticulous articulation of body line all bring forward the surface contours of Ailey's choreography. The recording Williams dances to here is noticeably slower than the recording used by Truitte in 1962; the difference in tempo requires Williams to sustain balances longer and display an impressive physical strength.

Folk singer Leon Bibb's recording of "Sinner Man," used in this performance of *Revelations*, veers furthest from Ailey's original musical choices. Performed here as a male solo accompanied by banjo, bass, and drums, the recording employs a pulsating shuffle tempo with strong accents on the off-beats. This rhythmic device gives the piece a honky-tonk, traveling-music feeling, more suited to a celebration of movement than the dramatic escape from purgatory suggested by Ailey's choreographic scenario.

Still structured in three parts consisting of group opening, three contrasting solos, and a group closing with musical tag, "Sinner Man" is now embellished with technically demanding feats. Its three male performers wear jazz shoes, which provide more traction than bare feet and allow for fast, multiple turns. "Sinner Man" now contains extravagant reaching balances on one leg followed by perilous drops to the floor; expansive, turning leaps performed with gasping urgency across the stage space; and high, explosive jumps articulated with contorted body positions. The musical score now includes a complete rhythmic break after the third man's solo. Ailey's revised staging mirrors the musical break with a freezing of motion; all three men suddenly pose in a wide stance on two feet, their arms held up toward the skies and heads thrown back in agony. The sudden rhythmic rupture increases a sense of anticipation and excitement, lending additional impact to the final phrases of the dance.

The final, gospel church service section of *Revelations*, danced by Ailey's full company of thirteen to recorded music by Brother John Sellers, now begins with character vignettes of greeting performed by the seven women. The lights rise to reveal a lone woman, positioned toward the corner of the space, dressed in a bright yellow Sunday church dress. She fans herself against the hot sun, suggested by a projection against the upstage wall, and moves lazily to the recitative-style strains of "The Day Is Past and Gone." Gradually, six other women enter, each wearing a similar yellow dress and oversized yellow straw hat and bearing a short stool and an oversized straw fan. The women move with an air of easy familiarity, stopping to chat in small groups of two and three and gesturing in greeting to others across the stage. As the invocation to the sermon ends, they fan out across the space, look about to confirm that they all are met, and sit down in unison. Their stools stretch symmetrically across the space in lines emanating along diagonals from Jamison's central position.

As the women sit down, the staging shifts from its relaxed, conversational introductory mode to a bound, unison style. This shift of flow details the formal beginning of the church service. The women maintain serious facial expressions during the "Preaching Spiritual" that follows, performing the seated unison choreography with a frozen mask of dutiful responsibility. The dance progresses as a layering of rhythmic patterns that intensify, drawing the women off their stools to make small excursions into space while remaining in unison and close to their home positions. As the music shifts into a spoken section, six men rush on from the wings. Dressed in identical tight black pants, black shoes, pale yellow shirts open at the neck, and ornately brocaded yellow vests that hug the torso, the men meet their partners during the sermon already in progress. Jamison, seated center stage, continues without a partner.

"Preaching Spiritual" segues into "Rocka My Soul" with much of Ailey's original staging intact, its vibrancy intensified by the expanded number of dancers. In a staging gesture simplified from its 1962 version, the dancers rush toward the camera in two parallel lines, hands held on the hips, upper bodies erect, and shoulders turning in sharp opposition on each step. The high-back posture offers a surprising sudden variation of stance, while the dancers' flat, frontal orientation and direct eye contact with the camera enlist the viewer's engagement with the dance. *Revelations* ends as before, with the company stretched across the space in lines, and a turn and drop to the knees lead to a final held position: knees wide, upper bodies erect, the dancers raise their arms upward on the diagonals as they toss their heads back toward the heavens.

By 1969, the Ailey company owned an international reputation bestowed largely by the appeal of *Revelations*. Aware of their responsibility to promote that reputation, the newer dancers in the company were likely responsible for the veneer of solemnity that covered the dance in this era. In 1969, Ailey's expanded company included four dancers new to the repertory (Harvey Cohen, John Medieros, Renee Rose, and Danny Strayhorn) and five dancers in only their second season with the company (George Faison, Linda Kent, Michele Murray, Alma Robinson, and Sylvia Waters). None of the four senior members of the company—Consuelo Atlas in her third year, Judith Jamison in her fourth, or five-year veterans Kelvin Rotardier and Dudley Williams—had been involved in the creation of *Revelations*. Long-time associate artistic director James Truitte left the company in 1968; by 1969, Ailey himself provided the only link to the original dance.

Ailey encouraged his dancers to fill out movement patterns with deeper knee bends and longer leg extensions ("I've Been 'Buked"), yielding, almost romantic passion ("Fix Me, Jesus"), and advanced combinations of turns and jumps ("Sinner Man"). He allowed his dancers to demonstrate their mastery of formidable techniques, gained from prestigious dance institutions such as the Juilliard School and Boston Conservatory of Music, within his nearly decade-old choreographic ground plan. In doing so, he rejected traditional concert dance conventions of "fixed" choreography for a more fluid, generational model that not only accommodated but *expected* changes in performance standards.

Ailey did not develop a dance technique that allowed him to train dancers before they performed his choreography. His dancers joined his company with their training from other schools, then honed their performance skills onstage. Like a jazz conductor, Ailey expected his dancers to bring a unique, individual method of expression to the company, to "play" his choreography as best suited their talents. This redefinition of the input of dancers offered a paradigm shift that allowed concert dance to resonate with other forms of Africanist expression, including big band jazz.

As presented on the WGBH program, *Revelations* enacted a dialogue of "historical beauty" with the more explosive, personalized "contemporary rage" depicted in *The Black Belt*. By 1969, Ailey intended *Revelations* to balance his company's repertory need for works glorifying Negro heritage with the need to render contemporary African American life; *On Being Black* confirmed his company's ability to embody both modes of performance. The depiction of violent rage in *The Black Belt* brought forward political concerns important to many African Americans, even as it aestheticized racism for theatrical consumption. The mask of reverence held throughout the 1969 version of *Revelations* honored a mythologized African American past, even as its dancers embellished its choreographic content. Taken together, the two works suggested the breadth of Ailey's enterprise: to depict a range of representation for dancing black bodies on the concert stage.

Dudley Williams, Loretta Abbott, Lucinda Ransom
(with umbrella), Takako Asakawa, and Morton Winston in
"Processional" from Alvin Ailey's *Revelations*, circa 1964.
Photographer unknown

█ Versioning

Versioning, the generational reworking of aesthetic ideals, is probably my favorite strategy of African American performance. At once postmodern and as ancient as the hills, versioning is a way to tell an old tale new or to launch a musty proverb into the contemporary moment. Born of transplanted modes of African orature, it has given rise to decades of popular music styles and dances, from ragtime to hip-hop, from the cakewalk, a nineteenth-century parody of European ballroom processionals, to the running man, a subtle satire of celluloid superheroes. The transformative agility central to versioning is highly prized in African American culture and typically noted in the individual's ability to switch meanings and tonalities from one moment to the next. Versioning, and its sibling, inversion, allow us to critique, to uncover, to rediscover, to realign, to mark the common as personal, to read (as in "someone's beads"), to make something *work*.

Music theorist Dick Hebdige writes about the importance of versioning in the realm of Caribbean popular music, where its practice gave rise to reggae and, after the era of Hebdige's study, rumpshaker beats. According to Hebdige, versioning "is at the heart of reggae but of *all* Afro-American and Caribbean music: jazz, blues, rap, r&b, reggae, calypso, soca, salsa, Afro-Cuban and so on."[4] Because versioning refers to an individual's creative interpretation, it is typically aligned with vernacular practices, that is, creative practices that are commonplace and available to anyone. But versioning requires skill to be effective, and its most successful practitioners work well outside any definitions that might mark them as amateurs. Why, then, is versioning considered a "vernacular" practice? More important, when is the moment of invention aligned not with re-creation, an interpretive mode, but with authorship, its generative cousin? Is versioning interpretive or generative?

It may be that in black American culture, distinctions between generative and interpretive modes can be easily elided. For example, many of Katherine Dunham's versions of Caribbean ritual dances arranged for the stage amplified certain movement sequences she found of interest, but minimized others. Is Dunham's vision of Caribbean dance, in the work *Shango* (1945), for example, more important than the cultural practices it represents? Surely not. Similarly, Pearl Primus restaged African dances she learned on the continent after her Rosenwald-sponsored research there in 1948–49.[5] But Primus had little intention to "refine" the dances when she taught and arranged them for the concert stage, as in her *Fanga* (1949). Rather, she intended to act as a guide for the audience, as an individual able to open a window onto diasporic dance practices.

My intention here is not to denigrate the accomplishment of Dunham or Primus as enormously gifted creative artists. But I do follow Hebdige, who asserts that in many African, Afro-American, and Caribbean musical forms, "the collective voice is given precedence over the individual voice of the artist or the composer."[6] Something similar occurs in certain concert dance formations, when the contributions of the group of dancers outweigh the choreographic plan of an individual artist. This paradigm allows for a generational "versioning" of dance materials, often without regard for a choreographer's, or a specific choreography's, original intention.

Versioning is also aligned with youthful innovation; in terms of dance, new versions of existing forms typically offer heightened physical risk. In this, dance becomes an activity propelled forward by the young. In black America, the dances of the youngest have the most power: social power, power as identity formation, as affirmation of self, as confirmation of creativity and individuality. Breakdancing offers an obvious example of this constellation of generational empowerment. Born in the crucible of poverty lining the South Bronx of New York circa 1970, breakdancing began as a form of gang fighting, a mixture of physically demanding movements that exploited the daredevil prowess of their performers and stylized punching and kicking movements directed at an opponent. A relative of capoeira, the Brazilian form of martial arts disguised as dance, breaking developed as the movement aspect of rap music when breakdancers—"B-Boys"—filled the musical breaks between records mixed by disc jockeys at parties and discotheques. Breaking, and its related forms of pop-locking, rose to mainstream cultural prominence in movies and music videos, including Charlie Ahearn's *Wild Style* (1982), the first film to document emergent hip-hop culture, *Flashdance* (1983), which pushed the form to international attention in a thirty-second sequence of street dancing, *Breakin'* (1984), which starred Shabba Doo (Adolfo Quinones), an important breakdance choreographer from Chicago, and Harry Belafonte's *Beat Street* (1984), which featured the New York City Breakers. By the late 1980s, breakdancing had become a youth culture fad, practiced by young men and women in many parts of the world.

But notice that the social dances we now watch on MTV are born in particular locations and at particular moments, and typically where young African, Latino/a, and Caribbean Americans respond to their contemporary musicians. We might realize that dance is indeed life in these situations: it is the creative throes of youth in conflict with maturity, the power of the body in formation and without fear of injury. The young bodies in these circumstances may tell more about the possibilities of moving than the careful, age-mediated movements of adults burdened by physical mishaps or musical missteps.

Brenda Dixon Gottschild calls this quality *ephebism*, or the power of youth; it is one of her core theoretical principles of Africanist performance that "encompasses attributes such as power, vitality, flexibility, drive, and attack. . . . Intensity is also a characteristic of ephebism, but it is a kinesthetic intensity that recognizes feeling as sensation, rather than emotion."[7] In this definition, the sensation of motion overrules its potential emotional impact; technique conquers expressivity; what one can do becomes more important than what it might mean.

The dancers of Ailey's 1975 company inherited roles made on dancers who came before them; the ways these younger artists signified on their predecessors' portrayals marked their performances as both unique and, in this paradigm of generational versioning, black. By amplifying their command of technique, the younger dancers confirmed their arrival in the company as bearers of the dance; they came to be known to their audiences and each other through their versions of the dances.

The best of these young artists are generative interpreters, if you will. They are dancers who honor and signify on the past by renewing it with their own individual version of its memory.

▌ Multiracial Concert Dance

To foster growing public enthusiasm for his company throughout the 1960s, Ailey constantly situated concert dance along a continuum of American art making that could appeal simultaneously to African Americans and others. For black dancers, concert performance offered an escape from the cruelties of racialized daily life in America. In 1966, Ailey and *Dance Magazine* writer Amelia Fatt referred to the liberating emotional climate in Europe and Africa that allowed his dancers to hone their performing skills: "'Finding that they were considered beautiful, the girls became beautiful. Respected as artists and as beautiful women, they became different performers.' What any dancer needs to blossom, and what the Negro dancer especially needs, is 'the devel-

Linda Kent and Clive Thompson in "Fix Me, Jesus" from Alvin Ailey's *Revelations*, circa 1972. Photograph by R. Faligant

opment of a feeling of respect about himself.' As self-respect develops, so does performance."[8]

Ailey also wanted to bring forward concert dance as a socializing tool available to young African Americans searching for identity through the 1960s upheavals of civil rights activism. During a short-lived residency at the Brooklyn Academy of Music (BAM), Ailey sponsored free classes for children and young adults geared to channel formidable youth rage into art. A press release dated 18 June 1969 and titled "Dance Riot in Brooklyn" claimed that Ailey-endorsed dance classes, offered through the cooperation of BAM and the Hanson Place Central Methodist Church, caused "many cases of radical personality change in young potential trouble-makers who have found that someone cares, and that they, themselves, can accomplish something meaningful for their own self esteem."[9]

Ailey found the 1969 arrangement with BAM unsatisfactory for at least two reasons: cramped quarters caused by shared resident status with the Merce Cunningham and José Limón companies, and BAM director Harvey Lichtenstein's attempts to exploit Ailey's racial identity. In February 1969, Ailey's company performed for a loose coalition of middle-class businesspeople, most of them "active in the community, social and political affairs." According to the *New York Times*, Lichtenstein used the occasion to elicit financial patronage "from the Negro community to support a Negro company. Not just financial, but to get across the feeling that the company belongs to the community."[10] Less than two months later, Ailey expressed his disdain for racialized business tactics: "It's terrifying in this day and time to keep after the black community to support my company. What about my white dancers? Should the [Brooklyn] Academy ask White businessmen to pay their salaries?"[11]

Like many conservatively minded African American artists his age, Ailey resisted stating a commitment to the emergent black aesthetic of the late 1960s. He maintained a steadfast allegiance to his integrated company and his freedom as an artist to evade the separatist demands of black nationalism: "I feel an obligation to use black dancers because there must be more opportunities for them but *not* because I'm a black choreographer talking to black people. . . . We talk too much of black art when we should be talking about art, just art. . . . Black composers must be free to write rondos and fugues, not only protest songs."[12]

Ailey's strict integrationist stance fit neatly with his company's audience and funding realities. By 1969, the company's fledgling African American audience base could not support its financial or critical needs. Still, Ailey sought to widen the public perception of art and concert dance, speaking in an interview of his company's efforts "to do something about the spiritual isolation of our times through dance." Opining that the country was "castrating itself culturally" through racial and artistic separatism, Ailey offered his organization as a model of racial harmony: "We consider ourselves a company of artists," and color should be "an irrelevant factor in the world of dance."[13] He described his company as one that began "to show the black cultural heritage in dance and music" but changed over the years "to be an integrated company. I believe in that very strongly. This country has a multiracial society. I believe in black pride and a black renaissance but I do feel that we have to learn to come together."[14]

Ailey's comments distanced him from a growing nationalist trend among black artists to define art politically by, for, and about black people. Choreographer Eleo Pomare became an outspoken advocate for culturally specific work: "I don't create works to amuse white crowds, nor do I wish to show them how charming, strong, and folksy Negro people are—as whites imagine them—Negroes dancing in the manner of Jerome Robbins or Martha Graham." For Pomare and like-minded black choreographers working to align dance to the black arts movement, concert dance had to be remodeled to "erase all white influences" and still dramatize the world of the black artist "in a dance language that originates in Harlem itself."[15] Clearly, *Revelations* could not fit this mandate.

Some critics recognized Ailey's dilemma. Writing in the *New York Times*, Clive Barnes offered a sustained essay on the wages of Ailey's stance that applauded his determination:

> It would be easier—and more acceptable—for Ailey to form an all-Black company, for then, as the obvious black leader in American dance, guilty foundations would have to beat a path to his door. But Ailey goes the hard way of his conscience. It is a very old-fashioned kind of militancy and, I suspect, it brings in less cash, yet there is the individuality of genius here. Also, when Ailey, I think our black leader in American Dance, demands such ethnic variety, and so successfully achieves this racial mix, can our "white" companies afford to stand aside?

Of course, Ailey had often been protected by "guilty foundations," including the U.S. government, and the notion that integrated casting in opera house concert dance could be considered "militant" seems, at best, dubious. But Barnes astutely underscored the comfort and consideration accorded Ailey by whites in American concert dance as well as integration-minded black audience members. Barnes continued:

> Ailey is black and proud of it. But he understands that the African culture is as much part of American life as European culture. He is no black apostle of apartheid, and I love him for it. Today his non-black dancers can keep up in his company's idiom, which, for the most part, is Afro-American. As a result—and I wouldn't stress this but rather take it as it comes—every performance he gives is the greatest lesson in race relations you are going to get in a month of Sundays."[16]

Here, Barnes presumes that the "lesson in race relations" goes in more than one direction. Certainly, Ailey's white audiences learned about black beauty as well as the resiliency of Africanist expression in each Ailey company performance. But as Ailey reached further and wider for a general audience, how his choreography spoke to young black people came to be questioned.

Modern dance had largely been created by artists to engage the individual psyche, to explore the impulses of a single artistic vision. This individualistic impulse contradicts a core tenet of black art: that art exists to serve the larger (black) community. In their study of the concurrent black arts literary movement, Abby Arthur and Ronald Maberry Johnson note how, in "advocating an art-for-people's sake, proponents of the black aesthetic emphasized the community, not the individual. The well-being of the collective group, of black persons everywhere, was more important than the needs of one person. In a similar manner, the evolving concerns of black literature were more significant than the artistic idiosyncracies and the reputation of the individual author."[17] To some nationalistic black audiences, Ailey's choreography seemed to serve the growing Ailey enterprise and its white audiences more than the black culture it purported to represent.

The problem Ailey faced involved at least commerce, race, and Ailey's own ambition to become a world-renowned success. Being stuck between the rock and the hard place of being a responsible leader among black artists, faithful to African American cultural wellsprings while nurturing European techniques of dance and choreography common to concert dance stages, tore at Ailey's sensibilities, especially during the height of the civil rights movement. His work could only lead a black audience willing to come into the proscenium theater to experience it; other black audiences could not understand some of his innovations without a sense of modern dance history. At the same time, Ailey's interest in ballet and Graham technique seemed a curiously apolitical response to the times, given his company's predominance and his widespread support from the government and audiences worldwide.

Ailey seldom acknowledged how his work stood in relation to the black arts movement, but he clearly expected his activities and company policies to speak for themselves. He often related his work to a traditional white lineage of American modern dance which included Isadora Duncan, Ruth St. Denis, Martha Graham, and his mentor Lestor Horton. In 1969, he called Graham's work the source for much modern choreography: "The major influence in modern dance in this century is Martha. She, the great mother, opened our eyes to using certain kinds of themes and costumes. The most important companies are off-shoots of her, making variations of her ideas."[18] Ailey's variation of Graham valued core tenets of African American musicality: participatory interaction of his dancers, an innovative approach to the act of choreography, and the subversive reclaiming of stage stereotypes to both honor and signify on the past. More than anything, Ailey sought to affirm the splendor of black bodies in motion, to unleash the healing power of (African American) dance: "I want to leave an idea about dancers, especially Negro dancers. I want to help show my people how beautiful they are. And not just Negroes. I want to hold up a mirror to the audience that says this is the way people can be, this is how open people can be."[19]

▋ *Revelations* 1975

Revelations attained its most extravagant proportions during the mid-1970s, when Ailey staged the dance to include a complement of nineteen dancers. The expansion of the ensemble magnified the dance's contours for viewing in the expansive space of the New York State Theater at Lincoln Center during the company's season there, 12–24 August 1975.

A huge phalanx of bodies cluster together as the curtain rises on "I've Been 'Buked." Throughout this section the thirteen dancers move together but not in strict unison, giving bending motions a supple, breathing variety that reaches the ground in waves. As in 1969, the dancers use their hands to provide visual punctuation at the end of phrases. Some changes in choreography appear: a unison sway to the right then left is now performed as a tightly controlled step to the right and left, accented by taut arms and tightly held torsos.

By 1975, Ailey's preferred dancer training veered heavily toward classical ballet technique, and the dancers here make pronounced categorical distinctions between balletic and modern dance movements. The dancers' shifting centers of weight describe the variations in idiom: the downward-directed, heavy bending motions that begin the work suggest modern dance, while buoyant, fluent turns performed with turned-out legs and arched, held torsos confirm ballet training. Varied articulations of port de bras also demonstrate the shift in company training. In group sections, tensely stretched arms reach toward the heavens, while gently curved arms prevail in solo variations.

Excepting "I've Been 'Buked" and the final gospel sequence, "The Day Is Past and Gone/Preaching Sermon/Rocka My Soul," other sections in the 1975 version of *Revelations* are not expanded to include more dancers. "Daniel" is still performed by two women and one man, now dwarfed by the enormous State Theater proscenium. Beginning in strict unison, the dancers seem to project formal shapes outward more than they connect movement patterns to any overarching dramatic narrative of redemption. The recording of the spiritual used here includes drummed rhythms that the dancers echo in sharp contractions and an overall percussive attack.

Other sections of the dance seem to be abstract meditations on the nature of devotional relationships. In "Fix Me, Jesus" the woman, Mari Kajiwara, is so much smaller than the man, Clive Thompson, that lifts and balances are effortless, performed without any sense of exertion or weight. They dance with an elongated, balletic stretch, prominently displayed in a lifted-posture walking cadence performed on the ends of arched feet. The combined ease of execution and stretched limbs heighten the dance's abstract qualities, lessening Ailey's original dramatic narrative of a woman in need of spiritual guidance. Kajiwara does not communicate distress or inward trouble; rather, she performs the movement to its fullest extent, and in the process pushes forward Ailey's outward choreographic design. Thompson dances with a subdued, purposeful intensity that similarly suggests a kinetic logic to Ailey's movement design. His technical facility forces the viewer's attention on gentle unfoldings, balances, and slow turns blurred or absent in earlier versions of the dance.

Dudley Williams gives a demure performance of "I Want to Be Ready" in which balances and levitations become technical chores rather than means of expression. He seems distracted, as if uncomfortable working on the stage without an audience present. Still, his performance reveals a heightened formal plan of contractions and releases, falls and recoveries, and circling motions of the arms and torso that contribute to an overall effect of physical expertise. The spare, abstract feeling of this particular rehearsal, however, may hold little relation to any of Williams's live performances in 1975.

An elongated, balletic carriage is also prominent on the seven dancers in the "Processional." The posture projects an effect of glamorous majesty contained by bodies moving in slow-motion pageantry. The dancers mark each step with a deep sway of the hips as they hold their upper bodies still. They take broad steps to cross the entire State Theater stage, and the spatial expansion dispels Ailey's central choreographic plan of a tight-knit community engaged in a religious ritual.

The final gospel church service of *Revelations* includes some eighteen dancers. The amplification brings the rhythmic structuring of Ailey's dance phrases into sharpened relief, especially as they perform pauses and accents embedded within the vivid spectacle of large-group unison dancing. Stretched across the State Theater stage, the dance loses any sense of intimacy that could be offered by its dancers.

The amplification of *Revelations* to fill the New York State Theater stage paralleled the considerable expansion of Ailey's company and school. The company counted some thirty-one dancers on its rolls during the 1975 calendar year; *Revelations*, the largest company piece in the Ailey repertory at the time, expanded to accommodate nineteen of the twenty-four dancers contracted during the company's State Theater appearance.

Ailey's desire to connect concert dance to a larger African American community drove him to contest traditional models of what concert dance could be. He adjusted the scale of *Revelations* to signal his company's viability as a major cultural representative, able, in this case, to command the expansive space of the New York State Theater. He allowed his dancers to bring themselves into the dance in subtle but telling terms of hairstyles and dance technique, a maneuver that honored core African American modes of expression through grooming and stance. Working without the benefit of any similarly styled

The Alvin Ailey American Dance Theater in "Rocka My
Soul" from Alvin Ailey's *Revelations*, circa 1972.
Photographer unknown

African American performing arts institution, Ailey evolved his company's standards to suit the needs of his changing audience and the larger sociopolitical
climate.

   Revelations represented cultural memory as body wisdom, a synthesis of
religious/folk song, formal technique, and social stance arranged as a series of
tasks that could be performed by shifting rosters of dancers. Changes in its scale
and the sound of its musical accompaniment echoed core principles of generational rebirth in black social music, a process that produced styles from doo-
wop to disco during *Revelations*' first fifteen years.

   By 1975 Ailey's company and *Revelations* set an African American standard
of concert dance performance. Burgeoning regional companies such as Dayton
Contemporary Dance Company (founded by Jeraldyne Blunden in 1968), Den-
ver's Cleo Parker Robinson Dance Company (founded by Cleo Parker Robinson
in 1970), the Philadelphia Dance Company (founded by Joan Myers Brown in
1969), as well as the soon-to-be-formed Dallas Black Dance Theatre (founded
by Anne Williams in 1976) and Lula Washington's Los Angeles Contemporary
Dance Theater (founded by Lula Washington in 1980) all adopted Ailey's model
of an integrated roster, mixed repertory by several modern dance choreogra-

phers, and a punchy synthesis of dance idioms as standard company technique. Eventually, the Ailey company's success caused *Revelations* to represent cultural history in and of itself. By 1975, the dance stood for achievement in the performing arts attained on a level unimaginable for African Americans before civil rights activism of the 1960s.

Touring, Touring, Touring

Ailey's company survived throughout the 1960s and 1970s only by extensive touring. Performances in out-of-the-way venues around the world guaranteed untried audiences potentially open to the artistic experiments of concert dance. The 12 July 1963 Fairfield, Iowa *Daily Ledger* reported the Ailey company's recent appearance there as "the first time dancing of this type has been presented in Fairfield," for which "the audience was appreciative and responsive." Typical of the company's barnstorming efforts throughout this period, the Fairfield engagement gathered an audience of nine hundred, "the largest attendance for a single performance" there.[1] The Ailey company consistently set attendance milestones for modern dance in such communities as Richmond, Virginia; Cleveland, Ohio; Holmdel, New Jersey, which counted 150 for a lecture-demonstration, and Minneapolis, which counted five hundred for a lecture-demonstration and five thousand for a single performance.[2]

Extensive touring inevitably wore on the company, whose members found little artistic development in strings of one-night performances. By 1971, two- and three-month stints on the road became commonplace. In an interview, dancer Kenneth Pearl described the "disastrous" effect of the hectic touring schedule: "Everyone has to keep learning their parts all over again with new partners and still perform each night. . . . It's good I suppose, all this performing. I mean, it's better than working for three months for two performances; but to work three days for months of one nighters is a bummer."[3]

However difficult for the dancers, the extensive touring attracted the interest of an audience newly introduced to concert dance. As early as 1962, Ailey realized that preperformance lecture-demonstrations offered another opportunity to feel the pulse of his audience. Interviewed immediately after the Far East tour of 1962, he acknowledged having

> learned more from students than anyone else. . . . Many wanted to know about dance techniques, choreographic ideas and how and where we had each studied. Obviously, this requires an educational process. Instead of just performing, future artists on tours such as ours should be given more time to give lectures and demonstrations, prior to the performances, for student and professional dancers as well as for the general public.[4]

After 1962, Ailey actively sought a college-age student audience for his company's performances.

Through these lecture demonstrations, Ailey attempted to familiarize audiences with the elements of modern dance technique and to suggest the inevitable collaboration of dancer and audience in creating the concert performance. When he told an audience in Holmdel, New Jersey, "I choreograph to communicate with the audience and with the dancers," he invited the audience to openly participate in a dialogue with concert dance. Ailey rejected the need for mediation by professional dance critics or aesthetes to attach value to his company's work. Rather, he actively sought a localized discussion of the immediate effects of concert dance. He also discussed how his dancers contributed to the choreographic process: "I do all the steps in the choreography myself. . . . However, my dancers are inspired people, and each of them is given the chance to add of himself or herself to the dance. They contribute to the dance personally."[5]

▌ *Quintet*

In 1968, Ailey turned to pop music for the first time in his choreographic career. Funded by a Guggenheim Fellowship awarded in the summer of 1968 for the creation of the new work, he made *Quintet* (28 August 1968) to six songs from Laura Nyro's album *Eli and the Thirteenth Confession*.[6] Finished quickly during the company's one-week stay in Scotland, *Quintet* debuted at the 1968 Edinburgh Festival.[7] The dance premiered in New York during the Ailey company's first Broadway season of January 1969 and remained in the company's repertory for two years.[8]

A backstage ballet about five members of a Motown-style girl group, *Quintet* describes the tension between public performances of glamour and the private despair and loneliness of offstage life. Ailey's choreographic notes subtitle

Consuelo Atlas in Alvin Ailey's *Quintet*, 1969.
Photograph by Jack Mitchell

the dance "The Tattered Souls," an attempt to create a "stream of consciousness [vision] of the song roots."[9]

The curtain rises to reveal five women posed identically in a tableau of de-fiant Motown glamour. With both arms raised overhead, they are sinuously ver-tical, outfitted in tight-fitting red lamé gowns, overdone makeup, smart high-heeled red pumps, and Hollywood-style blonde wigs. As the jazzy-pop strains of Nyro's "Stoned Soul Picnic" sound, the women slowly lower their arms to be-gin their singing group act, a simple arrangement of contemporary black social dances. They begin with the stone pony, a funky, four-count pushing step pop-ular in the late 1960s built on rhythmic isolations of the rib cage performed over a proudly wide foot stance. Suddenly, they drop the slow, elongated rhythmic phrasing of the stone pony to perform tiny walking steps toward and away from the audience. Mincing about the stage in a parody of high-fashion runway model posture, the women hold their hands underneath their breasts, offering them to the audience as if on a platter.

The dance continues with flagrant juxtapositions of bold, streetcorner-style movements to small, glamorous struts and shimmies. The women perform a catalogue of contemporary social dances and connecting material, arranged by Ailey to closely follow the contours of Nyro's music. As the recorded singers rise to a climactic high pitch, the dancers execute expansive turns across the stage, their arms circling overhead and down again in a staccato rhythm that mirrors the rock drumbeat. Mysteriously, dancers drop out of formation one at a time to move in anguish to some inaudible, private score. The number ends with the women once again posed luxuriously across the stage, knees bent deeply with arms raised overhead to approximate an allure of feminized celebrity.

Quintet continues through five more sections, roughly one for each woman, in which the wigs, dresses, and shoes come off and the performers reveal a private anguish hidden behind their show business drag. Recorded applause serves as a bridge between dances, satirically underscoring an oversized popularity of Ailey's mythic girl group. When the dancers return for subsequent group sections, the thrill of glamour dissipates, until eventually the women become steely and angry, defiant, and irreparably alienated.

The "offstage" dances suggest a bitterness born of disenfranchisement and neglect. In the third selection, "Poverty Train," the soloist removes the glamorous drag that imprisons her, revealing a nondescript gray slip. She angrily throws the high-heeled shoes binding her feet offstage; she drops her gown to kick it, exasperated, away. The ensuing dance gently mirrors Nyro's shifting musical moods: slow-motion contractions bending the body in agony toward the floor, followed by expansive rises to balance during legato interludes; searing, arrhythmic swaggers danced to the hesitations of six/eight drumming in bluesy verses; and repeated, sharp, two-count punching gestures timed to a prominent, screaming rhythm section lick. Toward the end of the solo, the dancer falls to the floor, rolls toward the audience, and rises to hide her face in her curled right arm while pushing away with her outstretched left hand. The image of constraint is followed by a slow-motion rise to balance with arms and neck stretched beseechingly upward. The dance ends when she collapses to the floor and pounds her fist, feebly, as Nyro moans the root of the problem: "Money." Taped applause sounds. Surprised, the woman suddenly notices her audience, gathers her gown from the floor, and exits, dazed, distracted, and wary.

Ailey maintained an integrated company with at least one white dancer on its roster after the 1962 Far East tour. The white minority dancers typically performed the same dances as the African American majority, and Ailey seldom choreographed work that dealt explicitly with race relations. When he did foreground race, either by design or, more frequently, the default of his casting, it inevitably signaled difference from an African American norm. In *Quintet*, the solo made for white dancer Linda Kent represented racial difference in its movement vocabularies and architectural structuring of foreground and background.

Clad in a diaphanous, floor-length white nightgown, Kent leads "Woman's Blues," a poignant depiction of a young, vulnerable woman struggling to maintain balance along a narrow path of innocence. As she treads in languid slow motion, swimming through the space in a series of alternating sideward balances, Kent is joined onstage by three women wearing chic miniskirts who perform an arrangement of social dance steps. Kent and the trio of women move through the stage space without relating to each other, and the two dances propose alternative physical narratives in terms of movement: Kent's modern dance steps, drawn from the vocabularies of Graham and Horton techniques, contrast with the trio's black social dance steps. These contrasting layers of dance vocabularies and costuming visually represent a split between public and private personae and heighten the sense of Kent's white difference from the black group.

As "Women's Blues" continues, its two layers of dance remain choreographically distinct, and the four women do not see each other. The dances arranged for the trio are hip-popping, soul steps built on rhythmic isolations of the hips, rib cage, and shoulders. The women move with an easy, fuzzy interior focus, dancing as if they are at a party, and seeming to sense each other's nearby presence and enjoy the dance as a cool physical response to the drumbeat. Kent's dance continues with slow-motion balances and treads skating through the space gingerly, which eventually progress to desperate kicks and reaching gestures. Her agitation rises until she loses control and repeatedly flings her leg toward the sky as if protesting her pathetic station. At one point, her movement converges briefly with the trio in a rhythmic unison motion of pitching the upper body toward the floor. This single unison gesture simultaneously confirms a continuity between the trio and the soloist and underscores their differences by its stark isolation.

As the rock drumbeat fades away, the trio begins to exit with a black power gesture: shaking their fists toward the skies, they two-step toward the side of the stage. Continuing in unison, they dance "the butt": with arms overhead, they drop down low to the floor, then rise, swinging their hips from side to side. Their dances become more demonstrative as Kent's become more pathetic. She collapses into a heap in the center of the stage, and the trio ignores her and exits, shaking their fists at the skies. Alone, Kent tries to repeat movements from the introduction, but by now she is exhausted and drained of any vestiges of innocence. She exits in a dramatic slow-motion walk, an extended gesture of mourning performed in silence.

Kent's solo describes the loss of innocence as a function of her difference from the group. The dance doesn't propose race as its organizing feature; rather, Kent's whiteness allows for a racialized interpretation of its construction. The trio of black women—Consuelo Atlas, Michele Murray, and Eleanor McCoy at the dance's premiere—are able to dance through the song, working in unison with social dance movements rife with intimations of power and self-control. The white soloist stutters and falls from her concert dance techniques, unable to sustain balance without, presumably, a connection to the larger group.

Quintet ends with "Love to Love Me Baby," a full-group finale that recaps movement ideas from the preceding dances. The five women enter singly, dressed again in their "onstage" gowns, to simultaneously perform phrase fragments from their solos. Searching through the space in slow motion, they move against Nyro's glib, pulsing rock beat without relating to the music or each other. When the music pauses before an ironically triumphant coda, the women converge in a line stretched across the stage. The dance ends with a recapitulation of the opening stone pony dance sequence, now enhanced by a harsh attitude of steely precision. Without warning, the women rush toward the audience, then retreat upstage, ending in their opening pose of feminized glamour.

With *Quintet*, Ailey continued his quest to create choreographic portraits of individuals. The "body level" of analysis—where the dancers go, what the movement motifs are—reveals only a portion of the dance. The psychological and emotional journeys Ailey coaxed from his dancers filled in the latent themes of disappointment and desire implicit in the scenario. The dance also presumed an audience versed in the oversized femininity of girl groups like the Supremes, an audience able to laugh along with a satirical take on pop culture glamour and then consider the price each woman paid for celebrity.

Quintet seems unfinished because the characters are not able to resolve their various private conflicts: the dance simply reveals their suppressed anger to the audience. Its first solo, "Lucky Says," ends when the other women rush onstage to remind the soloist of her duty as an entertainer. Dancer Michele Murray's anger and distraction, so diligently recounted in her solo, dissipate in the presence of the other women, and the girl group performance continues virtually unabated. "Poverty Train," "Women's Blues," and "December Boudoir" each offers glimpses of desperation and regretful longing, but the soloists find little consolation or hope in the act of dancing out their stories. Ailey draws convincing portraits of the sorrow behind the entertainer's mask but offers few suggestions as to how that generalized despair feeds into their celebrity.

Quintet eventually settled into the six-part format outlined above, but according to his notes, Ailey planned a larger piece that would include props and several male dancers.[10] "Woman's Blues" was to include a "primitive procession of hurt women waving big scarves, [executing] Congolese steps." Either "December Boudoir" or "Woman's Blues" was to include a "supported adagio for two women" consoling each other; among the iconic celebrity images he worked from were those of Gypsy Rose Lee, Billie Holiday, and Marilyn Monroe.[11] One rehearsal videotape of "December Boudoir" includes four men sitting on chairs reading newspapers and ignoring the dance soloist.

Paring the piece down to the five women allowed Ailey to focus attention on the lingering minstrel imagery associations surrounding black bodies as traditional entertainers for white audiences. Like many African American blackface minstrels before them, the women of *Quintet* are imprisoned by their public personae and able to reveal themselves only by discarding the masks that grant them visibility. Ailey's choice of Nyro's music reinforces the minstrel imagery: blonde black women dance to white blues singing.

In *Quintet* Ailey reverses the framing device of *Blues Suite,* implicating his audience in the false construction of celebrity. Where the earlier work suggested how social despair could be transformed into ebullient social dance steps, the later work aligns public performance with private sorrow. But in showcasing an idealized femininity, *Quintet* also exploits glamour and an assumedly masculine audience perspective. At times, the dance allows its women to be viewed as fantasy objects: naïve and hysterical "offstage," unresolved and essentially passive "onstage." Remarkably, this obvious binary construction contributes to the work's dramatic power as a critique of popular culture.

Though popular with general audiences, especially the college audiences the Ailey company taught in lecture-demonstration residencies, the dance was seldom favored by critics. Clive Barnes found the parody "neat, funny and effective. . . . Yet the joke goes on too long, and when the choreographer tries to reflect the very serious side of the music and lyrics he can never escape from the too firmly established sense of a put-on." Critic Stephen Smoliar recognized the "attempt to penetrate through the flashy exterior to the cold, underlying reality" of the pop singer, but wrote that the dance "never really dwelled on its argument long enough for the problem to hit home."[12] Whatever its shortcomings, *Quintet* opened a channel of communication to an audience of young people searching for concert representation of music and movement imagery familiar to them.

Swelling Popularity

Armed with *Quintet*, the Ailey company expanded its audience base and furthered its economic viability in the arts marketplace. The company repeatedly broke records for attendance and box office receipts. In 1971 the group grossed "close to $150,000" playing to "75% capacity" during its season at Manhattan's three thousand-seat City Center, "a definite and remarkable record for any modern dance company in history."[13] By 1972 the company opened at City Center "with what the management says is the biggest advance sale for any event, dance or nondance, in that theater's history."[14] That year the Ailey company settled into a steady performing arrangement with producing agent City Center, which provided advertisement, front-of-house support, including box office ticketing staff, backstage support, including stage hands, and a paid fee. This association continued unabated through 2003.

Ailey company performances appealed to a young-minded audience amenable to rock music in concert dance. The rousing enthusiasm with which audiences greeted the company caused critic Don McDonagh to wonder "whether it matters what the company is doing as long as it promises not to stop." Anna Kisselgoff noted in the *New York Times* that the company confirmed "a rumor" that modern dance "could be painless. The word has been that it might even be fun. It could perhaps be stirring."[15] Ailey embraced his company's swelling profile in an *After Dark* interview: "We're also show-biz. And I'm not ashamed of that. Black people have had a long tradition of that, and it's one of the things we, as a company, do very well."[16]

Among his most commercial work, Ailey made *Diversion No. 1* (14 July 1969) for a program his company shared with the singing group the 5th Dimension at the Greek Theatre of Los Angeles. This short work in three parts included dances to "Scarborough Fair" and the Edwin Hawkins Singers crossover pop-gospel hit "Oh Happy Day." Created quickly in two or three days, *Diversion No. 1* featured harlequin costumes by Rob Thomas with "lollypop colored string vests and feathered Restoration hats."[17] Ailey told the *Los Angeles Times* he intended the dance as a "mostly fun, not innovative" device to attract audiences to his company's upcoming UCLA season: "I look at it this way. The Greek seats more than 4,000 people, many of whom wouldn't be seeing us dance if we weren't on a double bill with a popular rock group. We're coming back to L.A. in the fall. If only 1,000 of these people who see us this week remember us and come to UCLA then they'll find out what we're all about."[18]

Tepid in comparison to its companion excerpts drawn from Talley Beatty's *Toccata* and *Revelations, Diversion No. 1* disappeared after its scheduled week of performances.

Kelvin Rotardier and Loretta Abbott in Alvin Ailey's *Blues Suite*, circa 1967. Photograph by Jack Mitchell

Jazz Dance

Jazz dance, or black vernacular social dance, has long been assumed to be the gestural foundation of black life. Because African Americans consider music and dance to be unified creative expressions, changes in black popular music have both been influenced by and prompted changes in African American movement styles. Easily achieved social dances, from the black bottom to the Charleston, the dog, the running man, and the Harlem shimmy, have arisen to accompany and encourage changes in popular music, from ragtime, to jazz, soul, hip-hop, and Dirty South beats. Because music and dance are completely imbricated in the social fabric of black life, social dance provides a potent marker of individual identity within the group and a process of socialization that allows black Americans to recognize each other.

Notably, the aesthetic structures surrounding black social dances and their music outlast any historical moment or movement/musical genre. Certain specific dance movements recur in different historical eras, as in the swiveling and swinging step of the Charleston in the 1920s that resurfaced as the mashed potatoes in the 1960s. In this case, the style of the music that accompanied the social dance changed, but the movements and their aesthetic imperatives—the importance of angularity in the positioning of the elbows and knees, the use of isolated rhythmic markers in the movements of shoulders and arms, the propulsive energy driving the motion—revealed a continuity of movement ideology. Black popular music and movements are unified in their approach through a shared percussive attack, allowance for individual expression within the group, repetition as intensification, strong reliance on breaks or abrupt ruptures of the underlying beat, and highly complex rhythmic structure.

Black social dance came to be called jazz dance when its companion music was known as jazz; when black popular music shifted to bebop in the 1950s, soul in the 1960s, and disco in the 1970s, jazz dance did not follow suit, but became the term to describe stage dancing based on black social dance forms.[19] In 1964, when Marshall and Jean Stearns published their seminal study *Jazz Dance: The Story of American Vernacular Dance*, they purposefully detailed the careers of a range of professional tap dancers, "shake" dancers, and vaudeville entertainers who could directly relate their performances to black social dance styles.[20] But even by then, "jazz dance" implied a nostalgic memory of a time when contemporary black social dances inevitably landed on Broadway stages and Hollywood screens.

By now, jazz dance doesn't imply contemporary black social dance movements at all. Instead, it implies a codified movement form based on the extrapolations of (mostly white male) American choreographers and teachers, including Jack Cole (1911–74) and Matt Mattox (1921–). Cole and Mattox rose to prominence in the 1940s and 1950s, respectively, as they distilled black social dances into component movements and a style of performance related to older dance forms, including tap dance, soft shoe, and the cakewalk.[21]

By now, students taking jazz dance in most colleges or dance studios work toward the physical articulation of complex meter through various body part isolations and historical reconstructions of social dances from the jazz age of the 1920s, typically executed with a fully stretched torso, emphasis on the achievement of precise physical line, and a balletically pointed foot. These classes may teach the outward, formal features of jazz dance as it appears in films or on Broadway stages, but they seldom encourage the spirit of performance invention at the heart of the jazz impulse.

Jazz invention is, of course, very hard to teach. However, it is nurtured and explored in the social dance spaces where African Americans have gathered for communal expression and release: the jook joints, discotheques, house parties, school dances, and night clubs defined as black spaces by their location and their clientele. Black social dances are no longer jazz dance, although these dances certainly provided the impetus and creative aesthetic that gave rise to the form. Sometime in the 1950s jazz dance went from being the catch-all title for (black) dances that were not ballet or modern and learned without a codified technique, to being the formal instruction of dance movements based in body isolations, angular body lines, percussive attack, complex rhythmic phrasing, and flamboyant, self-congratulatory technical virtuosity. Dances that were originally inspired by black social spaces, but then migrated out to

Broadway stages and Hollywood screens, ultimately became structured as a "technique" taught in studios and dance programs worldwide.

An open secret about jazz dance today is that there is no discrete jazz dance technique. Jazz classes typically mix a ballet barre warmup, used for strengthening and stretching the spine, followed by isolation exercises, used for improving physical articulation of line, followed by turns and struts across the floor, used for generating individual performance style and virtuosity, and ending with a combination learned and executed by the class, used to improve memorization and interpretation of movement material. Within this framework, teachers create their own system of jazz dance, usually determined by their own individual movement preferences and taste in music. But by now, virtually all professional jazz dancers have a facility and technique from study of ballet or modern dance techniques.

Although he had little experience in jazz dance "technique," Ailey taught the form in various New York studios during the early 1960s. Early in his choreographic career, his dancers were labeled jazz dancers in large part because this seemed closer to what the dancers actually did than ballet or modern dance. In works like *Been Here and Gone* and *Modern Jazz Suite*, Ailey's dancers engaged jazz dance as a distillation of social dance forms. But too often, the label jazz dancers reinforced the notion of an untrained black dancer moving "naturally," and Ailey carefully positioned his company's work in the realm of modern dance, a concert idiom recognized by all audiences as art. Ailey's challenge was to explore black culture on the concert stage without being reduced to the lower status of jazz dancer.

One strategy Ailey employed toward this end involved the oblique use of archetypal character vignettes, usually configured in a distinctive gestural shorthand. Through stance, rhythmical phrasing, and the undefinable but tangible affect of "attitude," Ailey often suggested a tintype of "down-home" characters who project an unassailable blackness. We see this method clearly in *Blues Suite*, *Revelations*, and *Been Here and Gone*, but it also comes forward in works like *Quintet*, *Cry*, *Night Creature*, *Pas de "Duke,"* *For Bird—With Love*, and *Opus McShann*. In each of these works, the performers embody a black affect, seldom sustained through entire dances or even sections of dances, but one that emerges, full-blown, in a single phrase or gesture. In *Quintet*, the women "hip pop"; in *Night Creature*, a woman dismisses friends and potential suitors alike with a fiercely efficient wave of the hand; in *Pas de "Duke,"* the dancers tease and strut with an unmitigated cool. The effect of these short passages grounds the dance characters in a black vernacular universe.

Significantly, these gestural tintypes emerge in works where the dancers portray people, but not in Ailey's thoroughly abstract works. In Ailey's world, people usually reveal themselves as black people, but that revelation rarely leads to jazz dance or black social dance movement.

▌ *Flowers*

Ailey next turned to rock music in 1971, when he made *Flowers* (26 January 1971). Set to music by Blind Faith, Pink Floyd, and Janis Joplin with Big Brother and the Holding Company, *Flowers* depicts the death of a rock star caused by an uncontrolled drug addiction. Obviously based on highly publicized accounts of the 3 October 1970 death of singer Janis Joplin, Ailey dedicated the dance in its original program note to a slew of rockers making youth-oriented electric music: "For Mick Jagger, Jimi Hendrix, Bob Dylan, Joe Cocker, Jim Morrison and Janice Joplin—With Love."[22] The central role was created for guest artist Lynn Seymour, a soloist of the London-based Royal Ballet, and subsequently performed by Ailey company members Linda Kent and Maxine Sherman.

Ailey's program note and evocatively assembled score provide the only substantive proof that *Flowers* relates to Joplin or rock culture. The ballet's central figure never sings or performs: her celebrity is a given circumstance from its opening gesture. In silence, a woman in an orange velvet jumpsuit strides onstage. She stops to strike a glamorous pose, and suddenly a group of eight men—photographers—rush on from all sides. Crowding around her, they snap their fingers in cacophonous clatter, eager to capture her flair. As Joplin's "Down On Me" pipes in, the audience understands the woman to represent Joplin backstage, satisfying her press. The photographers disappear as quickly as they appeared, and *Flowers* begins its tawdry depiction of a celebrity's steady downward spiral.

The Joplin figure is drawn as an indulgent seductress, a Bacchante careening toward disaster through substance abuse. In a sequence of exposition, she alternately poses for photographers and drinks from a flask, becoming more outlandish in each posed attitude, at one point dancing erotically with a bouquet of flowers. In a witty theatrical gesture that underscores her authority in this milieu, she waves her hand at an onstage stool, and it slides offstage. The first scene ends with the woman alone, seated at a small table, drinking.

The assembled score launches into "Do What You Like," a throbbing, repetitive groove recorded by the band Blind Faith, and the eight men return to the stage as members of Joplin's entourage. They sweep into the space singly with elevated balletic leaps, then settle into a fast-paced, floor-bound stepping dance of consecration. The men dance facing the woman as if in ritualistic submission to her charisma; when they face away from her, they enclose her as if to protect her from unseen adversaries. In this sequence, they represent a single impulse of adoration.

But as the Joplin figure becomes needy and demanding of the men, moving among them for balance or basic human contact, they retreat, breaking from their unison movements to physically push her away with increasing aggressiveness and disgust. One at a time, the men cast her aside, leaving her crumpled in a pathetic ball on the floor. A pusher, clad in black and silver cowboy clothes and ominous motorcycle sunglasses, saunters onstage. Dejected, the woman crawls to him and, without seeing him, walks her hands up his body. She looks to his face only when her hands securely grasp his waist.

The central pas de deux of *Flowers* depicts the Joplin figure's descent into drug addiction. It coincides with an extended electric guitar solo over the repeated paso-doble rhythmic gesture of "Do What You Like." The dance describes a gendered, symbiotic relationship, in which the pusher dominates Joplin physically and emotionally: he carries her upside down across the stage; he boxes her ears; he manipulates her into treacherous, awkwardly posed positions. The pusher maintains a menacing cool macho, expressed here by his resistance to dance movement. Throughout this section, he performs tasks of support, carrying, and motionlessness with an icy detachment. When he does dance a short solo in an effort to entice the woman to his drug supply, his movement comes in startling, idiosyncratic bursts of staccato activity.

The woman eventually receives her fix and a nightmarish, drug trip sequence ensues. The ensemble of men return, wearing skimpy tinsel underwear, to set the stage for the phantasmagoria in a short transitional dance. They overrun the stage with big, sweeping balletic leaps juxtaposed to slow, deeply anchored contractions of the torso. The woman rushes among them, now trailing a billowing red scarf trimmed with green feathers. To underscore the out-of-time, macabre quality of her hallucination, the men continue in excruciating slow motion, encircling the woman and reaching and pulsating toward her as they sink to the floor. The woman rushes about the stage without seeing them, even as the men gesticulate and scream, noiselessly, toward her. Finally, she is borne aloft and carried about like the masthead of a strange ship. Suddenly, the men leave her alone, taking the billowing cloth with them.

The music shifts to a spooky, electronic soundscape, and the woman dances a short solo, trying to hold balance while coming down from her high. She treads through the space, testing the fluidity of her upper body and undulating from the hips as she strikes curvaceous poses and precarious balances. Invariably, she falls out of her balances. Unable to find a place to rest, she slows down to a whimper, and the men reenter, now tormentors in her fearful delusions.

The men perform images and movement phrases borrowed from other Ailey works to suggest the depth of the woman's nightmare. At the cue of a big, screaming electric sound from the Pink Floyd recording, the men throw the woman into the air and then arrange themselves into two couples and a trio center stage. Shaking their torsos at each other like go-go dancers on speed, the men perform fragments of duets from the recent Ailey works *Streams* and *The River*. In a prominent homoerotic image, the men face each other, holding their hands at each other's hips, and press their groins together as their upper bodies lean away. They support each other in balanced poses, then rush toward the woman menacingly to encircle her, only to strike handstands and roll whimsically away. The action accelerates, and the men group into a tight phalanx with arms bent, holding each other at the shoulders, to tromp toward the woman, barely missing trampling her underfoot. Spent, the woman rolls offstage.

The men repeat the short transitional dance that introduced the drug hallucination, but this time, the pusher passes through the space, wryly victorious. With vacant disdain, he looks toward where the woman had been, then gestures

Lynn Seymour in Alvin Ailey's *Flowers*, circa 1971.
Photographer unknown

the men to reset the stage with table and chairs, as at the opening scene of the dance.

Joplin's "Kozmic Blues" provides the underscoring for the final scene of tragedy. The woman enters as she did before, but by now she is beaten down, wounded, and visibly older than at the beginning of the dance. She hides her face from the clamoring photographers. She guzzles from a flask, collapses into a chair, then rolls on the floor. The photographers keep coming, relentlessly taking photographs of the woman at her worst: drained, stoned, barely rational.

The woman performs a tormented solo of defeat. Barely able to walk, she staggers across the stage space, stops to gain her bearings, but suddenly collapses to the floor to reach for something—is it the drugs?—lost and confused. In a burst of bravado, she rises fully to her feet and defiantly knocks over the setting of table and chairs. As Joplin's taped voice rises to its pinnacle of intensity, the dancer moves to the center of the stage, poses, and then flamboyantly bows. An invisible force pulls her backward into a spasm of defeat. She tries to steady herself but can't, and finally collapses completely. Flowers are thrown onto her body from offstage. The photographers enter to capture a final shot of the woman lying, immobile, on the ground. The lights blackout decisively.

Flowers builds on themes broached in *Quintet*: the consuming power of celebrity; a deep despair and loneliness barely masked by public bravado; the implication of a ravenous audience in the construction of glamour. But whereas *Quintet* left these issues unresolved, *Flowers* presents an emotional and physical suicide as the logical end for the overtaxed celebrity figure.

Flowers includes movement phrases borrowed from a broad swatch of Ailey's earlier works: a sitting, "peekaboo" gesture from "Rocka My Soul" of *Revelations*; a strutting, swinging-hip walk from "Sham" of *Blues Suite*; a floor-bound series of contractions and leg extensions from "I Wanna Be Ready" of *Revelations*; a leaning and lifting pattern for couples from *Streams* and *The River*, both of 1970. As a whole, the nightmare section is reminiscent of portions of *Riedaiglia*; the men's militaristic stomping over the Joplin figure suggests the Minotaur of *Labyrinth*; and the procession with the Joplin figure borne aloft echoes Carmen de Lavallade's parades in *Ariette Oubliée*. For Ailey, these movement ideas and images suggest a nightmarish collapse of time: his previous dances converge in *Flowers* with disastrous results for its leading character.

Ailey often reworked movement phrases from his own oeuvre, tweaking the nuances of dance combinations to suit the landscape of a new scenario. He often choreographed quickly, pouring out phrases in a manner comparable to a jazz musician composing a spontaneous solo. Movements that pleased him, either structurally or kinetically, resurfaced in various contexts throughout his career. For the most part, he confined this practice of revisiting distinctive combinations to dramatic works like *Flowers*, works that depended less on the "steps" than on the dramatic sensibility surrounding them.

At its premiere, *Flowers* generated a mixed response from critics. Writing for the *New York Daily News*, Douglas Watt noted that guest artist Lynn Seymour's repetitive histrionics "got so she drew laughs each time she started to fall down." Anna Kisselgoff found that "the first part of the work . . . suffers from the conventionality of TV chorus-boy vocabulary," but continued to praise the work as a "tour de force" for Seymour. Marcia Siegel realized the implications of the work for Ailey's increasingly popular company: "*Flowers* hits at the very consumerism we're all taking part in by watching it and applauding it."[23]

Ailey intended the combination of sordid atmosphere and guest-starring presence of Royal Ballet artist Seymour to converge in a hybrid dance aesthetic combining rock music and classical concert dance vocabulary. Among the obvious precedents familiar to American dance audiences were the Joffrey Ballet's psychedelic work *Astarte* (1967), choreographed by Robert Joffrey to an original score by the short-lived group Crome Syrcus, and Gerald Arpino's *Trinity* (1970), also for the Joffrey Ballet, set to music by Alan Raph and Lee Holdridge. Where the Joffrey Ballet dances had built on classical technique, altered to "fit" the rock music, Ailey built Seymour's role from his own hybrid of Dunham, Graham, and Horton techniques, framed by his knowledge of theatrical and dramatic devices. Writing for the *New York Times* on the occasion of the dance's 1973 revival,

Clive Barnes noted, in a somewhat condescending review, Ailey's pioneering hybridity:

> *Flowers* is very indicative of Mr. Ailey's choreographic methods. First, its development over the years is typical of a choreographer who quite often seems to release half-finished works, and then returns to fix them up. Second, it shows the eclecticism and omnivorous appetite of Ailey. Many influences *seem* apparent here. John Butler's *Portrait of Billie*, for one, or, at the end, even Roland Petit's *Carmen*. But eventually the whole thing comes out as Ailey pure and simple.[24]

Ailey turned to rock music again in *Shaken Angels* (7 September 1972), a pièce d'occasion commissioned by the tenth New York Dance Festival for the Delacorte Theater in Central Park. He set the short work on two ballet-trained dancers, Bonnie Mathis of American Ballet Theatre and Dennis Wayne of the Joffrey Ballet, to recorded music by Alice Cooper, Pink Floyd, and Bill Withers. *Shaken Angels* told the harrowing story of "a boy and a girl, cornered into a relationship of violence and need, smoking pot and mainlining heroin."[25]

Reviewed as a theatrical portrait of an "Andy Warhol crowd couple very into hard rock, freaky clothes, sunglasses and smack," *Shaken Angels* told its story in terms of acted drama more than dance.[26] Ailey allowed the action to spill off the stage and into the aisles of the theater in a chase sequence that ended when Wayne caught Mathis, dragged her back to the stage, and stuck her with a (pantomimed) needle. The dancers sported "flamboyantly mod" clothes designed by Christian Holder and provided "morbid fascination . . . by the detailed realism of the boy giving himself a fix."[27] Ailey surely intended to startle his audience with a passionate depiction of drug addiction and its tragic aftermath. Like *Flowers*, *Shaken Angels* ended with the death of its protagonists. This "modern melodrama, saved by two stylish performers," disappeared after a week of performances.[28]

In all, Ailey's dances set to rock music encouraged a youthful dimension of concert dance that was built on a musical rejection of the concert stage status quo. He used rock music to bring more people into the concert hall; once there, he hoped to show them a range of material choreographed to a variety of music. *Flowers*, for instance, was regularly programmed alongside the historical music suites *Blues Suite* and *Revelations*. As he told the *Los Angeles Times*, "I want to get the general public interested in dance. I want to make dance reflect real-life experiences. I want to do large-scale productions incorporating ballet, modern dance, ethnic dance, films, jazz, electronic scores—everything."[29] Among the "real-life experiences" Ailey hoped to include in his dances was a familiar and seductive convergence of sex, drugs, and rock 'n roll.

▍ The Popular Audience

Throughout the 1970s, Ailey's company reeled precipitously from the prized adulation of an expanding audience of African Americans to the brink of financial disaster. In the fall of 1969, the company secured an invitation to represent the United States in a goodwill tour of the Soviet Union sometime in 1970. Facing a financial shortfall, the company finished its spring 1970 BAM season without sufficient engagements to pay the dancers or rehearse until the fall tour materialized. To force government intervention, Ailey cunningly played one situation off the other when he publicly announced the dissolution of the Alvin Ailey American Dance Theater due to financial difficulties. His announcement forced the U.S. Cultural Exchange Program to find suitable engagements for the company in the intervening months. Ailey's gambit worked, and the company toured North Africa in June 1970 before a six-week, six-city tour of Zaporozhe, Donetsk, Kiev, Voroshilovgrad, Moscow, and Leningrad begun in September 1970.[30] According to a *Dance News* journalist, the closing night performance on 1 November "surpassed the triumphant reception conferred until then upon the company when the ovation lasted for 20 minutes. Young people had been let in who, as standees, packed the sides of the auditorium."[31] Of his own work shown in the Soviet Union, Ailey included *Blues Suite, Revelations,* and *Streams; Quintet* and its mildly satiric depiction of disharmony stayed home.

The company's success abroad again enhanced its reputation in the United States and resulted in a spate of feature articles describing the company, its history, and its founder. Ailey's accomplishment garnered him several awards, including two honorary doctorates of fine arts in 1972 from Cedar Crest College of Washington, D.C. and Princeton University. Ailey's work resonated with that of recently formed Afro-American studies departments on college campuses, granting his company stature as a commended cultural ambassador to youth. Still, although the expansion of Ailey's audience meant more African American concert dancegoers, in the larger venues the proportions of this black audience shrank in relation to the whole. In the late 1960s, audiences for the Ailey company "were often at least 40 per cent black"; by 1974, journalists began recording the audience as "80 per cent white."[32] Writing in *The Afro American,* critic William Moore exclaimed, "All I want to do is to tell Black people to go see him so they can feel the indirect pride of achievement when this company brings audiences . . . to their feet in applause."[33]

As Ailey's audience expanded, some white critics began self-consciously wondering whether his company's success resulted not from its artistry, but in relation to its "multiracial character, its native populism, its ecumenical repertory . . . as a cause for good liberal Americans."[34] Reviews that disparaged the company's unequivocal popularity appeared under such titles as "Selling Soul," "Standing Still," and "Pleasing the Crowd."[35] For some critics, the Ailey company's astonishing success became tantamount to his choreographic banality. In 1971 critic Robert Pierce offered a fine example of the anxiety surrounding popularity and concert dance:

> When Alvin Ailey uses Negro derived movement in a modern balletic context, the works are interesting, and evocative. When he uses jazz movement, he is sometimes successful, depending most often on how

Illustration of Ailey superimposed on a map of Africa after his company's tour there. "African Odyssey," *Dance Magazine*, May, 1968: 50.

he handles his subject material. But when he tries to utilize neo-classical technique, he presents ballet in a manner which is mechanical, emotionless, and ostentatiously empty.

What Ailey offers America's expanding dance audiences is primarily decadent entertainment. But dance, like the other arts, is much more than merely entertainment. The appreciation of dance as an art requires effort, and for the most part Ailey requires none from his audiences. With some exceptions, he produces entertainment for the masses. It is rarely art, nor even art in an entertaining format. It is merely empty entertainment.[36]

In this passage, Pierce reveals himself to be unfamiliar with black musicality or social dance structure and unable to understand the participatory "effort" works like *Quintet* required of their audiences. Because critical paradigms seldom explored how African Americans valued qualities of performance, many professional critics may have felt "left out" of the process that allowed audiences to respond to, say, the trio of soulful women in "Woman's Blues" of *Quintet*.

For his part, Ailey, the former Broadway dancer, understood far too well how little was required to create empty entertainment; his rock ballets indicate that he sought to create something more than that. He understood social dance to be a site of pleasure and body knowledge, a "high" form of expression for many African Americans. In his dances, he situated "soul" proudly alongside ballet and modern dance forms, engendering a hybrid aesthetic with deep ties to African American cultural practices.

By 1974, Ailey felt compelled to respond to critics who connected his company's box office appeal to artistic pandering: "Some people are confused and think that 'popular' means an esthetic of lower caliber. It doesn't. I want my company to do a lot for a lot of people."[37] The lot of people Ailey served included scores of African Americans new to concert dance but proud of the company's obvious accomplishment in the field, and college students eager to connect rock music to theatrical performance.

Kelvin Rotardier and Leland Schwantes in Alvin Ailey's *Masekela Langage*, 1969. Photographer unknown

█ No Exit from Racism

The image startles: his white face ground into the floor, his mouth open to release a peal of pain, his body contorted with hands pulled useless behind his back, his leg extended tensely upward toward the ceiling. The soldier's decorations are askew, inverted by the momentum of his fall, untidy. Above him, the black man gazes impassively, his body not at all tense; he seems relaxed even, as though lifting an unwieldy but not particularly heavy object. The black man wears his collar open and his tie loosened a bit, as though he were on his way home from work; this job of disabling the white soldier is extra labor out of the norm, but not unexpected. He is prepared for it. His hat sits calmly on his head still, stylishly arranged as he placed it before he came out of his house, before he had the encounter with the white soldier, before he knew there would be a skirmish. He is cool, even in this posture of battle captured by a camera.

The energy of the image comes from the white man's face, from his immediate look of pain, eyes closed, back horribly contorted. The black man's face is cool and calm—we can't see his eyes, but they are surely trained on the white man. Was there a fight? Of course. Is the white man a victim? How could he be? Clad in military gear, the white man represents a political order, a system of control that lords over the civilians. The black man could be—anyone.

The violent imagery here suggests the literal inversion of political order, framed by the camera without setting or witness. It offers a racially constructed uprising, the fantastical turning of tables so that the black man is literally on top, ready to discard the white man, to pitch him away like so much useless dreck. The image presents a stark portrayal of retribution, in line with imagery created by artists working within the nationalistic aesthetic paradigms of the 1960s black arts movement.

The dance that this photograph represents is *Masekela Langage*, Ailey's most overtly "political" choreography from 1969, set in a no-name, no-exit bar in South Africa. Significantly, however, this photograph—in its depiction of racial politics— suggests a dance that doesn't really exist. I've seen *Masekela* a half-dozen times and never with the casting of a white man in either of these two roles. Of course, Ailey eschewed casting by "race," so the soldier might or might not be played by a white artist from Ailey's company at any performance. But this particular moment captured by the camera does not stand out in my memory of the dance itself. In the work, the fight that it represents is not one of triumph for either of its combatants; in fact, the soldier manages several body-slamming parries against the businessman character. In all, the photograph is a provocative red herring.

Still, *Masekela* stands as one of Ailey's few gestures toward politicized dance theater, and (white) critics continually refer to the work as a dance of protest. The work derives much of its power from the shocking "Epilogue" and its rote repetition of opening gestures, now danced over and around a bloodied dead man heaped on the barroom floor. The corpse becomes a ghost of those who have come and gone, those who have died in class- and race-based struggles worldwide who share the stage with those who dance there now. Wasn't he there, dead on the floor, from the beginning of the piece? Isn't he always there really?

At its premiere, *Masekela* must have drawn power from the sense of difference between audience and dancer. The characters must have seemed exotic to some modern dance audiences in 1969—angry black people in the theater at the same time as their educated white viewers—and as the photograph suggests, it delivered on the black arts movement promise of angry black bodies expressing a people's rage. But over time, as this dialectic collapsed to some degree, the characters lost their generic status as black and became, by default, working-class and neurotic. Seeing the dance today, I wonder at how odd the glamorous Ailey performers seem when dancing about people with limited strategies for survival. Isn't their dancing, in and of itself, a potent survival strategy?

Masekela held clear structural similarities to Eleo Pomare's landmark 1966 work *Blues for the Jungle*. Pomare had trained at New York's High School of Performing Arts and with José Limón before he formed the Eleo Pomare Dance Company in 1958. After traveling to Europe to study and perform with Kurt Jooss and Harald Kreutzberg, he returned to the United States in 1964 to revive and expand his company in explicit sympathy with the American civil rights movement of the 1960s. Outspoken, he proclaimed that "all art is political" and produced several protest works that depicted the degradation of black urban life. *Blues for the Jungle* included a cast of desperate characters who spilled from the stage as they shouted slogans and physically confronted the audience, accusing them of complicity in the construction of the American ghetto.

Like Ailey, Pomare formed an integrated company that explored black culture. Also like Ailey, his preferred movement vocabulary drew on several dance techniques, combined to best suit the theatrical moment. But unlike Ailey, Pomare never felt compelled to maintain any propriety in terms of race relations or the construction of "official" histories of black America. For example, his solo "Narcissus Rising" (1968), created for a composition class led by Martha Graham's musical collaborator Louis Horst, featured Pomare clad in a leather motorcycle biker's hat and g-string. Set to the sounds of a motorcycle, the work attracted notoriety for its frank belligerence. In 1967, Pomare directed the Dancemobile, a black arts project that evolved from theatrical experiments of LeRoi Jones and the Harlem Cultural Commission. The Dancemobile presented concert work on the back of a flatbed truck performed by the companies of Pomare, Raymond Sawyer, Louis Johnson, Rod Rodgers, Carole Johnson, Joan Miller, and dozens of other African American artists.[1]

Dance held a small role in the black arts movement overall, in part due to intimations of public dance performance and homosexuality. As a nationalistic project, the black arts movement erased diversities of class, race, and sexuality in the service of a singular, masculine-dominated "black" identity; gay men and lesbians held little status as proponents of the movement. In addition, for many audiences, concert dance became aligned with the individualistic subjectivity of "doing your own thing," a concept at odds with the political needs of the movement. Though they were seriously committed to change in the political order, few of the Dancemobile artists gained respect as bearers of the movement's creative soul, an honor that authors like Amiri Baraka (LeRoi Jones), Sonja Sanchez, and Ed Bullins enjoyed. For nationalistic black arts leaders, the acceptance of same-sex attraction as a function of everyday life in dance companies exempted concert dance artists from contributing fully to the movement.

Ailey's company seldom participated in the black arts movement experiments that might have directed its work exclusively toward a black audience. At the First National Congress on Blacks in Dance held at Indiana University in Bloomington 26 June – 1 July 1973, members of Ailey's company headlined a public performance event, but Ailey and his company's administration remained noticeably distant from conversations about how to advance the public perception and financial profiles of black modern dance companies. Ultimately, several of Ailey's contemporaries who were active in black arts projects, including Pomare, choreographed work for the Ailey company. But Ailey's strict integrationist stance implied the necessity of collaboration across races onstage, behind the scenes, and in the audience as the most valuable method of combating racism through concert dance.

Reflecting a Spectrum of Experience

Throughout the 1960s and 1970s, Ailey became increasingly known as a leading exponent of concert dance. He continuously spoke out for increased opportunities for African Americans in dance and geared his company policies specifically toward the canonization of a concert dance experience rooted in African American cultural history. In January 1969, some eight months before Arthur Mitchell and Karel Shook founded Dance Theatre of Harlem, Ailey wrote of founding the "Black American Ballet," a large company of dancers, singers, and musicians exclusively devoted to the cultural heritage of black America.[2] He made plans for a three-act ballet based on the life of Malcolm X, for a danced tribute to Langston Hughes, and for a Duke Ellington festival, finally realized at the nation's bicentennial in 1976. He wrote, "My greatest wish is for the black American dancer to enter, through the front door, the mainstream of American dance."[3]

For Ailey, entering the concert dance mainstream through the front door meant expanding the technical, thematic, and musical range of materials available to black dancers. Throughout the 1960s and into the 1970s, Ailey's company absorbed a number of dancers trained in classical ballet who could not find employment elsewhere because of pervasive racism in concert dance hiring. Judith Jamison joined the Ailey company in 1965 fresh from a limited engagement in

Agnes de Mille's *The Four Marys* at American Ballet Theatre. Sara Yarborough trained at the School of American Ballet in the 1960s; passed over by that school's parent organization, the New York City Ballet, she joined the Ailey company in 1970. While the founding of Dance Theater of Harlem provided opportunities for scores of talented classical dancers, the Ailey company counted ballet-trained soloist Mel Tomlinson among its ranks from 1976 to 1978, between his engagements with Dance Theater of Harlem and the New York City Ballet. Even as Ailey opened his arms to classically trained dancers of African descent, he remained a committed integrationist. His choreography and company policies rejected separatist doctrines of work labeled "black dance."

The black dance label came into use during the late 1960s. Although its articulation was perhaps intended by critics to favorably describe the hybrid aesthetic emerging from the studios of African American dance artists, the term quickly became reductive and dismissive. Carole Johnson, founding editor of *The Feet*, a publication devoted to concert dance made by African Americans begun in 1969 under the auspices of Modern Organization for Dance Evolvement, devoted several editorials to the impossible task of defining black dance:

> The term "Black dance" must be thought of from the broadest point that must be used to include any form of dance and any style that a black person chooses to work within. It includes the concept that all Black dance artists will use their talents to explore all known, as well as to invent new forms, styles, and ways of expression through movement. . . .
>
> Since the expression "Black dance" must be all inclusive, it includes those dancers that work in:
>
> 1 the very traditional forms (the more nearly authentic African styles);
> 2 the social dance forms that are indigenous to this country, which include tap and jazz dance;
> 3 the various contemporary and more abstract forms that are seen on the concert stage; and
> 4 the ballet (which must not be considered as solely European).[4]

In resonance with nationalistic strategies of other black Americans at the time, this broad definition sought to link all dance made by black people.[5]

Ailey consistently rejected blank capitulation to popular racial stereotypes in his choreography. His response to the debate surrounding his integrated company and black dance surfaced most vividly in the range of dances he made. In the four-year period between August 1969 and May 1973, Ailey completed sixteen dances, the musical staging for one Broadway show, and dances for five operas. Of these, only four works concerned themselves directly with prevalent constructions of "black art": *Masekela Langage*, *Cry*, *Love Songs*, and *Mary Lou's Mass*. Placed in context with Ailey's other work during this period, these four dances confirm the choreographer's broad vision of material to be made available to black artists, a vision that embraced several constructions of black art as a portion of African American identity.

Masekela Langage

Few of Ailey's dances broach racial politics directly. An exception is *Masekela Langage* (16 August 1969), created for a commission from the American Dance Festival. Ailey made the dance during a twelve-day residency at Connecticut College in New London. Described in the original program note as "five dances with prologue and epilogue based on the music of South African trumpeter Hugh Masekela," *Masekela Langage* received immediate audience acclaim. The dance has been revived intermittently by the Alvin Ailey American Dance Theater ever since. Initially performed by nine dancers at Connecticut College, the dance attained its final form featuring a company of ten dancers in the 1970s.

The curtain rises to reveal a startlingly explicit setting of a seedy South African jook joint, complete with potted tropical plants, a neon-lined jukebox, posters of beer advertisements, and an oversized, lazily spinning ceiling fan. Five men and four women are posed languorously across the front of the bar, seated in an assortment of stylish but mismatched wicker furniture. As the dancers simmer silently, faintly aware of the audience, the stage resembles a travel photograph in three dimensions.

The dance revels in a pungent mood and atmosphere reflected in hot, saturated lighting combinations of reds and greens and wisps of smoke rising through the leaves of potted palm plants. The dancers are costumed to represent assorted denizens: a lustful woman in a too-short, brightly colored dress; a capitalist businessman in a three-piece suit; an auto mechanic in dirty overalls; an alluring, mysterious woman in a short black dress; and so on. They remain motionless—on display—for an entire chorus of Masekela's "Sobukwe." At the song's second chorus, they rise individually, shift their focus to the front, and begin stalking the audience in carefully staged waves of slow walking.

As in *Blues Suite*, the walking slowly evolves into dance movement. Some characters taunt the audience with a seething cool, some entice, and still others run upstage, behind the chairs, to perform frantic bursts of turning phrases that cut, rhythmically, into the overall depressed mood. Methodically, the dancers drag their chairs to the back wall, where they are grouped in clumps around tables and plants already there. As the prologue music fades away, they turn their attention away from the audience and toward each other, placing themselves within the dramatic frame of a night in the bar. Clearly, these are the South African counterparts to the southern people of *Blues Suite*.

Unlike the earlier work, which telescoped an entire day at a barrellhouse into a twenty-minute suite, *Masekela Langage* evolves in real time, with dramatic events leading directly to consequences that invariably heighten the overall sense of frustration and urgency. After the group sits, a nervous and oppressive stillness fills the air as they eye each other suspiciously, each awaiting an action from the others. Finally, the businessman approaches the jukebox, and in a display of largesse intended to boost his vanity, deposits a coin. The jukebox, emblematic of life in this dilapidated, dead-end bar, doesn't work. The man has to beat the machine into action before he can invite a woman to dance "Fuzz," a grinding two-step, with him.

Three other couples join into the partner dancing, which builds as a competitive ritual of seduction. At one point, all eight dancers form a single throbbing line in the center of the bar. Crowded together, they grind their hips slowly while running their hands over each other's thighs and waists. Suddenly, they stare out toward the audience as a seething mass of barely repressed desire. This sexually charged image dissipates immediately, and the dancers move back into couples, slowing down as the jukebox music fades away. The momentary release afforded by social dancing falls apart as the characters become self-conscious and uncomfortable with their proximity, painfully aware of their inability to connect emotionally.

A single woman, partnerless witness to the group eroticism of "Fuzz," programs the jukebox to play "Morolo," a hesitant tune built from musical stutters and breaks. Her dance begins as an agonized plea for attention, answered uncertainly by two men who join her. Building on a basic mambo-style two-step, she swings her hips fiercely from side to side, simultaneously cutting through the air above her head with precise gestures of her arms. The men mirror her movements, their lower bodies articulating one rhythmical meter as their arms and upper bodies visually confirm another. The woman hardly looks at the men, but becomes increasingly distraught as she careens through the space. The men watch her closely, sometimes imitating her movements, at other times answering her with rhythmic counterpoint in slow-motion, weighty trudges across the bar. The men and woman never connect, and "Morolo" becomes a tale of missed communication, about the failure of the men to understand the woman's needs. Eventually, the men collapse into heaps at the side of the dance area, and the woman performs a series of silent screams: slow rises to a one-legged balance with arms extended upward as her face opens into an agonized screaming expression. "Morolo" ends with a reversal of its opening gestures, with the woman leading the men in the mambo step, then directing them back to their original seats in the bar. Defeated, she retreats through an inversion of her opening run for attention. Her hope to resolve her anger and loneliness through the act of dancing with the men has failed.

Seemingly disgusted by the woman's inability to resolve her emotions, the businessman rises to lead "Babajula Bonke." He controls the group with a series of gestural commands: directing them, with a wave of his hands, to sit on stools in a tight cluster at the side of the bar; leading them, with a circle of his arms, into a slow, unison sway. He bewitches the group with a series of traveling phrases, running toward them, then retreating with a stylized walking posture reminiscent of Afro-Caribbean religious dance. "Babajula Bonke" builds from the tension between the group's languid, submissive, unison movements and the businessman's tense, skittering phrases toward and away from them. He maintains absolute control over the group, his freedom of motion in stark contrast to their restricted movements on the stools.

But the businessman's authority carries a harsh liability: he has no peer among the bar's denizens, and his facile domination provides him no pleasure. His fury mounts in proportion to the group's submissiveness, even as he directs them to encircle him and become witnesses to, rather than objects of, his wrath. Seated, the group monitors his passionate attempts to come to voice, his enigmatic sways followed by sudden bursts of tense, counterpoised bending. Two people join into his dance briefly, echoing his movement, while the others sway and moan in audible response to his fervent calls. Like "I Cried" of *Blues Suite*, "Babajula Bonke" reveals the bottomless despair of a man grievously inarticulate. His anger propels a series of fragmentary movements that include simulations of self-flogging and gestures of railing against the skies. Frustrated, a man confronts the businessman in an extended choreographed fistfight. The businessman repels his attacker repeatedly, throwing him high into the air, apparently reveling in the physical release afforded by direct violence. The attacker counters with several solid hits, but the bout ends inconclusively, with the two men shaking each other to the floor, their arms locked around each other's throats. As the music fades away, the fighting men disengage and retreat to opposite parts of the bar. The onlookers, disappointed at the stalemate, swagger back into attitudes of detached languor.

This long sequence describing a man's staggering impotence, originally created by dancer Kelvin Rotardier, is balanced by "Bo Masekela," a long solo describing a shattered woman. As danced by Judith Jamison, "Bo Masekela" became the centerpiece of *Masekela Langage*, its stark depiction of desperation and barely suppressed rage rivaling its counterparts in *Blues Suite*, *Quintet*, and *Flowers*. This solo became the first important collaboration for Jamison and Ailey, and its success predicted the phenomenon of their collaboration three years later in *Cry*. It is worth noting that Jamison and Ailey clicked as collaborators only after Jamison was able to tap into an emotional reservoir of hard-edged desperation and rage that Ailey engaged in works like *Quintet* and *Riedaiglia*.

The next short selection, "U-Dui," is a simultaneously humorous and pathetic character dance, offered by a seated woman struck by a hysterical fit of laughter. Trembling from the shoulders and torso, her hysteria describes the neglect of dead-end life in the bar. Two men approach her—they may be concerned or predatory—and she rises, pushes them away, and tries to rouse the others into a party mood through a sequence of social dance steps. The dances she uses here are not familiar African American forms: they are Ailey's adaptation of South African movements.

Before the woman of "U-Dui" can provoke a change in mood, "Mace and Grenades" interrupts her dance, its pounding musical accents drawing the patrons away from her and toward the entrance to the bar. As they contemplate the outside world, their movements become frantic and formal, with fast-paced, dynamic phrases of nervous anticipation danced in waves by shifting groups of four and five dancers. A tattered and bloodied man bursts into the bar. The group first responds to this intrusion from outside with cowering fear, then frenzied sequences of running and turning that take over the barroom space. The tattered man tells his story of violent brutality at the hands of offstage (white) oppressors in a series of flamboyant and virtuosic turns, jumps, and leaps. The bar patrons respond with mounting anger and anguish, detailed in densely paced, increasingly difficult movement phrases. The tattered man dies, collapsing in the center of the bar. The others hide their faces as the music fades away.

In an "Epilogue," the dancers reverse the motions of the "Prologue," staring down the audience, taunting and enticing, moving their wicker chairs into place at the front of the bar. They ignore the bloody body lying on the floor. As the music fades, the bar patrons sit motionless, unchanged by the death in their midst. The curtain falls on this charged image of cyclical hopelessness.

A suite of dances that cumulatively depict the suppressed rage of a group, *Masekela Langage* contains obvious structural similarities to *Blues Suite* and *Quintet*. In this instance, however, Ailey allows his characters no costume changes, no entrances or exits from the oppressive squalor of the barroom, no relief from the miserable framing gesture of repetitious torpor. Its dramatic scenario ends ambiguously, with the characters repeating their opening gestures and moving by rote over and around the dead man's body. Structurally, the ending implies passive victimization as the only response available to these South African bar patrons. But emotionally, the ending of the dance proposes repetition with a difference. The air of the theater space has been charged by the unexpected intrusion of the dying man; the characters on stage, as well as the audience, must consider their own course of action in response to brutality happening just beyond the door.

The work trades in a circumstantial hopelessness tied to an unmitigated rage absent from Ailey's other works. The simple format of the dance—introduction, varied character vignettes, unexpected dramatic event, epilogue—allows the choreographer to explore aspects of anger and qualities of desperation in a sustained manner, to draw out distinctions between the characters and their responses to their shared, blank situation. The ending of the work echoes Katherine Dunham's famous *Southland* (1951), a dance that depicted a lynching and its aftermath in an unnamed rural southern American community.[6] As at the end of *Southland*, the characters of *Masekela Langage* await change; what they seem to demand of their audience is a measure of how long they may be willing to wait before they explode.

Ailey insisted that the dance had roots as a work of protest against the political, economic, and cultural impoverishment brandished by the racist South African system of apartheid. In 1977 he told Joseph Mazo that he made *Masekela Langage* "with the intention of drawing a parallel between events in South Africa and those in Chicago and to make a statement about the shooting to death of Fred Hampton, a leader of the Black Panther Party."[7] But the "statement" Ailey intended in relation to the Black Panther Party remains obscure, seldom born out by particularities of the choreography. None of the characters can be easily interpreted as Hampton or even as members of the Black Panther Party; the overall structure of the dance, though dramatically powerful, hardly references particular events in Chicago circa 1969.

In all, the intensity of emotion contained by the choreography offers the most clear reference to social and political dis-ease. In creating a dance of failed gestures and missed communications, Ailey describes a world in rehearsal. When the patrons of the South African bar "click" with each other—when they can finish their danced expressions of desire and hope, celebration, outrage, and anger while communicating directly with each other—the world outside the bar and, by extension, the concert dance theater, will be challenged and transformed. The dance predicts a change in the local order through action that can occur only after the curtain has descended.

Initial critical response to *Masekela Langage* was mixed. Writing for the *New York Times*, Anna Kisselgoff found the dance's narrow focus confining: "In its present form, the work relies entirely upon an unexpected dramatic climax for its impact—the actual choreography offering only a pale version of the striking uses Ailey has made of jazz and modern vocabulary in his best dances." Walter Terry noted the difficult mixture of dramatic intensity and emotional release offered by social dancing: "Or is Ailey saying that this is life with introspection, introversion, loneliness in the midst of conviviality, shaking hips, and the shudder of death? It is a stirring work, for it succeeds in being entertaining and disturbing at the same time, and that, in the classic sense, is what theater is all about."[8]

Masekela Langage succeeds as a dance of protest only to the degree that its audience understands an implicit dialectic of unequal power relations between black and white people. The dance's framing device tests the terrain of difference between the black characters and an assumed white audience, resulting in the "disturbing" tone acknowledged by Terry and other critics. The racist actions and political circumstances that have led these characters to their impermeable, blank existence remain offstage. But the character's victimization at its climax implicates the audience as collaborators to these political circumstances, made complicit by the act of witnessing the dance.

For Ailey, a dance that made any gesture toward uneasy American racial tensions may have been overtly political, dangerous, or messy. He certainly intended the work to stand as a South African counterpart to *Blues Suite*, confirming, through its choreographic structure, similarities between the grossly racist system of apartheid and strained civil rights efforts in the United States. Ultimately, his self-defined "protest" work probably challenged the idea of concert dance as an expressive idiom during times of great political strife more than any particular political event.

The politics of *Masekela Langage* surfaced infrequently in Ailey's oeuvre; most of his dances instead explore varied qualities of motion. For example, Ailey made *Gymnopedies* (23 April 1970) to the three-part Satie score of the same name. Set in a rehearsal studio, the solo premiered with American Ballet Theatre soloist Keith Lee as "a young man [who] lolls about, smokes a cigarette . . . dances, stops, reverts to ordinary movement and begins again, this time as if he were choreographing the dance on the spot."[9] A small, conceptual piece about a dancer at work in a studio, *Gymnopedies* obviously resembled Jerome Robbins's 1953 ballet *Afternoon of a Faun*. The dance depended on the dramatic abilities of its dancer to convey an unforced, engaging simplicity.

When Ailey next created a dance for his own company, he turned to a chance score by Andre Boucourechliev. The score for *Archipelago* (18 January 1971) had been commissioned by the fourth Festival of Contemporary Music at Royan, France in 1967. Described by the composer as "completely free in its sonorities, in its development, as well as in the duration of its sections," the tape-recorded accompaniment for the dance featured two pianists and two percussionists in two distinct recordings of the work.[10]

Ailey premiered the work at the opening of his company's Broadway season at the American National Theater and Academy. Its two contrasting sections offered formal explorations for varying groupings of dancers: "Version I" featured eight men and one woman; "Version II" included fourteen dancers. In both versions, the dancers wore neutral-colored practice clothes designed by A. Christina Giannini. Built from "continual asymmetry, use of spins and jetes as means of locomotion . . . arabesque turns and reaching arms," *Archipelago* began "with a group of men slowly rising and stretching, gradually going into huge leaps and big open attitudes."[11] "Version I" included a duet for Consuelo Atlas and Kelvin Rotardier, as well as a solo for Dudley Williams. "Version II" began with a group of women in place of the men, and included a trio of women in pointe shoes. An intense exploration of movement abstraction, the dance continued with "big sculptural designs, out of which some suggestions of a pas de deux begin to surface" before ending with a time-compressed variation of preceding movement ideas.[12]

The unprecedented formality of *Archipelago* confounded critics used to the dramatic scenarios and obtrusive humanism of Ailey's earlier work. Writing for the *New York Post*, Frances Herridge disparaged the musical selection as the source of the dance's weakness: "It is a long way from the definite beat and electrifying drive of the music Ailey usually works with. And it sends him on a different style of movement, more hackneyed, more nebulous, more derivative of classroom technique. It cannot keep up with the overwhelming clang of some of the music, and wanders vaguely with the rest, perhaps hoping it will be a voyage of discovery."

Joseph Mazo, writing for *Women's Wear Daily*, found structural formalism a liability because "the pace of the dance never seems to alter decisively; there are no major changes of mood. Because of this, the entire work seems suspended in water—which may have been Ailey's intention—and is difficult to respond to kinesthetically. . . . *Archipelago* . . . reaches the eyes and the mind, but rarely penetrates to the body and the emotions, which are the target areas of dance."[13] No film of the dance was made, and *Archipelago* disappeared after a single season.

As if to answer critics who found *Archipelago*'s formal abstraction unsatisfying, Ailey embellished his next abstract work with obvious religious/ritualistic overtones. Set to six dances from Benjamin Britten's *Gloriana*, *Choral Dances* (28 April 1971) premiered during the Ailey company's spring season at City Center. An austere, mystical ritual for a tightly knit community, the dance successfully resisted recurrent criticism typifying both "black dance" and Ailey's "show business" choreographic palette.

Ramon Sagarra and members of the Alvin Ailey American
Dance Theater in Alvin Ailey's *Archipelago*, 1971.
Photograph by Martha Swope

Choral Dances began with Kelvin Rotardier onstage, moving with measured weightiness through a solo of preparation danced in complete silence. Costumed in a long frock coat and pants, he acted as a devotional leader, preparing the space for his congregation. Rotardier moved to the side of the stage; as he crossed back toward the center, he was followed by the company of thirteen dancers walking in measured silence. The several dance episodes that followed engaged the stage space with an impressive visual architecture created by blocks of dancers often moving in silence. The dance ended in silence, with the group following Rotardier offstage in a continuation of their opening movement.

Writing for *The Village Voice* about an alternate cast, Deborah Jowitt found *Choral Dances*

reminiscent of some of the sober architectural pieces of early modern dance, of those choreographers who seemed to be trying somewhat sententiously to say that dancers were not empty-headed butterflies, but mature men and women who were serious about life. So, Ailey's dancers are dressed in subdued colors, the women in long jersey dresses,

The Alvin Ailey American Dance Theater in Alvin Ailey's
Choral Dances, 1971. Photograph by Mario Ruiz

their movements are weighted and their joy is devoid of any hint of fri-
volity. Their leader (Clive Thompson) begins by elevating an important chalice of some sort and leads the group in solemn processional
that suggest the endless flow of time."[14]

Ailey's strong historical sensibility may have inspired him to create a
"throwback" work; if so, *Choral Dances* revised conceptions of a historical legacy
of American modern dance to include a large company of African American
dancers. Ailey's ritualistic scenario matched the musical score while simultaneously expanding the familiar stage personae of pious black men and women. In
Choral Dances, the company's detached solemnity suggested a Puritan-like con-
servation of energy expended in small, contained bursts by a community of the
devout who are eager for order. The dance resists racial stereotyping and forced
audiences to see beyond the racially polarized moment: "And in the moments
without music, the dancers somehow seem to be removed from us, encased in
silence and moving through some other time, in some other place."[15]

Filling in for an unavailable Jerome Robbins,[16] Ailey created choreography for Leonard Bernstein's mammoth *Mass* (8 September 1971). Commissioned as the opening work of the twenty-two-hundred-seat John F. Kennedy Center for the Performing Arts in Washington, D.C., *Mass* absorbed the entirety of the Alvin Ailey American Dance Theater into its large cast of performers. A high-profile, youth-driven reworking of the complete Latin text of the Mass, lavishly hyped to match the pomp of the Kennedy Center opening, the work aroused great controversy and curiosity.

Working quickly, Ailey created incidental dances to fit into Bernstein's "rich amalgam of the theatrical arts," described by the composer simply as a "reaffirmation of faith" written "out of love and affection for [slain President] John Kennedy."[17] Bernstein subtitled his work "A Theater Piece for Players, Singers, and Dancers," composed in a format that encompassed "everything from churchly exaltation to the gaiety of street dances, and climaxes in a kind of Golden Calf bacchanal."[18] The sprawling nature of the work, which included a rock combo, boys choir, and marching brass band, as well as its Broadway-style staging disappointed several critics, including Jack Anderson writing for *Dance Magazine*: "The basic reason for the superficiality of 'Mass' lies in its attitude towards religion. Essentially, it depicts how a Celebrant (a role sung and mimed with fervor by Alan Titus) loses and regains his faith while conducting a service. Doubt, however, is expressed in banal lyrics . . . and the presentation of faith is sheer sentimentality."[19]

Although Bernstein claimed to consider dance integral to the construction of the *Mass*, he and his collaborators offered Ailey stringent confines. The severe spatial limitations of Oliver Smith's setting forced much of Ailey's choreography onto a small raised area, placing "the focus on arms and torso—in the manner of his celebrated 'Revelations.'"[20] Photographs of the *Mass* reveal stationary clusters of dancers split into two distinct groups: acolytes clad in brightly colored vestments, and an ensemble of young people clad in contemporary street wear.[21] Noting the "limit to what can be done from a stationary base," *Washington Post* critic Jean Battey Lewis observed: "Dance is part of the whole in that [this] is a fused theater piece. [But] there is no opportunity for dance to make a profound statement[;] instead it is called on to provide a visceral impact."[22]

Although he received double billing as choreographer and costager with Gordon Davidson, Ailey admitted in an interview that the collaborative arrangement had been less than satisfactory: "'I can't tell you what problems we had with all those on stage. I'd work something out and the next day they'd say, 'You can't have your dancers there. Lennie wants the marching band there.' Finally I stopped doing anything till all the directors were there to tell me if it was physically possible."[23] However unpleasant the circumstances, Ailey and his company were committed by contract to repeat their contributions to the *Mass* a year later, in a series of performances in Washington, D.C., Philadelphia, and at the Metropolitan Opera House in New York City in June 1972.

Ailey continued to explore a religious sensibility with *Mary Lou's Mass* (9 December 1971), set to a two-year-old score by composer Mary Lou Williams. Billed

John Parks, Dudley Williams, and Kelvin Rotardier in Alvin Ailey's
Mary Lou's Mass, 1971. Photograph by Rosemary Winckley

as a latter-day *Revelations*, the dance included some fourteen sections shaped in the manner of a Catholic Mass: Invocation, Processional, Kyrie, Gloria, Sermon, Credo, Offertory, Sanctus, Agnus Dei, Communion, and Recessional. Williams's jazz-inspired score offered a spectrum of African American musical styles: spirituals, contemporary gospel, blues, bebop, and hints of ragtime. A large-scale work for Ailey's entire company, *Mary Lou's Mass*, subtitled "Dances of Praise," inspired a spate of feature articles probing the historical connection of religion and modern dance, as well as the suitability of dance as prayer.

The piece also offered an alternative take on religion and theater to what Ailey's company had presented in Bernstein's *Mass* earlier the same year. Where Bernstein's *Mass* had been self-consciously youth-driven but created by men who were not young, Ailey's version celebrated Williams's music as the source of religious meditation. The dance emerged as homage to Williams's accomplishment, and Ailey clearly enjoyed publicly celebrating her through the dance. He told the *New York Times*, "One of my plans in life is to identify black music . . . to make it audible."[24]

Ailey turned next to Igor Stravinsky's "Symphonies of Wind Instruments" for the short ballet *Myth* (15 December 1971). A small, mythic work performed entirely behind a scrim, the dance featured Consuelo Atlas as a woman alternately pursued and protected by Clive Thompson, Kenneth Pearl, and Freddy Romero. Sensitive and imaginative lighting by Chenault Spence created "projections of bare tree branches that get warmed by an orange solar orb, and finally sprayed with a bloom of white dots as the three men hover protectively over Miss Atlas in a final tableau."[25]

The dance continued Ailey's fascination with an arrangement of ballet technique, Graham technique, and black social dance styles. He constructed the work with customary architectural dispatch: an introduction for all four dancers, followed by duets for Atlas with each of the men, and a short concluding section for all four. Glamorous in design, especially A. Christina Giannini's costumes, "suggesting a Vogue magazine on a very expensive safari," *Myth* offered Ailey's audiences a slight meditation on the power and beauty of a woman bound to three men whose sole purpose could be found in serving her.[26]

By 1972, Ailey's preferred structural form was the suite. His clearest successes had come in works built from a series of short dances connected by an overall dramatic or musical theme, including *Blues Suite, Revelations, Hermit Songs, Quintet, Masekela Langage, The River, Streams, Cry,* and *Mary Lou's Mass.* The suite form obviously appealed to his sense of architectural storytelling, as it allowed him to reveal facets of personality, both emotional and compositional, as portions of a larger whole. In Ailey's choreographic cosmology, these small units add up to a whole conceptually greater than the specifics of any of its parts.

The Lark Ascending

The surprise work of Ailey's spring 1972 season at City Center was a through-composed, fifteen-minute idyll set to Ralph Vaughan Williams's *Romance for Violin and Orchestra. The Lark Ascending* (25 April 1972) represented a significant breakthrough in Ailey's choreographic range. Created to showcase the lyrical capabilities of Judith Jamison, who led a company of twelve at its premiere, the dance met greater acclaim as a vehicle for Sara Yarborough in the 1970s, Maxine Sherman in the 1980s, and Elizabeth Roxas in the 1990s. *The Lark Ascending* has continually remained in the repertory of the Alvin Ailey American Dance Theater.

Ailey created the dance as a tribute to the bucolic Scottish countryside he enjoyed during his company's tour in 1968.[27] A lyrical, romantically styled dance, *The Lark Ascending* made extensive use of the Ailey company's balletic abilities, tempered by Horton-style lateral balances and Graham-inspired contractions of the torso. Ailey tiered the dance balletically, with roles for a principal couple (Judith Jamison and Clive Thompson at its premiere), a demisoloist couple (Linda Kent and Hector Mercado), and an ensemble of four men and four women (Ronald Dunham, Leland Harper, Rosamund Lynn, Clover Mathis, Kenneth

Pearl, Gail Reese, Freddy Romero, and Leland Schwantes). The dance explored hunting as a metaphor for male-female coupling, suggesting the transformative ability of heterosexual partnership to enable growth from puberty to maturity.

The dance brought forth a softness and suppleness unmined in Ailey's recent work. In its opening passage, danced behind a scrim, a lone hunter poised on his knees listens expectantly to the ground. As he awaits his prey, he meets a group of fellow hunters traveling through the woods with slow, weighty trudging motions, and a joyous demisoloist couple, dancing in a vibrant, animated rhythm built from expansive, sweeping jumps interspersed with gently curving lifts. The hunters celebrate this couple's buoyant union in softly bending sways, then leave to find partners of their own. Four women shimmer through the space, falling into and out of unison passages arranged from balancés, jumps, and arching turns, happily greeting the mated woman, then skittering about the edges of the stage. Suddenly, the ballet's leading woman—the lark—enters to greet the demisoloist with a soft gesture of her arms. As the score crescendos into its first full melodic idea, the scrim flies out, exposing the stage fully for the lark's first solo. The effect is glorious, like the fog lifting from the Scottish countryside.

The lark's first solo is a dance of intuitive joy told in small jumps set between balanced poses and flowing, floor-bound traveling phrases. An awkward, turned-in levitation on one leg recurs as a gesture of the lark's immaturity, but mostly she dances for the joy of moving, her yellow leotard and filmy pastel skirt floating in front of a speckled scrim background. Her dance is fast-paced and requires almost constant motion, with quick directional shifts and continual adjustments of the arms peppering her striving for grace and lightness. Her dance expresses a lushness of breath suggested by Williams's score.

The Lark Ascending contains extended unison passages bereft of dramatic overlay, a compositional maneuver uncommon in the Ailey repertory. In a long variation for five women, balancés, cabrioles, grand jetés, and slow promenades vary the quality of the stage space through shifting geometric groupings and an effective layering of canon and unison phrases. The staging billows, rising and falling as the women break into and out of movement symmetry. Partnered, the dancers become lovers in a countryside rather than hunters and birds, enabled by their mating to engage in joyous passages of unison movement.

In her second solo, filled with reaching and spinning motions, the lark floats, arches, balances, and flies. In a gesture that reveals her growing pains, she flaps her hands together at her wrists while seeming to nurture a mysterious sense of regret. The other women return as if to reassure her, and together they enjoy a short unison dance of avian memory, filled with pitching gestures toward the sides embellished by fluttering arm motions. When the men return, the dancers couple up for a long unison sequence of partnership, with the women frequently manipulated into balance by the men. In one inventive gesture, the men lean backward to the floor, their hands and feet supporting their upward-facing torsos crab-style, while the women rest on the men's thighs and flap their arms luxuriously. This sequence ends with the lark embracing her hunter with an awakened maturity, then leaving him to finish her transformation offstage.

Ronald Dunham, Gail Reese, Clive Thompson, Sara Yarborough, Hector Mercado, and Linda Kent in Alvin Ailey's *The Lark Ascending*, 1972. Photograph by Rosemary Winckley

The dance offered Ailey's company a formidable challenge of sustained lyricism. The hunter's short solo is built from a seamless arrangement of bounding jumps followed by controlled rolls across the floor. His stiff articulations of port de bras, which contrast neatly with the women's softer arm gestures, do not break the flowing momentum of his dance so much as they underscore his urgent anticipation of the lark's return. When she returns, the entire company reassembles, the men cartwheeling onstage as the women leap to their partners for a short sequence celebrating her transfiguration. The dance ends in a tableau, with the ensemble women supported by their seated partners in positions framing the center symmetrically; the demisoloist couple lying tranquilly on the ground in the center; and behind them, the lark as woman, balanced on her partner's thigh, leaning away from him as she reaches toward the heavens in celebration of her newfound identity.

A simple dance about the qualities of beauty, *The Lark Ascending* challenged its dancers and audiences to expand conceptions of the lyrical to include Ailey's hybrid aesthetic of balletic carriage and stretch, modern dance contraction and release, and sculptural design. The dance allowed its dancers an unfettered engagement with innocence within a single overarching narrative. In context with other works in the Ailey company repertory, such as Donald McKayle's tale of chain-gangs, *Rainbow 'round My Shoulder*, and Brian Macdonald's harsh ritual of mating, *Time Out of Mind*, both revived in the 1972 season, Ailey's dance offered an unrivaled purity of intention.

Surprisingly, white critical reaction to *The Lark Ascending* varied little, from tepid to condescendingly polite acknowledgment. Writing for the *New York Times*, Anna Kisselgoff suggested that the dance delivered an appealing lyricism, but in a work derivative and old-fashioned by white modern dance standards: "The fact that most of these possibilities have already been mined by Martha Graham kept getting in one viewer's way, but for those who have not seen 'Diversion of Angels' and 'Dark Meadow,' such considerations are basically irrelevant." Marcia Siegel found its simple format a liability: "For me, just to be able to look at those dancers moving around aimlessly doing balletic extensions with Ailey's famous fluidity isn't enough."[28]

Although offered negatively, the comparison of Ailey's work with Graham and his company's obviously rising facility in ballet technique signaled a breakthrough in portraiture for African American artists in concert dance. If *The Lark Ascending* only reworked ideas previously engaged by Graham, it did so with a large company of committed, trained black dancers able to meet its challenge of sustained lyricism. Throughout this period, Ailey's company stood alone as representative of an opera house–style African American presence in concert dance. In one analysis, *The Lark Ascending* stood as proof that a company of African American dancers could convincingly project, at least, physical lightness and balletic innocence, a truth previously unexplored by American choreographers.

Hidden Rites

The next group work Ailey made for his own company featured a familiar combination of a mythic community, ritual, and a percussion musical score. In terms of movement quality, though, it offered dramatic counterpoint to the lyricism of *The Lark Ascending*. *Hidden Rites* (17 May 1973), set to "Les Cyclopes" by Patrice Sciortino, included nine sections at its first performance, which were later pruned to eight. A watershed work that defined a choreographic style extending well into the 1990s, *Hidden Rites* provided a virtual catalogue of Ailey's hybrid movement aesthetic. The work has been intermittently revived into the active Ailey company repertory since then.

Hidden Rites details an enigmatic ritual of heterosexual mating told in terms of hard-edged movements performed with suffocating precision. The work begins with an "Incantation" duet, originally danced by Judith Jamison and John Parks. Posed center stage, the couple is revealed in a sharp pool of downward-directed light that traps them like objects on display. Their opening

Charles Adams and Judith Jamison in Alvin Ailey's *Hidden Rites*, 1972. Photograph by Bert Andrews

pose is reminiscent of sub-Saharan statuary: with feet planted wider than shoulder distance, both knees bend as they lean their weight into their right hips. Arms are held akimbo, with their left hands placed low on the left thigh and the right hands on the right hip, and their faces are turned in sharp profile. The opening pose contains an angularity unprecedented in Ailey's oeuvre, its sharp edges heightened by costumes of form-fitting leotard and tights.

As the percussion score begins its layered array of rhythmic tones, the dancers strike out into a series of exacting positions; they crackle through briefly held stances set in sharp rhythmic accord with percussion accents. They dance to bring down the spirits, to prepare the ground for the longer ritual that follows. At times, they mirror each other, dancing as reflections across an imaginary line drawn at the center of the stage floor; at other times, the woman seems to lead the preparations, guiding the man into an unexpected series of ecstatic turns. Suddenly, the woman jumps onto the man's shoulder, sits, and opens her arms decisively on a final cymbal crash. The duet hits hard, a bombastic series of sculptural positions connected by simple gestural and turning actions.

"Spirits Known and Unknown" follows, a dance introducing the entire company of sixteen in roles split sharply according to gender. Four men hit square, angular positions exactly on bell tones sounded in the score, while four women enter simultaneously with a sinuous swing of their hips. As the women cross the space slowly with their distinctive rhythmic pattern, they surround a female soloist, an initiate, who strides among them in measured slow motion. This woman reaches the center of the space to dance alone, ferociously slashing through the air with her body, balancing precariously on one leg as she tips her torso forward toward the floor, then pushing against the air with her arms in a staccato gesture of stuttering.

The elders of the mysterious *Hidden Rites* are distinguished through costuming and varying movement vocabularies. "Spirits Descending," a solo for a man wearing a feathered headpiece, proceeds with an assortment of sweeping, circular movements: sideward swings of the hips and briefly held poses that always sit, sideways, into the hips. Originally danced by Kenneth Pearl, the solo has a fast, Jack Cole jazz dance sensibility, evidenced in smooth quickness and surprising percussive accents. This solo also contains gestures that suggest physical stuttering; for example, balances in arabesque position are broken by sharp contractions from the stomach as the dancer moves toward a new balance. Several neo-African traveling steps require the dancer to skip across the space with a triplet rhythm in the feet phrased against a duple rhythm swing of arms and upper torso. The solo layers styles in a spontaneous-seeming manner: surprising balances are followed by hip-swinging traveling steps, balletic turns in a high attitude position, and sharp stops in sculptural poses timed to coincide with accents in the musical score. The soloist ends lying on the stage floor, his final faun-like pose timed to the final drumbeat.

A section for six women, "Of Women," begins with a long solo originally created to display the dizzying technical facility of Mari Kajiwara as an elder in red. The dance includes a pas de deux for the elder and the female initiate, danced by Kajiwara and Sylvia Waters at its premiere. Structurally similar to a number of duets Ailey made for a man and a woman, this supported adagio for two women assumes a supporting presence (Kajiwara) who alternately steadies and manipulates a mutable presence (Waters) in preparation for the mating ritual. In "Of Men," the initiate's male counterpart is prepared by an ensemble of four men in a dance of largely unabated unison movements. Whereas the female initiate had been physically prepared by an elder, the male initiate leads the male ensemble through a series of square postures connected by leaping turns and weighty motions that sink toward the ground. Here and elsewhere, *Hidden Rites* assumes an intractable difference between its male and female celebrants.

Two contrasting duets titled "Of Love" form the compositional centerpiece of the work. The first "Of Love" duet builds on a motif of fluttering motions begun in the wrists that develop into a swinging of the hips performed in opposition by the man and woman. The second duet builds through a series of startling frozen poses, including a perilous balance by the woman on the man's kneecaps, and an unexpected sudden jump from the floor to a seated position on his shoulder. Each dance has a competitive urgency and moves with a sense of inevitability toward its final gesture of harsh rancor: in each case, the man is suddenly clutched by the woman as the lights black out.

The adversarial brutality of the "Of Love" duets presages the surreal misogyny enacted in the ritual proper, titled "Of Celebration and Death." The dance describes the sacrifice of the initiate woman to the entire ensemble of men. At its climax, four men lie on their backs in a star-shaped formation around the initiate. Holding the woman by her shoulders, two other men dip her, in turn, on top of each of the prone men. The men respond to her contact with a fervent contraction of the torso. When all the men have been serviced in this manner, the woman is placed on the ground, spent. The men gather around her briefly, as if to confirm her death, then move away to assume positions for the ceremony of her spiritual ascendence.

The ensemble women spin onstage for the final section, "Spirits Ascending." The plumed elder picks up the lifeless body and carries her offstage as the other dancers partner up for a short celebratory gesture built from swinging hip motions and fluttering hands. The plumed man leads a recessional bearing the dead woman and the celebrants follow, dancing movement patterns varied according to their station in the community. The recessional extends into silence, and *Hidden Rites* ends with the woman from the opening "Incantation" remaining behind, standing center stage in an entrapping pool of light. She shakes her hips and arms at the sky, then settles into her opening pose reminiscent of African sculpture, her profile directed sharply along the path that led her clan away.

Where *The Lark Ascending* explored the pure joy of movement, *Hidden Rites* revealed Ailey's expansive facility at movement invention. The dance unfolds like a series of carefully wrought snapshots, each moment packed with visual energy. It presents a highly ordered community bound, in movement terms, by a formal sculptural precision. As an exploration of line and the ability of body line to convey an oblique narrative, *Hidden Rites* succeeds as an opus of architectural abstraction.

The combination of cool architectural abstraction and awesome technical precision Ailey required of his dancers in *Hidden Rites* spawned a style of choreography that extends well into the 2000s. The work of choreographers Donald Byrd, Ulysses Dove, Garth Fagan, Dwight Rhoden, and Kevin Wynn, each of whom was associated with Ailey and his school during the 1980s and 1990s, continues this unique stylistic blend of abstract movement driven by oblique narrative and tempered by an exploitation of the technical facility of its dancers.

Critics writing at the premiere of *Hidden Rites* noted the choreographic significance of Ailey's watershed ballet. Frances Herridge thought the dance added "a new mood and new facet to the repertory. . . . [Its] mood and style are a fascinating blend of Siamese, African, even ancient Egyptian, as are the Bea Feitler costumes." Anna Kisselgoff wrote that *Hidden Rites* "falls into that compartment of the Ailey repertory that includes 'Streams,' 'Myth,' 'Choral Dances' and 'Archipelago.' . . . These works share a deliberate ritual cast. Under the guise of pure movement, relationships and emotional states are depicted, often without the audience's being immediately aware of them. . . . We see the weak stomped by the strong and an acceptance of such as the order of things in this world." Writing for *New York Newsday*, Bob Micklin noted Ailey's "ability to project the essential psycho-sexual and physical qualities which separate, yet unite, man and woman." Micklin continued to define Ailey's choreographic quest as it seemed to impinge on Martha Graham's oeuvre: "I have the feeling that Ailey is somehow reexamining and rethinking the influence of Martha Graham on his work. That he is concerned with pruning out any traces of sheer imitation and trying to build his own, new, modern choreographic style which will recognize Graham's dramatic innovations but which will not rely on her established movements."[29] Ailey "relied" on Graham's movements in much the same way he "relied" on postures from classical ballet or African statuary, as elements arranged toward the end of composition.

Indeed, by 1973 Ailey had moved far beyond the "hermetically sealed" universe of *Revelations* to make works that explored an expansive range of scenarios, musical formats, and movement idioms. His choreographic strategies depended heavily on the musical accompaniment he used; happily, he was drawn to an eclectic array of compositions and musical forms. As *New York Times* critic Anna Kisselgoff intimated in her review of *The Lark Ascending*, general audiences for Ailey's company in the early 1970s were invited to consider dancing black bodies in a broad range of roles, portraying qualities of movement largely absent from American stages, including the stifling depiction of anger of *Masekela Langage*, the sustained lyricism of *The Lark Ascending*, and the precise physical geometry of *Hidden Rites*.

More specialized dance audiences—spectators and critics who frequented ballet, Graham, Cunningham, or other dance theater performances—may have lost interest in Ailey's work during the 1970s to the degree that their desire vacillated between works that explored "Negro heritage," like *Revelations*, and experimental, individualistic postmodern choreography. Ailey's creativity flourished somewhere between these poles, and he worked in that middle space to enlarge on representational possibilities for African Americans in modern dance. In terms of its overall choreographic structure, Ailey's work remained decidedly modern, with a commitment to recognizably human-scale gestures and movements that would be accessible to a large audience regardless of class or educational background. For some audiences, this facile use of concert dance as an accessible medium, available to audiences without reference to extensive program notes or training in Western aesthetics, condemned Ailey and his enterprise to the status of imitators. But Ailey remained committed to an Africanist aesthetic trajectory that embraced shifts in taste and style as communal and generational paradigms rather than responses to the will of an individual. In this analysis, his expressive palate did shift frequently, but always in direct collaboration with the sensibilities and abilities that dancers brought to his company. His creative innovations came not because critics or aesthetes demanded them, but because he and his affiliated artists forged them together.

With *Hidden Rites*, Ailey confirmed a standard of technical precision hinted at in works like *Myth* and *Archipelago*. The work offered its dancers an outlandish array of technical requirements, challenging them to prove heightened mastery of several dance techniques within the cryptic dramatic outline of a ritual ceremony. Unlike *Masekela Langage* or *The Lark Ascending*, *Hidden Rites* depends mostly on its surface architecture—the physical shapes made by the dancers—to convey its story.

The three dances described in detail in this chapter contain important choreographic devices Ailey returned to throughout his career. These include a turn with arms held upward and to the sides in an angular, broken U-shape; the Horton-inspired upper-body tilt toward the floor performed while balancing on one leg, the working leg stretching upward to the side or back of the torso; the elevated woman, balanced on the turned-out thigh of her male partner; and the classically placed, turned-out arabesque line. This final device is perhaps most surprising, given Ailey's background in modern dance. But his interest in classical ballet, stimulated by his choreography commissions for several ballet companies through the 1960s and 1970s, expanded as his own company grew. In Ailey's choreography, the arabesque became a symbol of balance, proportion, and flexibility, used frequently among Graham- and Horton-derived movements as a reference to ballet technique.

In creating many of the dances described in this chapter, Ailey responded to financial as well as artistic motivation. His dances filled his company's need to offer premieres in order to remain in the public eye. Always working fast and programming several premieres as works-in-progress, Ailey approached a range of thematic and musical material. Invariably, he adjusted and revised the dances after their premiere. This fluid system of dance composition allowed him to fit his choreography to the dancers at hand, to shape the work to the contours of its present performers. Ailey choreographed to bring his dancers forward, in front of the dances they performed; the works he made for his own company would have been impossible without the specific interpretive input of his dancers. He offered them a variety of structural outlines, a spectrum of musical, thematic, and movement approaches to the act of concert dance performance. By constantly expanding the range of approaches available to his dancers, Ailey hoped to explore fragments of African American experience that fell outside of traditional categories of black art.

SEVEN

Other Dances

By 1973, journalists routinely compared Ailey company practices to those of ballet troupes. Policies of alternate casting, an expansive and varied repertory, and opulent dances outfitted with elaborate lighting and decor set the Ailey company apart from other modern dance companies. In interviews, Ailey professed his respect for ballet as a standard of dancer training: "What I like is the line and technical range that classical ballet gives to the body. But I still want to project to the audience the expressiveness that only modern dance offers, especially for the inner kinds of things."[1]

In creating several pieces for ballet companies, Ailey broke through conventional distinctions between American modern dance and ballet. His landmark work *Feast of Ashes* (1962), choreographed for the Robert Joffrey Ballet, was among the first works created by a modern dance artist for a ballet company. He created two works for American Ballet Theatre, *The River* (1970), to a score by Duke Ellington, and *Sea Change* (1972), to music by Benjamin Britten, as well as several dances for the Harkness Ballet, the Joffrey Ballet, the Paris Opera Ballet, the Royal Danish Ballet, and La Scala Opera Ballet. These commissions inserted Ailey's particular stylistic concerns as a prominent author of an emergent Africanist concert dance aesthetic into arenas previously closed to the performance legacy of the African diaspora.

▋ Feast of Ashes

During the summer of 1962, Ailey worked with the Robert Joffrey Ballet at Rebekah Harkness's Watch Hill, Rhode Island retreat. He based the ballet he made there, *Feast of Ashes* (preview 30 September 1962; premiere 30 November 1962), on Federico García Lorca's 1936 tragedy, *The House of Bernarda Alba*. Successful productions of the work were later mounted on the Harkness Ballet (1964), Ailey's own company (1974), and the Maryland Ballet (1976). A rehearsal film of the work survives from the Harkness Ballet production of 1964.

In Lorca's play, subtitled "A Drama about Women in the Villages of Spain," Bernarda Alba's family mourns the passing of her second husband, Antonio María Benavides. Bernarda maintains an oppressively moralistic Catholic household in which she binds together her five adult daughters through her tyrannical adherence to tradition. Angustias, the oldest daughter (age thirty-nine), inherits a significant portion of money from her stepfather's estate; her four half-sisters receive notably less. Pepe el Romano, a handsome, twenty-five-year-old farmer, proposes to Angustias although he is in love with Adela, Bernarda's youngest daughter (age twenty). One of the other daughters, Martirio (age twenty-four), also loves Pepe. Martirio reveals Adela and Pepe's illicit affair to the family. By this time, Adela has become pregnant and unwilling to submit to Bernarda's tyranny; she reveals that she and Pepe plan to escape the village before he is to marry Angustias. Bernarda acts quickly: she scares Pepe away with a shotgun. Afflicted with grief, Adela commits suicide. As the play ends, Bernarda Alba orders her daughters to stony-faced silence: "I want no weeping. Death must be looked at face to face. Silence! Be still I said! Tears when you're alone! We'll drown ourselves in a sea of mourning. She, the youngest daughter of Bernarda Alba, died a virgin. Did you hear me? Silence, silence, I said. Silence!"[2]

Ailey might have been drawn to Lorca's depiction of a close-knit family unit bound by tradition but unable to contain the desires of its rebellious youngest member. Like Adela, Ailey had nurtured his passion (for dance) against his mother's knowledge, at one point winning himself a backstage slap in the face from his shocked mother, who was surprised to see her son in stage makeup.[3] Ailey understood the need for family and tradition but, like Adela, felt compelled to resist the established order of things to fulfill himself.

Ailey's adaptation veered significantly from Lorca's text. Where Lorca's play had only female characters, its action bound to the oppressive interior of the Bernarda Alba household, Ailey opened up the narrative to include scenes in the village and the local tavern/whorehouse. Ailey also included men in his ballet: among its principal roles are Pepe el Romano and an allegorical character, Señor Muerte. Other roles included Bernarda Alba, her five daughters, and an ensemble of seven men and three women to round out the company of eighteen. The musical score was assembled from two previously composed works by Carlos Surinach: *Doppo Concertino* and part of *Ritmo Jondo*.[4]

According to copious notes Ailey wrote in preparing the ballet, he originally intended the dance to include live singing of Lorca poems to set the mood and convey important plot points.[5] Owing to personnel or circumstances, he settled instead for a trio of "Women of the Street," three dancing Fates who establish the milieu for the ballet. As the curtain rises, these women are discovered in a corner of the town square, posed dramatically with oversized fans held high overhead. In a brief prelude, Adela and Pepe rush toward each other, and he lifts her high overhead before they embrace. Shooing Adela away, the Fates warn the lovers of the approaching funeral procession of Adela's father and escort Pepe offstage to join the trudging line of mourners.

To create the oppressively religious atmosphere of a rural Spanish village, Ailey expanded on choreographic devices and the use of props that had enhanced *Revelations*. Bearing a wooden cross and a tree branch high overhead, a priest leads the procession of Alba family mourners in a slow sway of misery, rocking forward and back from the knees as stiffly held upper bodies resist the impulse to cry. The Alba women wear black mourning shawls that vary the stage picture: at one point, the women spread out across the stage, kneel, and stretch their arms outward, fanning their shawls like the broken wings of injured birds. A group of village men join the women's processional, first echoing the creakily swaying gesture of mourning, then sobbing in rhythmic counterpoint to the women. In a potent and eerie image, the men lift Bernarda overhead in a rigid standing position, and she floats above and behind her daughters, who continue their mournful procession, their shawls wrapped dutifully over their heads. The men bring on five sturdy, high-backed chairs and exit, and suddenly the stage represents a drawing room in the house of Bernarda Alba.

Ailey's ballet distinguishes only Angustias and Adela of Bernarda's five daughters and establishes tension between the sisters in a pantomimed confrontation over one of the chairs. Bernarda resolves the argument decisively, striking Adela and seating Angustias in the central place of honor. Bernarda's domineering authority fuels the taut mood of the household, reflected in a seated dance of mourning performed by the sisters. Reaching outward, with their hands held tensely wide, the women avert their gazes from each other as they sob through a series of hard contractions of their torsos. Bernarda oversees their dance, hovering implacably behind Angustias.

As the score sounds a macabre, spare violin solo, Adela moves away from her sisters to turn and arch against the space in anguish, reaching to her mother with questioning gestures of yearning uncertainty. Bernarda strides toward her, striking strong, rigid postures, her chest released forward and high, in poses that suggest classical Spanish dance. Bernarda performs turns traditionally reserved for male dancers, her working leg stretched aggressively to the side and physically consuming the space around her daughter, as if to squash Adela's inquisitiveness. An inventive gesture describes the troubled relationship between mother and daughter: Adela grabs her mother's waist as she pitches her own torso forward toward the ground and balances precariously on one leg. Bernarda circles around Adela, causing her daughter to revolve slowly in a motion that echoes the physical support offered Bernarda by the priest in an earlier

The Robert Joffrey Ballet in Alvin Ailey's *Feast of Ashes*,
circa 1962. Photographer unknown

scene. But Bernarda does not intentionally support her daughter at all. Instead, she holds her arms up and away from Adela, her hands stretched wide in condemnation.

As a whole, *Feast of Ashes* is driven by its plot, with set dances arising to further the dramatic narrative derived from Lorca's play. Bernarda literally kicks after Adela to force her back to her rightful place among her sisters, then leads Angustias forward for a short duet that further confirms her domination. Bernarda assumes a supporting role, manipulating Angustias into balances, then pushing her down to the floor in submission. Two men enter, Pepe and his uncle, Señor Muerte, and Bernarda presents Angustias to Pepe. Coercion fills the moment of betrothal: Bernarda and the uncle slowly force Pepe and Angustias to kneel in symbolic accord, then rise; the younger couple falls limply into the arms of their elders. They recover to lead a mournful procession out of the house, followed by the Alba family swaying as before. Defying her mother's glance, Adela remains behind to dance out her frustration in a solo of barely modulated constriction.

Adela's dance conveys immaturity through its overdrawn description of impotent anger. The dancer emotes, carrying much of her expressive power in her hands, at times extending them tensely outward, toward the heavens, at other times holding them at her throat as if to choke herself or clenching them tightly into fists and pounding feebly against the chairs. In a burst of assertive action, she knocks over the row of chairs, and Pepe suddenly appears. Tentatively, the lovers tread toward each other to furtively caress each other's face, pausing only to look for interlopers. Convinced of their seclusion, they dance the central duet of the ballet.

Their pas de deux is constructed almost entirely from lifts, many of the balanced positions adapted from *Blues Suite* and *Revelations*. Balanced on Pepe's thigh, Adela reaches outward with an arm and leg three times, a sequence borrowed from "Backwater Blues." Still balanced on his leg, she reaches upward in a high arabesque position, the closing image of "Fix Me, Jesus." Pepe lies on his back and Adela balances above him, supported at her shoulders and raised legs, the striking levitation from "Fix Me, Jesus." In this context, the balanced positions convey Adela's desire to escape the earthly prison of Bernarda's household, to float away on wings of Pepe's love. The choreographic structure also underscores Adela's naïveté, in each instance keeping her from looking directly at Pepe.

The lovers end in each other's arms on the floor, where they are discovered by Adela's sisters. Creeping onstage, their faces hidden by their shawls, the sisters entrap the lovers with a series of fast turning motions and sharply accented, jabbing extensions of arms and legs. At the entrance of Bernarda and Señor Muerte, a momentary freeze of stage action, timed to coincide with a crashing orchestral flourish, brings the power of the elders into sharp relief. Bernarda and Señor Muerte drag the lovers apart, but Pepe escapes to run into the streets of the town.

The ballet follows Pepe into the town square, where he dances a stylized entreaty for happiness using gestures borrowed from classical Spanish dance: heel stomps, flamboyant kicking flourishes ending in drops to the knees, and a recurrent stance with the arms curved overhead while the back is released majestically forward. Six men bearing five blood-red chairs enter and surround him, threatening him obliquely. Again he escapes, running away as the three Fates enter the space, now transformed by lighting and gesture into a whorehouse/saloon.

Events in the saloon reveal a culture of machismo, driven by men who dance for each other and the attentions of the three Fates. Searching for Pepe, Adela interrupts a long divertissement danced by the rowdy, posturing men in the saloon. The men steal her shawl and taunt her before allowing her to escape. Bernarda follows closely on Adela's heels, her entrance to the saloon prompting the hurried exit of the three Fates and the dissolution of the scene. This saloon interlude provides a heightened context for Bernarda's belligerent matriarchy, her very presence strong enough to obliterate the men's rambunctiousness.

Angustias and her sisters steal onstage from all corners of the space, each entering the town square with an outstretched hand shaking at the side of her mouth to signify questioning and emotional confusion. Bernarda leads them in a furious dance of wrath, attacking the space with a tautly held body, at times writhing and rolling on the floor in indignant rage. The daughters kneel behind their mother and gesticulate toward the heavens in unison motions of fear and distress. Señor Muerte approaches, unsuccessful in his attempt to find Pepe, and Bernarda threatens him with a series of dramatic postures and flamboyant kicks, goading him into action. He races offstage, followed by Bernarda, who whirls her shawl in the air like a bullfighter's cape.

The pursuit of Pepe and Adela occurs amid a set piece of social dances performed by three townsmen and the three Fates in their earthly incarnation as women of the street. Adela and Pepe pass through this erotic carnival, searching for without finding each other. Wielding a knife, Señor Muerte leads a trio of men through the landscape of couples, and the chase mounts chaotically through a series of dovetailed crossings. Pepe and Adela finally meet in a lift that echoes the opening gesture of the ballet's prelude. In a surreal turn, the lovers are married by the town priest, who bears his cross and tree branch, their hurried ceremony witnessed by two of the women of the street. The chaos abates for a short dance of lyrical joy by the lovers, built from gently rising, falling, and swaying motions. Unlike their previous duet, the couple now dance together, seeing each other.

A hail of melodramatic action moves the ballet toward its inevitable tragedy. The lovers are discovered and separated by a sudden rush of the entire company. Led by Bernarda and Señor Muerte, the crowd encircles Pepe and Adela at opposite sides of the town square, at one point raising them aloft to reach, impotently, toward each other. In a flurry of action, Adela breaks free and escapes. Pepe is held, and an angered Señor Muerte stabs him in the stomach. Adela returns, grabs the knife, and tries to kill herself, but Bernarda intercedes. The women struggle until Adela wins the knife and stabs herself, rolling to die atop Pepe.

The final scene of the ballet describes Bernarda's emotional breakdown. In heaving gestures of newly minted physical anguish, she cries out in agony toward the heavens. The priest enters and reveals through gesture that he had married the couple, adding to Bernarda's dismay. The dead couple is borne aloft by the men and carried offstage, followed by the others in a physical recapitulation of the opening procession of mourning. Bernarda remains behind, emotionally bruised and unable to follow the group. The three Fates enter, and Bernarda rushes to them, irrationally seeking comfort. The women ignore her, and the ballet ends with Bernarda center stage, crumpled and distraught, writhing and sobbing on the ground. The three Fates assume their opening poses of implacable authority as the curtain falls.

Drawn as a broad series of vignettes, *Feast of Ashes* endures, like Lorca's play, as a "photographic document" of life in and around Bernarda Alba's home.[6] Ailey's ballet is rich in visual imagery, with any single moment full of carefully crafted compositional design. The creative use of props as agents of scenic transformation offers a fluid solution to the problem of frequently shifting locales.

Prominent among the successful narrative expansions of Lorca's play in Ailey's original libretto is the ballet's final depiction of Bernarda's emotional collapse. The ending allows for a sympathetic, humanistic portrayal of the mother's tyranny, a dimension virtually denied in Lorca's play.

Critics recognized the ballet's looseness with regard to Lorca's central plot points of Pepe's betrothal to Angustias, and the rather sketchy conception of Pepe himself, "who was too much of a cardboard figure for one who is such a dominating factor in the lives of them all."[7] Clive Barnes noted the freedom of Ailey's adaptation, which resulted in "a dance phantasmagoria of a girl caught between family duty, mother church and sexual desire."[8] As a whole, critics writing at the time of its premiere praised Ailey's achievement of a "personal form of expression, using modern movement naturally based on a firm substructure of the academic classical vocabulary."[9]

After the success of *Feast of Ashes*, Ailey outlined a ballet based on Lorca's *Blood Wedding*. According to his notes, he planned this second Lorca ballet for his own company, casting himself in the pivotal role of Leonardo.[10] *Blood Wedding* was never produced.

Ailey began his next ballet during the summer of 1964 at Harkness's Rhode Island retreat. Completed in the fall of 1964, *Ariadne* (12 March 1965) premiered at the Opéra Comique in Paris as part of a fund-raising project for "L'Association Franco-Amèricaine Atlantique, an organization to strengthen cultural ties between France and the United States."[11] Ailey collaborated with composer Andre Jolivet on the libretto for the ballet, with some material surely borrowed from the choreographer's earlier dance detailing the battle of Theseus and the Minotaur, *Labyrinth* (1963). Created to feature ballerina Marjorie Tallchief, the ballet depicted the legend from the point of view of its title character.

Danced by the newly formed Harkness Ballet, which was composed largely of dancers from the temporarily disbanded Joffrey Ballet, *Ariadne* made its strongest effects through processionals and "scenic pageantry."[12] The dance began with the birth of the Minotaur from Pasiphae's womb. Depicted as "a 10-foot naked-breasted priestess of Crete, long hair flying about her white face . . . writhing and twisting,"[13] Pasiphae raised her left arm majestically, then contracted and circled her torso faster and faster until the Minotaur popped out from between her legs.

According to reviews, photographs, and a rehearsal film made in 1967, Ailey employed a wealth of stage props, including a throng of men bearing large flags on poles, an elaborate litter that bore Theseus at his first entrance, and a series of red ribbons stretched across the stage to represent Ariadne's thread out of the labyrinth. According to Ailey's notes, Ariadne had three costume changes during the ballet. On her first entrance, she wore an oversized cape attended by two ladies-in-waiting.[14]

Ailey and Jolivet's strongest innovation came in extending the libretto to follow Ariadne's story after Theseus kills the Minotaur. Theseus celebrated his victory with Ariadne, then deserted her, leaving her alone for a final solo of anguished solitude. The ballet ended with Pasiphae's menacing indictment of Ariadne as responsible for her own fate, expressed in a powerful single pointing gesture. Abandoned and spent, Ariadne collapsed to the floor.

Ariadne allowed Ailey to frame the pathetic despair of a love-driven woman with the grand pageantry and theatrical monsters of Greek mythology. Tallchief garnered consistently strong reviews in the title role, which Ailey designed to complement her considerable acting and dance abilities. To convey the half-man, half-beast motivations of the Minotaur and his several minions, Ailey relied on a "primitive" movement vocabulary: feet planted firmly apart with knees bent, the upper body undulating in sinuous waves, extended balances and jumping sequences performed with turned-in legs and flexed feet. Costumed with considerable flair by Broadway designer Theoni Aldridge, the dance remained in the Harkness Ballet repertory for several years.

Rebekah Harkness paid Ailey handsomely for his efforts, and he enjoyed the opulence of both her ballet company's Watch Hill studio and frequent high-profile European engagements.[15] In an interview, however, he admitted a pedagogic difference between ballet dancers and modern dancers: "It was very had working with these kids. I'm so used to working with our own kids and literally wrenching something out of them. But these classical kids just stood around in rehearsal just waiting to be shown what to do. It's a hard life."[16] At the very least, Ailey showed the ballet dancers how to project tension and palpable despair through his blending of classical and modern dance techniques.

Ailey returned to the Harkness company a year later to create two new works: *Macumba* (11 May 1966) and *El Amor Brujo* (8 June 1966). Both works featured dancers from Ailey's own company, absorbed for the season into the Harkness Ballet. Neither work attracted critical or audience enthusiasm.

Ailey imagined *Macumba* as an "evocation of the sea goddess" Yemanja, a meditation on "her fatal charm [and] the legend of the sirens."[17] He created the dance to feature Judith Jamison as the goddess, partnered by Avind Harum as Xangô, and a large corps including Ailey company dancers Miguel Godreau and Morton Winston. Rebekah Harkness composed the score, and José Capuletti created a series of extravagant Brazilian carnival costumes for the ballet.

Ailey researched the dance during his company's brief trip to Brazil in 1963. He surely intended the dance as an homage to the transfigured Yoruban deities and an extension of his personal exploration of Afro-Brazilian fetish worship. But *Macumba* aroused slight attention. A rehearsal film of the twenty-eight-minute work reveals the components of a formidable ballet: considerable use of kaleidoscopically shifting groups of dancers; rhythmically sophisticated, low-to-the-ground passages; myriad hip-swaying variations, staged in processionals for men, women, and couples; a fight sequence between two men set within a rite of possession; and several sections featuring the powerful jumping abilities of Godreau. Given time, Ailey certainly might have pared the dance down to a compact, workable format; as performed for a single Harkness season, however, *Macumba* "rambled."[18]

Ailey fared worse with *El Amor Brujo* (8 June 1966). A vehicle for Marjorie Tallchief, partnered by Miguel Godreau leading a company of twelve, the dance "never came to life."[19] Performed for a single week on a makeshift outdoor stage at the Paris Festival of the Marais, *El Amor Brujo* could not rise above its "unfortunate outdoor setting, plus threatening rain."[20] The dance disappeared quickly.

Ailey made incidental dances for the premiere of Samuel Barber's *Anthony and Cleopatra* (16 September 1966), the opening production at the new Metropolitan Opera House at New York's Lincoln Center. Working with dancers from the Metropolitan Opera Ballet, Ailey's slight contribution to the opera occupied "a hectic four-minute dash on a Roman galley . . . with the girls as very decorative galley slaves, all sinuous writhing and chiffon. The episode opened with sailors . . . entering and waving a few banners in a manner reminiscent of Mr. Ailey's ballet *l'Ariadne*."[21] Ailey's "agreeable" choreography added to the overwhelming pomp of the opening night, but, as Walter Terry observed, "the dancing in *Anthony and Cleopatra* is truly trifling, and the only point in even talking about it at all is that it represented Alvin Ailey's debut as a choreographer at the Met."[22]

Sallie Wilson and Keith Lee in Alvin Ailey's *The River*, 1970.
Photograph by Martha Swope

▌ Black Dancer, White Dance

Can we consider a postcolonial theory of the dancing body? What would it look like? Whom might it serve? Would we do better to consider postcolonial representations of the body on stage? But what of the dancing bodies themselves? Do dancing bodies perform cultural identity only as representation, in the ways that audiences see them? Or can we actually consider the ways that dancers mean to embody cultural identities through their motions? Can dance construct itself, in a generative fashion, in its very gestures, or is it always circumscribed by the peculiar geographic, historical, and racialized circumstances of its performance?

Ailey's gambit to achieve a wide visibility for black dancers involved the actual dance techniques he explored. His success was not solely related to the fact of his black dancers in concert halls and on opera house stages; it stemmed also from his use of classical ballet as a means of expression. Balletic carriage allowed Ailey's dancers a way to be seen that was familiar to their largest audiences. Significantly, the company's discreet use of ballet did not distance it from its growing middle-class African American audience.

An African American presence in classical ballet, unequivocally confirmed by the founding of Arthur Mitchell's Dance Theatre of Harlem in 1969, grew slowly alongside general American interest in the European form of theatrical stage dancing.[23] During the 1960s, as Ailey's company struggled toward financial security, painfully few opportunities existed for African American dancers to achieve careers in professional ballet. Although classical ballet fit into assimilationist scenarios of African American upward mobility, in reality it attracted only a small African American audience nationwide. Black audiences may have welcomed the opportunity to confirm common aesthetic ideals with the whites who loved ballet, but the pervasive lack of black representation on ballet stages eventually squashed the hope for a committed black ballet audience. Ballet technique, in and of itself, is not racist, but the people who teach it, as well as its company managers, artistic directors, patrons, critics, and choreographers, live in a racist society and succumb to its vicissitudes.[24]

More than this, ballet's basic aesthetic is not necessarily of continual interest to black audiences. If ballet is concerned with lightness, unbroken flow, the illusion of effortlessness, and, physically, a rigid torso that moves as one piece, maybe it cannot, on its own, offer a satisfying corporeal paradigm to African diaspora dancers and audiences. Africanist dance values downward-directed energy, insistent rhythmicity, angularity of line, the percussive rupture of underlying flow, individualism within a group dynamic, and access to a dynamic "flash of the spirit" that is spontaneous and unpredictable. Its core styles diverge neatly from ballet's conception of strictly codified body line, a silenced and motionless audience, and movement as metaphoric abstraction.

Still, Ailey assumed that the benefits of ballet technique outweighed its liabilities and that it could somehow be folded into a mix of dance techniques for his dancers and his audiences. For Ailey, balletic carriage meant majestic black bodies, bodies endowed with opened trunks and lifted sternums, highly developed balance, and the effortless lifting and full extension of legs and feet. Unlike Mitchell's Dance Theatre of Harlem, Ailey felt no need to constantly prove the ability of black bodies to inhabit ballet technique. In works he made for his own company, he incorporated ballet as a movement idiom equivalent to Horton, Dunham, and Graham techniques. This mixing allowed the company to remain inflected as "black," even as occasional balletic stances afforded it a visual currency with Europeanist forms of dance representation. Over time, the function of ballet technique in Ailey's work took center stage or moved back into the wings according to the dancers in the company.

As it grew, Ailey's company became one of the largest proponents of balletic line in modern dance. Other choreographers resisted the arrival of ballet as a technique basic to modern dance expression; modern dance had been born of a rejection of ballet, and its dancers typically worked to reveal rather than conceal the body's effort and weight. Graham, Horton, and Humphrey had each developed a technique that positioned the visible manipulation of weight as a cornerstone of dance training, and Ailey's early works exploited these techniques in their visible effort. But when (white) postmodern artists emerged from downtown New York dance spaces like the Judson Church in the 1960s, their emphasis on everyday bodies without recognizable dance training veered sharply from Ailey's interest in heightened dance technique and theatrical spectacle. This divide widened, and by 1975 Martha Graham explained to the *New York Times* that "ballet dancers learn by line instead of volume," and "modern dance is a different idiom—it's like playing a different instrument."[25] During this period, Ailey's company, marginalized by racism and, ironically, its overt interest in sharing dance with a wide general public, moved steadily toward ballet as a foundational technique.

Two works revived by the Ailey company traded in neoclassical balletic invention: Louis Johnson's *Lament* (1953; revived Alvin Ailey American Dance Theater 1964; revived, second version, Alvin Ailey American Dance Theater 1985) and John Butler's *After Eden* (1966; revived Alvin Ailey American Dance Theater 1974; revived Alvin Ailey American Dance Theater 1999). Johnson's work, set to two selections of Heitor Villa-Lobos's *Bachianas Brasileiras*, told a story of romantic love rent asunder by the implacable will of mysterious social "keepers," a community of elders who, for reasons not divulged in the ballet, separate a young couple. Butler's *After Eden* described the relationship between Adam and Eve after their expulsion from the Garden of Eden. In this short pas de deux, set to a commissioned score by Lee Hoiby, Adam and Even dance alternately with and against each other in an effort to decide their own fate as individuals.

The leading female roles in both of these works were performed on pointe at times, a decided rarity for the Ailey company. Because classical ballet in general, and pointe work in particular, had been defined as "white" idioms for most audiences, Ailey's black dancers staged the "ruins" of colonialist encounter as they worked through these mythic tales of romance on pointe. For audiences who viewed the Ailey company as bearers of a native blackness, these works enacted a suture of the black (pre)modern dancer and the white classical dance that, presumably, both amazed and confounded. For audiences attendant to the limits of modernism, modern dancers performing on pointe signaled an ending of the modern as a singular construction in dance. In the context of the Ailey company's diverse repertory, which might have included neo-African works, jazz dances, or abstract modern works on the program with either the Johnson or Butler works, these pointe performances sounded a postmodernist playfulness in their alignment of formal techniques toward an end of "American Dance Theater."

When postmodern dance emerged on stages in the 1960s, its aesthetic concerns veered sharply from the highly trained physicality and narrative storytelling that Ailey's company routinely achieved. Still, Ailey's repertory and its embodied hybridity—in terms of diverse racial identities and movement techniques—predicted postmodern, if not postcolonial, assemblage as an aesthetic resource. By the 1980s, postmodern dance shifted profoundly, and its leading choreographers leaned into the individualistic virtuosity that ballet training provided and, not coincidentally, Ailey's dancers had long accomplished. By now, ballet is universally regarded as a useful tool in modern dance training and choreography. In at least one analysis, then, Ailey's company embodied a postcolonial theory of dance practice long before the idea gained academic currency.

▌ The River

Ailey achieved his greatest success on a company other than his own in his 1970 collaboration with composer Duke Ellington for American Ballet Theatre. *The River* (25 June 1970) premiered as a work-in-progress with six sections: "Spring," "Lake," "Vortex," "Falls," "Riba (Mainstream)," and "Two Cities." In June 1971 an expanded version of the dance added "Meander," "Giggling Rapids," a duet entitled "The Sea," and a reprise of "Spring." By 1972, *The River* achieved its final format of eight sections: "Spring," "Meander," "Giggling Rapids," "Lake," "Falls," "Vortex," "Riba (Mainstream)," and "Two Cities."

Ellington conceived the score as a programmatic contemplation of the life of a young man "who grows from childhood through the phases of water into maturity, finally emerging as a glorious, full human being."[26] Ellington included extensive program notes describing all thirteen sections of the score in his 1973 autobiography *Music Is My Mistress*; however, it is highly unlikely that Ailey consulted these notes at all during the frantic choreographic process.[27] Ailey, who usually choreographed in response to existing music, received the score in bits and pieces, with the bulk of material arriving after rehearsals had already begun.[28] Rushed, and aware of the pressure to produce something extraordinary for the high-profile American Ballet Theatre, Ailey rose to the occasion to create a work that both confirmed his own mature hybrid aesthetic and conformed to an emergent Africanist standard of choreography. The work has been revived often for several companies, including American Ballet Theatre, the Alvin Ailey American Dance Theater, the Pennsylvania Ballet, and the Dance Theatre of Harlem.

Choreographed in suite form, the abstract ballet describes the flow of a river from stream to estuary. Ailey interprets the water metaphor as a facet of human coupling, with prominent gestures of awakening desire, courtship, jealousy, and loving providing continuity among its sections. In the opening, "Spring," a man rises from the ground, born into a pool of light in a corner of the stage. His tentative awakening and tremulous first steps are set against the extended movements of fourteen paired corps dancers, representing a stream already in motion, who enter in waves from the side of the stage. They represent life in motion; the single man, an immature being born through the water's flow.

The soloist crawls, pulling himself along on the ground with his elbows, rolls on his back, and finally rises, managing a series of increasingly confident sideward balances. Having discovered his gait, he runs across the stage with abandon, joyfully jumping and turning with his arms raised high overhead. The ensemble dancers form a wedge behind the newborn man, and for a moment, he leads them forward, skittering on his knees, pushing against the space in front of him with his open hands. Moving their arms in waves, the ensemble follows him, reaching downward, upward, and forward, their rhythmically layered gestures forming an oscillating visual pattern behind the man. In this opening section, the newborn man's movements build on modern dance conventions of everyday gesture and the visible release of breath, while the ensemble maintains a classical balletic carriage of held upper body and full extension of the limbs.

William Carter and members of the American Ballet Theatre in
Alvin Ailey's *The River*, 1970. Photograph by Martha Swope

The two physical vocabularies suggest a conflict of idioms that is not resolved by
the dance.

In other sections, Ailey's choreography surprised audiences by teasing the
star system of ballet protocol with startling movement juxtapositions. He made
"Giggling Rapids" for American Ballet Theatre principal dancers Natalie
Makarova and Erik Bruhn as a frothy parody of the virtuosic exhibitionism inherent in pas de deux convention. After a bristling entrance of dynamic balances
interrupted by fast, running steps, the woman stops dancing to pose, noticeably

149

bored, as the man indulges in a series of flamboyant leaps. He gestures her off-stage with a flip of his hand and continues a solo built from the contrast of child-ish skipping steps, turns performed with the working leg held in various paral-lel and turned-out positions, and big jumps embellished with multiple beats. The dancer consistently underscores his technical bravado with playful joking and ends his variation by pretending to fall off balance and offstage.

The couple continues through a series of flagrant juxtapositions: jazz walks, sinking into the floor with a leading hip, followed by unexpected leaps set with frantic abandon off the beat, and Horton-inspired tilts to the side, interrupted by dynamic turns timed to stop precisely with musical accents. At one point, the man supports the woman as she strikes a balance in arabesque, only to be swat-ted away by his triumphantly poised partner. The dancers express giddy play-fulness in terms of exaggeration: overarticulated beats of the feet, flamboyantly oversized port de bras, and patently unballetic shimmies of the shoulder.

The musical and choreographic centerpiece of *The River* is "Lake," a lush adagio created for Cynthia Gregory partnered, originally, in alternate casting, by Ivan Nagy, Gayle Young, and Marcos Paredes leading an ensemble of fourteen. Ailey's staging complements the romantic quality of Ellington's music, described in the composer's autobiography thus:

> *THE LAKE:* The lake is beautiful and serene. It is all horizontal lines that offer up unrippled reflections. There it is, in all its beauty, God-made and untouched, until people come—people who are God-made and terribly touched by the beauty of the lake. They, in their admira-tion for it, begin to discover new faces of compatibility in each other, and as a romantic viewpoint develops, they indulge themselves. The whole situation compounds itself into an emotional violence that is even greater than that of the violence of the vortex to come. The lake supports them until, suddenly, they are over the top and down.[29]

The dance begins with a solo for Gregory, clad simply in an aqua leotard, short rehearsal skirt, white tights, and pointe shoes. She enters from the side, stepping onstage into a high arabesque balance with her head arched dramati-cally backward, her left arm directed away from her torso to echo the ramrod-straight line of her raised leg. She wears her hair down, and its free motion ac-centuates the lyrical sway of her attack. Her solo features a recurrent "water bearer" posture, an arabesque balance with one arm held in front of the body as if holding a vessel of water. Several times she performs a harrowing pitch toward the ground: balanced on one pointe, she hurls her torso forward, holding her arms along her thighs, and reaching upward with her back leg. The movement would be difficult partnered; performed solo, its kinesthetic impact startles.

In several extant films of this section, Gregory dances with a combination of clear precision and abandon, a synthesis of technique and style that suits Ai-ley's choreographic method. Her articulation of body line brings forward sub-tle distinctions in movement idiom and allows her to achieve a lyrical synthesis of classical ballet positions, jazz walks, floor work, and upper-body contraction.

She connects the movements easily with cool authority, imbuing them with the sort of generous flow Ailey regularly expected from his own dancers.

Ellington's score for "Lake" develops a two-part melodic theme set in alternating minor and major modes. Ailey's choreography develops this binary as a tension between romantic partners. A shirtless man enters suddenly from the side of the stage. The woman becomes wary, discarding her lyrical freedom to move with sharpened precision, retreating from his pursuit. He reaches her and manipulates her into a series of awkward, sharply angled positions. Eventually she surrenders to his advances to dance with, rather than against, him. Her acquiescence is timed to a melodic swell and release into a major mode articulation of the musical theme.

Ailey's humanistic staging for "Lake" treats the corps de ballet as a consensual community rather than a company of dancers, who bestow ritual authority on Gregory and her partner as leaders of a tender, erotic rite. An ensemble of fourteen unitard-clad couples enters from both sides, with the men carrying the women overhead in a stiff sculptural pose. As the men set the women onto the ground, their movements soften, and the ensemble encircles the principal couple, moving in soft, blurry waves of acknowledgment, undulating gently as they kneel and stand with their arms about each other. The leading couple kneels and embraces; the ensemble echoes their motions. Like ripples on a small pond set in motion by a skipping stone, the ensemble members rush away from the center, then bounce off the shore; they lie on their backs encircling the principal couple to move their arms and legs in a suggestion of rolling water emanating from the pool's center. As Ellington's score rises in rhythmic intensity with the addition of conga drumming, the ensemble partners up for an interlude of sensual lovemaking. Two same-sex couples dance in this sequence, positioned in the foreground of the stage, directly in front of the principal couple. The actual sequence of movements differs for each couple here, underscoring a humanistic portrayal of individualized sensuality. Led by the principals center stage, all of the couples rise from the floor for a final gesture of catharsis: facing each other, they stand close, holding outstretched hands at their partner's hips. In a gesture of consummation, timed to a prominent swelling of the score, they lean together at the pelvis while stretching their heads backward. "Lake" ends with the ensemble crowded around the principal couple, consecrating first the woman and then the man with a lift upward, and finishing with the woman standing with one hand raised toward the heavens as the others fall, languidly, to the ground.

Ellington's spare "Vortex" features percussive outbursts of arpeggiated chords sounded against an incessant snare drum roll. Ailey's choreography matches the angular oscillations of the score with a virtuosic woman's solo designed to test the balance and rhythmic ability of its dancer. Composed mostly of whirling motions interrupted by steely sculptural poses, the dance demands a focused, hard-edged precision in complete contrast to the preceding "Lake."[30]

The virtuoso demands of "Falls" offer male counterpart to "Vortex" in a pure dance variation for four men. The dance is arranged according to Ailey's preferred short-dance ground plan: an opening for the quartet, followed by contrasting solos for each of the men, and rounded out by a short, unison coda. Unlike the male variations of "In the Evening" of *Blues Suite* or "Sinner Man" of *Revelations*, however, "Falls" is shorn of dramatic narrative; it is explicitly concerned with the technical rendering of densely ordered virtuosic feats.

As *The River* continues, its Africanist hallmarks become more pronounced from both Ellington and Ailey. Where "Lake" forces the American Ballet Theatre dancers to "play gay" in discreet sequences of same-sex partnering, "Riba (Mainstream)" demands that the dancers "play black" in a jokey parody of Cotton Club routines and the cygnets of *Swan Lake*. Mining a tradition of derisive dance as parody, "Riba" signifies on stereotypical modes of public black performance suggested by Ellington's hard-swing, twelve-bar blues.[31]

To a thumping rhythmic motif, a male trickster character enters (Dennis Nahat in the original production), performing an exaggerated hipster walk. Hunched over from the waist, he ambles onstage, gesticulating feverishly with his arms and wagging his hips with each step. He stops to gesture toward the wings, and a row of four women prances on, their arms linked at the shoulders, chorus-girl style. Three other groups enter the stage in this manner: two rows of men and another row of women, each group performing a rhythmically complex traveling sequence marked by an exaggerated sway of the hip.

The trickster orchestrates the dance, prancing from one group to the next, joining into their motion as he pleases, and indicating, by gesture, changes in direction and placement on the stage. As he jitterbugs and bunny hugs, rummaging through a catalogue of 1940s social dances, the four lines of dancers move contrapuntally across the space in a visual representation of comping figures played against the score's persistent rhythmic bounce. At times, the trickster joins the group as they gather for a unison passage; eventually, he leads the ensemble men in a kickline across the front of the stage. As the women move offstage, their arms linked in front of their bodies in a parody of the celebrated *Swan Lake* swans, the men cavort through Rockette-style high kicks. The trickster directs them to exit, and he finishes his dance bopping toward the upstage horizon, pausing to wave goodbye to the audience along the way.

The River follows the giddiness of "Riba" with the solemnity of "Two Cities," a gospel hymn of reconciliation. A man and a woman are discovered on opposite ends of the stage, reaching and grasping as they try to move toward each other but seemingly trapped in stationary pools of light. They dance in complementary waves of rising and falling breath, the man often pausing in immobile stances while the woman gestures ornately through eddies of fluid motion. Their gestures visually balance the slow, steady pulse of Ellington's score.

Eventually, the dancers meet in the center for a short pas de deux. The woman gives herself to the man, allowing him to manipulate her through a series of exquisite arching positions and balances. At one point, he supports her on his turned-out thigh, then passes her body, limb by limb, over his head. The woman arches backward toward the floor, revolving in acrobatic slow motion until she lands in a fully extended penché arabesque at his side. Unlike the combative partners of "Lake" or the joking partners of "Giggling Rapids," the partnership of "Two Cities" suggests yielding acquiescence in consensually defined roles for man and woman.

The ensemble enters singly in the background of the scene to pulse up and down individually, creating another pattern of gentle oscillation. The principal couple continue their duet of romantic deliverance, finding their way into a floor-bound position quoted directly from "Fix Me, Jesus" of *Revelations*. As the music swells to a sweeping finale, the couple reaches toward each other only to be repelled by the massed ensemble—now representing the river—which moves between them. The man and woman fall to the floor at the sides of the stage, separated as at the beginning of the dance, with the stoic river frozen between them as the curtain falls.

The original casting of "Two Cities" featured white ballerina Sallie Wilson and black dancer Keith Lee, with the other (all-white) dancers of American Ballet Theatre as the angry river that separates them. Several critics commented on the racial implications of the casting: writing for *Newsweek*, Hubert Saal observed that "their pas de deux, touching in the complexity of intertwined limbs and intricate lifts, makes a wordless comment that lays waste racial distinctions."[32] The adjustments Ailey effected to "Two Cities" when he revived the dance for his own company in 1981 support the assertion that he intended the casting as a commentary on race relations. In the later version, typically performed by two dancers of similar hue, the partners perform a stuttering motion toward each other, with one foot edging along the floor as the other, stationary leg holds them apart. The movement makes explicit powerful external forces that separate the dancers, forces that hold them at bay in distinct sections of the stage. When Ailey originally choreographed the work for African American dancer Lee, he may have assumed that these forces were intimated by Lee's very presence onstage with Wilson as a member of the American Ballet Theatre. "Two Cities" offered racial collaboration—and its collapse at the hands of a white mainstream—as the logical ending point to a work describing the flow of life on a historically segregated American ballet stage.

In all, *The River* explored several grand themes that resonated deeply for Ailey: human interaction, the nature of desire, flow and its inevitable rupture, and the utopian possibility of a world without stylistic limits in terms of its musical score or movement idiom. Each of these themes fit Ailey's career-long project to enlarge possibilities for dancers and audiences to consider public portrayals of African American subjectivity, same-sex desire as a facet of community, the necessity of the "break" as a component of continuity, and the promise of play to release social power. In terms of length and ambition, the work rivaled *Revelations* with its tiers of casting and as a sustained suite that gathered power cumulatively.

The work also provided a dramatic exercise in scale, as the vast architecture of Ellington's score offered a slippery ground for the various solos, duets, and trios of Ailey's staging. For example, "Meander," the second section of the work, features a trio, in which two men alternately partner a woman as a playful representation of a curving tributary. Ellington's score here sounds a full-bodied bellowing, low-register, rhythmic call repeatedly answered by delicate, arrhythmic solo flute passages. The dancers, alternating partners and movement sensibilities as if in conversation with the score, shift frequently from portentously weighted strides to light bourées, the whole requiring broad physical projection. The total effect of the sequence, echoed at least in "Lake" and "Two Cities," suggests the fragility of human gesture framed by the rushing flow of orchestral jazz.

With *The River*, Ailey and Ellington provided American Ballet Theatre a historical sampling of African American modes of dance performance. The work challenged its dancers to engage a range of performance strategies beyond their traditional ken, in, for example, Horton-inspired tilting motions, versions of African American social dances, and sequences of bald humor and sensuality. In an interview, Ailey admitted his pleasure in challenging dancers Natalie Makarova and Erik Bruhn with Africanist demands of physical polycentrism:

> The first days of rehearsal were really hilarious, because she's so used to having every *finger*—I mean, "One is here, two is here," and I was saying, "Now it's one and a two and a three and . . ." and she just sort of "Oh!" Erik jumped right in and just started *doing* it. . . . It can be a *shock*, to a classical dancer, moving the hips, moving the joints in a certain way, which they are taught to *freeze*, so imagine being taught that for twenty years and somebody comes and says, "Pull your hips out; move your head over like this!"[33]

Critics noted the expansive virtuosity of Ailey and Ellington's collaboration with American Ballet Theatre. Writing for the *New York Times*, Clive Barnes compared the dance favorably to *Revelations*, citing its overall "ease and style," its "blend of classic ballet, modern dance and jazz movement, [to make] a most rewarding hybrid." Among other flattering reports, Harriett Johnson of the *New York Post* commented on Ailey and Ellington's achievement of "a fluid, cumulative structure and vivid suggestive power."[34]

Ailey and Ellington's efforts were not unilaterally appreciated, however, and more than one ballet critic seemed dismayed that Ellington and Ailey had arrived at American Ballet Theatre. Writing for *Dance News*, Nancy Goldner asserted that "the main problem is the music, which is diffuse and self-conscious, as though aware that its subject matter (life) is Important, and trying to be symphonic in content as well as in sound. The score is pompous and the worst thing, quasisymphonic. Accordingly, the ballet lacks punctuation and a sense of boundary."[35] Goldner doesn't support her definition of "quasisymphonic" musical pomposity, or how she determines the music to be "self-conscious" for Ellington's oeuvre; not surprisingly, these two claims are seldom in evidence in the voluminous Ellington scholarship. The unwarranted virulence of Goldner's attack on Ellington, echoed by several white ballet critics, implies judgments and concerns beyond the particulars of *The River*.

Ailey revised *The River* twice, when he restaged the ballet for the classically shaped Ballet Internacional de Caracas in 1978, and then again for his own company in 1981. For the Caracas company, he endorsed a "Latin translation" of the piece, set to a "re-orchestrated" score with Latin rhythmic underpinnings.[36] For his own company, Ailey shifted "Falls" to follow "Lake," undoubtedly to provide his male dancers some measure of rest before "Riba," and made subtle choreographic alterations in each section. For the most part, the changes simplified the technical demands of the dance while fleshing out its implied dramatic narratives. For example, in "Two Cities," the massed ensemble representing the river actually pushes the entwined dancers away from each other with an added wave of outstretched hands.

For Ailey, *The River* signaled a creative renewal, a stylistic and technical breakthrough in terms of its sweeping variety, grand scale, and comfort with classical idiom. His wry teasing of the balletic standard in "Giggling Rapids" and "Riba" subversively forced the American Ballet Theatre dancers to consider concert dance in an African American grain. For his part, Ailey recognized his growing interest in classical technique: "As a result, I think that I, too, have been affected by the ballet people; my own company now has become more balletic because I believe so strongly in the ballet technique. There's no doubt about it, there's the placement, alignment, the way they stretch; the kind of balance and line it gives you."[37] Around the time of his work with American Ballet Theatre, ballet class became a standard, daily technique required of dancers at the Ailey school and in the company.

Ailey worked with the City Center Joffrey Ballet during their 1971 season, overseeing a new production of *Feast of Ashes* and offering a world premiere ballet to the music of bassist Charles Mingus. *The Mingus Dances* (13 October 1971), subtitled "Five Dances and Four Episodes Suggested by the Music of American Composer Charles Mingus," enigmatically explored a representative sample of the bassist's music through a flamboyant juxtaposition of ballet and whiteface minstrelsy. A lengthy work, the ballet included veiled references to contemporary race relations, vaudeville and minstrel stage conventions, contrasting public and private personae, and events drawn from the composer's recently published autobiography.[38]

Ailey organized the dance strictly, separating its five pure dance episodes with four "vaudeville" episodes. Each section of the dance was titled according to its tempo marking and the name of its Mingus tune: "Dance No. 1: Andante Con Moto (Pithecanthropus Erectus)," followed by "Vaudeville: Prestissimo (O.P.)"; "Dance No. 2: Adagio Ma Non Troppo (Myself When I Am *Real*)," followed by "Vaudeville: Pesante (Freedom)"; "Dance No. 3: Lento Assai (Half-Mast Inhibition)," followed by "Vaudeville: Vivace (Dizzy's Moods)"; "Dance No. 4: Andantino (Diane)," followed by "Vaudeville: Scherzo (Ysable's Table Dance)"; and the final "Dance No. 5: Allegro Marcato (Haitian Fight Song)." The four vaudeville scenes took place "in one," on the front of the stage, replete with "colourful bright lights and dressy costumes" by Thomas Skelton and A. Christina Giannini, respectively, while the pure-dance episodes occurred in front of Edward Burbridge's "peacock-patterned [back]drop."[39]

No film of *The Mingus Dances* survives, but descriptions provided by puzzled critics, as well as a few production photographs, give a sense of the ballet's nightmarish substance. In the four vaudeville turns, a "nastily pert Southern belle treats her two escorts like performing dogs; a gang of cops strut and swing their billyclubs; a rather macabre group of doughboys salute and march and fall; a terrible nightclub flamenco trio snarl and stamp." Among the pure dance sections, a pas de deux featuring Christian Holder and Nancy Robinson seemingly casts Holder as "an angry ghetto youth who escapes death by murdering a white temptress in peacock feathers." Other sections "fade into existence behind a scrim," sometimes beginning with "a large, slowly moving cluster of bodies, which expands in soft, irregular spouts of movement."[40] A photograph of one of the pure dance sections reveals Dennis Wayne and Rebecca Wright in a familiar Ailey posture: Wayne balances Wright on his turned-out thigh as the ballerina arches magnificently upward toward the heavens.[41] In this photograph, Wright, in toe shoes, stands with both feet together, a subtle variation on Ailey's recurrent "elevated woman" choreographic gesture.

If, as several critics surmised, Ailey sought to satirize blackface stage conventions and contemporary race relations, *The Mingus Dances* failed. According to Lester Abelman of the *New York Daily News*, its flaws "center on the excessive length of the piece and the obscurity that results in some of the set pieces . . . because Ailey was apparently trying to make a statement. The statement remained unclear." Writing for the *New York Times*, Clive Barnes thought the dance "apparently sets out to portray two Americas—the America of America's own ideals and the tawdry gimcrack America of contemporary reality. Therefore we find the pure classic dances of heroes, interspersed with puppet-like comedy routines that grotesquely parody the more mechanical of life's attitudes. There is a great deal of symbolism here, but the symbolism seems to be either too obvious or too obscure."[42]

Clearly, *The Mingus Dances* embraced the discord between ballet and minstrelsy. Its greatest success may have been the public attention its performance provided Mingus and his music. Trombonist Alan Raph, assisted by Jaki Byard, expertly arranged the nine Mingus compositions for symphony orchestra, and jazz enthusiasts reveled in the spate of feature articles devoted to Mingus.[43] As a ballet attraction for the usual Joffrey audience, however, *The Mingus Dances* proved "long and complex, full of stunning moments and diverting little surprises, but on the whole too long and too complex."[44]

Ailey worked with the students of the Juilliard School to create dances for the world premiere of Virgil Thompson's *Lord Byron* (20 April 1972). Seven years in the making, the production, directed by John Houseman for the Juilliard American Opera Center, climaxed a series of tributes to the seventy-five-year-old composer.[45] Commissioned by the Ford and Koussevitzky Foundations, the opera speculated on the burning of Byron's memoirs, Byron's homosexuality and incestuous relationship with his half-sister, and the controversy around his burial, which had been refused by Westminster Abbey. Framed as a flashback, the opera begins and ends in the moment of Byron's death.

Ailey's significant contribution to the production included a fifteen-minute ballet in the third act that depicted the entirety of Byron's life in exile from England: "in Switzerland writing poetry, his beginning friendship with Shelley, carnivals and debaucheries in Venice, Shelley's drowning in a storm off Pisa," and "his own death of a fever at Missalonghi."[46] An admittedly "tough assignment," the ballet intended to "show the frantic quality of Byron's life after he has been renounced by his sister."[47] Favorably reviewed, the ballet made use of "a series of clever mirror dances" performed by Byron, Shelley, a contessa on toe, and a pageboy; its entirety "choreographed with a strong sense of structure and balletic flair."[48]

Ailey returned to American Ballet Theatre to stage *Sea Change* (26 October 1972), set to Benjamin Britten's "Four Sea Interludes" from *Peter Grimes*. American Ballet Theatre scheduled the ballet's New York premiere for 6 July 1972, but the dance was not presentable until later that fall.[49] It premiered in Washington, D.C. during the company's season at the Kennedy Center.

Sea Change embraced "themes of life, death and transcendent love to illustrate the very pictorial Britten music." The dance portrayed events in a village after a fisherman had drowned. To Britten's "Dawn," "women of the village, shawls covering their heads, mourn his death, as the men, hands linked, thread their way across the back of the stage." The second section, "Sunday Morning," introduced a woman—the fisherman's widow, portrayed by Sallie Wilson—"alone and remote" from a "whirling buoyant corps of young men," led by Fernando Bujones. Next, to "Moonlight," the woman and the fisherman's ghost, portrayed by Royes Fernandez, danced the work's central duet of tender love. The final, "Storm," brought back the ensemble for a finale in which "the Fisherman and his wife [were] lifted high surrounded by the grieving villagers."[50]

From Patricia Barnes's detailed description, the only extant account of the ballet, *Sea Change* seems to be a reworking of themes familiar to Ailey from *Feast of Ashes*: a rural community lamenting the passing of one of its members, with set pieces of mourning women contrasted with dances of masculine bravado. In photographs, Frank Thompson's tunic-style costumes for the men and a long, dark dress for Sallie Wilson suggest the contours of a mythic town pierced by the grief of loss. But Ailey allowed the *Sea Change* protagonists a false and rapturous ending. A small, lyric work that caused little excitement, *Sea Change* disappeared quickly.

Ailey staged the incidental dances for the Metropolitan Opera's new production of Georges Bizet's *Carmen* (18 September 1972). Conducted by Leonard Bernstein, the production followed the staging ideas of recently deceased Met general manager Goeran Gentele, who had died in an automobile accident before rehearsals began. Gentele had conceived a stylish, impressionistic production that eschewed naturalism; Ailey, accordingly, rethought the uses of Flamenco-derived movements in the opera: "When people think of Spanish dancing they think Flamenco, with high heels, standing on tables, toe and heel tapping. I am using bare feet."[51] Although the production garnered a favorable review in the *New York Times*,[52] Ailey's work went completely unremarked and undocumented.

Sallie Wilson and members of the American Ballet Theatre in Alvin
Ailey's *Sea Change*, 1972. Photograph by Judy Cameron

Ailey returned to the Metropolitan Opera to stage Virgil Thompson's *Four Saints in Three Acts* (20 February 1973). The work was produced for the Mini-Operas at the Met, a short-lived special project presented in the three-hundred-seat Forum Theater at Lincoln Center. Working on a small, three-quarter-round setting proved a hindrance for Ailey, who admitted to the *New York Times*, "I like a stage on which I can make very strong groupings."[53] The opera received a successful three-week run, with critics noting the "bold and free direction of Alvin Ailey, whose saints nimbly marched and turned," and Ailey's "Martha Gra-hamish dances, modest and simple."[54]

Ailey embodied a pioneering presence as an African American choreographer working frequently with American classical ballet companies. The commissions he made for these mostly white companies fed his impulse to create concert structures in which the dancing black body would be considered classical. Working with his own company, he capitalized on the technical strengths his dancers brought to him. On at least two occasions, these strengths included pointe technique, which Ailey employed in *Sonera* (1959) and *Archipelago* (1971). Although his usual choreographic strategy cultivated a strong coherence of dancer to dance, he sometimes became frustrated by the inability to predict precise body line. Working at times in the classical ballet idiom granted him access to a technique structured around specific postures. As Ailey's choreographic interests veered away from humanistic narratives and toward the abstract throughout the 1970s, ballet joined the lingua franca of required Ailey company training alongside Horton, Dunham, and Graham techniques.

EIGHT

Ailey Celebrates Ellington

In interviews, Ailey repeatedly stressed his goal of preserving a modern dance repertory of "great works": "Marvelous dances would disappear after one performance. So I decided that one of the things I wanted to do was to preserve works of modern dance so that we could have a showcase for it the way classical companies have for classical works. I started of course with the black choreographers because they were the most neglected."[1] By 1974, the Alvin Ailey American Dance Theater had revived a wide range of works originally made for other companies. These included *The Road of the Phoebe Snow* (1959, revival 1964) and *Come and Get the Beauty of It Hot* (1960, revival 1966) by Talley Beatty, "To José Clemente Orozco" (1953, revival 1964) and *The Beloved* (1947, revival 1964) by Lester Horton, Anna Sokolow's *Rooms* (1955, revival 1964), Joyce Trisler's *Journey* (1958, revival 1964), Lucas Hoving's *Icarus* (1964, revival 1964), *Lament* (1953, revival 1965) by Louis Johnson, Paul Sanasardo's *Metallics* (1964, revival 1966), Geoffrey Holder's *Adagio for a Dead Soldier* (1964, revival 1970), Brian Macdonald's *Time Out of Mind* (1962, revival 1971), Katherine Dunham's *Choros* (1943, revival 1972), Donald McKayle's *Rainbow 'round My Shoulder* (1959, revival 1972), Ted Shawn's *Kinetic Molpai* (1935, revival 1972), José Limón's *Missa Brevis* (1958, revival 1973), John Butler's *Carmina Burana* (1959, revival 1973) and *After Eden* (1966, revival 1974), and *Fanga* (1949, revived 1974) and *The Wedding*

(1951, revived 1974) by Pearl Primus.[2] In this revisionist practice, Ailey positioned his company as heir to a common legacy of work made by both white and black American choreographers. In many instances, these revivals inserted black dancers into works originally created on white dancers, furthering Ailey's mission to expand the range of material available to dancing black bodies. The strategy also allowed him to refigure the historical chronology of "great works" represented by his company's repertory to include neglected dances by African American artists.

Ailey's interest in the history of modern dance, especially its African American pioneers represented in his company's repertory, paralleled his interest in the history of African American musical forms, especially modern jazz. The classically trained jazz musicians Ailey collaborated with included Keith Jarrett, Jay McShann, Charles Mingus, Charlie Parker, Max Roach, and Mary Lou Williams. The bulk of Ailey's jazz ballets, however, were created to music by Ellington. By creating eleven ballets to music by Ellington, Ailey hoped to align his own ascent to that of his favorite composer.

▌ The Ellington Connection

By 1970, music critics regularly acknowledged Ellington's preeminence as an artist working beyond traditional categories of musicianship.[3] Ellington's sustained achievement as a resilient, celebrated, "official" representative of African American culture provided Ailey an enviable prototype of creative leadership, social savvy, and apparent personal fulfillment. According to Ellington associate Don George's biography, Ailey's esteem for Ellington grew considerably as they collaborated on *The River* in 1970: "One Afternoon Ailey said to me . . . 'He's become a model for me: a man who can lead his organization, with their background and history, and still go on and do the performances and find time in his life for new creative projects.'"[4]

Ellington's death on 24 May 1974 accelerated Ailey's plans for an Ellington festival of ballets to honor the composer at the nation's bicentennial in 1976.[5] Offered a commission by the CBS Festival of Lively Arts for Young People, Ailey created *Ailey Celebrates Ellington*, a one-hour special of six dances made for the young dancers of the newly formed Alvin Ailey Repertory Workshop. Hosted by popular singing star Gladys Knight and including cameo appearances by Ailey and veteran performer and teacher Fred Benjamin, the program was first telecast on Thanksgiving Day, 28 November 1974. Reviewed favorably by several television critics, the program included two long works later adapted for the stage, *Night Creature* and *The Mooche*, and several shorter pieces that disappeared after the television taping, "Such Sweet Thunder," "The Blues Ain't" from Ellington's 1943 *Black, Brown, and Beige*, "Sonnet for Caesar," and "Praise God and Dance," the finale of Ellington's *Second Sacred Concert*.

The shorter works Ailey made for the program rely on costuming and musical milieu to carry the dancing, with each work sounding a single, evocative tone sustained only for the short duration of the Ellington selection. The program opens with "Such Sweet Thunder," an abstract jazz dance for the entire ensemble. Most noticeable here are the flamboyant costumes designed by Randy Barcelo. Capitalizing on an emerging exotic disco-glamour look, Barcelo outfits the dancers with garish designs: an orange bell-bottom suit with matching "pimp hat"; a gold sequined tube top, accessorized with huge, dangling hoop earrings, red shorts trimmed in gold sequins, and knee-high leather boots; hot-pink, form-fitting slacks; and ornamented hair styles, including cornrows, oversized Afro wigs riddled with flowers, glittering headbands, and sequined skullcaps. Barcelo's costumes, designed to suggest an exotic late-night party in Harlem, all but overwhelm Ailey's choreography. Underneath the glad rags, Ailey offers a familiar portrait of strutting Uptown city slickers, showing off for each other and celebrating their own cool in an arrangement of exaggerated walks, stances, shrugs of the shoulder, and careless lifts of the leg that precede incredible volleys of turns and sweeping backbends.

Ailey first choreographed "The Blues Ain't" in 1963 as part of Ellington's *My People (First Negro Centennial)*. The revised television version of the dance features a couple engaged in an amorous ritual of reconciliation witnessed by an ensemble of five men and five women. Close in tone to "Backwater Blues" of *Blues Suite*, the short dance confirms a correlation between heterosexual courtship and the blues suggested by Ellington's rhymed couplet which introduces it: "The blues is the accompaniment of the world's greatest duet—a man and a woman going steady. And if neither one feels like singing them, then, the blues just vamps 'till ready."[6]

Program narrator Gladys Knight describes "Sonnet for Caesar" as "in complete contrast" to "The Blues Ain't." A short abstract work built from gentle unfoldings, rises, and falls, the dance features a male soloist as the leader of an obscure rite, suggested by Jane Greenwood's skin-colored "tribal" costumes for a large, mixed ensemble. The male dancers wear only short skirts, while the women wear billowy brown dresses over tights. All of the dancers have geometric patterns painted in white on their torsos, although the male soloist is visually distinguished by a large medallion and beaded headband. The costume accentuates the soloist's physique, and the camera focuses in for several close-ups, lingering on his musculature. The haziness of Ailey's staging of "Sonnet for Caesar" may stem from Ellington's languid score. Essentially a tone poem, the score offers few obvious rhythmic markers, and is performed with an understated languor. Ailey returned to this music in *Pas de "Duke"* (1976) with more success.

The television program ends with "Praise God and Dance (Sacred Concert)," a lively, theatrical dance for the entire ensemble of twelve and guest artist Fred Benjamin. Ailey and Knight introduce the score as among Ellington's "most important works," a "fitting" subject for Ailey and his collaborators. "Praise God and Dance," however, expands only slightly on the range of religious dances Ailey made before 1974. This unremarkable dance ends exactly as *Revelations* does, with a turn, fall to the knees, and stretching of the arms outward on the last beat of the drums.

Each of these short works encourages exoticized modes of spectatorship that build on stereotypical images of African Americans on stage. In succession, the dancers portray garish party-goers, aggressively impassioned lovers, tribal members, and ecstatic religious worshipers. *Night Creature* and *The Mooche*, the two longer works positioned as centerpieces for the television show, contain less predictable imagery and stronger choreographic content.

Ailey ends his on-screen introduction to *Night Creature* with a quote from Ellington's description of the work: "Night creatures, unlike stars, do not come out at night, they come *on*, each thinking before the night is out he or she will be the star."[7] Conceived in 1955, the score for Ellington band and symphony offers variations on short big band musical themes interrupted by soaring string passages. Ailey's choreography similarly employs an instructive catalogue of 1940s social dance steps offset by passages of ballet and contemporary classroom jazz dance. The whole is arranged by Ellington and Ailey as a coherent confirmation that black bodies, classical technique, Ellington band, and symphonic orchestrations could converge in concert dance.

In "First Movement," Ailey pits men and women against each another, as women search out partners in a humorous nighttime romp. The choreography follows the contours of the score closely, differentiating couples according to shifts in musical tone. A funky, percussive back-beat phrase is matched by a jive-stepping, man-eating woman; a sweeping phrase for string ensemble is matched by a lyrical "ballerina" seeking a cavalier. After duets for each couple, the eleven dancers—five women and six men—meet in a single-file, tightly positioned throbbing line borrowed from *Masekela Langage*. As in the earlier work, the dancers here look first to their various partners, then suddenly shift focus toward the camera, implicating the viewer in the construction of the dance. They jump away from the pulsating center on a rhythmic accent in the score and slink out of sight as the first movement ends, leaving dancer Agnes Johnson posed in the center of the space.

"Second Movement" begins with a teeming, teasing strut that moves the dancers toward and away from the camera. The rhythmic complexity of the company's unison stalking pattern butts against Ellington's spare, walking-bass motif, effectively revealing a range of submerged rhythmic variations. Ailey himself appears in this dance, partnering Johnson in *Night Creature*'s central pas de deux. Supported by constant visual counterpoint by members of the ensemble, Ailey and Johnson embody the recorded Ray Nance violin solo in a unison duet performed almost entirely side by side. Ailey's charisma obliterates his partner's presence, as they dance a variation of the work's opening strutting pattern. His focused precision, evident in rhythmic swings of torso, hips, and knees, and traveling phrases that simultaneously float above and sink into the floor suggest a cool duality of motion that complements the sultry reserve of Ellington's score as well as the unlikely articulations of jazz violin playing.

The choreography for "Second Movement" develops as a conversation between jazz dance and ballet, a visualization of Ellington's scored exploration of continuities between his band and symphonic ensemble. As the strings launch into a bouncing, dotted-note motif, five dancers perform a complex petite allegro ornamented with multiple beats. The buoyant movement phrasing here surprises the viewer, with unexpected jetés toward the camera and sudden changes of direction popping out of a classroom-style exercise danced by three women and two men. When Ellington's band wails through a series of brazen chords, Ailey's dancers strike a sequence of difficult balanced pose and change body line in response to each crashing chord. Performed in unison by the entire company spread across the space, the dancers physicalize the musicians' efforts by hitting poses with sharp accents. "Second Movement" ends with an inversion of its opening sequence, the dancers exiting singly from a repeat of the dance's first, strutting, unison passage. Johnson finishes the dance alone, reacting to Ellington's rhythmic accents with defiant stops timed to each thumping articulation.

In large part an exercise in television special effects, "Third Movement" contains as much choreography for the camera as dancing. The piece begins with an extended overhead shot, the camera looking down on a tight group of dancers who wave tensely stretched hands toward and away from a central female soloist. "Third Movement" continues with a soft layering of samba movements, its five women first dancing separately from five men, then pairing up as the music shifts into a heavy swing finale. The dancers perform a series of running and leaping phrases, but the movement sequences are obscured by superimposed images, fast-motion editing, and video montage. *Night Creature* ends with a close-up of soloist Johnson spinning, her image echoed and layered onto itself, blurred, phantasmagoric, and indeterminate.

Night Creature is followed by *The Mooche*, Ailey's dance portrait of three female stage personae. Gladys Knight's introduction sets a provocative and worshipful tone: "Long before black became officially beautiful, Duke Ellington was writing musical portraits of black artists. He wrote 'Black Beauty' as long ago as 1928. Alvin Ailey uses it now, along with two other numbers . . . to accompany his impressions of a musical star, a dancer, and a blues singer. They are introduced by 'The Mooche,' a funky Harlem dance from way back in the 1920s."[8] Knight's introduction again validates Ailey's dance as an homage to "official" African American culture.

As presented on the television program, however, *The Mooche* provides a thinly drawn character sketch of three undeniably glamorous stage archetypes. Costumed with considerable flair by Barcelo, the women are visually distinguished by chic 1920s-style dresses, each in a single bold color of black, white, or red. Arranged as a suite of dances, *The Mooche* begins with a group introduction, followed by three contrasting dances and a short, full-group coda.

Ailey sets the female dancers against an ensemble of eight men in black who portray chorus boys, eager fans, and, in the final selection, impassive angels of death. The staging is tightly contoured to the musical selections: in the first solo, "Black Beauty," a woman in black tap dances as the men perform basic, vaudeville-era time-keeping steps; in the second solo, "The Shepherd," a woman in white struts and shimmies as the men ogle her and comically beg her attentions; in the final dance, "Creole Love Song," a woman in red pantomimes a gen-

Estelle Spurlock and members of the Alvin Ailey American Dance
Theater in Alvin Ailey's *The Mooche*, 1975. Photograph by Johan
Elbers

eralized state of agony as the men, their faces now covered by ominous white masks, alternately taunt and ensnare her. *The Mooche* ends startlingly, with this woman in red's death: after rolling across the floor in despair, the men position an arrangement of benches over her supine body as a casket, and the other two women cover the benches with a flower-laden shroud.

As screened on the television program, *The Mooche* functioned most convincingly as a costume parade that confirmed an alluring brand of theatricalized feminine glamour. A dance heavy in concept but embryonic in its 1974 television realization, *The Mooche* achieved a fuller and more lucid form in a stage version premiered the next year during Ailey's Ellington festival.

Although Ailey rushed to make the dances for *Ailey Celebrates Ellington* and, in the process, thrust the junior dancers of the Alvin Ailey Repertory Ensemble into a premature national spotlight, reviews of the television program were generally complimentary. Writing for the *Philadelphia Inquirer*, Lee Winfrey appreciated the simplicity of the program's format: "The nice thing about this show was that I never got the feeling that the music was being 'interpreted,' that dreadful word. Ellington's music is so danceable that the show is more like just watching a set of good movers work out." John O'Connor of the *New York Times* found the program provided "a superb and broad catalogue of black contributions to the culture of American music. Mr. Ailey . . . illustrates the sounds with wit and sass, street-jive hustle and spiritual tension."[9] Screened as convincing mainstream television fare, the program successfully advanced Ailey's alignment with Ellington in the public imagination.

Dudley Williams and members of the Alvin Ailey American
Dance Theater in Alvin Ailey's *Three Black Kings*, 1976.
Photograph by Johan Elbers

█ Heroes

Throughout his career, Ailey planned dance tributes to individuals. Although most of them went unrealized, his eclectic group of proposed subjects included Ernest Hemingway, Henri Christophe, Langston Hughes, Harriet Tubman, and Malcolm X. The choreographer's impulse to canonize significant personalities intended to counterbalance the astonishing absence of heroic mythologies in the public imagination resonant to African Americans.

The causes for this absence are many. Before the invention of multiculturalism in the 1980s, which explored the relational subjectivities of cultural processes, and identity politics in the 1990s, which explored the individual subjectivities of people in the context of mainstream hegemonies, African Americans had little recourse to widely dispersed public mythologies, or more explicitly, heroes. Multiculturalism brought to the classroom an increased awareness of historical African American innovation in fields such as the arts and sciences, and identity politics allowed students to consider themselves inheritors of long-standing legacies of resistance and survival. But before the 1970s, American public school education paid only the tiniest bit of attention to African American history in terms of the people who shaped it. It was, and probably still is, possible for students to reach college without a working understanding of individual African American achievement in any field beyond professional sports, entertainment, or a blending of the two.

Ailey took the creation of stage heroes as a task worth pursuing for the good of all his audiences. But heroes present difficult subject matter for dance. By definition, the heroic exceeds the everyday, and conferral of hero status is contingent on an excessive achievement attained by few. Consequently, in the heroic depiction of a particular action, series of actions, or even the "life well lived," everyday nuances of individual character are minimized. Heroes have little subtlety or inner psychological conflict of conscience; their usefulness in the public imagination stems from their ability to exist, in patently oversized terms, far outside everyday social norms. The heroic gesture is exceedingly difficult to translate into terms of dance, where nearly every gesture already exists outside everyday praxis.

The several works Ailey made that were inspired by or dedicated to historical figures honor a range of politicians, musicians, and religious leaders. The central characters in these works are not immutably heroic, but Ailey meant to honor their memory by telling their stories—or a version of their stories—on public stages. The religious archetypes of *According to St. Francis* and *Passage*, the entertainers of *The Mooche*, *For Bird—With Love*, *Flowers*, *Au Bord du Precipice*, and *Opus McShann*, and the political leaders of *Three Black Kings* and *Survivors* all fit into Ailey's plan to increase public visibility for figures he felt to be important.

In staging these dance tributes, Ailey aligned himself with older traditions of black art that valued social responsibility alongside aesthetic appeal: an exploration of function with form. These dances celebrate—and, at times, mourn—the heroic measure of their subjects, and in the process refer to social history as relevant to the production of concert dance. They also allowed Ailey to shape his work as a "center" of black dance production, a pole of creation that was neither iconoclastic nor demure in its subject matter. Ailey always counted white subjects among his source material, including the Italian Roman Catholic friar St. Francis of Assisi of *According to St. Francis* and the tragic fiery rock singer Janis Joplin of *Flowers*; he also made works about dignified civil rights exponents Martin Luther King Jr. in *Three Black Kings* and Nelson and Winnie Mandela in *Survivors*, as well as an entire evening-length tribute to his dance theater heroine, Katherine Dunham, in *The Magic of Katherine Dunham* (1987). With Ailey's mythologizing impulse at the "center" of public dance possibilities, other choreographers working for the Ailey company could embrace or resist the pull of heroic representation; they could make quirky, self-referential works like Bill T. Jones's *Fever Swamp* (1983) or jokey explorations of jazz dance and pop music, like the revival of George Faison's *Tilt* (1979).

Younger postmodern choreographers working with African-inspired materials owed a debt to Ailey's public hero worship, as well as his traditionally shaped concert works like *Revelations*, because these dances at least represented the kind of work they did not make. These choreographers could reject the "upward mobility" rhetoric that works like *Revelations* and *Three Black Kings* espoused to focus more carefully on abstract qualities of motion and movement invention that stood in contrast to Ailey's work. Several artists have actively worked to deconstruct *Revelations* in their own pieces made for the Alvin Ailey American Dance Theater, including Donald Byrd's *Shards* (1988) and the thematic organization of Ronald K. Brown's *Grace* (1999). Both of these works assume the existence of *Revelations* as a starting point for their movement explorations. The Byrd dance reconfigures elements of Ailey's actual movement lexicon, and the Brown work offers a contemporary depiction of the intertwined sacred and profane interactions of a group of African Americans framed by Duke Ellington's neospiritual "Come Sunday."

Because the Ailey company stands as a preeminent site of black creative expression, many choreographers commissioned by Ailey followed his lead in an attempt to canonize black history. George Faison's *Gazelle* (1971, revived 1976), later titled *Slaves*, included references to a mythic African past, and both Donald McKayle's sprawling *Blood Memories* (1976) and Dianne McIntyre's intriguing if unsuccessful *Ancestral Voices* (1977) attempted to describe connections between black history and contemporary black life.

These dances fulfilled Ailey's mandate to give artistic voice to African American experience, yet they seemed decidedly old-fashioned to many artists and audiences interested in forward-looking depictions of multivalent black identity. Two extravagant examples of quixotic "hero worship" created for the Ailey company outline the limits of how far younger choreographers felt comfortable reaching from Ailey's original plan. Ailey engaged iconoclastic choreographer Louis Falco to create *Caravan* for the Ellington Festival in 1976.[10] Falco's dance combines a free-wheeling, loose-limbed movement vocabulary with constantly shifting decor and an irreverent score created by Michael Kamen. The work begins and ends with coups de théâtre: at the curtain's rise, a group of dancers lay marley on the stage and proceed to tape the dance floor down, ostensibly so that the dance can proceed. A single woman, Jamison at the work's premiere, dances enthusiastically in comic bursts of movement, then stops suddenly to jokingly admire her own allure. Fabric panels designed by William Katz descend, then disappear; a large company of dancers in bright sweatpants and flesh-colored leotards bounce and play through the space, while a mysterious man on foot-tall wooden clogs paces mysteriously behind various scrims. At one point, the front curtain descends behind this man, then rises just enough to reveal the entire company standing atop similar oversized wooden shoes, where they proceed to perform a soft-shoe. At its conclusion, the dancing company makes its way through the space single file, caravan-style amid the fabric scrims, to exit the back stage door of the theater, now shorn of all scenery and in full audience view. The most surprising aspect of the work had to be its irreverent musical score, which veered precipitously from one classic Ellington tune to another in various unexpected musical styles and prominently featured tongue-in-cheek disco arrangements of "I Got It Bad (And That Ain't Good)" and "Sophisticated Lady." As a whole, *Caravan* teased both Ellington and Ailey's expertise with a jokey, playful subversion of the musical "tribute" format and a patently simplistic movement vocabulary at odds with the Ailey company's preferred sleek performance style.

Nearly a decade later, Bill T. Jones and Arnie Zane created a more controversial "tribute" work with *How to Walk an Elephant* (1985). Modeled on George Balanchine's *Serenade* (1934),[11] the Jones-Zane work visually referenced sections of Balanchine's choreography in groupings and patterns performed here by Ailey company dancers rather than ballerinas in pointe shoes. General audience response to the piece was mixed, but critical response to the work was uncompromisingly harsh. Many ballet critics who loved Balanchine's work could not brook, for example, the sight of two men performing a central pas de deux quoted in the Jones-Zane composition. That the men were black and that the revisioning of Balanchine took place on Ailey's company surely added fuel to the controversy surrounding the dance. Jones, for his part, claimed ownership of the Balanchine legacy as an artist committed to concert dance; like Ailey, Jones saw the Euro-American heritage of neoclassical ballet as an important aspect of his own choreographic explorations.

Unlike Ailey's preferred scheme, neither of these two experimental works paid homage to an individual. In this, they enjoyed a certain freedom from literalness that inspired a buoyant self-confidence without the lugubrious solemnity that accompanies many dance tributes. If Ailey's plan to create black heroes in concert dance foundered at times, it may have been the result of the inevitable tension between the proportioned measure of any canonization and the necessary spontaneity of dance performance.

Ailey Celebrates Ellington

*What I really want to do is to bring to audiences the profundity
of this man's contribution—to illustrate not only his music, but
his philosophy of life. The public knows him only by his pop
pieces. Black composers have a way of disappearing and we
want very much for this man to take his rightful place in
American and international music history. To me, Duke was a
man who spoke to all mankind, a poet, a voice crying out
against darkness and negativism. He was a man whom the
Black community revered; a man who to us was a God.*
—Alvin Ailey, *Ailey Celebrates Ellington* program note

Ailey began to realize a stage version of his "monument in movement" to Ellington during the spring season of 1975.[12] He planned thirteen of his own works to
Ellington music and sought contributions from other choreographers: "I've sent
music to a lot of other choreographers and asked them to work in the festival.
I've talked with George Balanchine, Talley Beatty, Donald McKayle, George Faison. I want to ask Jerome Robbins, too."[13] In publicity leading up to the festival,
Ailey aggressively associated his festival with the recent Stravinsky festival, with
which Balanchine and his New York City Ballet had honored Igor Stravinsky in
1972. In a shrewd publicity effort, Ailey emphasized the multiracial American
nature of his own enterprise, in sharp contrast to the white Russian émigré roots
of New York City Ballet efforts.

The first of Ailey's new Ellington ballets to reach the stage was an adaptation of *The Mooche* (15 April 1975). Expanded from the 1974 television version to
include a fourth dance soloist, Ailey's new program note made the historical
portraiture explicit: "For Florence Mills, Marie Bryant, Mahalia Jackson, Bessie
Smith." Framed by an exquisitely overwrought setting by Rouben Ter-Arutunian,
the stage version featured several mirrored panels, billowing smoke, and a neon
light fixture that spelled out "The Mooche" in art deco–style lettering. Randy
Barcelo embellished his television costumes, adding a multicolored, floor-length
tunic for the tribute to Mahalia Jackson. Ailey also expanded on the function of
the ensemble of eight men in black, now listed in the program as "People, adoring audiences, chorus boys, saints, pimps, members of the Ku Klux Klan, people who keep the faith, strangers who never knew them, shadows, remem-
brances, bringers of flowers, those who will never forget . . ."[14]

Changes in the dance from the television version to the stage emerged from
the addition of the fourth dance portrait and the advanced technical facility of
the dancers of Ailey's first company. By 1975, dancer Sarita Allen had graduated
from the Repertory Workshop ensemble to the parent Alvin Ailey American
Dance Theater; she retained her role in a tribute to dancer Marie Bryant, joined
now by Estelle Spurlock in a tribute to Broadway entertainer Florence Mills, Sara
Yarborough in a tribute to gospel singer Mahalia Jackson, and star dancer Judith
Jamison in a tribute to blues singer Bessie Smith.

Jamison's presence in *The Mooche* all but overwhelms the work's modest intention as historical homage. In a filmed rehearsal of the dance made in 1976, Jamison's authority, her commanding precision of gesture in the slightest articulation of body line, and her fervent devotion to the choreographic structure effectively wipes out the solos that come before her. By 1976, Ailey added a new selection for Jamison that allowed her to hold forth in a simple arrangement of jazz dance steps. In constant motion, she struts, shim-shams, snake-hips, and sails across the stage, dancing at the audience with the ferocity of her own allure. She seems to confront the audience with the circumstance of her own celebrity as a dance star; she embodies a force of black female celebrity that aligns her with her subject, Bessie Smith.

In the Ailey repertory, *The Mooche* functioned as a much-needed spectacular showpiece laden with a sumptuous theatricality common to the stages of ballet companies. Clive Barnes found the work "more a superb and spectacular realization of show business, or even the crystallization of a show-business era, than a masterly piece of choreography." Writing for *Dance News*, Walter Sorell recognized the strength of Ailey's designer/collaborators: "I felt that Alvin Ailey tricked me with all the extraneous theatrical marvels. But they were so marvelous that I did not mind being tricked."[15]

A strange, moody work, *The Mooche*, like *Quintet*, matches its obvious trappings of glamour with dark tensions simmering just below its mirrored surface. In the stage version, the ensemble of male watchers don white masks for the final death sequence of "Creole Love Call," their eerie, measured movements in spooky contrast to the female soloist's histrionic undulations. As in *Flowers*, the women of *The Mooche* convey the isolation and distance from an adoring public inherent in a carefully constructed stage persona. Unlike either previous work, in *The Mooche* Ailey relies on his onstage ensemble of men to portray an entire range of demons and well-wishers, a general public alternately adoring, demanding, demeaning, and menacing. The shape-shifting abilities of the men underscore Ailey's macabre construction of the women as figments, who "slip in and out of the mirrors, appearing and disappearing like ghosts troubling our minds and memories; it's not happy nostalgia."[16]

More than one critic noted the campy, drag show milieu inhabited by the women of *The Mooche*, as evidenced in the overwrought costumes and grand processional catwalk struts that each character uses to enter the stage.[17] In asking his dancers to engage, literally, in a fashion parade during the dance's titular selection, Ailey again stretched their range of performance material. The Marie Bryant tribute includes a bit of tap dancing absent elsewhere from the Ailey repertory. Ailey used *The Mooche* to capture antiquated modes of African American social dance for his dancers and their audience; *The Mooche* encouraged its dancers to reclaim rhythms and movements long absent from the social sphere.

Night Creature (22 April 1975) benefited greatly in its transference from television to the stage. The stage adaptation brought forward Ailey's choreographic dialogue between ballet technique and jazz dance as a visualization of Ellington's whimsical interplay between symphony orchestra and jazz band. The dance was

The Alvin Ailey American Dance Theater in Alvin Ailey's
Night Creature, circa 1980. Photograph by Ron Reagan

an immediate success among critics and audiences and remained a staple of the
Alvin Ailey American Dance Theater repertory.

Ailey effected few substantive alterations in the choreography, mostly filling in sections obscured by the pyrotechnics of the television camera. For example, the revision of "Third Movement" for the stage builds on the strange,
slow-motion undulations of its television predecessor. The dance begins simply,
with Ellington's sinuous Latin motif matched by wavering arm movements that
metamorphose into quivering lunges performed by the entire body. But when
the score launches abruptly into a hard-swing version of the opening Latin musical motif, the dancers rush through the space, running first in a variety of partnered lifts and next in a series of running leaps. Suddenly, the seven couples ar-
rive onstage for a section of partnered jitterbug dancing performed in couples
spread evenly across the stage. The stage version of *Night Creature* ends decisively with this suggestion of an ordered system of 1940s-style social dance.

Positive critical reaction to the stage version of *Night Creature* focused on
Ailey's use of historical social dances and his successful combination of varying
dance vocabularies. Critic Robert Kimball called the dance "a kinetic backward
glance at the loose and free-swinging spirit and essence of the jazz dancing,
Jitterbug-Lindy days of the Savoy Ballroom and the big band era." Writing for

the *New York Times*, Anna Kisselgoff wondered at the choreographic savvy with which Ailey "gets away with it—all those girls doing their developpés into arabesques penchés, not to speak of their entrechats, assemblés and brisés and still being part of the hip-jutting wiggling pulse that colors the entire ballet." Five years later, Kisselgoff revised her comments to declare *Night Creature* "one of Mr. Ailey's happiest works. It has a joyful pulse, a sophisticated entente with its sophisticated music that carries on the best of the Ellington tradition. A serious work, 'Night Creature' is also entertaining."[18]

Ailey's next Ellington premiere, *Black, Brown and Beige* (11 May 1976), survived only a single week of performances. Working with five excerpts from Ellington's 1943 masterpiece of the same title, Ailey imagined a panoramic sampling of African American history told in terms of dance, "from pre–Civil War slavery, through the struggle for freedom and dignity, to a celebration of emancipation and an optimistic look to the future."[19] A large-scale production featuring a cast of thirteen and a series of projections executed by Maurice Van der Lindern, the dance included a revised version of "The Blues Ain't" from the 1974 *Ailey Celebrates Ellington* television special. Dancer Clive Thompson led the work in the ambiguous role of "Ancestor," a sort of flying Dutchman character "dressed like an overseer, but supposedly representing the Black man's guiding spirit," whose function was to link disparate historical eras.[20] Tepid audience reception must have discouraged Ailey, who, in an uncharacteristic gesture, abandoned the piece rather than rework it into an acceptable format.

Pas de "Duke"

Ailey fared far better with the premiere of *Pas de "Duke"* (11 May 1976), a pièce d'occasion arranged for the season fund-raiser gala featuring Judith Jamison and Russian ballet dancer Mikhail Baryshnikov. Widely previewed in the popular press as "a meeting of two worlds,"[21] the pairing of Jamison and Baryshnikov offered an obvious array of dynamic contrasts: race, gender, nationality, technical background, physical stature, and, of course, relationship to choreographer Ailey. An immediate success, *Pas de "Duke"* capitalized on Ailey's mature choreographic synthesis of ballet, social dance, and modern dance techniques. The duet remained in the Ailey company repertory.

Ailey's staging carefully creates excitement around the entrance of the dancers by delaying their arrival on stage. The curtain rises to reveal designer Rouben Ter-Arutunian's elaborate background scrim of several hundred metallic discs, floating in a random, rhythmic design in front of Chenault Spence's turquoise backlighting. The rhythmic motor of Ellington's "Such Sweet Thunder" sounds before the dancers appear, introducing the dance with a firm, steady backbeat. As Ellington's horns sound a raucous countermelody, the two dancers stride boldly onto the stage from opposite sides, stopping back to back, in a pose of wry appraisal. Pausing only for a moment to check each other out—as if in a sudden photo opportunity—they stride across the stage in gulping steps timed to the driving four-

Judith Jamison and Mikhail Baryshnikov in Alvin Ailey's
Pas de "Duke," 1976. Photograph by Martha Swope

count beat to pose briefly at the corners of the stage. The dancers repeat this ritual of teasing and testing each other before meeting center stage to begin the dance proper. A powerful, star-caliber entrance to the stage, these movements as performed in 1976 by Jamison in a shiny, black unitard and jacket with Baryshnikov in a shiny white unitard and jacket must have been combustive.

The dance develops formally as a challenge between dancers, with shifts in movement quality timed to coincide exactly with changes in the musical accompaniment. At times, the dancers appraise each other coyly, one striding about the periphery of the space as the other solos in the center. When the score eases into an improvised trumpet solo, the woman dances a solo of understated excess, consuming the space with sliding, arching runs ending in multiple turns and unexpected, flamboyant flips of the wrists. At times, she stops to gesture, teasingly defiant, to the man. The man's contrasting solo builds on multiple turns performed with unlikely leg positions, each difficult turn repeated to both sides, and stopping, unexpectedly, in an extended balance on one leg. The dance ends with a sudden moment of intimacy, when the man reaches toward the woman. She rejects his advance and moves to the far corner of the stage in silence. Rebuffed, the man moves away, and like prizefighters before a bout, they stalk out territory at opposite ends of the stage.

The recitative-style piano introduction of "Sonnet for Caesar" initiates a sultry exchange between the dancers. Eyeing each other with wary fascination, they peel off their jackets and approach each other, catlike. Their dance develops as a sensuous exploration of their emergent relationship, a romance told in terms of reaching toward each other with oblique innuendo. Swaying with generous movements of the torso and arms, they lay hands on each other in a teetering embrace. Each moment of contact dissipates quickly, and the dancers break apart to perform sweeping phrases of turns and melting contractions toward the floor on opposite sides of the stage. The duet continues as a sensual challenge, constructed at times in mirror image across an imaginary center axis, with movements at once smooth and lush, matching the sustained intensity of Ellington's score. The dance ends with a sudden rapprochement, as the dancers meet center stage with one arm extended overhead and the other wrapped around their partner. As the lights dim, they sink into the floor, caressing each other rapturously.

The two contrasting solos Ailey devised for Baryshnikov and Jamison describe the dancers' differences in terms of bravura showmanship, celebrating their technical facility in familiar movement idioms while gently challenging their ability in other idioms. For Baryshnikov, Ailey's choreography indulges a demonstrative, outward-directed energy, building on big kicks, exuberant struts, and flamboyant turning combinations. Several passages are directed toward the audience in a "showing off" manner, forcing the audience to acknowledge his mastery in several difficult turning and jumping passages, then suddenly undercutting that accomplishment with a wink and a shrug toward the house. Following ballet protocol, Ailey allows the dancer a bow after his solo, effectively breaking any cumulative momentum of an overall choreographic plan for the dance as a whole.

Jamison's following abstract solo develops around oppositional directions and controlled releases of energy. Working with an angular piano solo, "Clothed Woman," the dancer teases the space in bursts of at first hard and sudden, then soft and sustained contractions of the arms and torso. Her movement is far more weighty and curvaceous than that of the man, yet it also contains an elevated, upward reach, suggesting a balletic revision of Graham-inspired contractions and Dunham-based traveling phrases. The dance ends as the woman spirals to the floor, recovers to her feet, and, in an unexpected coda, settles into a sassy, showgirl pose, her gaze directed suddenly at the audience.

Pas de "Duke," and the guest-starring appearance of Baryshnikov, provided the Ellington festival with an important newsworthy cachet. Curiously, its strongest sections are its first two selections and not the contrasting solos Ailey made for his high-voltage performers. In the opening sections, "Such Sweet Thunder" and "Sonnet for Caesar," Ailey best teased out the differences between his dancers' abilities and the audience's expectations of their performances. The cat-like struts and social dance steps performed by Baryshnikov, juxtaposed to the balletic extensions held by Jamison, spoke eloquently to Ailey's desire to expand the public perception of his company and strengthen the entertaining and instructive import of his work with Ellington's music.

The final piece Ailey created for the Ellington festival was the highly anticipated posthumous premiere of Ellington's *Three Black Kings* (7 July 1976). Working with a three-part score completed by Ellington's son, Mercer Ellington,

Ailey created a tribute to three historical figures canonized in African American history: King Balthazar, King Solomon, and the Reverend Martin Luther King Jr. Elbert Watson, Clive Thompson, and Dudley Williams embodied the three kings, respectively, leading a cast of eighteen through a suite that explicitly aligned sovereignty with the dancing black male body.

Ailey rehearsed the dance quickly for its premiere at Artpark in Lewiston, New York, and it underwent some revisions before its New York City premiere on 13 August 1976, the official opening night of the Ellington festival at the New York State Theater.[22] Although *Three Black Kings* remained in active repertory only a single season, a rehearsal tape of the ballet made in 1976 reveals a characteristic schematic plan with movement closely aligned to musical contours and character distinctions among the kings relayed in broad strokes of costuming and movement vocabulary.

Strongest in its conceptual promise as an homage to three revered men of African ancestry, *Three Black Kings* never reached a successful finished form. Like *Pas de "Duke,"* the ballet did generate a significant amount of publicity as both the premiere of Ellington's last musical offering and a gesture of goodwill to its subjects. Coretta Scott King, widow of Martin Luther King Jr., introduced the ballet at its premiere, adding a measure of pomp and authenticity to Ailey's endeavor to chronicle African American history in music and dance.

Ellingtonia

The official Ellington festival played two weeks at the New York State Theater at Lincoln Center, 10–22 August 1976. The festival included fifteen dances set to Ellington music, five of which were made for the young dancers of the Alvin Ailey Repertory Ensemble: *New Orleans Junction* by Alvin McDuffie, *Still Life* by Christyne Lawson, *Forty* by Gus Solomons Jr., *Afro-Eurasian Eclipse* by Raymond Sawyer, and *Deep South Suite* by Dianne McIntyre. Four dances set on the senior company made by choreographers other than Ailey included a restaging of Talley Beatty's *The Road of the Phoebe Snow* and a new version of Lester Horton's *Liberian Suite* (1952) staged by James Truitte. Two new works commissioned for the festival were *Caravan* by choreographer Louis Falco, a former member of the José Limón company, and *Echoes in Blue* by Ailey company member Milton Myers. Ailey's six stage works—*Night Creature, Three Black Kings, The Mooche, Black, Brown and Beige*, a revival of the solo "Reflections in D," and *The River* as performed by guest artists of American Ballet Theatre—rounded out the festival repertory.

Each performance of the festival began with a medley of Ellington songs performed by the Duke Ellington Orchestra led by the composer's son, Mercer Ellington. Each performance was also introduced by a celebrity reading from program notes supplied by Ellington biographer Stanley Dance. The eclectic collection of celebrities included political figures such as Mrs. Betty Ford, Mrs. Coretta Scott King, and Mrs. Maynard Jackson; actors Ossie Davis, Ruby Dee,

Ellen Holly, and Al Freeman Jr.; and pop singing stars Patti LaBelle and Ashford and Simpson. Ruth Ellington, the composer's sister, represented the Ellington family at several performances with greetings and words of goodwill toward the entire Ailey enterprise.

As a whole, *Ailey Celebrates Ellington* confirmed the cultural and political capital accorded Ailey's dance enterprise by 1976. Many dance critics, however, found the choreographic offerings of the festival slight. Writing for the *New York Post*, Robert Kimball thought the festival "came up short in a number of ways," and noted the absence of a coherent festival book with information on Ellington, biographies of the choreographers, or a discography of the music played. Deborah Jowitt found *Three Black Kings* vague in places: "Ailey . . . seems to have strong feelings only about the last of these men; the other two appear simply as handsome, one-dimensional dance heroes." Wayne Robbins described *The Mooche* as a "rather slender" addition to the Ailey repertory, the dance being "simultaneously grandiose and pedestrian in its ambitions. At the sudden end, you realize there has been an attempt at a statement about life and death (a flower-draped coffin doesn't allow many other interpretations). But it *still* looks like a fashion show." Writing for *Dance Magazine*, Amanda Smith wondered at the volume of output the festival required of Ailey: "As a whole, the movement in *Black, Brown and Beige* was clichéd Ailey, and the appearance of the Falco work in the same season points up what a rut Ailey has gotten himself into in using the Ellington music—simply because that music seems to remind him repeatedly of the same movement."[23]

This last criticism may be valid in a way, considering Ailey's remark in an interview: "I've tried to make the music visual."[24] But Ailey and Ellington both worked within and outside of established traditions in choreography and music, as Moira Hodgson shrewdly noted in a *Dance News* feature: "Ailey says that just as his work is a marriage of jazz, ethnic and classical styles of dance so Ellington combines all styles in his music. 'Even the popular pieces have classical constructions. I like to use whatever styles please me at the time when I work. Ellington is that way too. They all merge and become one.'"[25] In this way, both creators were able to explore Africanist compositional strategies such as rupture, as in Ellington's unanticipated heavy-swing finale to *Night Creature*, and inversion, as in Ailey's flamboyant all-male kickline in "Riba" of *The River*. In both of these examples, a new motif emerges suddenly, suggesting a convergence of idioms through the portrayal of seeming opposites. In this, the "action" of the composition—what "happens" in the music and the dance—trumps the method of expression: the melodic or choreographic gestures employed by the composer and choreographer. As in jazz, what is played becomes, at times, less important than how it is played. Critics eager to evaluate Ailey's work as a "product" in these moments may have missed out on how the work represented a "process" in its performance.

A triumph of marketing and public relations, the Ellington festival focused attention on an honored statesman of African American artistry, a man who, like Ailey, had fostered an integrationist stance amid drastic changes in the prevalent political/racial dialogue. Ailey's homage, published in the program notes to the festival, was intended to counteract dismissive and reductive assessments of Ellington's artistic oeuvre and social tenacity:

> Ellington was the first authentic genius I ever met. He had collected around him a group of superbly gifted men—musicians—who were like his Stradivarius. I want to speak in this Celebration to his uniqueness, his daring, his beauty, his wit, his enormous spirit. . . . I want to say something about this great man who through his music, through his personality and through his love of humanity, healed some of the wounds of this century. . . . To me, Duke was a man who spoke to all mankind, a poet, a voice crying out against darkness and negativism.[26]

By virtue of his interracial school and company operations, Ailey himself clearly hoped to "heal some of the wounds of this century" through an engagement with the historical dimensions of modern dance.

NINE

Gender and Spectatorship

As a whole, Ailey's dances suggest an egalitarian configuration of female and male physical presence. His dances seldom privilege male bodies over female bodies in terms of either technical challenge or stage time. For many years the women of the Ailey company had stronger technical capacity as dancers, often having begun formal dance training in childhood or adolescence. Ailey's male dancers, like Ailey himself, typically came to dance as adults and gained technical expertise as they performed with the company. As a choreographer, Ailey ignored this lopsided, gendered dance background, insisting on the same punchy mixture of Horton technique, ballet, Graham technique, jazz, and social dance from all his dancers.

In works built from dramatic scenarios, however, Ailey's choreography often exploits traditional constructions of feminine emotivity juxtaposed to masculine immutability. Dances like *Revelations*, *Feast of Ashes*, *Masekela Langage*, and the coed draft of *Quintet* describe categories of feminine neurosis, demonstrated in passages of overwrought emotional outbursts, that stand in contrast to masculine stability, demonstrated in passages of cool meditation. The woman of "Fix Me, Jesus" searches for spiritual consolation; her male guardian angel offers her support and direction. In *Feast of Ashes*, Adela knocks over chairs in anguished protest over her misbegotten love, while Pepe stands immobile, waiting for her passion to subside before they dance together. The demonstrative solo "Bo Masekela" and the hysterical woman laughing through the "U-Dui" in *Masekela Langage* follow the soberly cool combat of two men fighting; the men's battle is told in terms of slow-motion parries and extended strangleholds, while the women's dances exhibit fervor in high-pitched passages of movement. In a draft of *Quintet*, the woman of "December Boudoir" dances for four men who are sitting and reading newspapers, effectively ignoring her protestations.

Ailey constructed *Quintet*, like *The Mooche* and *Flowers*, to present female characters as objects of an explicitly capitalist masculine audience gaze. Even as he sought to critique the assumptions within this construction, underlining pitfalls of feminized American celebrity in each of these dances, he nonetheless perpetuated this imagery by recreating it. As dance critics bore out, a large portion of the appeal of these three works lay in their spectacular depiction of glamour, made available to their paying audiences.

Ailey's work consistently encouraged gay male spectatorship in its varied depictions of glamorous masculinity: from the hypermasculine working men of *Blues Suite* to the sensitive but sensually deprived religious archetypes of *Revelations* and *Hermit Songs*. The extravagant costume and setting design of works like *Quintet*, *Riedaiglia*, *Flowers*, and *The Mooche* fit a prevalent mold of campy excess enjoyed by some gay audiences. Working in acquiescence to socially inscribed dictums to mask homosexuality, Ailey's company and choreography provided a veiled but safe performance space for the contemplation of (black) gay culture.

Instead of dealing closely with issues of sexuality, Ailey's presentation of black bodies in heightened states of grace encouraged a consumption of glamour welcomed by gay and straight audiences. Through time, works that originally held little promise of glamour acquired it; for example, the inwardly motivated slave-era archetypes of the "Pilgrim of Sorrow" section of *Revelations* took on an outward-directed, elegant, and upright bearing by the mid-1970s. Other kinds of glamour that Ailey's choreography promoted included the mystique of religious ritual, displayed in works like *Choral Dances* and the riverside baptism of *Revelations*; the elegance of a man's physical bearing, as in *Gymnopedies* and *Love Songs*; and the mythic glory of African American history embodied by choreography for the entire Ellington festival. The kinds of glamour Ailey allowed to become a cornerstone of his company's presentations spoke specifically to an African American audience hungry for such staged confirmations of beauty. Through the aesthetic display of his dancers' bodies and the cultural memories their movements provoked, Ailey created a stage on which traditional conceptions of black masculinity and black femininity could intersect fruitfully with his audience's divergent desires.

As in his subtle adjustment of minstrel stereotypes, Ailey gently sought to adjust gender-stereotyped imagery in roles he made for women and men. His largest success in this came in the plotless dances he made, beginning with "Reflections in D" of 1963. Originally created as a solo for himself, Ailey later assigned "Reflections" to both Dudley Williams and Judith Jamison,[1] a succession that confirmed the choreographer's at times flexible conception of gender and movement.

The unique stage personae of Jamison and Williams offered Ailey effective collaboration in his project to redefine gender imagery. Jamison combined her tall stature, unconventional dark-skinned beauty, close-cropped Afro haircut, and obvious femininity with a hard-edged bodily precision and technical grounding in classical ballet to create powerful, multivalent women. Williams allowed his slight stature and unassuming projection of masculinity to merge with a passionate reserve and tendency toward softness onstage to create dance depictions of soulful, sensitive men. Ailey drew on these oppositional qualities in two solos he made for these dancers in the early 1970s: *Cry* (4 May 1971), the ballet that made Jamison a star, and *Love Songs* (18 November 1972), created for Williams. Considered successes largely on the strength of their original interpreters, both dances remained in the repertory of the Alvin Ailey American Dance Theater after their premieres.

▌ *Cry*

Ailey created *Cry* as a present for his mother, Lula Cooper.[2] Choreographed quickly, with only five days of rehearsal, Ailey made the dance "to say something about the huge influence that black women have had in my life."[3] Dedicated "to all black women everywhere—especially our mothers," the sixteen-minute, three-part plotless solo tells of life, work, and spiritual rebirth as experienced by an everywoman figure.[4] Considered something of a "family heirloom" by its many performers, the work has been successfully interpreted by Jamison, Estelle Spurlock, Donna Wood, Sara Yarborough, Deborah Manning, Toni Pierce, Renee Robinson, and Nasha Thomas. As originally performed by Jamison, Ailey's choreography presented a coherent relationship between the dancing body and the experience of living black in America.

The dance achieves an evocative tone through an economy of gestures in its opening moments. The curtain rises to reveal a dancer swathed in a white leotard and voluminous white skirt, bearing a long white scarf upward as a totem to the gods. She sways easily to Alice Coltrane's electronic score "Something about John Coltrane," then opens the cloth to bear it forward ceremonially, at arm's length, in a series of weighty, serpentine lunges. She kneels and throws the scarf outward to the sides, recoiling from each sideward toss with a mighty, percussive lurch of her torso. Rising, she begins a series of incantatory gestures toward the fabric, including a low-to-the-ground pulsating isolation of the torso borrowed from neo-African dance forms.

The dancer's attitude toward the prop transforms it from a scarf to an infant's swaddling cloth to an object of potent ritual consequence. At times, she seems to react to the fabric, moving away from it almost fearfully before falling to her knees to return to it, grudgingly. Grabbing the scarf, she runs through the space, trailing it majestically, then falls to her knees again to use the cloth as a

Judith Jamison in Alvin Ailey's *Cry*, 1971.
Photograph by Rosemary Winckley

cleaning rag, desperately scrubbing the floor. She rises again to wear the cloth as a shawl, then steps on its ends as if bound by it to the ground. Finally, she wraps it around her head to run in a circle, becoming a priestess in royal costume. Repeating the opening phrases of the dance, she bears the cloth forward to the ground, again spreading it out along the front edge of the stage. She backs away from the cloth to dance as the score shifts subtly into an extended saxophone solo.

Skittering through a rapid juxtaposition of posed stances and purposely undeveloped movement ideas, "Something about John Coltrane" develops in a fragmentary manner. The arrangement of images meshes with Coltrane's electronic soundscape to convey a mystical mood of indeterminate time. Lighting design by Chenault Spence adds to the fantastical sensibility with oversized, abstract shapes projected onto a scrim behind the dancer. The dance presents a charged temporal and physical space, dominated by the dancer's constantly shifting embodiment of roles and functions; at times she seems to be laborer, mother, priestess, slave, lover.

The second movement of *Cry* describes an emotional sorrow inextricably linked to roles suggested in "Something About John Coltrane." Set to Laura

Nyro's disconsolate song "Been on a Train," the dance details the woman's despair, precipitated by the actions of offstage men, through a confident layering of dramatic gesture. Nyro's transformed twelve-bar blues scored simply for piano and voice tells of a woman witnessing a man's death from drug addiction.

The dancer contorts her body vigorously, timing dramatic gestures of supplication directly with percussive piano accents. She moves constantly, venturing through the space with gestures of reaching and searching, at times grasping her head in anguish. Her dance follows the contours of Nyro's song closely, rising in physical intensity with a series of leaps as the singer wails a lament, then stopping suddenly as a piano interlude falls silent. In a pungent silence between verses, she performs a slow rise to balance on one leg while simultaneously stretching her arms upward. Her excruciatingly slow unfolding occurs amid a series of contorted postures of sorrow; as performed by statuesque Jamison, the stunning visual effect of physical expansion suggests a vast reserve of power submerged within the performance of grief. "Been on a Train" ends with a slow bodily release to the floor followed by a gentle rise to both feet, a final supplication of the arms toward the heavens, and a collapse of the torso toward the ground. The final posture mirrors the opening posture of the dance, suggesting a cyclical, inevitable progression of frustration and despair.

The final section of *Cry* is set to the Voices of East Harlem recording of "Right On, Be Free," a gospel song about the triumph of will and spiritual rebirth. Structurally simple, the dance features an array of transformed spiritual dancing. Patting complex rhythms with her feet, torso, neck, shoulders, and arms, the woman moves easily throughout the space, reaching upward and outward with an exuberant flash of the spirit. At times, she matches gestures to the words of the song, as in a circling, wing-like flapping of the arms and legs set to the lyric "high flying bird." Her dance is infused by the joy of triumphant perseverance, through traveling hitch kicks, simple walking phrases, and surprising freezes timed to hard rhythmic breaks in the music. *Cry* ends with the dancer center stage, performing a full-bodied dance of divination. Tearing at the earth and sky simultaneously, she moves in unabashed ecstasy, embellishing subtle variations in rhythmic accent with her hands, shoulders, and feet as the curtain falls.

The power of *Cry* emanates from its defiantly shifting images of identity in its first section, the bottomless abyss of sorrow approached in its second section, and the transcendent quality of ecstatic faith engaged in the third section. *Cry* became emblematic as an act of simultaneous defiance and release. As a depiction of contemporary African American identity, the dance liberated audience and dancer in its modernistic layering of movement genres, especially its conspicuous use of neo-African body part isolations. Programmed often as a pièce d'occasion in gala performances by Jamison and Wood at American Ballet Theatre, the San Francisco Ballet, and elsewhere, the dance proposed a defiant interpolation of African American experience onto stage spaces typically empty of black bodies.

Cry enhanced the creative bonding between Ailey and Jamison begun in the solo "Bo Masekela" of *Masekela Langage*; it became Ailey's first full-length, free-standing solo created for a woman, and it featured Jamison prominently as recent works in the company's repertory had not. In terms of movement, the dance facilitated a shockingly percussive, hard-edged style of performance that later became standard for Ailey's company. Following the prototype set by Pearl Primus in dances like "Strange Fruit" of 1943, Jamison's oversized projection embodied heroic qualities rarely associated with black women in concert dance: strength and resiliency, defiance and triumph.

Love Songs

Ailey made *Love Songs* as a companion to Jamison's *Cry*, a tripartite solo for long-time company member Dudley Williams. Working with three popular recordings by soulful singers Donny Hathaway and Nina Simone, Ailey introduced *Love Songs* in sections, premiering "A Song for You" by itself on 25 April 1972 and the entire suite on 18 November 1972. Other strong interpreters of the work include Aubrey Lynch II, Michael Thomas, and Matthew Rushing.

Love Songs presents an introspective emotional journey of a man contemplating an absent (male) presence. Its musical score includes three selections whose lyrics intimate a sensual and caring relationship between the dancer and his absent friend. Although the movement content of the dance is not explicitly homoerotic, *Love Songs* can easily be viewed as a romantic offering to an offstage male lover.

"A Song for You," the first of the love songs, explores lyricism in the rhythm and blues musical grain. Leon Russell's song details a conciliatory offering from the singer to his lover, a scenario caused by the singer's popularity: "I've been so many places in my life and times, I've sung a lot of songs, I've made some bad rhyme. I've acted out my life in stages, with ten thousand people watching. But we're alone now and I'm singing this song for you." Although the song lyric never specifies a male-male configuration of speaker and witness, it also resists a conventional male-female interpretation with its intimations of secrecy and transcendence of the everyday: "You taught me precious secrets of the truth, withholding nothing: you came out in front, and I was hiding. But now I'm so much better, and if my words don't come together, listen to the melody, cause my love's in there, hiding. I love you in a place where there's no space or time, I love you for my life, you are a friend of mine. And when my life is over, remember when we were together. We were alone and I was singing this song to you."[5] The privacy sought by the singer brings to mind closeted spaces occupied by Ailey and other gay black men who studiously avoided public discussion of their sexuality.

Ailey's choreography matches Hathaway's expressive vocal with abstract sculptural postures connected by emotive gestures. The effect is a visual correlation of Hathaway's "romantic blues"—a balance of graceful expression within sadness. Wearing a bright blue unitard, the dancer is revealed standing still in a

185

Dudley Williams in Alvin Ailey's *Love Songs*, 1972.
Photograph by Fred Fehl

distant corner of an expansive space. He begins with a series of heavily weighted, sculptural poses, carving at the space around him with slow gestures of his arms and upper body. As he slowly makes his way across the stage, he falls into still poses that coincide rhythmically with hesitations in Hathaway's vocal phrasing. An abstract narrative of mounting desperation emerges as he tries, but fails, to corral the space around his body through sculptural posturing. At times, his mimetic gestures coincide with Hathaway's sung lyrics, as in sequences of waving toward his absent friend. The dancer holds his body very erect and his face consistently upward to perform the dance outward, as if toward a member of the audience. He ends with a gesture of giving, kneeling on one knee with his weight pitched forward as he stretches his arms outward to offer his heart to someone in the audience.

The dancer asserts an introspective, meditative quality as he finds his way into "A Field of Poppies," set to Nina Simone's cautionary drug song describing heroin addiction. Passing through a series of frozen poses wrought as if in iconographic representation of grief, longing, or regret, the dancer seems to embody the loving, woeful partner of a drug addict. His dance ends inconclusively when he collapses to the floor in a distant corner of the space, apparently unsuccessful in his bid to divert his partner from tragedy.

The final selection of *Love Songs* intends to convey the man's physical journey of passage and emotional absolution to the strains of Donny Hathaway's "He Ain't Heavy, He's My Brother." Performed as a gospel spiritual, the song tells of a man bearing witness for a fallen brother: "The road is long, with many a winding turn, that leads us to who knows where, who knows where. But I'm strong, strong enough to carry him. He ain't heavy, he's my brother." As in "A Song for You," the lyric suggests a sensual tie between the singer and his subject without explicit reference: "If I'm laden at all, I'm laden with sadness, that ev'ryone's heart isn't filled with the gladness of love for one another. It's a long, long road, from which there is no return. While we're on our way to there, why not share? And the load doesn't weigh me down at all; he ain't heavy, he's my brother."[6] Ailey's choreography builds on the song lyric's prevalent associations of burden and love.

Rising from the floor slowly, the dancer begins with gestures of beseeching, his arms raised upward, indicating a burden—the partner from "A Field of Poppies"?—too heavy for him alone. Driven to the floor, he crawls across the stage, moving in intensely elongated slow motion through postures of physical oppression. His movements correspond closely to Hathaway's vocal: as the singer releases a high note, the dancer stretches upward with an open, reaching hand, his chest released forward, his head tilted backward. When the singer riffs downward in a decorative vocal phrase, the dancer manifests the melismatic sound with sequential, isolated ripples of his back, shoulders, neck, and head.

Like "A Field of Poppies," "He Ain't Heavy" explores a narrow spectrum of movement invention and rhythmic variation. The dance rarely veers from its halting rhythmic construction, even when Hathaway's recording provides prominent rhythmic breaks. It ends inconclusively, when the dancer performs a stiff two-step motion with his arms jutting out to the sides as he arches his upper body backward, a movement quotation suggesting turbulent frustration borrowed from the final section of *Blues Suite*.

Love Songs achieved a success that stemmed from Ailey's deft musical selection of two works by an enormously popular musician, recordings that struck an immediate chord of emotional recognition for Ailey's large African American audience, whether they recognized a homoerotic subtext or not; its heroically demanding test of endurance as a twelve-minute solo; its affirmation of masculine sensitivity in a form typically dominated by women; and in Dudley Williams's consummate artistry, unanimously lauded by dance critics. Like *Cry*, *Love Songs* provided its dancer a challenging exercise in sustaining mood. The dance fit Williams well, offering him an extended, abstract work suited to his passionate reserve and command of weight, attack, and grace. A former Graham company dancer, Williams brought a careful resolve and purpose to his performances of the dance, always certain to tender his expression to his audience in a sober, transparent manner.

Although *Cry* and *Love Songs* utilize a similar movement vocabulary, the dances underscore Ailey's divergent conceptions of stage personae appropriate to gender. As a whole, his collaboration with Jamison suggested a malleable, multifaceted, and profoundly empathetic presence. Working with Williams, Ailey created a yielding but emotionally unresolved presence whose actions seem masked by secretiveness. The woman of *Cry* finds emotional synthesis of several personae in the ecstatic dance that ends the work; the man of *Love Songs* finds no such synthesis, and his dance fades away in a gesture of physical and spiritual turbulence. The woman is palpably emotive; the man, troubled but reserved.

Masked Spectatorship: Ailey's Representation of Sexuality

To be sure, a large portion of the association of masculinity and guarded stoicism in Ailey's work stemmed from the choreographer's need to deflect his audience's potentially negative connotations of male homosexuality from modern dance. By 1972, mainstream American culture offered little public space for the representation of black homosexuality. Ailey and Williams, both gay men deeply concerned with the mainstream reputation of the Ailey enterprise, felt compelled to perpetuate conventionally masculine stage personae.

Critics and audiences routinely associated Ailey's early work with familiar stereotypes of black sensuality, and Ailey pragmatically toed the heterosexist line. By 1969, he attributed his childhood interest in dance to the screen movements of Gene Kelly and Fred Astaire, from which he "learned that dancing could be a masculine thing. I found out that dance doesn't have to be a sport for fairy queens." *New York Newsday* writer Bob Micklin asked Ailey about the prevalence of eroticism in contemporary work, and Ailey allowed a veiled reference to his own situation as a closeted gay artist: " 'Dance like any other art form, reflects the times. And these are troubled times. So when you get eroticism showing up in dance, well, eroticism shows up in the theater and movies too. And eroticism is easy to suggest in an art that uses human bodies.' Asked why much of contemporary dance seems to center around sexual conflict, he laughed. 'Maybe a lot of choreographers have sexual hang-ups,' he said."[7]

Ailey seldom used autobiography as a tool of narrative composition, and he carefully guarded his public persona of masculine virility dissociated from homosexuality. He matured and spent much of his adult life in a society that openly critiqued his professional accomplishments on racial grounds; as a closeted gay man, he avoided an additional burden of political judgment surrounding his sexual identity. In his posthumously published autobiography, Ailey presented his homosexuality as something of a footnote to an adult life of emotional insecurity and mental illness.[8]

Still, Ailey managed to create dance imagery that acknowledged male and female homosexuality in abstract work he made for the American Ballet Theatre (*The River*) and his own company (*Streams*). These two dances, both created in 1970, include sections that recognize a sensual, intimate bond between men and women in dances of same-sex partnering framed by opposite-sex encounters.

Joan Peters and members of the Alvin Ailey American Dance
Theater in Alvin Ailey's *Blues Suite*, circa 1964. Photograph
by Eva F. Maze

▌ Sex

I came to consider the complexity of my own sexuality as I gazed at the photograph
on the wall: the Alvin Ailey American Dance Theater performing Ailey's *Blues Suite*. In
the world of this photograph, the men are heroically muscular, with biceps and
quadriceps straining against the skin that encases them; the women are strong and
unafraid, defying the satin and sequins that cover their lean physiques. I had hung the
page from the program on my bedroom window at the age of thirteen. For me, the
Ailey company became a totem of possibilities for my body and my desires.

Associations of concert dance and homosexuality lean into time-worn American
stereotypes of male dancers being queer. But concert dance does attract queer people, in no small part simply because it doesn't shun them. More than this, concert
dance traffics in the aesthetic medium of the body; it is the body that initiates desires
within and without heterosexual norms, and concert dance encourages contemplation of physical form. Why wouldn't dance invite queer arousal? What better way is

189

there to marshal the impulses of a queer body than to look to an accepted expressive idiom for the body—to look to the dance?

Ailey was homosexual, although he never defined himself in terms of his sexuality. In his autobiography he wondered that his secret lives—as a poor black man and as a gay man—were responsible for his illness in some way: "Still, I find it impossible to consider on the gasping distance between small town Texas and ending up dancing on the Champs Elysees in Paris, a heavy load to carry. . . . The cultural distance between those two points certainly had something to do with my illness."[9] The illness Ailey refers to here is his manic depression, but he contracted and succumbed to AIDS. Throughout his life, Ailey remained squarely in the closet, even as he allowed for same-sex desire to be discreetly depicted in some of his work.

For the most part, African American communities have not enjoyed open discussions of sexuality or its implications. Still, while most official narratives of African American culture resist gay male or lesbian presence, queer people of color have long been embedded in African American social structures. Recent explorations of African American cultural history have revealed an enduring queer presence in realms of politics, finance, sports, arts, education, health care, and elsewhere; since 1994, the Web site www.blackstripe.com has offered biographies of gay and lesbian African diaspora figures of note, including Ailey himself.

The Ailey company has always counted lesbians and gay men among its company members and, of course, its core audience. Ailey performances provide gay audiences of color a welcome opportunity to assemble publicly. Because Ailey dancers are consistently lauded for their preeminence, the public assumption of gay dancers on stage works to strengthen associations of queer black people and excellence. Queer audiences enjoy a particular place of pride at Ailey performances, and enjoy the fantastic landscapes of beautiful black men and women working together physically, but without regard to sexual orientation.

Although no choreographer made explicitly queer work for the Ailey company during Ailey's lifetime, Ulysses Dove may have come closest to expressing queer black desire in terms of concert dance. Dove joined the Ailey company in 1973, then retired from performing in 1980, when he started making dances at Ailey's urging. Several of his works explored dysfunctional relationships bound by inexplicable attractions.[10] His dance *Episodes* (1987) describes a harsh landscape of men and women who rush toward each other as if to connect emotionally, but are inevitably repelled by the very force of their (e)motion. Dove's movements here are hard-edged, punchy, and invariably violent in their intensity. Clad in chic, form-fitting black, the men and women of this dance are pinned, rather than revealed, by shafts of blinding white light focused as a diagonal crossroads on the stage. The overall mood is unrelentingly tense, in no small part due to the extreme physical demands of Dove's choreography. When slow-motion phrases emerge, they offer little release from the overall drive and fervor of the staging.

Episodes offers a queer landscape in its urgency and sense of danger. Its men sometimes work in same-sex partnership, but with an intensity that suggests extraordinary tension and risk. In this reading, the risk of erotic tension between men reveals itself as an excessive attack in specific movements and a harsh, uncompromising view of relationships drawn without tenderness or vulnerability.

Like much of Dove's choreography, *Episodes* became very popular among Ailey's black audiences, who recognized the overwhelmingly violent exertion of his movement phrasing as an expressive response to the random racism of everyday American life. Dove's pairings of men with men and women with women occur within a heteronormative frame, in which men and women repeatedly confirm their inability to communicate. The dance offers no solutions or answers to its contentions; rather, it reflects a world without emotional end. This unrelenting way of being in the world also resonates for black gay men and lesbians who function in black society without a full expression of their sexuality as a part of their identity.

▌ *Streams*

Ailey made *Streams* (15 April 1970) as one of two premieres for his company's 1970 Brooklyn Academy of Music season. Set to an eight-part percussion score by Miloslav Kabelac, the dance became Ailey's first full-length plotless work. Choreographed for the company's full complement of fourteen dancers, *Streams* proved a critical success and remained in the Ailey repertory.

An intricate curtain-raising work designed to introduce its dancers to the audience, *Streams* lists no costumer credit for the pale blue unitards for the women and tights-only worn by the men. The work begins with "Corale," a slow-motion, two-part processional of the entire company along the diagonals of the stage. Composed as a layered arrangement of fragments taken from a long movement phrase, the dance explores the architecture of bodies in space.

Led by a single woman testing gravity with swimming motions of her arms and legs in an upstage corner, a group of women joins singly into a flowing phrase of movement exercises derived from Horton technique. They glide across the stage single file in fluid, measured steps. A second brigade of dancers led by a man joins the procession with slow-motion rises into balance on one leg, turns, and slow, pliant walking. Occasionally, a sudden drop toward the floor in a deep, first-position plié breaks the even tenor of the processional, as do strikingly angular articulations of the arms in several positions. Eventually, all fourteen men and woman pass along this diagonal path, dancing phrases drawn from a limited vocabulary of balances and drops toward the floor. They return along the opposite diagonal in different groupings: a trio of women, a mixed-gender group of six, a male duet, and a single man who strides, simply and majestically, along the center of the path. Holding his head and chest raised proudly, this "seeker" figure keeps his eyes intent on a vision in the far distance, passing amid the groups of dancing bodies without relating to them. His passage provides the first hint of an oblique narrative of humanity that permeates the whole of *Streams*.

Two combative duets, separated by solos for women, provide contrasting models of movement designed for female-male and male-male couples. "Giubiloso," created for John Parks and long-time company member Michele Murray, describes an intense, violent bond between counterparts. The woman enters first, running and unfolding along a diagonal axis, pulling and pushing at the space around her as if treading water. The man enters from the opposite corner, moving toward the woman with gestures of kicking and punching. They avoid visual contact even as they dance in unison, falling into similar sculptural poses by rote or seeming coincidence. Finally, they touch for a brief section of partnering, the man manipulating the woman harshly into a series of dynamic poses, until he lifts her overhead and carries her offstage.

Where "Giubiloso" describes a hardened familiarity between partners, "Scherzo," a duet for two men set to a powerfully aggressive arrangement of xylophone and trap drums, emerges as a danced competition. The two men are defined in terms of oppositions: one man displays flashy technical expertise, performing huge, flamboyant jumps and double tours en l'air approached without obvious preparation. The second man trades in body sculpture, carving out space with asymmetrical positions of his arms and torso, suggesting an authoritative cool through simple traveling motions. The dancers fall into and out of unison passages and sections of physical mirroring, heightening the obvious contrast in their styles. Their competition ends inconclusively, with a simultaneous grand jeté offstage timed in the space after the percussion score ends.

"Giubiloso" and "Scherzo" each depict partnership as a battle. In the entirety of his abstract and narrative ballet output, Ailey created few depictions of reciprocal romantic alliances between two people. As he became increasingly interested in ballet technique and creating abstract work, the combative nature of duets he made became absorbed by the display of dance technique. Although he rarely veered toward the romantic in his work, Ailey masked the convention of fighting (romantic) partners depicted in dances like "Scherzo" and "Giubiloso" by casting them as danced abstraction.

As a whole, the choreography for *Streams* employs a limited palette of treading, arching, and sharply etched frozen positions to create imagery of either water in motion or bodies reacting to the flow of water. Two solos for women demonstrate these perspectives. "Recitativo," created for Consuelo Atlas, suggests a woman in harmony with aqueous flow who moves through dense passages with the quiet intensity of a rolling wave. "Lamentoso," made for Judith Jamison, explores a body resistant to the crushing flow of water in weighted movements performed with the dancer's upper body held rigid.

The yielding softness in the solo Ailey made for Atlas offers distinct contrast to the hard precision of work he typically made for Jamison. As a dancer, Atlas's stage persona filled a category of feminine pliancy Ailey responded to deeply. Like Carmen de Lavallade, Atlas capitalized on a demure intensity in performance, projecting a conventional, delicate beauty underscored by her slight stature and classical ballet technique.

As *Streams* continues, a narrative of human interaction that coincides with its formalistic construction becomes apparent. "Danza" pits four women against three men in a pugnacious display of technical prowess. The dance begins with the sudden leaping entrance of a woman from a distant corner of the space. Three other women join her, dancing an extended phrase of frozen positions connected by pulsing pliés and sharp, isolated sways of the neck and hips. Three men rush onstage, their abrupt appearance driving the women away. Like the women, these men move in unison through an arrangement of two-dimensional postures featuring bent arms, knees, and tensely flexed hands. The women's leader reenters cautiously behind the men, clearing the space with a mysterious circling gesture of one hand about her face. "Danza" continues as a cat-and-mouse game defined by gender, the women rushing offstage when the men return, the men exiting when the women reclaim the space. Eventually, six dancers partner up for a violent sequence of simultaneous combative duets, each couple staged with distinctive physicality. The women's leader dances alone in frenzied agony center stage until the three couples exit, and she collapses with a sweeping fall to the floor performed in the silence after the music ends.

Dudley Williams, Michihiko Oka, and Carl Paris in Alvin
Ailey's *Streams*, circa 1978. Photograph by Johan Elbers

A visual meditation on the nature of partnership, "Aria" presents a layered, kaleidoscopic unfolding of line, arranged as an extended canon danced by couples pulsating gently to a mysterious vibraphone score. The dancers approach each other indifferently, striding with measured, slow gait to a neutral, face-to-face position. Their duets begin with a teetering, breathing motion, a rocking of their bodies toward and away from each other without moving arms or feet. Varied only by rhythmic approach, each couple proceeds into an exquisitely slow adagio built from gentle leanings onto each other, giving weight to each other in stretching gestures toward the ground and reaching outward and upward from each other to balance in elevated positions. At one point, the woman of each male-female couple balances on the turned-out thigh of the man, arching upward in the signature arabesque silhouette that effectively ends "Fix Me, Jesus" of *Revelations*. Following the hard-edged belligerence of previous sections, the frank pliancy of "Aria" soothes.

"Aria" premiered in 1970 with five mixed-sex couples, but sometime between 1970 and 1973 Ailey added two same-sex couples into its lyrical counterpoint. He allowed the additional couples slight variations in the canon phrase: the two women forgo lifting motions for mirror-image balances in arabesque position, while the two men end the original phrase just before the signature, upward-reaching arabesque balance on one leg. Both the original and revised versions of "Aria" end as the dancers exit the stage slowly, some remaining in couples while others separate and back away from each other. One man skitters away from his partner and collapses to the floor in an abstract gesture of grief or repulsion. "Aria" ends as it began, with a single dancer performing a short, floor-bound solo in silence.

"Diabolico," the final section of *Streams*, features a series of fast-paced unison passages split among varied mixed-gender groups. Staged as a pure dance coda for the entire company, the dance builds on classroom-style traveling steps, turns, and kicking phrases. The staging builds to a unison phrase of simple directional oppositions—up followed by down, a reach left followed by a reach right—performed by the dancers spread in even lines to cover the entire stage space. *Streams* ends like "Rocka My Soul" of *Revelations* and "Sham" of *Blues Suite*, with a rhythmically complex arrangement of treading motions, abstract shapes and fast turns, stopping in a lunge toward the audience. As the last percussion sounds fade away, the dancers raise their arms upward into the silence, and the curtain falls.

Ailey conceived *Streams* as a plotless ballet, but, according to its original dancers, he talked about it as a reflection of relationships in the company at the time of its premiere.[11] As "Scherzo" depicted a competition between Williams and Miguel Godreau, building on their unique abilities while assuming a challenge dance format within its very structure, it also suggested an elusive bond between gay men in the Ailey company. Later in the dance, during "Aria," Ailey positioned this male couple prominently among the softly flowing encounters, allowing them to end the sequence with their slow-motion exit. The adjustment in choreography subtly encouraged audiences to acknowledge homosexist bonding within the company, even if, as Anna Kisselgoff noted, "the final plea for all kinds of love—both heterosexual and homosexual—is stated so subtly that many might miss the message."[12]

In this sequence, as in "Lake" of *The River*, Ailey carefully embeds same-sex encounters within a larger group framework of opposite-sex partnering. This strategy of subtle intimation stands closest to Ailey's lifelong project to propel marginalized identities toward the mainstream of modern dance. The slow-motion nonchalance of the two same-sex couples in *Streams* suggests an offhand continuity between homosexual partnerships and a dominant heterosexist model. Ever so gently, Ailey enables a dialogue between his audiences and his dancers about the nature of same-sex partnering, in this instance with all of the dancers invested in the same movement vocabulary. In this, Ailey used concert dance to imply an inherent dignity of homosexuality, embodied in a movement lexicon that aligned it explicitly with the charged heterosexuality that characterized his work.

The four dancers who best embodied Ailey's choreographic construction of the masculine and feminine during this era were the hard-edged and precise Jamison, the softly vulnerable Atlas, the yielding and quietly passionate Williams, and Ailey himself. As a point in this quadrilateral, Ailey built a stage persona from an alluring sensuality improbably linked to his football player's physique as he created roles like the hypermasculine lover of "Backwater Blues" in *Blues Suite*. But he seldom created work that confronted these gendered categories directly. Instead, he explored them separately and distinctly, as pieces in a mosaic of African American identity embodied by his company, to be presented side by side in works like *Streams, Love Songs*, and *Cry*.

As a choreographer, Ailey rarely ventured into the humorous, and gestures of overt comedy are remarkably rare in his large oeuvre. When humor does appear, it is inevitably tied to assumptions surrounding gender stereotypes or sexuality. A clutch of nine church-going women beat their fans furiously at the beginning of the "Yellow Section" of *Revelations*, gossiping in a broad, exaggerated pantomime. In "Riba" of *The River*, a prancing trickster orchestrates a campy parody of ballet and black social dance structures transformed for the stage. During the final section of *Blues Suite*, a wrong-way Casanova gets between couples at play on the dance floor, interrupting several erotic trysts as he mistakenly "feels up" the wrong men and women. Writing about *Blues Suite* in 1966, Marcia Marks found an example of this latter humor excessive: "The role of Miguel Godreau as one of the young men was particularly ambiguous, shifting from flamboyant homosexuality to undistorted conventionality. The unit detracts from the rest of the suite and almost seems the seeds of a new work."[13]

In both *The River* and *Blues Suite*, Ailey constructs the trickster figure as "queer": uncommon, outlandish, and vivacious, given to eccentric dancing featuring sassy thrusts of the hips and fierce pops of his wrists, with the whole colored by a self-serving exuberance. Outwardly joyous, the queer trickster steals the spotlight for a brief moment before his inevitable isolation. Discarded by the larger group, he ends his dance alone and without partner.

Ironically, even as Ailey shunned a public declaration of gay identity for himself, gay audiences claimed the company as a touchstone of accomplishment and a shorthand designation for black gay presence. In 1996, black gay romance novelist E. Lynn Harris published *And This Too Shall Pass*, a story detailing a man's discovery of his homosexual identity.[14] In the novel, Sean, a gay African American sportswriter, is preparing a feature story about Zurich, a professional football quarterback. During his background research, Sean learns that Zurich has a twin brother who danced with the Alvin Ailey American Dance Theater. This fact allows Sean to conclude that Zurich's brother is gay and that Zurich might be as well. In Harris's novel, black male presence in the Ailey company points to gay male presence in the world, a configuration Ailey might have denied, but that his company's gay audiences, at least, understood.

Nat Orr, April Berry, and Carl Bailey in Alvin Ailey's *The River*,
circa 1981. Photograph by Bill Hilton

Black Atlantic Dance

Do dancing black bodies always dance black? For many African American cultural historians, the critical category of "black dance" encompasses only social dance. In the realm of the social, the dancing bodies and their audiences merge. As Frantz Fanon writes, "The circle of the dance is a permissive circle: it protects and permits. . . . There are no limits—inside the circle."[1] But what happens outside of the circular realm of the social? Does the black body, publicly displayed, automatically become a privileged "racial" sign? How does concert dance created and performed by African American artists fall into and outside of the circle that protects and permits?

In many circumstances, African American dancers break open the circle that protects and permits. British cultural theorist Paul Gilroy writes of contemporary black social dance: "Instead of taking our places in the circle of the dance where subordination was ambivalently enacted, transcended, and transformed . . . we are invited to consume particularity just like any other commodity. The ring shout gives way to polite applause."[2] Here, the performer no longer dissolves into the crowd, thereby enacting a relationship of black identity in antiphonal call-and-response forms. Instead, the dancer offers stylized movements as objects to be casually consumed by immobile spectators.

To think through the mechanisms that mark black bodies in public spaces, we must consider a counternarrative of public spaces as "white spaces." I contend that a public space, at least in terms of concert dance, is a white space, a space of production and consumption, a modernist space, a fetishized space, a Europeanist space. A display of the black body in any of these spaces confers a responsibility on the artist, who assumes "custodianship of the racial group's most intimate self-identity. The black body makes explicit the hidden links between blacks and helps to ground an oppositional aesthetic constituted around our phenotypical difference from 'white' ideals of beauty and a concept of the body in motion which is the residue of our African cultures."[3] Significantly, this public space is outside the circle that protects and permits.

Black Atlantic theory means to allow us a common dialectic as Africans in diaspora. According to Gilroy and others, antiphony, or call and response, is the principal formal feature of its artistic practices and expressive cultures. Antiphony works best in physical intimacy, in a circle where all can see the other dancers across the way.

Moving into the circle, I ask: Where is the Black Atlantic located in concert dance gesture? Richard Wright locates its expression in the diasporic tradition of bitterness; Gilroy calls this the condition of "being in pain."[4] Either articulation suggests that we will recognize the Black Atlantic in concert dance through a pervasive dissatisfaction with existing modes of expression, a need and desire to remake concert dance, that is, dance of the open circle, in some unique idiom or perverse restructuring of what came before. If the circle that permits and protects must be opened, it will deny its audience's expectations of comfort; it will force you to mourn, or shout, or become enraged that you might enter into dialogue with its bitter tongue, that you might somehow close the circle that permits and protects. The Black Atlantic gesture in concert dance intends to force its audience to presence, that we might see each other across the footlights.

Consider a concert dance of the Black Atlantic, Katherine Dunham's *Choros*, created in 1943 and revived by the Ailey company in 1972.[5] The five-part work presents a theatricalized social dance, a pas de quatre based on a Brazilian version of the French quadrille. *Choros* begins with a man and a woman who approach each other from opposite sides of the stage to pose in a series of balletic postures. When the music shifts into a driving rhythmic motif, they launch into a high-spirited unison dance marked by fast footwork and grand leaps toward each other. As they join hands, another couple enters suddenly to traverse a similar floor pattern with unison jumps through the space. The two couples engage in a figured dance studded with hopping on one foot, multiple pirouettes, balancé combinations in triple meter, and fast striding promenades between musical phrases. Throughout, the basic quadrille figures are punctuated by complex rhythmic breaks, and the short fourth part includes rhythmic variations for the men, danced in unison. At one point, the melody disappears, and drumming patterns lead all four dancers into a series of clapping and low-to-the-ground stamping steps.

Performed without scenery but with extravagant black-and-white costumes of long white skirts and slacks topped by intricately brocaded shirts, *Choros* is clearly related to the American cakewalk as an African version of a European social dance form. Dunham's innovations in staging the dance involve the degree to which she reconceived its structure from a figured dance to a proscenium format. As, literally, a "square" dance, the original quadrille is opened in Dunham's version, so that the audience can view the flirtations and competitions among the four dancers on stage. *Choros* intercuts balletic turning motions with recognizable "get-down" stepping passages. More than this, the work exists as the creative invention of an African American woman's response to a Caribbean version of a Brazilian social dance based on a French social form. As Black Atlantic theory is constantly concerned with hybridity, *Choros* offers a fine example of the possibilities of Black Atlantic dance.

My body understands how to be inside and a part of the circle that protects and permits. The practical activity of my dance—my gesture, my words, and what I mean to tell you by my stance—all contribute to how I construct my own black identity. It is not a singular construction; it has no proscriptive limits of gender, sexuality, or caste. My life as a black person is coherent and always changing. My experience follows Gilroy in its complexity; I am aware that "the fundamental, time-worn assumptions of homogenous and unchanging black communities whose political and economic interests were readily knowable and easily transferred from everyday life into their expressive cultures has . . . proved to be a fantasy."[6]

This takes us back to vernacular dance and the problem of conflating the everyday gesture with the extraordinary. Concert dance is never vernacular; dance that is prepared can only make reference to dance that emerged within closed black spaces. So what of our circle? Is it exclusive to black dancers in "core black cultural spaces"? Can "black dance" stretch to accommodate work by white choreographers? Certainly. Its aesthetic principles can be learned, and then the protective circle can form around a new, hybrid dance. We certainly see this in white hip-hop, in cheerleading, in some concert dance choreography by choreographers who do not claim African ancestry. But this reformation often inspires failures in readings, as audiences, dancers, and choreographers don't necessarily understand their relationship to the circle. The circle protects and permits. When it is opened, we are no longer protected, although we may be permitted. Gilroy reminds us that "the globalization of vernacular forms means that our understanding of antiphony will have to change. The calls and responses no longer converge in the tidy patterns of secret, ethnically encoded dialogue."[7]

But this change in locality that Gilroy predicts needn't be conceived as a loss; in terms of dance scholarship, it may most definitely be a gain. The migration of African diaspora dance forms from the closed circles of social spaces to the open circle of the concert stage allows us an enormous opportunity to document performance and its vital impact on culture in re/formation. The transformations of African-derived movements through the Middle Passage, and their emergence in the Americas and Europe as elements of concert dance, hold special significance for scholars working to construct histories of the body in motion. These particular histories—of black bodies dancing black—form the body, the corporeal essence, of any study of black dance.

TEN

Later Dances

Ailey's choreographic output slowed considerably after the Ellington festival. Despite numerous requests for his work,[8] he made no new dances for his company or any other for two years, a gap representing the longest break in his creativity since 1958. Meanwhile, the Ailey enterprise continued to expand during this period. By 1976, Dance Theater Foundation managed the Alvin Ailey Repertory Ensemble, founded in 1974 and headed by Sylvia Waters since 1976; the Alvin Ailey Student Workshop, composed of advanced students from the Ailey school, which performed in hospitals, schools, and longer in-school projects under the direction of Kelvin Rotardier; and the Alvin Ailey American Dance Center, the dance school supervised by Thomas Stevens.[9] The "first company" Alvin Ailey American Dance Theater continued to tour extensively and represent the United States as an effective cultural ambassador in overseas tours, including a second Far East tour of Japan and the Philippines in 1977.

The advent of a strong executive board in 1974, led by corporate lawyers Howard Squadron and Stanley Plesent, relieved Ailey of day-to-day pressures related to the management of the company such as payroll and tour logistics. But as corporate sponsorship and grant procurement tactics became more sophisticated, so did the logistical pressures on Ailey to predict his future needs and aspirations, sometimes two and three years in advance.[10] Ailey responded poorly to these changes in infrastructure, becoming wan and withdrawn, appearing alternately lonely and aloof.[11] Several journalists sensed that the powerful board, ultimately responsible for the fiscal vitality of the Ailey enterprise after Ailey's death, actually alienated Ailey from his work. As the company ran efficiently even with his diminished creative input, Ailey settled into choreographic hibernation and psychotherapy.[12]

Still, the Ailey enterprise had reason to celebrate. The accomplishment of twenty years of fairly continuous company maintenance spawned the first book-length publication devoted to the company, *The Alvin Ailey American Dance Theater*, with text by dance writer Joseph H. Mazo and photographs by Susan Cook. Mazo's text includes brief critical descriptions of several Ailey dances and other works from the Alvin Ailey American Dance Theater repertory. Ostensibly laudatory, Mazo's text manages a derisive tone in its depictions of the company's popularity and highlights a "danger" in Ailey's "emotional approach" to choreography, in which "the artist can oversimplify his statement, fail to fully extend the music into visual terms, repeat himself too often, or complete a work only to find that, like the canvases of the 'primitive' or 'naive' painters, it presents its subject in only two dimensions." Later, Mazo compares Ailey disparagingly to others:

> Balanchine, Graham, and Cunningham are among the great molders of the art. They have changed the way we see dance and the way we see ourselves. Alvin has not. . . . Ailey is a theatrically imaginative choreographer rather than a kinetically inventive one. He relies on a fairly limited choreographic palette. His work relates directly to the music rather than augmenting it. . . . Ailey maintains a commitment to emotional honesty that, despite his weaknesses in aspects of formal dance composition, makes him valuable.[13]

In this passage, Mazo offers a fine example of the parochial platform many white dance critics assumed in relation to Ailey's work and the Ailey enterprise throughout the 1970s. He writes as if Ailey's mission to explore African American cultural history holds little promise to "change the way we see ourselves," while dismissing as irrelevant the startling revision of stage personae Ailey engendered for dancing black bodies. He reduces the stature of Ailey's accomplishments to insinuations of imitation, fervency, and commercialism. All this is accomplished in a volume marketed as a tribute to the Ailey company's achievement on the occasion of its twentieth anniversary. Startlingly unimaginative criticisms like these hounded Ailey throughout his lifetime, lending purpose to his ambivalence at both his company's success and his own role as a spokesman for black presence in modern dance.

The spring 1978 premiere of an in-house marketing newsletter titled *Revelations: The Friends of Alvin Ailey* promised an Ailey premiere for the upcoming spring season: "Cello Suite," a "solo-showcase for the unique talents of Judith Jamison," set to music by Howard Swanson.[14] That piece never materialized, but Ailey instead created *Passage* (3 May 1978) as a solo vehicle for Jamison. The work marked Jamison's return to the Ailey company after a short professional absence.[15] Performed to the 1976 composition "Ritual and Incantations" by prominent African American composer Hale Smith, the work united Ailey with visual artist Romare Bearden, who designed the setting, costumer Normand Maxon, who had designed costumes for Ailey's *Ode and Homage* in 1958, and resident lighting designer Chenault Spence.

According to the program note, Ailey intended the dance as a historical homage to Marie Laveau, "the most powerful voodoo queen in the history of this country, her ceremonies involving snake worship, mystical spells and magic. Beyond her role as a priestess, her influences extended deeply into the social and political fabric of 19th century New Orleans."[16] In an interview, however, Ailey downplayed the historiographic aspects of the work and suggested that the dancer "could represent any woman facing herself in various stages of development."[17] In comments to writer Olga Maynard, Ailey outlined the difficult, dual-purpose nature of creating for superstar Jamison: "I made *Passage* for Judith because she is a dancer of mythical nature. . . . Part of the effect comes from Judith as the person, part from the intensity, the dynamism of her approach to dancing. Judith is a modern woman but she understands ritual, she understands the piety of incantations."[18] Ailey worked quickly on the dance, apparently without disclosing his imagery to the dancer. Jamison, for her part, hesitated to define the work or her role in it, telling one journalist, "I'm not really sure. You should really ask Alvin."[19]

Ailey astutely chose Smith's 1976 score, cryptically described by the composer as "an objective evocation of ritual and incantational phenomenon."[20] A portentous and elliptical composition for orchestra, the fifteen-minute selection suited a choreographic essay on Laveau in its fragmentary patches of melody and seething rushes of brass scored against a yawning, dissonant soundscape. A rehearsal film of the dance, made without Bearden's setting of platforms, suggests an expressionistic work with elements reminiscent of Martha Graham's *Lamentation* of 1930 or one of Mary Wigman's "Witch Dance" series of 1926.

The curtain rose to reveal Jamison standing atop "a monumental platform (like a series of stone tables) with her head and face hooded by a huge crimson cloth whose ends are attached to the floor on either side of the stage." Wearing "a simple long black dress slit on one side to accommodate her powerful extensions," the dancer began a series of harsh, percussive incantatory gestures with her hands and elbows, pulling at the crimson fabric, as "she sinks into deep pliés, seeming to gather in with her arms the unseen forces around her."[21] The cloth reflected her bodily movements "as ripples in a pond"[22] until, at a climactic crescendo in the score, she raised her arms and cast the cloth away. She descended from the platform and its cloth to dance the remainder of the work on the level stage floor.

Ailey's movement vocabulary here included some innovative ideas: pedestrian-style walking patterns, which resist transformation into struts or lyrical glamour; galloping chassé phrases performed as hopping gestures with both arms glued downward to the sides of the body; and a vicious, crawling idea that placed the dancer on all fours, pushing ferociously against the ground. For the most part, however, Ailey relied on his signature vocabulary of extended balances, unfolding limbs, pitch turns, and sculptural poses connected by unexpected variations in rhythmic phrasing. During a central section of the dance, Jamison took hold of a long swath of fabric and used it as a mantle to suggest a transformation of character, from a priestess, to a bird in flight, to a vibrating force of energy writhing on the floor with her body completely sheathed within its confines. Eventually, she ascended the platforms, replaced the larger cloth over her head, and strained her body forward against it. The music suddenly stopped, and the dance ended in this enigmatic image of confinement.

With its series of platforms and expressionistic use of prop, *Passage* represented yet another departure in style for Ailey. But the dance disappeared after a single season of performances. Critics uniformly disparaged the work as a whole, terming it a "stuffy" and "aimless . . . dance of foreplay" burdened with "an emptiness that Miss Jamison did her most to disguise."[23] Some critics recognized the startling metaphor of possession projected by the dancer's body bound in taut fabric; others respected the extreme technical challenge presented by the series of platforms. Most writers, however, found *Passage* too long and unabashedly derivative of Graham works featuring commanding women, architectural structures, and voluminous capes. But even if Ailey had intended no more than to allow Jamison a harsh, Grahamesque vehicle, he succeeded, as critics and audiences responded to Jamison's charismatic presence in the work. Writing for the *New York Times*, Anna Kisselgoff offered: "*Passage* is an abstraction. It shows a woman going through stages of development, into a trance and then into rest. She is as affected as those she is trying to affect, and in her concentration and commitment, Miss Jamison carries off a tour de force."[24]

Sometime in the spring of 1978, Ailey visited the Bat-Dor Company in Israel to set *The River*, *Streams*, and *Myth* on that group. He also created an extravagant new work for the company entitled *Shigaon! Children of the Diaspora* (17 August 1978). Details about the work remain sketchy, although an eroded, incomplete rehearsal videotape of the work in the Alvin Ailey American Dance Center archives marked "Disco Ailey," reveals a forty-minute, large-company suite staged to contemporary dance music by diverse artists, including Earth, Wind and Fire, Laura Nyro, Donna Summer, Heatwave, LaBelle, Diana Ross, the Rolling Stones, and Peabo Bryson. A diffuse piece set in a discotheque, *Shigaon!* reworked signature choreographic strategies, including pulsating lines of dancers staring down the audience from a motley assortment of chairs, familiar from *Masekela Langage*; extended, classroom-style jazz dance phrases set in unison on alternating groups of men and women, familiar from *Blues Suite*; dramatic solo dances for women juxtaposed with frothy, demonstrative solos for men, familiar from *Quintet* and *Blues Suite*; and the sheer joy of dancing, without inhibition, for an audience. In an interview, Ailey termed the dance "a kind of conceptual ballet, a disco ballet . . . aimed at getting the younger people into the theater."[25]

Passage and *Shigaon!* served as prelude to the Ailey company's twentieth anniversary celebration, a homecoming party staged at the City Center Theater on 1 December 1978. The celebration brought a number of guest artists back to the Ailey fold to celebrate the company's success and financial perseverance. The four-hour gala performance, marked by speeches, amplified versions of Ailey dances to incorporate generations of Ailey dancers, and recent choreography by members of the extended Ailey family, included a surprise dancing appearance by Ailey himself as partner to Hope Clarke in "Backwater Blues" of *Blues Suite*.[26]

Ailey allowed the 1978 gala to stand as his farewell to performing, and he made no definite plans to return to choreography for his company's spring 1979 season. On the opening night of that season, however, he announced the un-scheduled premiere of a solo homage to bassist Charles Mingus, "finished the day before."[27] Ailey dedicated *Solo for Mingus* (2 May 1979) "to the memory of that great bassist, composer, rebel, bandleader—SPIRIT—Charles Mingus," who had died 5 January 1979.[28] Set to "Myself When I Am Real," a 1963 piano im-provisation by Mingus that Ailey had used in *The Mingus Dances*, the short, ab-stract work was premiered by Peter Woodin.

Quite long for an abstract solo shorn of explicit dramatic narrative, the eight-minute dance moved from idea to idea like an essay of free association. This sensibility embodied the gist of Mingus's experiments in collective im-provisation and episodic structuring, suggesting something of a choreographic doodle to be performed confidently with intermittent flashes of intensity. But the dance acquired a troubled, self-conscious quality when performed by Woodin. In two rehearsal films from 1979, *Solo for Mingus* seems remarkably ill-suited to the dancer, demanding an expansive, demonstrative technique at odds with his brooding, internalized persona.

Ailey probably intended the casting of Woodin, the sole white man in his company at the time, as a gesture of gentle irony. Mingus, like Ailey, had been precocious, unpredictable, and volatile in his art and lifestyle, as well as errati-cally outspoken in matters of racial inequity and African American identity.[29] White-skinned Woodin's stage persona hinted at the transcendent quality of Mingus's achievements, while sidestepping easy associations of black rage, cul-tural fragmentation, and free jazz in Ailey's homage to the composer. Sub-sequent performances of *Solo for Mingus* by African American and Jamaican dancers Dudley Williams and Clive Thompson garnered better reviews from critics; Anna Kisselgoff thought Thompson gave the work "the high-pitched emotional quality it did not have opening night."[30]

The casting of Woodin in *Solo for Mingus* fit a pattern in which dancers who stayed with the company for several seasons were rewarded by principal casting in an Ailey dance. Although the company officially eschewed ranking, and a dancer in the corps of one work might be a featured soloist in another, Ailey rec-ognized seniority and loyalty when creating and casting new works. He intended for his choreography to facilitate a congenial communication between dancer and audience, and usually created work that could offer its performer a visceral and modernistic platform for expression. In the choreographer's later works, he continued to explore dance making as an act of gift giving by creating technically challenging abstract works that revealed the strengths of younger, athletic dancers and by designing dramatic roles that underscored the emotionally expressive abilities of veteran company members.

▌ *Memoria*

Joyce Trisler's death on 6 October 1979 threw Ailey into a tailspin. Trisler, who had been a friend of Ailey's from the Lester Horton Dance Studio and a respected teacher at the Ailey school, suffered a fatal heart attack while she was alone in her apartment. Her death at the age of forty-five served as a portent to Ailey; it also inspired his grandest mature choreographic achievement.

Ailey dedicated *Memoria* (29 November 1979) to "the joy . . . the beauty . . . the creativity . . . and the wild spirit of my friend Joyce Trisler."[31] Set to two Keith Jarrett works, "Runes" and "Solara March," the dance depicted a woman, obviously Trisler incarnate, traveling through a two-part landscape titled "In Memory" and "In Celebration." Ailey staged the work in three weeks, augmenting his senior company with members of the Alvin Ailey Repertory Ensemble and the Alvin Ailey Student Workshop to bring the total cast to forty-seven, the largest group he ever choreographed.[32]

Memoria begins with excruciating formality: the woman soloist stands center stage, clad in an elegant pale lavender dance dress, her arms tensely elevated with hands clasped overhead like an inverted divining rod. Two men positioned at the downstage corners enclose the space, facing her with an erect simplicity of purpose, awaiting her need. Jarrett's music bleeds into the air, a quivering soundscape of string ensemble, acoustic bass, and piano that suspends time effortlessly, its elongated melodic phrases organized around subtly shifting tonalities. The woman responds to the music and her own muses, moving with intense interior focus throughout this first, "In Memory" section, only once seeing the male guides who accompany and partner her.

The dance builds on a layering of rhythmic foci. Three couples pass through the space between the soloist and her guides, dancing lyrical partnering phrases in an accelerated tempo. The Trisler figure and her guides maintain their own deliberate rhythm, pausing at times to monitor their steady progress toward the center of the space. The passing couples perform increasingly time-compressed crossings until they surround the soloist. As she searches the sky in slow motion, the ensemble and guides link hands to rise and fall repeatedly from a crouching position, contracting percussively as if sobbing. The contrasting rhythmic motors converge at an aural break in Jarrett's score, when the dancers singly rise and squat around the motionless soloist in a poignantly simple rolling gesture of breath.

A solo for the woman created to Jarrett's first piano improvisation builds on Trisler's signature treading gestures and sweeping spirals to the floor. In a videotaped performance of this section, the searing lyricism of Ailey's phrases benefit from the halting urgency of dancer April Berry's movement, from the projection of physical release she allows her lateral balances and spitfire turns. Always searching, the woman rushes through the entire stage space as if seeking a place to rest.

At a musical shift marked by the entrance of string ensemble, a woman draped with a strangely translucent skirt overlay rushes onstage to mirror the Trisler figure. The women respond to each other directly, as the new woman consecrates the ground around the Trisler figure, then blesses her form with mysterious fluttering gestures of hands passing up and down her body. They melt into a striking image of mutual support: one woman in a deep penché arabesque, the other in a high-extension side balance. This striking, unexpected held pose suggests a resolution for the Trisler figure, a place of momentary rest activated by her connection to the other woman. Their bonding allows the guides and ensemble to reenter and dance an extended section of searching and treading through the space gingerly, as if seeking peace. The two guides partner the Trisler figure alternately and reverently, consecrating her form with wavering fingers around her head. Unexpectedly, the entire company arrives at a demanding unison passage: balanced on one leg, they lean forward, focusing on the ground as they unfold a working leg skyward, then raise their torsos to emerge in an arched-back, turned-out position à la sèconde. The sequence echoes a passage in "Second Movement" of *Night Creature*, but here it is performed not as a display of prowess, but as an expression of courage in the face of rising urgency. "In Memory" ends as the company pauses in physical quiescence to witness the Trisler figure's exit, flanked by her guides, as she treads upstage and away into the silence after the music ends.

"In Celebration" introduces a second wave of some thirty-eight dancers separated into age groups: six members of the senior Ailey company clad in gray jersey wedged center stage, flanked by two groups of dancers from the Alvin Ailey Repertory Ensemble and a lengthy single file of young dancers trudging slowly around the periphery. Each group works separately, building bulbously expanding and contracting waves of leaning and swaying gestures that emanate from the center of the stage. The groups of dancers weave through canon phrases, bestowing a formality reminiscent of the dance's opening idea to the constantly flowing patterns. Images of physical restraint and emotional defeat permeate the dance in a lurching, low-to-the-ground lumber used to travel through the space and an expressionistic pile of bodies, with heads stacked gently atop each other. The staging flows constantly, passing through formations and groupings with a relentless lyrical agility.

The largest group of young dancers, clad in nude-colored tights and unitards, respond to a shift in lighting by rushing into an extended diagonal column. The Trisler figure reenters, now wearing a blood-red dance dress. As she moves inexorably forward, her treading motions spark a complex canon of falls, crawling gestures, and levitations performed in sequence by the line of thirty-two dancers she passes. The fantastical brilliance of her red dress against the beiges and browns of the falling and rising bodies underscores an ethereal quality to the sequence: the bodies become the clay of the earth that her movements

Donna Wood and the Alvin Ailey American Dance Theater in Alvin Ailey's *Memoria*, 1979. Photograph by Kenn Duncan

effectively shape. The guides return and lift her up to be encircled by the teeming mass of bodies in a visual gesture of apotheosis.

Memoria moves beyond the deification of Trisler's memory to end with a celebration of her legacy. The score shifts to an animated rhythmic idea, and a new principal man appears to briefly partner the Trisler figure. Dancing side by side, they lead a steadily rising ecstatic dance of spiritual deliverance. The movement phrases cascade atop each other without obvious beginning or middle, allowing the dancers to open their focus and see each other, to respond to each other's presence with casual playfulness. The youngest dancers reenter dressed in brightly colored street clothes, filling the stage as they join into a simple sequence of shoulder, torso, and hip isolations. Finally, the dancers form four circles around the Trisler figure, moving in opposite directions as she works her skirt rapturously in the center. The dance ends with the company grouped around the woman, who is suddenly raised heavenward with her arms pointed directly upward as at its beginning.

Ailey filled *Memoria* with imagery related to Trisler's life and works: gestures clearly borrowed from Trisler-choreographed works, including *Journey* (1958); a group of dance students completing classroom-style exercises with the dedication and precision she inspired; a woman in red at the center of a party in constant, fluid motion. The shadowed woman figure of the first section could represent Doris Humphrey, one of Trisler's mentors; the two guides might be Lester Horton and James Truitte, her teacher and partner, respectively.[33] Her cavalier in the last section could be Ailey incarnate, appearing unexpectedly for a short dance to match her controlled abandon with an effortlessly designed Afro-Caribbean sway of his hips. Ailey manages to transform Trisler's death— her physical absence—into a dance of flowing presence, a loving description of a woman's journey to an afterlife protected by a continuous, circling pulsation of dance.

In *Memoria*, Ailey achieved a rare synthesis of movement lexicon, theme, and overall effect, and the dance remained in the active Ailey company repertory. After his death in 1989, performances of the work seemed as much a tribute to Ailey as to Trisler, an apt memorial to their common dedication to students and a work that effectively introduced several generations of dancers to the Alvin Ailey American Dance Theater stage. Writing for the *Wall Street Journal*, Peter Rosenwald found the dance itself to be "a particularly poignant memorial to . . . Mr. Ailey's belief that each new generation of dancers is a celebration of the life of an art form which he loves and to which he has contributed so much."[34]

On 18 October 1979, the Ailey company studios and offices moved into the newly furbished Alvin Ailey American Dance Center located in the Minskoff building at the corner of 44th Street and Broadway. The school had been located at 229 East 59th Street since May 1971, where it started with an enrollment of 125 students; by 1979, the enrollment ballooned to 5,000. Among the amenities promised by the new location were a well-appointed reception area, a student lounge, changing rooms with showers, and four large studios with three-story windows that overlooked Times Square. Ailey's office was located in a suite of nine administrative offices on the ninth floor of the building. Under his supervision, the school initiated the Arts Connection, a program funded by the U.S. Office of Education, the National Endowment for the Arts, and the New York State Education Department and Division for Youth.[35] Arts Connection auditioned children designated as from "disadvantaged communities" to identify and train potentially gifted dancers.

According to his autobiography, Ailey had begun heavy cocaine use during the choreographic process of *Memoria*.[36] Escalating drug use and unresolved personal tensions led to his highly publicized nervous breakdown on 7 March 1980, when police arrested the choreographer at International House in Manhattan.[37] Journalists attributed his emotional rupture to drug use, diminished contact with his company, and an overwhelming frustration with the need to maintain distinct public and private personae.[38] Diagnosed by doctors at the Cornell Medical Center as manic-depressive, Ailey began a regimen of lithium that he continued until his death.[39]

Ailey made thirteen dances after his hospitalization, eight for the Alvin Ailey American Dance Theater and five for European ballet companies. These dances approached a characteristically broad range of thematic and musical materials, varying greatly in scale, tone, and theatrical concept. *Phases* (5 December 1980), the first of these later works, premiered just six months after Ailey's return from the hospital. A large ballet for fifteen dancers originally comprising six parts, *Phases* used a contemporary score of fusion jazz recordings by saxophonist Pharoah Sanders, trumpeter Donald Byrd, and drummer Max Roach. As was often the case in his later works, Ailey allowed his choreography here to stand only for itself in an ebullient, unselfconscious manner.

Phases began with "Astral Traveling," a soft group piece for fourteen dancers framed by images of community and coherence. The dancers began massed in a soft sphere center stage, carefully arranged in a three-dimensional grouping that sloped backward from the front of the stage. In sensitive unison, they worked through a series of gentle undulations, fanning away from the center with tautly stretched torsos and arms finished by softly held hands. This kaleidoscopic unfurling of limbs, set to the cool pulsations of the Sanders recording, was phrased in lush, extended series to convey an effect of soothing homeopathy, a visual laying on of hands. The passage suggested a throbbing continuity among the dancers, emanating from a powerful, unseen force—perhaps the spirit of Ailey himself—at its center.

Other sections of *Phases* depicted members of Ailey's dance family in bounding states of happiness. "Thembi," the second movement, offered a joyous dance of freedom, expressed as a frothy, happy pas de deux by company veteran Maxine Sherman and relative newcomer Gary DeLoatch. The dance projected the feeling of a jam session, with comping phrases for each dancer as the other soloed in front. Donald Byrd's "Makin' It" provided a fast, funky duet for Marilyn Banks and Masazumi Chaya. Their short, high-energy dance interspersed partnered social dance steps with gulping traveling turns and jumps to detail an encounter between jazz dancers. Frothy like "Thembi," but silly where the first duet had been joyful, "Makin' It" ended almost sensually, with Banks swirling in Chaya's arms, spinning offstage as the lights and music faded.

"It's Time," the final section of *Phases*, emerged as a visualization of the propulsive score by Max Roach staged in a style reminiscent of the hyperpowered choreography of Talley Beatty (in, for example, *Congo Tango Palace* of 1960) and George Faison (in, for example, *Suite Otis* of 1971). Utilizing the entire company of fifteen, the dance featured Dudley Williams as the embodiment of an extended saxophone solo who matched gestures and movements to riffs of the musical recording. Staged at a frenetic tempo to match Roach's drumming, the dance used groups of bodies as visual support to Williams's solo, with shifting groups of men and women rushing in to comp Williams's movement. Ailey's choreography clearly built on his reaction to shifting musical colorations, presenting, in essence, "jazz music in motion."[40]

For Ailey, newly returned to making dances after his nervous breakdown, this successful foray into buoyant, self-referential jazz dance must have proved therapeutic. As a whole, *Phases* created stage imagery of holistic communities and cooperative mutual support in group passages and duets. Its final section

The Alvin Ailey American Dance Theater in Alvin Ailey's
Phases, 1981. Photograph by Jack Vartoogian

contained a relentless drive unmatched in any of his previous work for a large group, suggesting the choreographer's desire to challenge his dancers and excite his audiences.

Where *Phases* suggested an optimism born of working with his company, Ailey's next dance suggested a cynical glamour surrounding celebrity dancers and company fund-raising. Working with the assistance of former American Ballet Theatre dancer Keith Lee, Ailey created *Spell* (3 December 1981), a pièce d'occasion for his company's gala opening night. Set to Keith Jarrett's "Invocations," the fifteen-minute duet described an encounter between Judith Jamison, cast again as the embodiment of priestess Marie Laveau, and Bolshoi Ballet defector Alexander Godunov, who plays a wayward traveler caught in her spell.

Costumed with grotesque glamour by Randy Barcelo, *Spell* began with Jamison's emergence, in flowing gold-and-black gown, from a bank of fog. Powerful gestures of her arms summoned Godunov, clad entirely in black, "his face blank and his body stiff, advancing like a sleepwalker."[41] Her presence awakened him for a first duet during which Godunov lifted Jamison, fell prone, and became enchanted by her ministration, performed as she straddled him.[42] Godunov exited briefly, and returned stripped down to a "fishnet loincloth" for his solo variation, in which Ailey capitalized on "the Russian dancer's mix of virility and softness."[43] Jamison performed a brief solo, then, with Godunov's help, stripped down to a "maillot asparkle with glitter and finished in ankle-length fringes."[44] The dance ended with a short erotic duet and embrace, the couple disappearing into a bank of fog.

Spell exploited the star presence of its dancers, titillating the gala audience with the seductive appeal of their physical majesty. Critics thought little of the work as a whole, terming it "visually, if not choreographically, entertaining."[45] While Godunov managed "some of the necessary sinuous flow" of Ailey's choreography, Jamison was, "choreographically speaking, given very little to do except to *be*."[46] *Spell* disappeared after its single performance, fulfilling Anna Kisselgoff's prediction that the dance stood "to make the history books on more factual than artistic grounds."[47]

Ailey's interest in dance history began to surface aggressively in works he made for his company that probed movement idioms and musical scores previously explored by others. *Landscape* (11 December 1981), inspired by Bela Bartok's "Piano Concerto No. 3" and dedicated to the composer's centenary,[48] featured Mari Kajiwara and Stanley Perryman as initiates in a ritualistic celebration performed by an eight-member ensemble of townspeople overseen by elders Dudley Williams and Marilyn Banks. The dance suggested a landscape reminiscent of Martha Graham's *Dark Meadow* of 1946 or *Primitive Mysteries* of 1931.

Ailey separated the dance into four thematic sections: "Legend," "Touchstone," "Romance," and "Terror."[49] Williams, as a "man who embodies a rather abstract notion of an earth father," opened the work, surrounded by four men; later joined by Banks and four women, the townspeople consecrate Kajiwara and Perryman separately. The initiates met for a sustained pas de deux in the "Romance" section, and the townspeople saluted their union with the "rather cheerful celebration" of the final, strangely titled "Terror" section.[50]

A mythic work that described an insular community with well-defined roles for each of its inhabitants, *Landscape* garnered supportive critical reviews, especially the "exceptionally pretty costumes by A. Christina Giannini" of "long dresses for the women, jump-suits for the men, all in a picturesque array of bright colors," and Kajiwara's "almost transparent dancing," which provided "the key to the work."[51] Critics commended Ailey's apparently newfound choreographic freedom, its "buoyant ease and evident mastery," and its "depth of feeling, a passionate sadness, that climbs into the movement and breaks it apart."[52] Critics also noted the distinctive idiom of the work, which "could be described as 'treated Graham.' "[53] Ailey's treatment of Graham, represented by *Landscape*, probably intended to honor her legacy through a choreographic adaptation tailored to his dancers and audience. Ailey realized that the general audiences his company attracted regularly in the 1980s were not likely to have seen Graham's company; for them, critical comparisons to her work offered little advantage. Ailey, for his part, wanted to bring dance to as many people as possible, and he used elements of Graham technique and diction as he did ballet, theatrical jazz, and social dance structures: as elements in a larger process of dance making.

If *Landscape* offered a meditation on Graham, Ailey's next work revisited the world proposed by Vaslav Nijinsky's *L'Après Midi d'un Faune*. Set to Maurice Ravel's luscious "Introduction and Allegro for Harp, String Quartet, Flute and Clarinet," *Satyriade* (3 December 1982) imagines another mythic landscape, this one populated by a trio of nymphs and their decorously lascivious satyrs. Set in a wood grove complete with hanging blossoms, the work premiered with the capable cast of Mari Kajiwara, Maxine Sherman, and Donna Wood partnered by Keith McDaniel, Gary DeLoatch, and Kevin Brown, respectively.

The curtain rose to reveal three nymphs lying down asleep, wearing "the Nylon Age equivalent of Isadora Duncan's flowing chiffon Greek robes . . . Mari Kajiwara in orange, Maxine Sherman in yellow and Donna Wood in pink."[54] Ravel's music sets a pastoral tone, and, like the people of *Blues Suite*, the nymphs slowly awoke, stretched, and shook off their slumber. As they danced in tightly spaced unison, three satyrs appeared in the background, clad in shredded leotards and headbands fitted with goat's horns. The satyrs posed in a series of hard-edged, angular tableaux, watching the nymphs swirl and pose through a range of soft, melting unison phrases. After each nymph accepted a flower blossom offered by a satyr, they partnered up for a sequence of duet variations. The trio of contrasting duets emerged in sharply gendered relief: flexed feet and extended arms for the men contrasted with turned-out legs, pointed toes, and softly curved arms for the women. *Satyriade* concluded with a propulsive section for all six dancers and the sudden exit of the satyrs, which left the nymphs to return to their opening positions asleep in the grove.

A dreamy idyll, characterized by one critic as reminiscent of a childhood fantasy game of "Let's Pretend," *Satyriade* found halting praise from critics and audiences, who couldn't tell if the dance took itself seriously.[55] Clive Barnes thought it "an affectionate, half-camp and probably only a quarter-serious tribute to those old-style Bacchanalias beloved alike of Ballet Russes choreographers and candy-box painters," an effort swept along by Ailey's "unerring musicality." Anna Kisselgoff praised Carol Vollet Garner's costumes and settings and the overall thrust of a work, "where the rightness of the movement is always apparent. 'Satyriade' is danced with just the right put-on quality and excellent technique by all the dancers—to the enjoyment of all." Critic Tobi Tobias astutely noted the worthiness of the new work in the extant repertory, even as her visual sensibility was policed by race: "Ailey's own new work . . . makes a fine foil for the Beatty. . . . And there's a delicious touch in the casting of a black, a white, and an Oriental woman as the nymphs. . . . Together they are so captivating you hardly notice the silliness of their material."[56] The "race" of the dancers was hardly a "casting touch" for a company composed entirely of black, white, and Oriental dancers; few African American critics of *Satyriade* commented on the race of its performers as if it could be detached from their dancing.

Satyriade was not the hit of the Ailey company's 1982 season; that honor belonged to Talley Beatty's new commissioned work, *The Stack-Up* (1982). Set in a chaotic urban milieu complete with gangs, drug pushers, and discotheques, *The Stack-Up* tells a cautionary tale of a man overtaken by drugs in a bold layering of theatrical and social dance movements. With its incorporation of rap music into its musical score, Beatty's work more than satisfied the company's mission to reflect contemporary African American experience in music and dance. *Satyriade*'s premiere dovetailed nicely with Ailey's alternative mission to deflect ethnic pigeonholing by his dancers, audiences, or critics.

With the aggressively autonomous Dance Theater Foundation Board managing the Ailey enterprise, Ailey allowed himself more freedom to choreograph for other companies. In 1983, he worked in France at the Paris Opera Ballet and Italy at the Aterballetto of Reggio Emilia; in 1986, he traveled to Denmark to work with the Royal Danish Ballet; and in 1988, he returned to Italy to stage a work for the La Scala Opera Ballet. Overall, the works he made for these foreign companies paled in comparison to the dances he made for his own company. Working with unfamiliar dancers in strange settings without the cultural landmarks that allowed him to calculate and then subvert expectations, Ailey's choreography languished, filling up with passages borrowed wholly from earlier works.

Au Bord du Precipice

Still, Ailey made his best choreography in response to particular dancers, and Paris Opera Ballet étoile Patrick Dupond inspired the greatest excitement of *Au Bord du Precipice* (8 April 1983). Created for the Paris Opera Ballet's novelty program of three commissioned modern dance pieces,[57] the thirty-minute ballet offered a splashy, theatrically daring look at the life of a rock musician. Working with a cast of twenty-six led by Dupond, Ailey set *Au Bord du Precipice* to a rushing, layered score by Pat Metheny and Lyle Mays titled "As Falls Wichita, So Falls Wichita Falls." He intended the dance to detail the rise and crushing fall of a rock star: "*Precipice* is inspired by the lives of certain stars of pop music, notably Jim Morrison and Jimi Hendrix, who, at the peak of their success, were constantly driven toward self-destruction. It is in some ways a ballet about loneliness—a ballet where a hero, an idol . . . a star, trapped by the paradox of his times, finds himself at the top—at the edge of the precipice."[58]

A controversial, popular success, *Au Bord du Precipice* premiered in New York on 10 July 1984, danced by the Alvin Ailey American Dance Theater under the title *Precipice* during their summer season at the Metropolitan Opera House.[59] A 1983 film of the Paris Opera Ballet company, made in a rehearsal hall without costumes or scenery, survives.

Precipice describes its central figure's fragmentation succinctly in an opening solo. Clad entirely in white, Dupond runs and skips through expansive circling patterns, taking over the open space with a gallop, then stops suddenly to size up his audience, staring out with a curious detachment. Undaunted, he continues with a joyous running dance, sweeping through a flamboyant series of turns and leaps. At times, he stops dancing to walk a few steps and abruptly pose. His variations in mood are arranged as an incoherent conversation between styles: a balletic leaping passage answers a questioning, stationary pose. His dance ends with a tentative restatement of its opening choreographic motif and a sudden wavering leap offstage.

Subsequent scenes of the ballet detail the causes of the protagonist's psychosis, attributed to the harsh actions of people surrounding "He": "Those Close to Him (His Entourage)" and "Those at a Distance (His Admirers)." Pulsating in eerie slow motion to a recorded soundscape of voices, the large group of dancers begin in a chance canon, waving their bodies up and down, then toward and away from the center of the stage in individual rhythms. Gradually, a melodic idea emerges from the cacophonous recording of voices, and the admirers and entourage settle into a slow unison pulsation danced by the full company spread evenly across the space. They hold their faces expressionless and maintain an accusatory stance directed at the audience. When the music shifts into turbulent phases of electronic sound, the company adjusts to encircle He, reaching and pulling at him in slow-motion waves, edging toward him in waves of greedy hunger. Unquenchable, the mass breaks off into smaller groups of expressionless, undulating bodies, now circling and reaching at each other as He is left alone. He writhes in angst, needing their attention but unable to attain it.

As in *Quintet* and *Flowers*, *Au Bord du Precipice* implicates the theater audience in the construction of the protagonist's celebrity and downfall. A musical shift into drumming signals the entrance of "She (His Woman, His Desire, His Drug)," borne aloft by a group of six men. Wearing long streamers attached to an oversized headpiece, She circles the stage space in an entrance reminiscent of the trip sequence of *Flowers*, before descending to the floor to seduce the audience with a slow, serpentine cross from the back of the stage rife with deep pliés and sinuous, curving rolls of the hips. The men exit, and She launches into a fast-paced variation. Danced in the rehearsal film by original interpreter Monique Loudières on pointe and with her hair down, the solo builds from a dizzying array of fast turns, kicks, and sudden stops in balance, all marked by a hard-edged attack. The men's ensemble reenters to bear She aloft, carrying her offstage as He returns, now clad in black leather and boots, to chase after her. A hallucinatory dream sequence featuring the men follows, staged as a tumescent display of technical excess in a manner reminiscent of "Falls" from *The River*. The men rush onstage in overlapping sequence to perform explosive solo feats and, without pausing, rush offstage. In effect, the men's technical prowess is offered as a thrilling, but ultimately empty, feature of a landscape of corruption.

Ailey treats the entourage surrounding He, familiar from works like *The Mooche*, with a compelling expressionistic dispatch. In a subsequent scene, He is tempted first by a clutch of clawing seductresses and then by She. A gang of men accompany She, mirroring her movements while striding arrogantly with a low center of gravity, their hips thrust lasciviously forward. After the ballet's central pas de deux, the crowd reenters for a short section of cool posturing staged in slow-moving waves, creating the effect of a cinematic dissolve to a new scene. As He moves slowly through the crowd, they first ignore him, then grope at him as they peel offstage singly or in pairs. Unlike the crowds in *Flowers* or *The*

Patrick Dupond and Monique Loudières in Alvin Ailey's *Au Bord du Précipice*, 1984. Photograph by Johan Elbers

Mooche, which merely reacted to their protagonist's excesses, the crowd here is clearly part of the cause of a rising emotional paralysis suffered by He.

A second solo for Dupond depicts his further withdrawal and edging toward the precipice. Danced in a severely restricted section of the stage, the solo builds on excruciatingly slow rises to balance and slow promenades on one leg, separated by low bends toward the ground and elongated backward stretches. His movements and phrasing are strongly reminiscent of the woman's dance in "Fix Me, Jesus" from *Revelations*, but performed here without the benefit of a stabilizing partner. Accordingly, his solo search for spiritual conciliation fails, forcing him into increasingly broad and tense movements without resolution.

The crowd rushes onstage in waves of groups, and She enters bearing a white cape which He greedily takes. Dancing in high heels, She orchestrates a nightmarish bacchanalia, gesturing couples together throughout the space, then dancing with He center stage. The staging again evolves in an excruciating slow-motion rhythm, with the orgiastic partnering set in slow, canon waves that melt into an occasional full-stage unison tableau. Fragments of partnering passages from "Lake" of *The River* and "Aria" of *Streams* emerge in the pairs of inter-twining bodies, danced as a pulsating frame for He and She in the center. He is alternately reverent and abusive to "She," holding her tenderly to lift her high overhead, then casting her violently to the floor. The phantasmagoric sequence builds to a frenzied climax of unison turns performed by the entire company separated by gender, whirling toward and away from the center of the stage. The crowd suddenly assumes a throbbing tableau, with She hoisted atop the men's shoulders with her white cape arranged majestically behind. The crowd rises and bends vacantly, now ignoring He and waving toward a new star performer on the offstage horizon. He is left alone, dazed and depleted, again abandoned.

The score launches into a recapitulation of the opening theme, and He attempts to repeat his opening solo. But now he can't finish the dance: he staggers between skipping phrases; he falls to the floor out of his signature, provocative poses directed at the audience. Gradually, he disintegrates and collapses to the floor to roll about in circles. *Precipice* ends with He center stage, prone, his arms stretched to the sides in a cross position, entirely alone and lost.

Like *Flowers* and the earlier *Quintet*, *Au Bord du Precipice* caused a sensation with its youth-driven narrative, its outlandish fashion backdrop supplied by designer Carol Vollet Garner, and its theatrical convergence of sex, drugs, and rock 'n roll in a ballet presentation. The piece "generated a storm of invective" from many French critics, including Gerard Mannoni's accusations of wasting the talent of Dupond and Loudières in "an enterprise of such bad taste . . . treated in a naive and linear manner."[60] American critics noted the sweeping scale of Ailey's effort, its "dreamlike quality that, perhaps intentionally, set up and maintained an unsurmountable distance between it and the audience."[61] One critic noted Ailey's vibrant "body references to Morrison; his prancing poses, his over-the-shoulder glances, his shamanic stance, his two-arm, self-embracing hug" peppered throughout the work.[62]

The most severe criticisms of the work centered on its obvious, conventional narrative of decay, barely transformed from earlier Ailey works like *Quintet* and *Flowers*. Reviewing the 10 February 1984 U.S. premiere of the work at Berkeley, California, Marilyn Tucker thought *Precipice* "never made us care much about the mess of the main character's life." Rob Baker wondered at the slight impression Ailey allowed She, who seemed "merely the wispy phantom of an LSD dream. . . . At present the relationship posed [between She and He] is not nearly as interesting as that between the Morrison figure and his public." Clive Barnes noted that Ailey again offered his leading dancers enormously virtuosic opportunities to stretch themselves in terms of dance technique and dramatic presence.[63]

Precipice, like *Quintet, Flowers, The Mooche*, and *For Bird—With Love*, depicts an impossible ambivalence dividing celebrity from self-awareness. The theme resonated deeply for Ailey, reflecting his stature as a statesman of dance, forced by that position to maintain a closeted, affable mainstream persona even in the aftermath of his own nervous breakdown. The theme also resonated to scores of African Americans engaged in dual cultural processes of African American and mainstream configurations of identity. Built on commonly held recipes for survival known to black Americans for generations, these dances depict the dangers of advancing too far beyond what is expected and the peril of landing in a spotlight outside of the familial community. Disappointment and disenfranchisement may await those who reach too far, and it may be better to function surreptitiously within the mainstream.

Ailey made *Escapades* (4 July 1983) for the Aterballetto of Reggio Emilia. Set to a pulsating jazz score for instrumental quartet and choir by Max Roach, the four-part, plotless jazz dance bore a conceptual resemblance to *Phases*. Performed by a corps of eight, led by artistic director Amedeo Amodio and Luciana Cicerchia in principal roles,[64] the commissioned work provided Ailey another opportunity to create sustained, self-referential passages of movement arranged to test the dancers' ability to project strength, virtuosic technique, and clarity of line. *Escapades* concerned itself mostly with the emotional release of dancing to jazz music.

Ailey configured the dance in bold, purposeful sequence: an opening section for the male soloist and mixed ensemble; a second section featuring the female soloist and mixed ensemble; a transitory sequence of solos for the principal couple leading into the central pas de deux; and a final section for the entire company of ten. A performance videotape of the Aterballetto company made in 1983 reveals a familiar arrangement of Ailey's choreographic lexicon in the first section: rushing waves of dancers moving toward and away from a soloist positioned center; phrases filled with fluid reaching, sweeping, pulling, and unfolding motions; and virtuostic passages of tilts and pitch turns phrased to reveal the muscular dynamism involved in the performance of the movement.

Buoyed by Chenault Spence's punchy lighting design with kaleidoscopic shifting colors and Carol Vollett Garner's sleek costumes and attractive abstract backdrop, *Escapades* proved a success for Aterballetto, praised for the "zest *cum* precision with which the company . . . performed it."[65] Clearly conceived but overlong, the dance again proved Ailey capable of explosive patterned choreography similar to the signature style of Talley Beatty. Whatever its virtues, however, Ailey didn't think enough of *Escapades* to set it on his own company during his lifetime.

Ailey settled into a steady pattern of making at least one new work each year. Enjoying his organization's carefully managed maturity, the choreographer would rehearse a new work in the fall, preview it on the road during the company's extensive touring season, and premiere the dance in its finished form during the company's December season in New York. For the company's twenty-fifth gala anniversary, held at New York City Center on 30 November 1983, he arranged a pièce d'occasion for sixteen Ailey alumni to the Lionel Richie recording "Can't Slow Down." A sort of teasing strut, equipped with spotlit variations for each dancer, the short processional dance showcased veterans Delores Browne, Merle Derby, Nat Horne, Judith Jamison, Keith Lee, Audrey Mason, Charles Moore, Ella Thompson Moore, Michele Murray, Joan Peters, Harold Pierson, Lucinda Ransom, Dorene Richardson, Renee Rose, James Truitte, and Liz Williamson. The 1983 season also featured the opening solo from *Au Bord du Precipice*, titled "Going, Going, Gone" (3 December 1983), danced by guest artist

Patrick Dupond. Ailey titled his major premiere *Isba* (3 December 1983), a twenty-four-minute work set to George Winston's piano solo "Autumn." Rehearsed throughout the fall and first performed in Richmond, Virginia, the dance realized an arrangement of ornate lyricism surely aided by its long onstage gestation period.

Ailey conceived a ceremonial rationale for the dance, a precept that dictated the formal organization of the work as well as its dancers' roles. *Isba* describes a mythic community of ten men and women celebrants, led by Kevin Brown as a "priestlike figure in a silk sari skirt,"[66] engaged in a rite of communal regeneration organized into scenes of preparation, consecration, initiation, and celebration. The dance featured Sharrell Mesh and Michihiko Oka as initiates, brought together in a ritual of arranged coupling.

The first scene of *Isba* describes the ritualistic preparations for the initiates' union. The community is defined by strictly ordered gender roles, with the bulk of preparatory work falling to the women. The dance begins with a short gesture sequence performed in silence, in which the priest/leader consecrates the ground in the presence of the celebrant women. A long section of anticipatory dancing follows, built from a limited vocabulary of turning gestures varied by articulations of the arms, torso, and head. Wearing long, full dance skirts, the women spin and tilt in shifting kaleidoscopic patterns, pausing for suspended tilts or hard stops in held poses that signal the passing stages of the ceremony. The dance relies heavily on Chenault Spence's shifting series of lighting effects, which shape the stage space in pulsating swathes of color. At a musical shift to a contrasting theme, the celebrant men enter and augment the circular patterning, their silken jumpsuits visually tying each man to a female counterpart. As the priest figure winds through the group, his presence a powerful reminder of communal obligation, the couples assume poses of mutual dependence. This opening section maintains a strict formal organization, with each shift in mood marked by repeated turning patterns that visually frame the priest. The preparations end with a recessional, the celebrants walking toward the priest simply, then suddenly cascading from a single-file row in a series of running and leaping offstage, exiting as the music fades away to finish the sequence in silence.

The slight dramatic conflict of *Isba* stems from the woman initiate's apprehension at coupling. In the scene of consecration, the priest prepares the initiate couple, clad by costumer Carol Vollet Garner in white. The woman first completes a short dance of discovery, testing her ability to control the space around her through tentative stretching and turning ideas. The priest consecrates her with a circular flourish, then summons the male initiate. For a moment, the scene strongly echoes "Wade in the Water" of *Revelations* in its white costuming and dramatic architecture of an initiate couple set in front of a devotional leader. Here, however, the priest exits before their dance begins, leaving them to discover each other alone.

The man begins a dance of courtship, preening in a series of deep pliés in a widespread leg position, swaying his hips in an effort to attract the woman. She seems impassive at first, involved in her own ritual of preparation as she backs away from him. She resists his advance by maintaining her own rhythmic identity. Eventually, she succumbs to join in his dance, and a group of four celebrant men enter in the background to oversee their courtship. These men visually augment the stage picture in a series of posed tableaux, then lift the woman up and display her to the man in several glamorous posed positions. Convinced of their preparation, the entire ensemble swirls onstage to surround the couple in a sunburst tableau timed to the end of the music.

The formal initiation scene focuses again on the woman's anxiety in an exposed, dramatic solo witnessed impassively by the entire community. Left alone, the couple begins a second duet staged as two simultaneous solos, the woman still apprehensive, the man eager to soothe her. They manage to reach some resolution, indicated by a short embrace, and begin a formal dance of partnership. First she gives her weight to him in sways, balances, and lifts; eventually, the couple find their way into a series of mirrored movement. The duet ends with this suggestion of conciliation, with the couple dancing together in generous unison.

The final celebration sequence features a fluid series of solo, duet, and group variations performed by the entire ensemble. At times, the dancers work against the flowing repetition of Winston's piano score, attacking precise gestures on prominent rhythmic pulses, adding percussive, visual accents to the whole. Eventually, the full company joins in a long unison phrase built from a challenging mixture of tilted balances, sweeping turns, deeply arched layouts, and loping strides from side to side. The dancers finally join hands and run downstage in a line, pausing at the edge of the stage to gesture ecstatically with an arm reaching toward a vision in the horizon. *Isba* ends as the company recedes upstage to again form a sunburst tableau, framing the initiate couple and priest as the curtain falls.

The flowing, pulsating eddies at the base of Ailey's movement design for *Isba* surprised audiences and critics with an unabashed lyricism and consummate craftsmanship.[67] Although its obvious narrative structure offers few dramatic surprises along the way, critics responded to the "balance, ease and continuousness of its plan . . . undoubtedly the work of a well-practiced creative hand."[68] The dance contains Ailey's single choreographic gesture toward minimalism, reflected in its musical choice and seeming concern with "extracting the most from a limited range of repetitive movement."[69] The recurrent circling imagery, embedded in a ritualistic scenario of coupling, suggests an optimistic, "peacefully meditative" awareness of the life cycle, bound here by the meeting of gender and the maintenance of order.[70] But these parameters also bestow a hazy simplicity on the dance, allowing it a curiously antiquated, "primitivist" veneer.

By 1983, Ailey's choreography consistently evoked a modernist aesthetic reminiscent of Lester Horton's work, dependent on scenic design and dramatic narrative, a mode discarded by younger, postmodern choreographers. Even in ostensibly abstract works like *Isba*, Ailey veered toward mythically coherent communities with well-defined roles for each of its members. Increasingly, he sought to create work that placed his movement sensibility in historical scenarios or atemporal locales far from the realities of his everyday life.

219

A burgeoning relationship between Ailey and the Gentlemen of Distinction, a group of African American community leaders from Kansas City led by Allan Gray, sparked the experiment of an extended residency for the Ailey company in the Midwest. The company enjoyed a lavish reception there in 1983, and Gray spearheaded a successful community awareness drive that led to the formation of a strong fund-raising arm called the Kansas City Friends of Alvin Ailey. A year later, for the company's 1984 residency there, Ailey created a long-deferred ballet about saxophonist Charlie Parker. *For Bird—With Love* (6 October 1984) premiered with a length of one hour and fifteen minutes,[71] but was later cut by Ailey to forty-five minutes for its New York premiere on 12 December 1985.

Ailey worked with a representative sampling of music from the Parker era, with original connecting material commissioned from composer Coleridge Taylor-Perkinson. The dance spawned the most extravagant array of costume and scenic elements Ailey ever enjoyed while working with his own company, including some four drops, two scrims, projections, voice-overs, and a total of thirty costumes for the company of thirteen. Clearly excited by the opulence of Randy Barcelo's designs, Ailey launched into extensive research of "what he called 'the Parker mystique,' reading books, listening to recordings and talking with musicians who played with the legendary saxophonist."[72] The resulting work combined a biographical diligence and surreal, evocative milieu unmatched in the choreographer's recent work.

Against a backdrop of Parker's passport photo, Dudley Williams begins the dance as the mysterious "Man Who Came Before," a tuxedoed conjure man who oversees and links several disparate scenes. Armed with a prop saxophone, Gary DeLoatch, as Bird moves through sequences describing his musical upbringing in the gospel church, Kansas City jazz club beginnings, preeminence in New York clubs like Birdland, his nervous breakdown, and an extended dance of deliverance in an open-spaced afterlife. Other dancers portray "Men Close to Him—Musicians" in his band, "Women Close to Him—3 Singers and a Pianist," and the eerily glamorous "Two Chorus Girls—One from New Orleans, the other from Kansas City."

The centerpiece of the work, set to "The Song Is You" and "A Night in Tunisia," depicts Bird and his band performing in New York City nightclubs. As two statuesque, heavily sequinned chorus girls edge around the space in nightmarish slow motion, four women seated at small tables shout, prod, and cajole Bird and his six-man band through a series of character dances that correspond to the instrumental solos of the Parker recordings. With nonchalance, the dancers sometimes mime playing instruments as they dance; at other times, their dance physically represents the music. With a remarkable economy of actual dance movement, the staging suggests the multilayered, fragmentary, participatory essence of jazz musicianship in solos that move freely from blatant exhibition to casual struts about the stage, occasional and spontaneous duets between musicians, and the vibrant vocalizations of the dancers throughout the sequence. The dance evokes African American signifying practices in subtle

Gary DeLoatch in Alvin Ailey's *For Bird—With Love,* 1984.
Photograph by Donald Moss

physical details: a man throwing a handkerchief at the feet of a dancing musician; a woman wiping Bird's brow after a particularly sublime passage.

Ailey filled *For Bird—With Love* with fantastical visual imagery. During Bird's breakdown, DeLoatch dons a straitjacket for a sequence of spinning, and his jacket's untied sleeves arc through the space in graceful counterpoint to the tumultuous trembling of free-form jazz drumming. In an image reminiscent of Jamison's entrapment in *Passage,* DeLoatch lunges forward violently, restrained by the ends of the straitjacket sleeves. As Bird tries to revive himself in the sanitarium, he manages a tentative dance step, inexplicably backed by the Two Chorus Girls and the Man Who Came Before. The ballet ends with DeLoatch in a white suit, surrounded by his sidemen, now clad in red jumpsuits, dancing Bird's transfiguration on a bare stage.

Powerfully overwrought, *For Bird—With Love* confused critics and audiences with its bizarre layering of biographical narrative thrust, portentous archetypal characters, dancing, and surreal theatrics. Anna Kisselgoff proclaimed the work to contain "the most brilliant examples of character dancing to be seen anywhere," and Joseph Mazo thought the "dramatic montage . . . not Ailey's most inspired work," as it contained "too many suggestions of earlier pieces."[73]

With *For Bird—With Love* Ailey sought again to canonize an African American artist in a work that managed to revere its subject without disguising the rough edges of his life. The choreographer's own experiences as a prominent African American artist recently fallen from a pedestal of figurehead importance clearly fed the work, as dancer DeLoatch noted in an interview: "For this characterization, I think of the 'struggling artist.' Bird was that, so is Alvin. I'm pretending I'm Alvin."[74] For his part, Ailey claimed kinship with the tenacity of Parker's accomplishments: "I don't identify with the self-destructive part of him that made him abuse his body and finally took him out. I identify with the parts that are revolutionary—that changed the lives of the artists he worked with— and the parts that are loving."[75] Indeed, in this latter regard, the Parker role provided one of the very few emotionally expressive roles in a dramatic dance Ailey created for a male dancer.

In 1986, Ailey received a commission from Frank Andersen, newly appointed director of the Royal Danish Ballet, to stage a production of *The River* and create a large new work for the company. Ailey worked for two months on *Caverna Magica* (22 March 1986), a ritualistic work for nineteen dancers featuring company veteran Mette Høennigen as a goddess/priestess and Lars Damsgaard and Linda Hindberg as two initiates brought together during a rite of spring. Especially responsive to Høennigen's presence, Ailey also made a solo for her titled *Witness* (22 March 1986).

During his stay in Copenhagen, Ailey suffered severe bouts of depression unchecked by medication.[76] The two dances he made for the Royal Danish Ballet bore wounds of creative neglect: overwhelmingly familiar narrative concept, grotesquely extravagant theatrical design, and extensive use of movement phrases borrowed from earlier dances.

Caverna Magica reworked ideas from *Isba* and *Choral Dances*, with Høennigen cast as an omniscient leader presiding over obscure mating rites for a mythic community, in this case defined by the "magic cavern" in which the rites took place. Set to an electronic score by Andreas Vollenweider, the dance followed the familiar narrative sequence of preparation, consecration, initiation, and celebration. The production traded in spectacular stage effects, including rolling thunder and bolts of lighting summoned by Høennigen at its opening and closing, and a voluptuously dramatic scenic and costume design by Carol Vollet Garner. Garner's scenic design featured a shifting array of scrims painted in fantastical colors of oranges, plums, and pinks, which rose, lowered, opened, and closed between scenes, effectively changing the shape of the stage space. In one visually impressive sequence, the celebrants, clad in Oriental "harem" garb, processed through the "cave" bearing mystical orbs of light. The dance concluded with a bizarre double ending of bows to the audience, performed *during* (not after) the final company variation, followed by processional exits as the music faded away. Høennigen remained center stage, and as the scrims repositioned, she manipulated her extravagantly flowing chiffon cape vigorously, summoning the elements as the main curtain descended.

Witness (22 March 1986), a solo describing a woman's spiritual deliverance set to spirituals, revisited the territory of *Cry* and *Revelations*. Like *Caverna Magica*, the dance achieved its greatest effect through its scenery. Douglas Grekin and Patrick Venn's setting suggested a mystical sanctuary, with three stark wooden benches framed by dozens of burning votive candles floating against a darkened background. Clad in a simple, full white dress reminiscent of the costume for *Cry*, Høennigen appealed for mercy in an eight-minute solo set to Jessye Norman's recording of "My Soul Is a Witness for My Lord." Danish audiences applauded the dancer's convincing religious ardor, "at first expressed in tugs, jerks and twitches as well as enormous leaps and extensions," which concluded "as a happy, easy release . . . expressed by running, playful steps."[77]

Ailey allowed his company to perform both works in New York during the December 1986 City Center Season. *Caverna Magica* (New York premiere 2 December 1986) garnered barely modulated contempt from many of Ailey's most ardent critics and audiences, who slighted its "paucity of invention, with stylized swirlings and stampings too often filling in for real dances."[78] *Witness* (New York premiere 2 December 1986) fared slightly better, buoyed by Marilyn Banks's emotionally taut performances, though it too "nevertheless [fell] under the weight of Ailey's overly-familiar formulas for depicting a woman's agitation and exultation."[79]

Survivors

The surreal extravagance of these two works spoke to Ailey's intensifying depression. AIDS entered the Ailey company landscape around this time, taking the lives of two Dance Theater Foundation administrators.[80] Ailey himself was not formally diagnosed as HIV-positive until the last year of his life, when he succumbed quickly to the ravages of AIDS before dying on 1 December 1989. Still, his choreographic retreat into fantastical settings of monstrously oversized scale, in *For Bird—With Love*, *Caverna Magica*, *Witness*, and his final three works, suggests a deepening preoccupation with mortality. In his dances, Ailey sought to deflect these feelings through the creation of mythos. His next work, *Survivors* (Kansas City 13 November 1986, New York Premiere 9 December 1986), described the embodiment of black African tenacity in the face of apartheid as inspired by its living icons, Nelson and Winnie Mandela.

Ailey worked with Max Roach's two-part score: the 1957 composition "Survivors," composed for percussion, voice, and taped string ensemble, and the newly composed "Triptych," scored for percussion and solo voice. Roach and singer Abbey Lincoln Aminata Moseka performed the work live for all of its 1986 City Center season. The two harsh, through-composed musical offerings fit well with Ailey's conceptual narrative of actions and their consequences: political re-

The Alvin Ailey American Dance Theater in Alvin Ailey's
Survivors, 1986. Photograph by Johan Elbers

sistance that led to imprisonment, anguish, and resolution. Departing from the biographical impulse that fueled *For Bird—With Love*, Ailey declined to name the central characters of *Survivors*, instead dedicating the work "Especially for Nelson and Winnie Mandela, whose determination inspires the survivor in us all."[81]

The work describes survivorship as sustained participation in a march to freedom. It begins with trap-set drumming in darkness, sounding a raucous conversation of arrhythmic tones. A male figure in a dark suit emerges from the shadows (Dudley Williams) marching in suspended slow motion directly toward the audience. As more lights bleed onto the stage, a woman in a long, rust-colored dress (Sharrell Mesh) falls into his step slightly behind him. They march in focused accord, eyes pasted on a prize in the far distance, moving without reference to the fervent drumming. Other figures emerge from the shadows: wearing loose-fitting, African-inspired ensembles, three women and two men fall into slow-motion step, advancing inexorably toward the audience. Through this simple and evocative staging device, these few dancers suggest the omnipresence of multitudes, always poised in darkness but ready to join the march.

Sensing an impending change, Williams pauses to look out in the distance as the others advance and recede. At a sudden shift in musical texture, the dancers begin an emphatic movement visualization of the drumming, slashing the air with an array of fast turning phrases, sharp kicks, and angry, punching gestures. Driven by audible but unseen forces, they push and pull at Williams, then turn like cyclones away from him to exit suddenly. Alone, Williams dances an embittered solo of resistance, pushing against the air around him as he sculpts his body into attitudes suggesting physical oppression. His movements develop as a series of sharp, physical interruptions from fluid motions, with accents timed to coincide with chords sounded suddenly by a recorded string ensemble. He shies from the apocalyptic physicality suggested by the choreography and score, adding an interior, stoic gloss that draws attention to the actual movement vocabulary used in the dance. His performance echoes the popular American impression of Mandela as a martyr, a man whose measured actions are more significant than the person executing them.

Mesh enters for a duet with Williams, and the terms of their partnership become clear: where Williams is careful and conciliatory, Mesh exudes harsh precision, transforming leg extensions and turns into expressions of implacable power. These seeming opposites inspire a duet of mutual support in which each dancer holds the other in a series of reaching balances; each restrains the other as anger veers toward anguish. In this and the subsequent pas de deux for Mesh and Williams, Ailey created his sole stage depiction of a functional, loving relationship between a man and a woman.

The ensemble in *Survivors* represent motivating forces surrounding the Mandela figure, at times spurring him to action while at other times lamenting his fate. They enter for a short dance of mimetic fury, pounding against the sky with clenched fists and cutting the air with sweeping layout kicks to remind Williams of his responsibility. They follow him through the space until he collapses sacrificially and rolls helplessly toward the upstage shadows. The ensemble reaches toward him with tensely splayed fingers, but an unseen force holds them back, pulling them away into attitudes of anguish. As the drum sounds subside and a panel of jail bars descends, imprisoning Williams, they sob silently in the shadowy corners of the stage space.

The ballet continues to explore sustained emotional waves of action violently pierced by shards of sudden frenzy. The music shifts to "Triptych," and Mesh dances a long, mournful solo of mounting agony visually supported by the physical contractions of the ensemble. She responds to the moaning sighs of the vocalist, building her dance from excruciatingly slow unfolding motions suggesting perseverance, interrupted by sharply accented contractions suggesting pain and confusion. Williams watches her, at times poignantly echoing her gestures behind the cell bars. Mesh's grief rises in tandem with the vocalist's wails, until suddenly all emotional reserve breaks loose and the ensemble rolls crazily across the floor, skittering as if scalded by fire. The music climaxes with a piercing vocal howl, and the dancers cluster together, clutching each other tightly in a mass of trembling bodies. Repelled by unseen forces, they careen to the corners of the stage space, then manage to group together in time to cover Mesh, acting as a human shield against the unseen oppressor's lash. In a cathartic gesture of release, the music and lights lower, giving way to a moment of silence in darkened relief.

In a coup de théâtre, the central pas de deux of *Survivors* occurs through the bars of the cell. Reaching forward between the bars, Williams partners Mesh, supporting her in balanced promenades, effectively defying his imprisonment through their tender dance of solidarity. In phrases that suggest their emotional parity, they move in accord, creating mirror-image symmetry with their bodies across the bars. Mesh kisses Williams gently. He teaches her a fighting marching step, a triumphant stride of wide stance, proud, rolling torso isolations, and circling clenched fists. She shows him that she understands the movement, then leads the crowd in this new march toward freedom. Williams sinks onto his stool in the cell. Left alone, as the musical score sounds a heavy breathing motif, he stares out at the audience, watching, waiting for change as the curtain falls.

To choreograph *Survivors*, Ailey leaned heavily on company associate artistic director Mary Barnett, who suggested important structural enhancements such as the addition of the ensemble at the end of the dance.[82] Ailey clearly enjoyed the vibrant collaboration of dancers, choreographer, and musicians in the rare process of a commissioned score. As Anna Kisselgoff reported, the work became a "creative event . . . a fusion of each participant's contribution. The meeting ground is the commitment to the subject, the struggle against oppression."[83] From its title to its creative process and its political subject matter, *Survivors* proved to be Ailey in his mature form. The choreographer imagined a theatrically stunning, evocative tribute and simultaneous call to arms: an homage to the Mandelas, a choreographic gift to Mesh and Williams, and a bracing challenge to African American audiences preoccupied with themselves to the detriment of their South African kin. The dance resists analysis or interpretation on the level of the body; it isn't about the steps and movement it contains, but rather the array of emotions it provokes. Bolstered by an insightful stage design, *Survivors* realized Ailey's ambition for true dance theater, created in collaboration and responsive to an expansive vision of African American cultural heritage.

Ailey made *La Dea delle Acqua* (29 March 1988) for La Scala Opera Ballet, a commission designed to fill out a triple bill with *Streams* and *Memoria*. The surprisingly long work described a ritualistic mating ceremony performed by a mythic community. Unlike *Isba*, *Choral Dances*, or the baptism scene from *Revelations*, the scenario here dispensed with the separation of a priest/leader figure from the ceremony's novitiates, centering instead on a bejeweled priestess who both presided over the rites and participated as its central initiate woman. The dance traded in aqueous imagery, with pale blue costuming and speckled lighting effects and sensuous coupling phrases borrowed from *The River*. Made for a company of sixteen, *La Dea delle Acqua* aroused little attention and was not shown in the United States during Ailey's lifetime.

Opus McShann (Kansas City 4 November 1988, New York 11 December 1988), the last ballet Ailey showed during his lifetime, fulfilled a dual mission to honor both the legacy of Kansas City jazz pianist Jay McShann and the vigorous financial efforts of the Kansas City Friends of Alvin Ailey, who commissioned the work. A suite set to ten McShann recordings, Ailey imagined the dance as a "prequel" to *For Bird—With Love*, a sustained evocation of Kansas City in the late 1930s, where Charlie Parker had played in McShann's band. Structurally underdeveloped, the dance meandered through a series of glossy Randy Barcelo settings that alternately suggested a jook joint, a burlesque theater, a barrelhouse bedroom, and a celestial limbo reserved for jazz artists in transition.

Dudley Williams anchored the thirty-minute, large-company work as a tuxedoed interlocutor, clearly embodying the spirit of McShann. He began alone onstage, in silence, with a series of conjuring gestures that drew forth an assortment of Kansas City archetypes from the shadows. At his gesture the music began, and Williams alternately oversaw the nightclub proceedings and mimed playing an invisible piano. Striding in omniscient slow motion, he moved freely in and out of the various scenes, connecting its mixture of presentational dances, comic vignettes, theatricalized social dances, and private dramatic rituals of sexual role playing. In a gesture to historic authenticity, Ailey turned to choreographers Frank Manning and Norma Miller to stage a jitterbug sequence set in a jook joint. He then undercut this danced reminiscence with a fantastical turn: a group of masked Ku Klux Klan members somersaulted onstage, interrupting the dance with a series of strangely toned undulating gestures. Williams then removed his jacket to dance a solo of spiritual conciliation, attempting to drive the Klansmen away by the emotional force of his dance. Suddenly, the Klansmen dispersed, and the company reassembled onstage, now transformed into an expansive, celestial limbo. They grouped around dancer Gary DeLoatch as Williams dressed him in the costume jacket belonging to the Bird character of *For Bird—With Love*. *Opus McShann* ended when DeLoatch sat on a chair center stage, rocking tremulously, as the other dancers backed away, awaiting his musical suggestion.

Like *Blues Suite*, *Opus McShann* evoked a mythically coherent landscape of African American history, where music, dance, and sexual play converge in response to social oppression and the need for survival. Both works offer a context in which to situate blues and jazz as heroically vital forms of cultural invention and release. In the later work, Ailey eschewed the gentler implication of offstage oppressors he allowed in *Blues Suite*; the onstage Klansmen force the audience to consider political history as a component of African American music and dance.

Both suites grew from Ailey's responses to the music, from his understanding of the variety of rhythms, breaks, harmonic progressions, and improvisatory structures articulated therein that suggested an emblematic range of locale and mood. Each work included a centerpiece dance confrontation between a sequestered man and woman, with "Gee Baby Ain't I Good to You" of *Opus McShann* rivaling the "Backwater Blues" of *Blues Suite* as a concise essay in gender relations. In the later work, Ailey exploited the formidable virtuosity of dancer Sharrell Mesh-Alexander to represent female desire: her extended un-foldings and bodily precision contrasted with partner Andre Tyson's sullen in-difference and blockish formality of motion. In this section of his final work, Ai-ley came full circle to create a synthesis of modern dance technique and character-driven emotional narrative that successfully expressed several modal-ities of the blues.

Alvin Ailey, circa 1964.
Photographer unknown

Alvin Ailey, Public and Private

Writing about one person's body of choreography elicits more questions than it answers. How do we remember dance? What may be important about its memory? What did Ailey think of his own work, and how did he remember it? Was he ever happy with his achievement? Was his desire to make something big and bold, scaled to opera house stages, all-consuming? Is this desire what pushed him beyond what he seemed able to handle in his private life? Was he compelled to create an American Dance Theater because, to his mind, no one else had?

> Asked what is the nemesis of his own life, Ailey answers quickly, with a sweep of his hand. "This," he says. "Having a dance company. That is the great struggle, that has been the challenge of 30 years. Keeping it all together is still the problem, the constant battle to afford the engagements, the designers, the choreographers, to pay the dancers a decent wage. You have to keep proving that you have a right to exist."[1]

In the fall of 1988, Ailey received a John F. Kennedy Center Honor, awarded for Lifetime Achievement in the Arts, along with comedian George Burns, actress Myrna Loy, violinist Alexander Schneider, and theatrical producer Roger Stevens. This presti-

229

gious award came as his company searched for a new home and veered precipitously toward financial ruin. During Ailey's lifetime, his company never achieved financial stability. He was rarely celebrated by the largest New York community of choreographers, and criticisms that he had made his best works first—in *Blues Suite* and *Revelations*—persecuted his memory long after his death.

> It has to be constantly proven again and again to the powers that be that we are worthwhile. And I don't know whether that's the product of the inherent racism in the society, or my own personal feeling, but I feel it very strongly. I also feel that all of this takes place at a kind of an enormous personal sacrifice. It is something that is all-engrossing and it keeps me in a stage of turmoil all the time.[3]

Even as audiences grew steadily for Ailey company performances, and the Alvin Ailey Foundation operations expanded steadily, a suspicion that Ailey was not worthy of his own success hovered nearby. The unasked question, implicit in dozens of feature articles and reviews, seemed to be: How could a gay black man from dirt-poor, rural, Depression-era Texas, with limited dance training and no college degree, found and run the most successful modern dance company in the idiom's history?

> I don't know if I will ever choreograph again. Sometimes I think, "God, Jesus Christ, I don't ever want to do this again." It's the hardest thing I ever tried to do in my life. . . . Then, other times, when I feel like I really must do this right this moment, the company is on tour or we're involved in something else. So the fact that the company has become so structured has, in a way, become a hindrance. There isn't the freedom to do whatever I feel like doing.[4]

As a young choreographer, Ailey had no opportunities to try out movement ideas or play without the risk of damaging his professional reputation. He started as the resident choreographer for the nationally recognized Horton company, and after one workshop composition, every piece he ever made was reviewed by professional critics.

> It's a ballet . . . about choice. . . . I think Jim Morrison chose to fall. By the way he took himself out, with the alcohol, the drugs, the stress of trying to stay on top pulls him forward into the precipice. I think we all choose; you either choose to fall, or you don't. . . . Remember . . . despite the fall, the spirit still survives.[5]

Ailey's demons stayed close to him. He engaged in psychotherapy that was decidedly inconclusive; he used drugs frequently and recklessly; in later years, he pursued "rough trade" aggressively, picking up young men for sex who were by no means his equal. His ill-requited love for a young Arab man, Abdoullah, led directly to his nervous breakdown, but few of his closest friends knew much about Abdoullah or his relationship to Ailey. In interviews, those closest to Ailey confirm that he rarely discussed his private life at all and seemed to have few avenues of emotional support. Despite this, he submitted himself to interviews by journalists on hundreds of occasions.

Sometimes I will start with an idea, other times with a piece of music. However I do it, I find it difficult to do on schedule.[6]

Ailey's actual choreographic process remains shrouded in a casual mystery. He created an individual notebook for each of the dances he made. Each notebook contains, at most, an overall thematic depiction of the dance, detailed character descriptions, drawings of proposed settings and costuming, and casting ideas; each contains at least an outline of the counts to the music. In accounts of his rehearsal etiquette, he seldom discussed theme or the intention of his movement ideas with his dancers. Surely he expected his dances to speak for themselves, in their directness and recurring depictions of ritual order and transformation.

I think that people come to the theater to look at themselves, to look at the state of things. I try to hold up the mirror, although I try not to be too depressing about it.[7]

For years, Ailey's death from AIDS in 1989 remained a jealously guarded secret of the Ailey company and estate, maintained according to a concern over the public perception of the company by its assumed heterosexist audience. But in the early 1990s, we all felt the specter of illness at New York dance performances. Other African American choreographers, including Bill T. Jones, Donald Byrd, and Garth Fagan, explored emotional and kinesthetic landscapes drawn by AIDS; audiences could no longer pretend that sexuality belonged only to a marginal, offstage private world.[8] Ailey himself, though, belonged to an older generation, one that rarely spoke publicly about personal experiences or trials. For example, only those closest to him heard him discuss his 1967 arrest and overnight detention in New York at the hands of policemen who suspected him of having murdered four policemen in Cincinnati. The police were looking for a black male with a moustache and beard; Ailey, like a million other black men, fit the description.[9]

Also like many other black men, Ailey allowed his tastes, ambitions, and creative work to speak about the world he inherited, to remember its difficulties and hardships and celebrate its possibilities through the medium of dance. His interests in black people and their histories were never discarded or forgotten as he met and interacted with more and more white Americans and Europeans with power and influence; he never abandoned his sensibilities as they stood in an obvious Africanist aesthetic lineage that valued the actions of the group over the desires of the individual. Ailey was no martyr or saint; he was an enormously gifted artist who seems never to have quite savored the profound effect his actions had.

Mostly, thinking about Ailey's life makes me wish. I wish he had more close friends, I wish he had a healthy intimate relationship. I wish he had consistent patrons, mindful of Harold Youngblood's remark to Zita Allen, "Ailey did it without the help of a wealthy person. 'Martha Graham had that Rotschild woman. Balanchine had Lincoln Kirstein, and American Ballet Theatre had Lucia Chase. Who did Alvin have?' "[10] I wish he might have understood—and enjoyed—how much his energy and vision transformed so many lives in terms of dance.

ELEVEN

Concluding Moves

In a 1977 discussion of *The Lark Ascending*, Ailey informed journalist Peter Rosenwald that "the critics never knew what this ballet meant. The lark is ascending and the girl is becoming a woman. All my ballets are about transition."[11] A recurrent theme in Ailey's work clearly involves passage and the journey to reconfiguration, from the dysfunctional family scenarios of *Morning Mourning*, through the emotional voyage of the woman in *Cry* and the monk in *Hermit Songs*, to the initiations of procession-filled rituals in works like *Isba* and *Caverna Magica*. In Ailey's choreographic landscape, the liminal moment of transition, once established in some dramatic-narrative context, invariably proved ripe for dance.

Ailey choreographed most often in suite form. The suite allowed for imaginative variations around a theme of situation, as in *Masekela Langage*; around the musical selection, as in *Three for Now—Modern Jazz Suite*; around a theatrical conceit, as in *The Mooche*; or around an exploration of movement theme, as in *Streams*. The suite appealed to Ailey's lack of choreographic pretentiousness, it allowed him flexibility to continue developing a work after its premiere, and it allowed for a carefully mediated layering of movement tonalities within a single work.

In the suites and the narrative scenarios Ailey choreographed, solo dances often emerge as arias—extended dance meditations on the character's state of being. Typically, these solos offer no emotional resolution for their characters. Instead, they focus on subtle variations within a narrow emotional palette, as in Adela's first solo of despair in *Feast of Ashes* or the lark's first solo of joy in *The Lark Ascending*. The aria format, popular among modern dance choreographers of the 1940s and 1950s such as Martha Graham in *Appalachian Spring* (1944) and Anna Sokolow in *Rooms* (1955), fell into disfavor among postmodern choreographers of the 1960s and later. Ailey's use of the aria format as late as the mid-1980s in works like *Survivors* made some younger audiences and critics see his late work as old-fashioned.

Ailey's choreographic output testifies to a voracious catholicity of musical taste. He drew his choreographic structures directly from his musical scores, at times to the point of subservience to rhythm and shifts in tonality. Although he frequently used vocal music from several genres, his staging related more to rhythmic and harmonic structures than to song lyrics. His strongest works grew from musical sources with strong, shifting rhythmic underpinnings and clear percussive accents; his weakest, from repetitive music without clear modulation, as in *Witness* and *La Dea della Acqua*.

The importance of lighting to Ailey's theatrical vision cannot be overestimated. Remembering his lessons from the Horton studio, he relied on his lighting to significantly alter mood and the shape of the stage space. Through time, lighting design for Ailey works became more sophisticated and complex, until a short dance, such as "I've Been 'Buked" of *Revelations*, may contain as many shifts of lighting as it does verses and choruses. The complexity of these designs is often discussed as external to Ailey's choreography, as he rarely spoke of his design collaborators in interviews and rarely finished work in time to actually rehearse with lighting before premieres.[12] Some critics found the conspicuous design plots for Ailey's dances excessive. Writing for *Dance Magazine*, Suzanne Merry termed the design for *Solo for Mingus* "a terribly murky blue-green light that shifts excessively with perceived shifts in the music."[13]

Lighting for Ailey dances by his main collaborators Nicola Cernovich, Chenault Spence, and Timothy Hunter always guided the viewer through the space, amplifying the choreographic patterns by drawing the audience's eye directly to the dancers. In *Witness*, for example, Hunter's design casts circular pools of light at the center of the stage space in two colors of pale blue and white. The pools travel subtly about the space, following the dancer's movement across the stage. These lighting effects occur in front of a setting of flickering candles, a visual hindrance overcome only by Hunter's virtuosic design ability.

Working most often in a realistic idiom, Ailey relied extensively on costuming to signify character. For example, the congregation in the final section of *Revelations* wears clothes suitable for a Sunday church service; the hip people of "Such Sweet Thunder" from *Ailey Celebrates Ellington* sport garb likely to be seen at a party in Harlem. Extravagant theatrical costuming pushes forward the characters of *Quintet* and *The Mooche*, building on the trappings of show business to explore the theatrically heightened presentation of self. The choreographer's fascination with grotesque theatrical exaggeration reached a pinnacle in the two oversized chorus girls of *For Bird—With Love*. Clad in sequined g-strings and ornate head plumes, the women wander, usually in eerie slow motion, through the landscape of Bird's imagination. In this dance, the women surpass any vestige of humanity to embody only the netherworldly extremes of the theatrical.

These hypertheatrical "mannequins" appeared at regular intervals in Ailey's work. More often, however, he created dances that project archetypal characters, or social types, through an effective gestural shorthand. The presence of these "types" fed the movement lexicon in several works, providing thematic associations of gesture, stance, and even rhythmical phrasing. These characters were rarely sustained throughout entire dances, or even sections of dances; sometimes they emerged, full-blown, in a single phrase or gesture. Ailey usually used these types to populate his work with "down-home" characters.

In *Pas de "Duke,"* for example, Ailey allowed the archetypal "Harlemesque" characters to come forward in the movement itself. Audiences understood Jamison, Baryshnikov, and their successors to be strutting, Uptown types, showing off for each other and celebrating their own cool. Ailey conveyed this in the specificity of the dancer's walk, the man's stance, a shrug of the woman's shoulder, the careless lift of the leg that preceded an incredible volley of flamboyant turns. These archetypal motions suggested "black folks" as a type, a crystallization of stance and gesture equally available to the culturally divergent casts of dancers in his works.

According to Richard Philp, Ailey talked about his choreography in terms of snapshots of people he had known: "He often began a new dance with 'certain images, visual images that may occur in the dance, of groups of people, of patterns.' He talked in photographic terms of 'moving stills' and discussed blending, as in action photography, of 'several images that, in my mind, eventually become the dance.'"[14] This assessment provides a worthwhile insight into the recurrent posed tableaux in dances Ailey made throughout his career, from the opening silhouette of *Blues Suite* through the final tableau of *Opus McShann*. Ailey used the theatrical proscenium to frame his carefully arranged architectural visions, always aware of his own mediation of the dancer and the audience's perception of that dancer.

In Ailey's choreography, drugs served as a marker of contemporary significance and concern, and drug use afforded dramatic impetus in several works, including *Flowers, Shaken Angels, Au Bord du Precipice, Cry,* and *Love Songs*. In the first three works, onstage drug use provides access to an altered state appropriate to phantasmagoric dance expression. In the last two solo works, an offstage partner's drug use pushes the dancer to lament the destructive effects of the drugs. Notably, these five works are set in an explicitly contemporary time frame, where everyday social behavior may influence the theme and action of the dance. In this, Ailey staged actions from the world he lived in, actions that also concerned and resonated with his core African American audiences as truisms of modern urban life.

After Ailey veered structurally toward choreographic abstraction, his work strove to reveal the dancer as a person inside the act of dance, to evade the transference of stage gesture into intellectual abstraction. In a 1988 interview, he described his motives:

> I've always been interested in communicating to the common man without any kind of aesthetic condescension. A high artistic profile, yes, but I wanted the ordinary person to come and see their lives, their pain and their hope, on that stage. I'm constantly shouting at rehearsals, "You're boring everybody to death, dear. You're dancing about dance, not about life! Don't go out there and be a ballerina, reveal yourself! That's what's unique. Show us what you're feeling!"[15]

Even as Ailey made abstract dances about dance, as in *Phases*, he encouraged his dancers to perform the works dramatically, to create a personal narrative of growth and transition inside the movement, inside the act of dancing. He demanded that his dancers lay emotional claim to the stage, to perform his choreography as a confirmation of human presence.

A large portion of Ailey's success came from his ability to reveal dancers to their audiences. Speaking of his choreographic process, he told an interviewer in 1975, "I have to make it [a dance] on a person. The quality of the individual, how they look, how they feel the music, how well they interpret lyrical movements, are all influential."[16] For Ailey, the intellectual pursuit of abstract structure held limited choreographic currency; making dances meant creating movement for people to inhabit. In 1978, critic Marcia Siegel noted that Ailey's "best and most memorable works have been dances of character" and wondered if his method had been about "convincing us that not just modern dancers but his particular dancers could be stars."[17] In this latter vein, Ailey dances consistently succeeded, bringing forward a perennial roster of celebrated dance personalities in dances sharply tailored to their abilities.

The Ailey after Ailey

According to a 1992 *Dance Magazine* feature, the Alvin Ailey American Dance Theater began its 1993 season without any operating deficit whatsoever. This historic occurrence, possibly unique in the fiscal management of American modern dance companies, confirmed the palatability and power of Ailey's larger vision. Before 1992, the Alvin Ailey American Dance Theater earned "seventy percent of its $8.3 million annual operating budget," an "unusually high" figure for modern dance.[18] Following the trajectory set by Ailey, the company continued to tour extensively within the United States and abroad, attracting sell-out audiences augmented by its extensive lecture-demonstration programs, teaching residencies, and high-profile reputation for excellence as a repository for an African American tradition in modern dance.

Even as it expanded financially, the company managed to sustain systems of extended family, African American informality in its New York City galas. By the

1980s, the Ailey enterprise stood as one of the disappearing sites of interracial performance, an emissary of hope that African American culture processes could be engaged and sustained by an integrated public. In 1981, Anna Kisselgoff's disparaging review of Ailey's *Spell* also commented on the success of the evening as a whole:

> Ailey benefits are different from other dance-company galas, which nowadays tend to be stuffed-shirt affairs. Alvin Ailey, through the sheer force of his committed personality, manages to make these events intense family type gatherings. The mood in the theater is that of a friendly, homey living room. And if this might lead to an occasional piece that looks better in a closet than a parlor, that is all right, too. The spirit of the evening counts.[19]

Kisselgoff's comments approach an underlying truth of the Ailey enterprise: *what* the company danced could never compete with the fact of its continuity and the appropriation of that achievement as a measure of cultural pride.

Eventually, changes in the arts marketplace removed Ailey from tension with many dance critics and the nominal dance establishment that annoyed him throughout the 1960s and early 1970s. By 1975, critic David Vaughan noted, "It used to be that in New York there was something called 'the dance audience' that one used to see at any and every performance. Now it is clear that there are almost as many audiences as there are companies, which is why so many dance attractions can play simultaneously."[20] As Ailey's audience crystallized and the company began to program, and sell out, its season long in advance of performances, critics lost any sway over what the Ailey company produced or the company's public prestige. This significant shift, which accelerated and continued after Ailey's death, allows the company a robust financial existence, essentially detached from the troubled critical responses Ailey endured during his lifetime. The company proves its value and centrality to contemporary life in performances, whether critics appreciate its efforts or not.

Ailey's modern dance enterprise as a center of cultural growth continued in his company's Kansas City residencies. Before the New York opening of *Survivors*, *New York Times* reporter Jonathan Probber noted, "Mr. Ailey has fired interest in dance throughout a region not necessarily known for that, and his works have helped give Kansas City's substantial black population increased pride in their own large musical heritage. Furthermore, the planning and fundraising required to stage the two-week residency . . . helps unite the white and black communities of Kansas City."[21] In 2003, the Kansas City Friends of Alvin Ailey continues as an important fiscal partner to the company's continuity.

█ *Revelations* 2003

By the 1970s, audiences identified the Alvin Ailey American Dance Theater so completely with *Revelations* that critic David Vaughan described its perfor-

The Alvin Ailey American Dance Theater in "I've Been
'Buked" from Alvin Ailey's *Revelations*, 1999. Photograph
by Josef Astor

mance as mandatory: "The Ailey company without 'Revelations' is almost un-thinkable: each season, in fact, they attempt to make programs without it but before the end the public demand is such that they have to rearrange everything to put it on every night."[22] Even as the company acquired dozens of works by as many choreographers, and Ailey himself created dozens of additional dances, *Revelations* persisted as the signature work of the company, a venerable document of modern dance history and "perhaps the best known and most loved of all American modern-dance classics."[23]

Tensions surrounding what the dance had been in earlier manifestations and what it had become also persisted. Dance critics consistently compared with disfavor contemporary performances of the dance to their memory of earlier versions, typically citing changes in its scale and its dancers' technique. In 1978, a *Soho Weekly News* writer described current performances as being "executed as a tour of style and technique in an ambiance approximating Sammy Davis Jr.'s Vegas shows." In a feature article devoted to the thirty-fifth anniversary of the dance, *New York Times* writer Jennifer Dunning quoted several generations of Ailey dancers who mourned the lost "feeling of sharing and community" the dance previously contained: "'There is a sort of uniformity now,' Ms. [Ella Thompson] Moore says sadly. 'Everyone's leg has to go up to 6 o'clock, or maybe 6:10. Everyone has to do four or five turns.'"[24]

Indeed, by 2003 most dancers in the Alvin Ailey American Dance Theater had enjoyed advanced dance training either at the Ailey school or some other accredited institution. The younger dancers routinely had a stronger technical facility than any of Ailey's original company members. At times, the younger dancers performed elaborations of simple movements in *Revelations* as arrogant acts of appropriation—just because they could. The younger dancers took hold of Ailey's original movement design and amplified portions of it, often creating their own distinct version of its contents. Their performances shifted the range of interpretations applicable to the dance, from modernist correlations of physical slavery resolved through the group's spiritual uplift, to postmodernist explorations of dance technique framed by fragments of African American cultural history.

For some, this rearticulation of the work obscured its meaning and diminished its emotional power. As the younger dancers focused on the physical challenges of performing *Revelations*, they evaded the emotional truths contained by its choreography. Ailey company dancer Sarita Allen told Dunning, "They [young dancers] see a tape of an old performance and say, 'Look at how low that leg is.' . . . They don't see the richness. . . . Alvin developed 'Revelations' on adults. . . . They were adults with deep emotions. Those emotions require time. The younger dancers haven't suffered in the same way. In a way, that's good. Times have changed. But there's no way they can identify."[25]

In one sense, dancers and critics mourned the loss of a world in which the smaller version of *Revelations* could exist. The dance boom of the 1960s and 1970s expanded the audience and the accompanying infrastructure of company practice to such an extent that by 2003 an internationally renowned, eight-person company dancing to sacred music could only be esoterica. A consistent note sounded by Ailey in thirty years of interviews was his resistance to the notion of a privileged audience for dance. Ailey allowed *Revelations* to change in order to allow it to speak to the shifting rosters of dancers performing it. Performances of the dance in 2003 invited audiences to a display of beautifully trained bodies, moving in striking accord and physical magnificence to musical documents of African American history. The dancers no longer embodied the experience of the sacred music by their very presence as black bodies performing for mostly white audiences. Instead, the dancers worked *to* the sacred music, at times capturing its slippery truths in a humorous gesture here, a triumphant balance there. But in the era of postmodernism, the dance had come to represent itself as an inimitable achievement of choreographic invention. By

2003, there was no dance like *Revelations* in the company's wide repertory, and few contemporary choreographers commissioned by the Ailey company worked in the humanistic mode that had inspired *Revelations*. Performances of the dance reminded audiences of the Ailey company's endurance as a modern dance company and as a home for an international roster of black dance artists.

By 2003, Ailey's *Revelations* achieved a cogent counternarrative to the "dangerous" implications of African American modern dance suggested by Isadora Duncan and Martha Graham in the previous century. The work's careful alignment of a range of movement idioms, particular African American themes, and a structured deployment of the "psychic intensity" contained by gospel music and jazz dance effectively define the American "modern" in a way that no other dance work can. For contemporary audiences, the work enacted the crucible of race relations born of slavery, but through an emphatically systemized representation of order, dignity, and public possibilities for physical expression. In many ways, *Revelations* answered the call to create an American system of dance representation that might be inhabited by any dancing body, but would speak to an American history shared regardless of class background.

Ailey received numerous honors and awards throughout his career. He always used the opportunity of his acceptance speeches to reiterate his aims for his company and choreography. Receiving the 1975 *Dance Magazine* Award along with Cynthia Gregory and Arthur Mitchell, Ailey again stated his convergent political and aesthetic ideals: "I am celebrating the trembling beauty of the black American. I am not just a black choreographer. Black American culture is a part of the whole country's heritage. The dances are created to celebrate the human experience—to communicate to everyone—and through the concept, our dance is for art regardless of color."[26]

Still, according to his audiences and critics, Ailey's strongest success stemmed from his works exploring aspects of African American cultural history. Of eight "major works" cited by Ailey biographer Jennifer Dunning, only two, *Night Creature* and *Memoria*, have been performed by companies of mostly white dancers, and those are "abstract" works.[27] The other works on Dunning's list— *Blues Suite, Revelations, Quintet, Masekela Langage, Cry*, and *For Bird—With Love*—have been performed only by companies featuring dancers of African descent. Each of these dances presumes a tension surrounding the construction of black identity. Thinking about his company's twentieth anniversary, Ailey expressed an ambivalence about his work's encodings of race: "I've never been asked by another dance company for *Revelations*. I'm not so sure that it would work [for a white company]. Certainly the personal identification would not be there: It would work as choreography, it would work as structure, as dance, but as far as its being a statement about the black experience—which is an important part of its ethos—it would be lost. And I wouldn't be too anxious to have too many white companies do them."[28]

Ailey created a thriving cultural institution balanced on the double-edged sword of race. His choreographic success in six works Dunning cited comes because of his engagement with blackness as an inevitable political construction;

still, he wanted more than anything to reveal "art regardless of color." Several times he threatened to disband his company, wondering why "the inherent racism in the society" forced him to prove "again and again to the powers that be that we are worthwhile."[29] Ailey didn't live to see his company emerge financially solvent by 1993, a profound accomplishment in an era of diminishing resources for arts funding.

For Ailey, dance theater could not offer transcendence from the racial and political foundations of everyday life. He rarely attempted to use dance to promote ideals far beyond those he already knew to be present in his collaborators or audience. His choreographies of beauty, anger, desire, and community confirmed truths that his audiences understood, even as these dances allowed audiences a welcome, public manifestation of these ideas. The performance event, and its clear intimations of socialization represented by the mastery his dancers always embodied, fulfilled his intertwined aesthetic and political aspirations. In 1983, speaking at the occasion of his company's twenty-fifth anniversary, he described his original objective in creating work: "I wanted to explore black culture, and I wanted that culture to be a revelation."[30] In the realm of modern dance, at least, his choreography and company practices evinced African American cultural processes as revelations, available to the world but best contained by dancing black bodies.

Choreography by Alvin Ailey

APPENDIX

All punctuation and ellipses are as they appeared in original programs.

Afternoon Blues. Summer, 1953. Composition Workshop, Lester Horton Studio. Music: Leonard Bernstein (Selection from *On the Town*). Based on Vaslav Nijinsky's *L'Après Midi d'un Faune*. Original cast: Alvin Ailey.

According to St. Francis. 4 June 1954. Lester Horton Dancers. Music: Gershon Kingsley. Costumes by Larry Maldonado. Lighting design by Alvin Ailey. Decor by Alvin Ailey. Original program note: "A dance play in five continuous scenes after the life and spirit of St. Francis of Assisi . . . conceived as a play within a play." Original cast and order: "Player's entrance; 1. Play Dance . . . a poverty figure offers the deep life, 2. Francis returns to his revelries . . . but is troubled by a memory of fire . . . dance of rejection . . . interlude . . . a door is opened in the wilderness . . . vision offers life for death . . . 3. The deep life . . . canticle of love and faith . . . uncertainty . . . dance of joining . . . penitence . . . celebration . . . death. 4. Mourning . . . 5. Rebirth and celebration . . . players' exit." James Truitte as the St. Francis figure; Misaye Kawasami as the poverty figure, vision figure, figure of rebirth . . . and Lelia Goldoni, Joyce Trisler, Yvonne de Lavallade, Roland Goldwater, Alvin Ailey, Don Martin as players.

Morning Mourning. 4 June 1954. Lester Horton Dancers. Music: Gertrude Robinson. Costumes by Alvin Ailey. Lighting design by Diane Kadden. Decor by Alvin Ailey. Original order and program note: " 'I give you the truth in the pleasant guise of illusion . . .'

from Tennessee Williams' *The Glass Menagerie.*" *Morning*: Carmen de Lavallade as "The Daughter": Lelia Goldoni as "The Mother"; James Truitte, Alvin Ailey (alternating) as "The Father"; *Afternoon*: de Lavallade as "The Woman"; Truitte, Ailey alternating as "A Very Young Man"; Goldoni as "Another Woman"; *Evening—Mourning*: de Lavallade as "The Woman"; Truitte, Ailey (alternating) and Goldoni as "Two Strangers."

Creation of the World (La Creation du Monde). 13 July 1954. Lester Horton Dancers. Music: Darius Milhaud. Costumes by Ves Harper. Lighting design by Nicola Cernovich. Single performance in San Diego, California with the San Diego Symphony Orchestra.

Blues Suite. 30 March 1958. Alvin Ailey and Company. Music: Traditional blues, arranged by Paquita Anderson and Jose Ricci. Original scenery and costumes by Geoffrey Holder. Later versions, costumes and decor by Ves Harper. Lighting design by Nicola Cernovich. First performance: New York, Kaufmann Auditorium, 92nd Street YM-YWHA, Alvin Ailey and Company. Original cast and order: Clarence Cooper as A Blindman, Nancy Redi as The Woman Upstairs, Claude Thompson as Her Lover, Tommy Johnson as The Other Man, Charles Moore, Herman Howell, Charles Neal as The Men, Ella Thompson, Audrey Mason, Jacqueline Walcott, Minnie Marshall as The Women. "Good Morning Blues" (Cooper, Redi, Company), "Smoke Dream" (Claude Thompson), "Fare Thee Well" (Mason, Ella Thompson, Walcott), "New Broom" (Redi, Thompson), "In the Evening" (Cooper), "God Bless the Child" (Claude Thompson and Company), "Careless Love" (Mason, Marshall, Ella Thompson, Walcott, Redi), "Jack of Diamonds" (Cooper and Company), "Good Morning Blues" (Company).

Ode and Homage. 30 March 1958. Alvin Ailey and Company. Music: Peggy Glanville-Hicks. Costumes by Normand Maxon. Lighting design by Nicola Cernovich. Decor by Normand Maxon. Dedicated to Lester Horton. Original cast: Alvin Ailey.

Ariette Oubliée. 21 December 1958. Alvin Ailey and Company. Music: Claude Debussy. Costumes by Normand Maxon. Lighting design by Nicola Cernovich. Decor by Normand Maxon. Original program note: "How wan the face. O traveller, this wan/ Gray landscape looked upon. / And how forlornly in the high tree-tops/ Lamented thy drowned hopes.— Paul Verlaine." Original cast: Alvin Ailey as The Man; Don Price as The Clown; Carmen de Lavallade as The Moon; Audrey Mason, Dorene Richardson, Ilene Tema, Cliff Feats, and Tommy Johnson as the Company; Jeff Warren, Tenor.

Redonda/Cinco Latinos. 30 March 1958/21 December 1958. Costumes by Normand Maxon. Lighting design by Nicola Cernovich. A work in five sections, with titles that varied from performance to performance and included: Prelude, Liricas (music: Baxter), Rumba (music: Fields), Beguine (music: Prado), Rumbalero (choreography: Ernest Parham; costumes: Lew Smith), Rite (music: Black), El Cigaro (music: Fields), Bolero (music: Liter). First performance: New York, Kaufmann Concert Hall, 30 March 1958, Alvin Ailey and Company, Ernest Parham and Company; the work was entitled *Redonda* (Five Dances on Latin Themes) and included Lirica, Rumba, Beguine, Rumbalero, Rite. Costumes by Normand Maxon and George Mills. Second performance: New York, Kaufmann Concert Hall, 21 December 1958, Alvin Ailey and Company; the work was titled *Cinco Latinos* (Five Dances on Latin Themes) and included Prelude, Liricas (Dorene Richardson, Minnie Marshall, Ella Thompson, Tommy Johnson, Cliff Fears, Herman Howell, Alvin Ailey, and Audrey Mason); El Cigaro (Charles Moore and Jacqueline Walcott); Bolero (Claude Thompson, Lavinia Hamilton, and Ella Thompson); Rite (music: Knudson-Black): Charles Moore as The Shaman, Dorene Richardson, Minnie Marshall, Tommy Johnson, Herman Howell as Acolytes; Alvin Ailey and Audrey Mason as The Initiates. Program note (21 December 1958): "These are not intended as exact duplications of any ethnic form but creative interpretations of the mood, style and rich variety of the Afro-Brazilian-Caribbean heritage." Performance at Jacob's Pillow Dance Festival, 30 June 1959 included Prelude, Liricas, Rite (music: Gonzalez).

Mistress and Manservant. 1 February 1959. Shirley Broughton Dance Company. Music: Maurice Ravel. Costumes by George Mills. Based on "Miss Julie" by August Strindberg. Original cast: "The Mistress," Shirley Broughton; "Her Manservant," Robert du Mee; "Her Maid," Connie Greco; "Her Other Servants," Carole Eisner, Patti Morrow, Gene GeBauer, Danny Joel.

Sonera. 31 January 1960. Alvin Ailey and Company. Music: Alejandra Caturla. Costumes by Thomas Wendland. Lighting design by Nicola Cernovich. Original order and cast: "Sonera," "Camparsa," "Danza." Delores Browne, Betsy Dickerson, Joy Smith, Gene GeBauer, Jan Mickens, Dudley Williams.

Revelations. 31 January 1960. Alvin Ailey Dance Theater. Music: Traditional. Original scenery and costumes: Laurence Maldonado. Lighting design by Nicola Cernovich. Later productions (after 1960), costumes by Ves Harper. First performance: New York, Kaufmann Concert Hall, 92nd St. YM-YWHA. Original program note: "This suite explores motivations and emotions of Negro religious music which, like its heir the Blues, takes many forms—'true spirituals' with their sustained melodies, ring-shouts, song-sermons, gospel songs, and holy blues—songs of trouble, of Love, of deliverance." Original cast and order: Pilgrim of Sorrow: "I Been 'Buked" (arranged by Hall Johnson), The Company; "Weeping Mary," Nancy Redi; "Poor Pilgrim," Nancy Redi; "Round about the Mountain," Joan Derby, Minnie Marshall, Dorene Richardson; "Wonder Where," Merle Derby; "Troubles," The Company; That Love My Jesus Gives Me: "Fix Me, Jesus" (arranged by Hall Johnson), Minnie Marshall, Herman Howell; "Honor, Honor" (arranged by Howard Roberts), The Company; "Wade in the Water" (arranged by Howard Roberts), Joan Derby, Jay Fletcher, Merle Derby, Nathaniel Horne; "Morning Star," Nancy Redi, Joan Derby, Merle Derby, Minnie Marshall; "My Lord What a Morning," The Chorus; "Sinner Man" (arranged by Howard Roberts), Gene Hobgood, Nathaniel Horne, Herman Howell, Jay Fletcher; Move, Members, Move!: "Precious Lord," "You May Run On (God a Mighty)" (arranged by Howard Roberts and Brother John Sellars), "Waters of Babylon," and "Elijah Rock!," The Company. Later additions: "Daniel (Didn't My Lord Deliver Daniel?)" (arranged by James Miller), "Processional" (arranged and adapted by Howard Roberts), "I Wanna Be Ready" (arranged by James Miller), "The Day Is Past and Gone" (arranged by Howard Roberts and Brother John Sellars), "Rock-a-My Soul in the Bosom of Abraham" (arranged by Howard Roberts).

Creation of the World (**Second Version**). 31 January 1960. Alvin Ailey Dance Theater. Music: Darius Milhaud. Costumes by Ves Harper. Lighting design by Nicola Cernovich. Cast: Alvin Ailey, Matt Turney.

African Holiday. 26 February 1960. Theatrical Revue, Apollo Theater, New York. Music: Various. Codirectors: Alvin Ailey, Peter Long.

Jamaica (**Musical Comedy**). Summer stock, Lambertsville Theatre in the Round in Pennsylvania, 1960.

Knoxville: Summer of 1915. 27 November 1960. Alvin Ailey Dance Theater. Music: Samuel Barber. Costumes by Joop Stokvis. Lighting design by Nicola Cernovich. Original program note: "We are speaking now of summer evenings in Knoxville Tennessee in the time

I lived there so successfully disguised to myself as a child—James Agee." Original cast: Kevin Carlisle as the boy; Miriam Pandor, Yemima Ben-Gal, Myrna White, Herman Howell, Alton Ruff as the people he remembers. Revised version: Edinburgh, Church Hill Theatre, 28 August 1968, Alvin Ailey American Dance Theater. Cast: Miguel Godreau as "The Boy," Judith Jamison as "His Mother," Kelvin Rotardier as "His Father," Michele Murray, George Faison, Alma Robinson, Eleanor McCoy, Linda Kent, Ernest Pagnano, Michael Peters as "Relatives, Children, Visions."

Three for Now—Modern Jazz Suite. 27 November 1960. Alvin Ailey Dance Theater. Music: Jimmy Giuffre, John Lewis. A triparte work with a shifting order. First performance: New York: Clark Center, West Side YWCA. Original program note: ". . . in the spirit of fun . . ." Original cast: James Truitte, Yemima Ben-Gal, Myrna White, Herman Howell, Ella Thompson, Paul Roman. "Suspensions" (music: Giuffre), "Sun Dance" (music: Lewis), and "The Golden Striker" (music: Lewis).

Roots of the Blues. 12 June 1961. Alvin Ailey Dance Theater. Music: Traditional. Costumes by Ves Harper. Lighting design by Nicola Cernovich. Decor by Ves Harper. First performance: Boston, Boston Arts Festival Theatre. First New York performance: Lewisohn Stadium, 1 July 1961. Original order and program note: "From the fields, levees, barrelhouses of the Southern Negro sprang the blues—hymns to the secular regions of his soul . . . 'when you see me laughing/I'm laughing to keep from crying.'" "Waiting," "Jack of Diamonds," "In the Evening," "Backwater Blues," "Mean Ol' Frisco." Original cast: Alvin Ailey and Carmen de Lavallade.

"Gillespiana." 19 July 1961. Alvin Ailey Dance Theater. Music: Lilo Shifrin. Costumes by Ves Harper. Lighting design by Nicola Cernoivch. Added to *Three for Now.* Original New York cast: James Truitte, Alvin Ailey, Ella Thompson, Myrna White, Minnie Marshall.

Hermit Songs. 10 December 1961. Alvin Ailey Dance Theater. Music: Samuel Barber. Costumes by Ves Harper. Lighting design by Nicola Cernovich. Original program note: ". . . small poems of anonymous monks and scholars of the 8th to 13th centuries speaking of the simple life these men led—close to nature, to animals, to God." Original order: "At St. Patrick's Purgatory," "Church Bell at Night," "St. Ita's Vision," "The Heavenly Banquet," "The Crucifixion," "Sea Snatch." Original cast: Alvin Ailey.

Been Here and Gone. 26 January 1962. Alvin Ailey Dance Theater. Music: Traditional folk. Costumes by Ves Harper. Lighting design by Nicola Cernovich. Decor by Ves Harper. Original program note: "Anybody ask you who made up this song, Tell 'em Jack the Rabbit, he's been here and gone. . . ." Original cast: Brother John Sellars, Ella Thompson, singers; Alvin Ailey, James Truitte, Charles Moore, Minnie Marshall, Georgia Collins, Don Martin, Thelma Hill, Connie Greco, dancers. First New York performance: Delacorte Theater, Central Park, 9 September 1962. Cast and order: "Big Stars Falling" (Chorale), "Keep Your Lamp Trimmed and Burning" (Brother John Sellars, Hilda Harris), "Country Dance" (Company), "Boll Weevil" (James Truitte, Nathaniel Horne, Don Martin, Ray Gilbert) "Children's Song" (Thelma Hill, Geri Seignious, Altovise Gore, Minnie Marshall), "Marigolds" (Harris), "Fare Thee Well (Seignious, Marshall), "Big Boat up the River" (Sellars and Company), "Reprise: Keep Your Lamp Trimmed and Burning" (Company).

Creation of the World (**Third Version**). 9 September 1962. Alvin Ailey Dance Theater. Music: Darius Milhaud. Costumes by Ves Harper. Lighting design by Nicola Cernovich. Decor by Ves Harper. Original cast: Alvin Ailey, Minnie Marshall, James Truitte, Nathaniel Horne, Thelma Hill, Don Martin, Geri Seignious, Ray Gilbert, Altovise Gore.

Feast of Ashes. 30 September 1962. Robert Joffrey Ballet. Music: Carlos Surinach. Costumes by Jac Venza. Lighting design by Thomas Skelton. Decor by Irving Milton Duke. Libretto: Federico Garcia Lorca (*The House of Bernarda Alba*). First preview performance: New York, Fashion Institute of Technology. First performance: Lisbon, Teatro San Carlos, 30 November 1962, Robert Joffrey Ballet. Original cast: Bernarda, Françoise Martinet; Adela, Lisa Bradley; Angus, Suzanne Hamons; Sisters, Karina Rieger, Marlene Rizzo, June Wilson; Pepe el Ramono, Paul Sutherland; Señor Muerte, Felix Smith; O Frade, Vicente Nebreda; Hommes de Aldeia, Lawrence Adams, Finis Jhung, Vicente Negreda, Lawrence Rhodes, Helgi Tomasson, John Wilson; Mulheres, Elisabeth Carroll, Maie Paquet, Illona Issaksen.

"Reflections in D." 28 April 1963. Alvin Ailey Dance Theater. Music: Duke Ellington. Lighting design by Nicola Cernovich. First performance: Brooklyn Academy of Music. Original cast: Alvin Ailey.

Labyrinth. 28 April 1963. Alvin Ailey Dance Theater. Music: Lawrence Rosenthal. Costumes by Ves Harper. Lighting design by Nicola Cernovich. Decor by Ves Harper. First performance: Brooklyn Academy of Music. Original program note: "This ballet attempts to delineate in part the legend of the Greek hero Theseus and his encounter with the Cretan Minotaur—a beast half-bull, half-human to whom annual sacrifices were made. Given a magical red string by Ariadne with which to retrace his steps from the dark and complex maze, Theseus enters the labyrinth, engages the beast in combat and then emerges." Original cast: "A Man Like Theseus," Louis Falco; "A Woman Like Ariadne," Mariko Sanjo; "Three Men Like the Beast," Don Martin, Donato Capozzoli, Glen Brooks.

My People (First Negro Centennial). 19 August 1963. Theatrical production. Music: Duke Ellington. Costumes by Ves Harper. Lighting design by Ves Harper. First performance: Arie Crown Theater, Chicago. Dances included "The Blues Ain't," "Light," and "My Mother My Father." Co-choreographer with Talley Beatty on "Work Song."

Rivers, Streams, Doors. 6 September 1963. Alvin Ailey Dance Theater. Music: Traditional folk. Costumes by Ves Harper. Lighting design by Nicola Cernovich.

Jerico-Jim Crow. 12 January 1964. Off-Broadway production. Music: Traditional. Costumes by Ves Harper. Lighting design by Ves Harper. Langston Hughes play with music. Ailey codirector with William Hairston. Cast: Gilbert Price, Hilda Harris, Joseph Attles, Rosalie King, William Cain, Dorothy Drake, and the Hugh Porter Gospel Singers.

The Twelve Gates. 11 August 1964. Carmen de Lavallade and James Truitte. Music: Traditional spirituals, arranged by Brother John Sellars. Costumes by Geoffrey Holder. Decor by Geoffrey Holder. Original program note and order: "If I could I surely would/stand on the rock where Moses stood. . . ." "This small suite of songs and dances, inspired by the images of woman in the Bible, is respectfully dedicated to—Ruth St. Denis and Ted Shawn." "Amazing Grace," "Herod's One," "Oh Mary Don't You Weep," "Twelve Gates," "Little Boy," "Jezebel," "Jesus Met the Woman at the Well." Original cast: Carmen de Lavallade and James Truitte. Brother John Sellars, folksinger.

Ariadne. 12 March 1965. Harkness Ballet. Music: André Jolivet. Costumes by Theoni Aldridge. Lighting design by Nicola Cernovich. Libretto by Pierre-Alain Jolivet and Alvin Ailey. Decor by Ming Cho Lee. First performance: Paris, Opéra Comique, Harkness Ballet. Original program note and cast: "Réalisation moderne de la légende d'Ariane et Thésée et du Minotaure. Le livret qui sert de base pour ce ballet a été écrit par MM.

Pierre-Alain Jolivey et Alvin Ailey, et représente l'histoire vue du point de vue d'Ariadne." Pasaiphaé, Mlle. Suzanne Hammons; Minotaures, MM. Salvatore Aiello, Finis Jhung, William Jacobs, Kenneth Kreel, Vicente Nebrada, Dennis Wayne, Richard Wolf; Ariadne, Mlle. Marjorie Tallchief; Thésée, MM. Nicholas Polajenko; Les Porteurs d'étendards, Finis Jhung, Richard Wagner, Dennis Wayne; Les Hommes, Salvatore Aiello, William Jacobs, Kenneth Kreel, Vicente Nebrada, Richard Wolf; Les Femmes, Mlles Kathleen Bannon, Lili Cockerille, Hester Fitzgerald, Barbara Livshin, Karina Rieger, Sarah Thomas.

Macumba. 11 May 1966. Harkness Ballet. Music: Rebekah Harkness. Costumes by Jose Capuletti. Lighting design by Nicola Cernovich. Decor by Jose Capuletti. Also called "Yemanja." First performance: Barcelona, Spain, Gran Teatro del Liceo. First U.S. performance: Chicago Opera House, March 1967, under title "Yemanja." Cast and order at premiere (Original Program in Spanish)

I. Fiesta de la Candelaria, Candomble
Avin Harum, Judith Jamison, Kathleen Bannon, Jacques Cesbron, Alexis Hoff, Philip Kaesen, Barbara Livshin, William Jacobs, Bonnie Mathis, Vicente Nebrada, Carlyn Muchmore, Robert Vickrey, Sarah Thomas, Denis Wayne, Lili Cockerille, Miyoko Kato, Donna Stanley

II. Exu, dios del mal
Finis Jhung and corps de ballet

III. Yemenja, diosa del mar
Brunilda Ruiz with Alexis Hoff, Carlyn Muchmore, Jacques Cesbron, William Jacobs, Vicente Nebrada

IV. Capoeira, danza guerrera
Salvatore Aiello, Dennis Wayne, Kathleen Bannon, Lili Cockerille, Bonnie Mathis, Karine Rieger, Sarah Thomas, June Wilson, Jacques Cesbron, William Jacobs, Robert Vickrey, James Truitte, Miguel Godreau, Morton Winston, Kelvin Rotardier

V. IFA, Dios y diosa de la caza
Suzanne Hammons, Roderick Drew, Avin Harum, Dale Muchmore, Robert Scevers

VI. Carnival

a) Desfile
Hombre con sombrero: Vicente Negrada
Mujer con pájaros: Mary Barnett
Pastor y Pastora: Marlene Rizzo, Ali Pourfarrokh
Dos Egipcios: Barbara Livshin, Salvatore Aiello
Muchacha con Bandera: Consuelo Huston
Tres Rusos: Finis Jhung, Robert Vickrey, Miguel Godreau
Napoleón y Josefina: Miyoko Kato, Robert Scevers
Pareja excéntrica: Loretta Abbot, James Truitte
Dueto: Marlene Rizzo, Ali Pourfarrohk

b) Samba
Alexis Hoff and Loretta Abbot with
Bill Breedlove, Jacques Cesbron, William Jacobs, James Truitte, Kelving Rotardier, Morton Winston

First Variation: Miyoko Kato, Robert Scevers
Second Variation: Finis Jhung, Robert Vickrey, Miguel Godreau
Third Variation: Barbara Livshin, Salvatore Aiello
Finale with the whole company

El Amor Brujo. 8 June 1966. Harkness Ballet. Music: Manuel de Falla. Lighting design by Nicola Cernovich. Costumes by André Levasseur. Original cast included Marjorie Tallchief, Miguel Godreau, and [unnamed in the original program] members of the Harkness Ballet, featuring artists of the Alvin Ailey Dance Company. Original program title: *L'amour Sorcier.*

Anthony and Cleopatra. 16 September 1966. Metropolitan Opera. Music: Samuel Barber. Costumes by Franco Zefferelli. Decor by Franco Zefferelli. Dance ensemble included Sally Brayley, Nira Paaz, Rhodie Jorgenson, Hope Clarke, Jan Michens, Lance Westergard.

Riedaiglia. June, 1967. Alvin Ailey Dance Theater. Music: George Riedel. Costumes by Alvin Ailey. Lighting design by Nicola Cernovich. Directed by Lars Egler. Cast: Loretta Abbott, Enid Atych, Consuelo Atlas, George Faison, Miguel Godreau, Judith Jamison, Sharon Miller, Elbert Morris, Kelvin Rotardier, Lynne Taylor, James Truitte, Dudley Williams.

Quintet. 28 August 1968. Alvin Ailey Dance Theater. Music: Laura Nyro. Costumes by Matthew Cameron and George Faison. Lighting design by Nicola Cernovich. First performance: Scotland, Edinburgh Festival, Church Hill Theatre. First New York performance: Billy Rose Theater, 27 January 1969. Program note: "Little girl of all the daughters, you were born a woman not a slave!" Original cast and order: "Stoned Soul Picnic" (Consuelo Atlas, Michele Murray, Eleanor McCoy, Alma Robinson, Linda Kent); "Luckie" (Murray and Atlas; McCoy, Robinson, Kent); "Poverty Train" (Robinson); "Woman's Blues" (Kent and Atlas, Murray, McCoy); "December's Boudoir" (Atlas); "The Confession" (Murray, Robinson, Kent, McCoy, Atlas).

Diversion No. 1. 14 July 1969. Alvin Ailey Dance Theater. Music: Various. Costumes by Rob Thomas. "Scarborough Fair" and "Oh Happy Day." Original cast: Consuelo Atlas and Kelvin Rotardier, Dudley Williams, George Faison.

Masekela Langage. 16 August 1969. Alvin Ailey Dance Theater. Music: Hugh Masekela. Costumes by A. Christina Giannini. Lighting design by Gilbert Hemsley. Decor by William Hammond. First performance as a work-in-progress: New London, CT, American Dance Festival. First New York performance: Brooklyn Academy of Music, 21 November 1969. Original cast and order: "Prologue—Sobukwe" (Company); "Fuzz" (Judith Jamison, Renee Rose, Sylvia Waters, Harvey Cohen, John Medeiros, Kelvin Rotardier); "U-Dui" (Rose, with Cohen, Medeiros, William Hansen); "Babajula Bonke" (Rotardier and Company); "Morolo" (Michele Murray with Cohen, Medeiros); "Bo Masekela" (Jamison); "Mace and Grenades" (George Faison and Company); "Epilogue—Sobukwe" (Company). Program note: "For Katherine Dunham. Five dances with prologue and epilogue based on the music of South African trumpeter Hugh Masekela . . . and reflecting on the idea that South Chicago and South Africa might be somewhat the same . . ."

La Strada (**Broadway musical**). 14 December 1969. Music: Lionel Bart. Principal cast: Bernadette Peters, Anne Hegira, Lisa Belleran, Stephen Pearlman, Lucille Patton, Paul Charles, Larry Kert, and John Coe; Ensemble of singers and dancers: Loretta Abbott, Glenn Brooks, Henry Brunjes, Connie Burnett, Robert Carle, Barbara Christopher, Peggy

Cooper, Betsy Dickerson, Harry Endicott, Anna Maria Fanizzi, Jack Fletcher, Nino Galanti, Susan Goeppinger, Rodney Griffin, Mickey Gunnerson, Kenneth Krell, Don Lopez, Joyce Maret, Stan Page, Odette Panaccione, Mary Ann Robbins, Steven Ross, Larry Small, and Eileen Taylor.

Streams. 15 April 1970. Alvin Ailey American Dance Theater. Music: Miloslav Kabelac ("Eight Inventions for Percussion Ensemble"). Lighting design by Chenault Spence. First performance: Brooklyn Academy of Music. Original cast and order: "Corale" (Company); "Giubiloso" (Michele Murray, John Parks); "Recitativo" (Consuelo Atlas); "Scherzo" (Dudley Williams, Miguel Godreau); "Lamentoso" (Judith Jamison); "Danza" (Renee Rose, Linda Kent, Leland Schwantes, Sylvia Waters, Bobby Johnson, Mari Kajiwara, Mario Delamo); "Aria" (Jamison, Murray, Kent, Waters, Kajiwara, Kelvin Rotardier, Parks, Schwantes, Johnson, Delamo); "Diabolico" (Company).

Gymnopedies. 23 April 1970. Alvin Ailey American Dance Theater. Music: Eric Satie. Lighting design by Chenault Spence. First performance: Brooklyn Academy of Music. Original cast: Keith Lee; pianist John Childs.

The River. 25 June 1970. American Ballet Theatre. Music: Duke Ellington. Costumes by Frank Thompson. Lighting design by Gilbert V. Hemsley and Nicola Cernovich. Assistant to Mr. Ailey: Judith Jamison. First performance as a work-in-progress. Original cast and order: "Spring" (Jon Prinz with Robert Brassel, Richard Cammack, William Carter, Robert Gladstein, Dennis Nahat, Frank Smith, Gaudio Vacacio, Vane Vest, Amy Blaisdell, Zola Dishong, Deborah Dobson, Ingrid Fraley, Nanette Glushak, Rhodie Jorgenson, Naomi Sorkin, Marianna Tcherkassky); "Vortex" (Eleanor D'Antuono); "Falls" (Robert Gladstein, William Carter, Vane Vest, Richard Cammack); "Lake" (Cynthia Gregory, Ivan Nagy and Robert Brassel, Rchard Cammack, William Carter, Robert Gladstein, Dennis Nahat, Frank Smith, Gaudio Vacacio, Vane Vest, Amy Blaisdell, Zola Dishong, Deborah Dobson, Ingrid Fraley, Nanette Glushak, Rhodie Jorgenson, Naomi Sorkin, Marianna Tcherkassky); "Riba (Mainstream)" (Dennis Nahat and Robert Brassel, Richard Cammack, William Carter, Robert Gladstein, Frank Smith, Gaudio Vacacio, Vane Vest, Amy Blaisdell, Zola Dishong, Deborah Dobson, Ingrid Fraley, Nanette Glushak, Rhodie Jorgenson, Naomi Sorkin, Marianna Tcherkassky); and "Two Cities" (Sallie Wilson, Keith Lee and Robert Brassel, Richard Cammack, William Carter, Robert Gladstein, Dennis Nahat, Frank Smith, Gaudio Vacacio, Vane Vest, Amy Blaisdell, Zola Dishong, Deborah Dobson, Ingrid Fraley, Nanette Glushak, Rhodie Jorgenson, Naomi Sorkin, Marianna Tcherkassky).

Archipelago. 18 January 1971. Alvin Ailey American Dance Theater. Music: Andre Boucourechliev. Costumes by A. Christina Giannini. Lighting design by Nicola Cernovich. First performance: New York ANTA Theatre. Original cast and order: Version I: Dudley Williams, Ramon Sagarra, Kelvin Rotardier, Alphonso Figueroa, Hector Mercado, Ronald Dunham; Consuelo Atlas, Rotardier; Williams. Version II: Linda Kent, Sylvia Waters, Mari Kajiwara; Ramon Sagarra; Gail Reese, Lee Harper, Rosamund Lynn, Leland Schwantes, John Parks, Kenneth Pearl; Judith Jamison; Atlas, Rotardier; Williams.

Flowers. 25 January 1971. Alvin Ailey American Dance Theater with Lynn Seymour, guest artist. Music: Big Brother and the Holding Company, Pink Floyd, Blind Faith, and Janis Joplin. Costumes by A. Christina Giannini. Lighting design by Nicola Cernovich. Decor by A. Christina Giannini. First performance: New York, ANTA Theatre. Original program note: "For Mick Jagger, Jimi Hendrix, Bob Dylan, Joe Cocker, Jim Morrison and

Janice Joplin—With Love." Original cast: Lynn Seymour, Ramon Sagarra, and Leland Schwantes, Hector Mercado, Kenneth Pearl, Morton Winston, John Parks, and Ronald Dunham.

Choral Dances. 28 April 1971. Alvin Ailey Dance Theatre. Music: Benjamin Britten (Six dances from "Gloriana" Act II). Costumes by A. Christina Giannini. Lighting design by Nicola Cernovich. First performance: New York, City Center Theater. Original cast, order, and program note: "Time" ". . . yes he is time, lusty and blithe, time is at his apogee!" (Dudley Williams, Kelvin Rotardier, Judith Jamison and Company); "Concord" ". . . concord, concord is here our days to bless" (Jamison, Consuelo Atlas, Williams, Hector Mercado and Company); "Time and Concord" ". . . from springs of bounty, through this country, streams abundant" (Sylvia Waters, Rosamund Lynn, Gail Reese, Lee Harper, John Parks, Leland Schwantes, Kenneth Pearl, Ronald Dunham); "Country Girls" ". . . sweetflag and cuckoo flower, cow-slip and columbine" (Jamison, Atlas, Waters, Lynn, Reese, Harper); "Rustics and Fisherman" ". . . from fen and meadow in rushy baskets they bring in samples of all they grow" (Williams, Mercado, Rotardier, Parks, Schwantes, Pearl, Dunham); "Final Dance of Homage" ". . . these tokens of our love receiving" (Rotardier, Jamison, Atlas, Williams, Mercado and Company).

Cry. 4 May 1971. Alvin Ailey Dance Theater. Music: Alice Coltrane ("Something about John Coltrane"), Laura Nyro ("Been on a Train"), Voices of East Harlem ("Right On, Be Free"). Lighting design by Chenault Spence. First performance: New York, City Center Theater. Program note: "Dedicated to all black women everywhere—especially our mothers." Original cast: Judith Jamison.

Mass. 8 September 1971. Music: Leonard Bernstein. Costumes by Frank Thompson. Lighting design by Gilbert Hemsley. Decor by Oliver Smith. Libretto: Leonard Bernstein, Stephen Schwartz, and texts from the liturgy of the Roman Mass. Staging by Ailey and Gordon Davidson. First performance: Washington, D.C. at the opening of the John F. Kennedy Center for the Performing Arts. First New York performance: 26 June 1972 at the Metropolitan Opera House. Cast (1972) included dancing ensemble: Judith Jamison, Dudley Williams, Clive Thompson, Linda Kent, Kenneth Pearl, Sylvia Waters, Estelle E. Spurlock (Acolytes); Kelvin Rotardier, Sara Yarborough, Mari Kajiwara, John Parks, Hector Mercado, Leland Schwantes, Clover Mathis, Lynne Dell Walker.

The Mingus Dances. 13 October 1971. City Center Joffrey Ballet. Music: Charles Mingus, arranged by Alan Raph. Costumes by A. Christina Giannini. Lighting design by Thomas Skelton. Decor by Edward Burbridge. First performance: New York City Center Theater. Original order: Dance No. 1: Andante Con Moto ("Pithecanthropus Erectus"), Vaudeville: Prestissimo ("O.P."), Dance No. 2: Adagio Ma Non Troppo ("Myself When I Am Real"), Vaudeville: Pesante ("Freedom"), Dance No. 3: Lento Assai ("Half-Mast Inhibition"), Vaudeville: Vivace ("Dizzy's Moods"), Dance No. 4: Andantino ("Diane"), Vaudeville: Scherzo ("Ysable's Table Dance"), Dance No. 5: Allegro Marcato ("Haitian Fight Song").

Mary Lou's Mass. 9 December 1971. Alvin Ailey American Dance Theater. Music: Mary Lou Williams ("Music for Peace"). Costumes by A. Christina Giannini. Lighting design by Chenault Spence. First performance: New York City Center Theater. Original program note: "Praise the Lord from Heaven, praise Him in the heights, praise Him all you angels, praise Him sun and moon . . ." Original cast and order: "Introductory" (Mary Lou Williams and trio); "Entrance Hymn" (Company); "Act of Contrition" (Company);

"Kyrie" (Judith Jamison, Hector Mercado, Kenneth Pearl, Freddy Romero, Ronald Dunham); "Gloria" (Linda Kent, Mari Kajiwara, Rosamund Lynn, Lee Harper, Gail Reese, Estelle Spurlock); "Scripture Reading" (Dudley Williams, Kelvin Rotardier, John Parks); "Responsories" (Jamison, Rotardier); "Credo" (Parks, Rotardier); "Offertory Psalm" (Rotardier); "Sanctus" (Kajiwara, Mercado, Lynn, Reese, Harper, Spurlock, Pearl, Dunham); "Lord's Prayer" (Jamison); "Agnus Dei" (Williams); "Pax Communion" (Rotardier and Company); "Recessional" (Company).

Myth. 15 December 1971. Alvin Ailey American Dance Theater. Music: Igor Stravinsky. Costumes by A. Christina Giannini. Lighting design by Chenault Spence. First performance: New York City Center Theater. Original cast: Consuelo Atlas, Clive Thompson, Kenneth Pearl, and Freddy Romero.

Lord Byron. 20 April 1972. Music: Virgil Thompson. Costumes by Patricia Zipprodt. Lighting design by Joe Pacitti. Decor by David Mitchell. Libretto by Jack Larson. Directed by John Houseman for the Juilliard American Opera Center. Performed by the Juilliard Dance Ensemble: Gregory Mitchell (Lord Byron), David Briggs (Shelley), Maria Barrios (Contessa), and others.

The Lark Ascending. 25 April 1972. Alvin Ailey American Dance Theater. Music: Ralph Vaughan Williams. Costumes by Bea Feitler. Lighting design by Chenault Spence. First performance: New York City Center Theater. Original program note: "This beautiful short work was written by Vaughan Williams in 1914 but was laid aside at the outbreak of war and revised in 1920. It takes its title from a poem by George Meredith. The violin rises and soars aloft above a delicate orchestral accompaniment; there's a short folk-song-like middle section, and then the soloist again takes wing." Original cast: Judith Jamison, Clive Thompson, Linda Kent, Hector Mercado, Kenneth Pearl, Rosamund Lynn, Leland Schwantes, Freddy Romero, Gail Reese, Ronald Dunham, Lee Harper and Clover Mathis.

Shaken Angels. 7 September 1972. Dennis Wayne and Bonnie Mathis. Music: Various: Pink Floyd, Bill Withers, Alice Cooper. Costumes by Christian Holder. Lighting design by Chenault Spence. Decor by Christian Holder. First performance: 10th New York Dance Festival, Delacorte Theater. Original cast: Bonnie Mathis and Dennis Wayne.

Carmen. 18 September 1972. Metropolitan Opera. Music: Georges Bizet. Costumes by David Walker. Lighting design by Rudy Kuntner. Decor by Joseph Swoboda. Conducted by Leonard Bernstein. Production staged by Goelan Gentele.

Sea Change. 26 October 1972. American Ballet Theatre. Music: Benjamin Britten ("Four Sea Interludes" from *Peter Grimes*). Costumes by Frank Thompson. Lighting design by Chenault Spence. Decor by Oliver Smith. Assistant to Mr. Ailey: Karina Rieger. First performance: Washington, D.C. First New York performance: 9 January 1973. Original program note and cast:

> Full fathom five thy father lies;
> Of his bones are coral made;
> Those are pearls that were his eyes:
> Nothing of him that doth fade,
> But doth suffer a sea-change
> Into something rich and strange. . . .
> —William Shakespeare, *The Tempest*

> DAWN—Royes Fernandez with Amy Blaisdell, Christine Busch, Zola Dishong, Deborah Dobson, Ingrid Fraley, Nanette Glushak, Rhodie Jorgenson, Janet Shibata

SUNDAY MORNING—Sallie Wilson with Robert Brassel, Richard Cammack, Daniel Levins, Dennis Marshall, Richard Schafer, Frank Smith, Clark Tippet, Charles Ward, Buddy Balough, Frenando Bujones, Warren Conover

MOONLIGHT—Sallie Wilson and Royes Fernandez

STORM—Sallie Wilson, Royes Fernandez and the Entire Ensemble.

Love Songs. 18 November 1972. Alvin Ailey City Center Dance Theatre. Music: Donny Hathaway, Nina Simone. Costumes by Ursula Reed. Lighting design by Shirley Prendergast. Original order: "A Song for You" (premiered separately 25 April 1972) by Leon Russell, sung by Donny Hathaway; "A Field of Poppies" by Jeremy Wind and Leonard Bleacher, sung by Nina Simone, "He Ain't Heavy" by Bob Russell and Bobby Scott. First performance: New York City Center Theater. Original cast: Dudley Williams.

Four Saints in Three Acts. 20 February 1973. Music: Virgil Thompson. Libretto by Gertrude Stein. Costumes by Jane Greenwood. Lighting design by Shirley Prendergast. Decor by Ming Cho Lee. Conducted by Roland Gagnon. Direction and staging by Alvin Ailey. Assistant to Mr. Ailey: Karina Rieger. Mini-Met Metropolitan Opera Premiere. Cast: St. Stephen, David Britton; St. Settlement, Barbara Hendricks; St. Plan, Walter Richardson; St. Sara, Nancy Szabo; Commère, Betty Allen; Compère, Benjamin Matthews; St. Teresa I, Clamma Dale; St. Teresa II, Hilda Harris; St. Ignatius, Arthur Thompson; St. Cecilia, Doris Hollenbach; St. Chavez, Henry Price; St. Genevieve, Connie Barnett; St. Anne, Carolyn Val-Schmidt; St. Abelson, Melvin Lowery; Tenor, Arthur Warren; St. Vincent, Stephen Rowland.

Hidden Rites. 17 May 1973. Alvin Ailey City Center Dance Theater. Music: Patrice Sciortino ("Les Cyclopes"). Costumes by Bea Feitler. Lighting design by Chenault Spence. First performance as a work-in-progress: New York City Center Theater. Original cast and order: "Incantation" (Judith Jamison, John Parks); "Spirits Known and Unknown" (Company); "Spirits Descending" (Kenneth Pearl); "Of Women" (Mari Kajiwara, Sylvia Waters, Estelle Spurlock, Dana Sapiro, Nerissa Barnes, Donna Wood); "Of Men" (Freddy Romero and Hector Mercado, Kenneth Pearl, Michihiko Oka, Melvin Jones, Edward Love, Peter Woodin); "Of Love I" (Jamison and Parks); "Of Love II" (Tina Yuan and Clive Thompson); "Of Celebration and Death" (Mercado, Kajiwara, Waters); "Spirits Ascending" (Jamison and Parks); "Spirits Known and Unknown" (Company).

Ailey Celebrates Ellington. Televised 28 November 1974. Herman Krawitz, Executive Producer. Produced by Robert Weiner. Directed by Joshua White. Staged and choreographed by Alvin Ailey. Director of workshop and assistant to Mr. Ailey: Karina Rieger. Narration by Stanley Dance. Costumes for *Night Creature*, "Sonnet for Caesar," and "Praise God and Dance" (Sacred Concert) by Jane Greenwood. Costumes for "Such Sweet Thunder," *The Mooche,* and "The Blues Ain't" by Randy Barcelo. Art director: Robert Hoppe. Produced for the CBS Television Network. Original order and dancers: "Such Sweet Thunder," *Night Creature, The Mooche,* "The Blues Ain't," "Sonnet for Caesar," "Praise God and Dance" (Sacred Concert). Alvin Ailey, Sarita Allen, Fred Benjamins, Agnes Johnson, Dianne Harvey, and members of the Alvin Ailey Repertory Workshop.

Night Creature (**Stage Version**). 22 April 1975. Alvin Ailey City Center Dance Theater. Music: Duke Ellington. Costumes by Jane Greenwood. Lighting design by Chenault Spence. First performance: New York City Center Theater. Original program note: "Night creatures unlike stars, do not come *out* at night—they come *on,* each thinking that before the night is out he or she will be the star.—Duke Ellington." Original cast: "First Movement," Tina

Yuan and Dudley Williams with Enid Britten, Charles Adams, Mari Kajiwara, Warren Spears, Estelle Spurlock, Elbert Watson, Sarita Allen, Masazumi Chaya, Beth Shorter, Michihiko Oka, Jodi Moccia and Melvin Jones; "Second Movement," Tina Yuan, Kelvin Rotardier with ensemble; "Third Movement," Tina Yuan, Dudley Williams with ensemble.

The Mooche (**Stage Version**). 15 April 1975. Alvin Ailey City Center Dance Theater. Music: Duke Ellington. Costumes by Randy Barcelo. Lighting design by Chenault Spence. Decor by Rouben Ter-Arutunian. First performance: New York City Center Theater. Original program note: "For Florence Mills, Marie Bryant, Mahalia Jackson, Bessie Smith." Original order and cast: "The Mooche" (Estelle Spurlock, Sarita Allen, Sara Yarborough, Judith Jamison and Company: Charles Adams, Ulysses Dove, Melvin Jones, Kelvin Rotardier, Warren Spears, Clive Thompson, Elbert Watson, Peter Woodin); "Black Beauty" (Spurlock with Company); "The Shepherd" (Allen with Company); "Maha" (Yarborough with Company); "Creole Love Call" (Jamison with Company); "The Mooche" (Company).

Black, Brown and Beige. 11 May 1976. Alvin Ailey City Center Dance Theater. Music: Duke Ellington. Costumes by Randy Barcelo. Lighting design by Chenault Spence. Assistant to Mr. Ailey: Karina Rieger. First performance: New York City Center Theater. Original program note: "I was there when the angel/ drove out the ancestor/ I was there when the waters/ consumed the mountains—Bernard Dadie." Original cast and order: BLACK Ancestor: Clive Thompson; "Work Song": Elbert Watson and Estelle Spurlock, Melvin Jones, Enid Britten, Ulysses Dove, Sarita Allen, Carl Paris, Beth Shorter, Charles Adams; "Come Sunday"; Donna Wood, Enid Britten, Elbert Watson; BROWN "West Indian Dance"; Jones, Paris, Adams, Allen, Shorter, Anita Littleman; "The Blues Ain't"; Spurlock and Dove; BEIGE "Emancipation": Clive Thompson and the Company. Vocal solo by Carline Ray.

Pas de "Duke." 11 May 1976. Alvin Ailey City Center Dance Theater. Music: Duke Ellington and Mercer Ellington. Costumes by Rouben Ter-Arutunian. Lighting design by Chenault Spence. First performance: New York City Center Theater. Assistant to Mr. Ailey: Karina Rieger. Original order: "Such Sweet Thunder," "Sonnet for Caesar," "Hank Cinq," "Clothed Woman," "Old Man's Blues." Original cast: Judith Jamison and Mikhail Baryshnikov.

Three Black Kings. 7 July 1976. Alvin Ailey City Center Dance Theater. Music: Duke Ellington and Mercer Ellington. Costumes by Normand Maxon. Lighting design by Chenault Spence. First performance: Lewiston, New York, Art Park, 7 July 1976. First New York City performance: New York State Theater, 13 August 1976. Original program note: "*Three Black Kings* was the last major work written by Duke Ellington. As he lay dying in his hospital bed in 1974, he gave his son, Mercer, final instructions on how it was to be completed and orchestrated. The first movement with its African rhythmic motifs, depicts Balthazar, the black king of the Nativity; the second is concerned with King Solomon; and the third celebrates, with warm 'down-home' feeling, the triumphs of Ellington's good friend, Martin Luther King." Original New York cast and order: "King Balthazar"; Elbert Watson, with Masazumi Chaya, Peter Woodin, Melvin Jones, Ulysses Dove, Carl Paris, Sergio Cal, Marvin Tunney; "King Solomon": Clive Thompson, with Tina Yuan and Donna Wood, Valerie Feit, Jodi Moccia, Sarita Allen, Beth Shorter, Anita Littleman; "Martin Luther King": Dudley Williams and Estelle Spurlock with Jodi Moccia, Beth Shorter, Sarita Allen, Valerie Feit, Meg Gordon, Anita Littleman, Peter Woodin, Michihiko Oka, Melvin Jones, Carl Paris, Sergio Cal, Marvin Tunney.

Passage. 3 May 1978. Alvin Ailey American Dance Theater. Music: Hale Smith ("Ritual and Incantations"). Costumes by Norman Maxon. Lighting design by Chenault Spence. Decor by Romare Bearden. First performance: New York, City Center Theater. Original program note: "Marie Laveau was the most powerful voodoo queen in the history of this country, her ceremonies involving snake worship, mystical spells and magic. Beyond her role as a priestess, her influences extended deeply into the social and political fabric of 19th century New Orleans." Original cast: Judith Jamison.

Shigaon! Children of the Diaspora. 17 August 1978. Bat-Dor Company. Music: Various. Costumes by Tamara Yuval. Lighting design by Chenault Spence. Decor by Tamara Yuval. Assistant to Mr. Ailey: Mari Kajiwara. Music: Popular. Original program note: "For All the Young People of Israel . . . In Honour of Their Country's 30th Anniversary." Cast included Hannah Alex, Jonathan Avni, Jarck Benschop, Nathan Garda, Charla Genn, Moshe Goldberg, Miriam Hertz, Ronnie Huta, Mark Kessler, Graciella Kozak, Patrice Libeau, Lea Lichtenstein, Alan Maniker, David Rapoport, and Ilana Soffren.

Solo for Mingus. 2 May 1979. Alvin Ailey American Dance Theater. Music: Charles Mingus ("Myself When I Am Near"). Lighting design by Chenault Spence. First performance: New York, City Center Theater. Program note: "To the memory of that great bassist, composer, rebel, bandleader—SPIRIT—Charles Mingus." Original cast: Peter Woodin. Alternate casts: Clive Thompson and Dudley Williams.

Memoria. 29 November 1979. Alvin Ailey American Dance Theater. Music: Keith Jarrett ("Runes—Solara March"). Costumes by A. Christina Giannini. Lighting design by Chenault Spence. Assistant to Mr. Ailey: Mari Kajiwara. Original program note: "To the joy . . . the beauty . . . the creativity . . . and the wild spirit of my friend Joyce Trisler." Original cast: In Memory—In Celebration. Donna Wood, Alistair Butler, Gary DeLoatch, Sarita Allen, Marilyn Banks, Linda Spriggs, Michihiko Oka, Keith McDaniel, Ronald Brown, Sharrell Mesh, Pat Dingle, Danita Ridout, Masazumi Chaya, Milton Myers, Otis Daye with The Alvin Ailey Repertory Ensemble, Sylvia Waters, Director: Carl Bailey, Masha Clark, Susan Dillen, Jeffrey Ferguson, Arrow Holt, Regina Hood, Norman Kaunhi, Diane Maroney, Lauren Overby, Ted Pollen, George Randolph, Eugene Roscoe, Awa Rostant, Hideaki Ryo, Elizabeth Sung, Leslie Woodard; and The American Dance Center Workshop, Kelvin Rotardier, Director: Wally Alvarez, Basil Baker, Courtney Conner, Joseph Garcia, Jasmine Guy, Raymond Harris, Barbara Koval, David McCauley, Cheryl Ann Penn, Renee Robinson, Steven Rooks, Cheryl Lynn Ross, Elizabeth Roxas, Ronnell Seay, Robert Smith, Victoria Williams.

Phases. 5 December 1980. Alvin Ailey American Dance Theater. Music: Pharoah Sanders, Donald Byrd, and Max Roach. Costumes by A. Christina Giannini. Lighting design by Chenault Spence. First performance: New York City Center Theater. Original program note: "Six dances inspired by the dynamic sounds of Pharoah Sanders, Donald Byrd, and Max Roach." Original cast and order: I. "Astral Traveling" (Lonnie Liston Smith, composer; Pharoah Sanders recording): Marilyn Banks, Patricia Dingle, Sharrell Mesh, Barbara Pouncie, Danita Ridout, Maxine Sherman, Linda Spriggs, Roman Brooks, Kevin Brown, Masazumi Chaya, Ulysses Dove, Gary DeLoatch, Keith McDaniel, Stanley Perryman; II. "Thembi" (Pharoah Sanders, composer and recording): Maxine Sherman, Gary DeLoatch; III. "Flight time" (L. Mizell, composer; Donald Byrd recording): Spriggs, McDaniel, Dove, Mesh, Ridout, Perryman, Pouncie, Dingle; IV. "Makin' It" (J. Mason and L. Mizell, composers; Donald Byrd recording): Banks and Chaya; V. "Mr. Thomas" (L. Mizell and W. Jordan, composers; Donald Byrd recording): Sherman, Dingle, Pouncie, Mesh, Ridout; VI. "It's Time" (Max Roach, composer and recording): Dudley Williams and Company.

Spell. 3 December 1981. Alvin Ailey American Dance Theater. Music: Keith Jarrett ("Invocations"). Costumes by Randy Barcelo. Lighting design by Chenault Spence. Based on the life of Marie Laveau. First performance: New York City Center Theater. Original cast: Judith Jamison and Alexander Godunov.

Landscape. 11 December 1981. Alvin Ailey American Dance Theater. Music: Bela Bartok ("Piano Concerto No. 3"). Costumes by A. Christina Giannini. Lighting design by Chenault Spence. Assistants to Mr. Ailey: Mari Kajiwara and Michihiko Oka. First performance: New York, City Center Theater. Original program note: "For Bela Bartok in honor of his centenary . . . and for Miloslav Kabelac, the great Czechoslovakian composer, whose spirit soars above oppression." Original cast and order: "Legend—Touchstone—Romance—Terror": Mari Kajiwara and Stanley Perryman; Dudley Williams and Marilyn Banks; Patricia Dingle, Deborah Manning, Deborah Chase, Barbara Pouncie Beckles, Daniel Clark, Ronald Brown, Ralph Glenmore, Norman Kauahi.

Satyriade. 3 December 1982. Alvin Ailey American Dance Theater. Music: Maurice Ravel ("Introduction and Allegro for Harp, String Quartet, Flute and Clarinet"). Costumes by Carol Vollet Garner. Lighting design by Chenault Spence. Decor by Carol Vollet Garner. Assistant to Mr. Ailey: Michihiko Oka. Set design assistant: Michael White. First performance: New York, City Center, 3 December 1982; Alvin Ailey American Dance Theater. Original cast: Mari Kajiwara, Maxine Sherman, Donna Wood, Keith McDaniel, Gary DeLoatch, Kevin Brown.

Au Bord du Precipice. 8 April 1983. Paris Opera Ballet. Music: Pat Metheny and Lyle Mays ("As Falls Wichita, So Falls Wichita Falls"). Costumes by Carol Vollet Garner. Lighting design by Chenault Spence. Decor by Lyle Mays. First performance: Paris Opera Ballet. First U.S. performance, under title "Precipice": Berkeley, California, February 1984. First New York performance: Metropolitan Opera, 10 July 1984; Alvin Ailey American Dance Theater, with guest artists Patrick Dupond and Monique Loudieres; restaged by Ulysses Dove. Program note: "*Precipice* is inspired by the lives of certain stars of pop music, notably Jim Morrison and Jimi Hendrix, who, at the peak of their success, were constantly driven toward self-destruction. It is in some ways a ballet about loneliness—a ballet where a hero, an idol . . . a star, trapped by the paradox of his times, finds himself at the top—at the edge of the precipice." Original New York cast: He, Patrick Dupond; She (His woman, his desire, his drug), Monique Loudières; Those Close to Him (His Entourage), Ralph Glenmore, Masazumi Chaya, David St. Charles, Kevin Brown, Rodney Nugent, Michihiko Oka, April Berry, Debora Chase, Deborah Manning, Marilyn Banks, Sharrell Mesh, Renee Robinson; The Vision of His Parents, Mary Barnett, Dudley Williams; Those at a Distance (His Admirers), Patricia Dingle, Toni Pierce, Beth Lane, Christopher Huggins, Charles Epps, Carl Bailey, Daniel Clark, Marey Griffith, Norman Kauahi, Nat Orr.

Escapades. 4 July 1983. Aterbaletto, Reggio Emilia, Italy. Music: Max Roach. Costumes by Carol Vollet Garner. Lighting design by Chenault Spence. Decor by Carol Vollet Garner. Assistant choreographer: Ulysses Dove. First performance: Reggio Emilia. Original cast: Amedeo Amodio, Luciana Cicerchia and Company.

Isba. 11 November 1983. Alvin Ailey American Dance Theater. Music: George Winston ("Autumn," for piano). Costumes by Carol Vollet Garner. Lighting design by Chenault Spence. Decor by Carol Vollet Garner. Assistant to Mr. Ailey: Mari Kajiwara. First performance: Richmond, Virginia. First New York performance: City Center Theater, 3 December 1983. Original New York cast: Sharrell Mesh, Michihiko Oka, with Kevin Brown,

Patricia Dingle, Deborah Chase, Marey Griffith, Deborah Manning, Renee Robinson, Daniel Clark, Christopher Huggins, Nat Orr, Gregory Stewart.

"Can't Slow Down." 3 December 1983. Alvin Ailey American Dance Theater. Music: Lionel Richie ("Can't Slow Down"). First performance: New York City Center Theater. Original cast: Delores Brown, Merle Derby, Nat Horne, Judith Jamison, Keith Lee, Audrey Mason, Charles Moore, Michele Murray, Joan Peters, Harold Pierson, Lucinda Ransom, Dorene Richardson, Renee Rose, Ella Thompson, James Truitte, and Liz Williamson.

For Bird—With Love. 6 October 1984. Alvin Ailey American Dance Theater. Music: Charlie Parker, Dizzy Gillespie, Count Basie, Jerome Kern, Coleridge Taylor-Perkinson. Costumes by Randy Barcelo. Lighting design by Timothy Hunter. Decor by Randy Barcelo. Assistant to Mr. Ailey: Masazumi Chaya. First performance: Kansas City, Folly Theater. First New York performance: City Center Theater, 12 December 1985. Program note: "From all of us forever touched by his magic." New York cast and order: "Bird" (A man, a musician), *Alto Sax*: Gary DeLoatch; Men Close to Him—Musicians, *Trumpet*: Carl Bailey; *Tenor Sax*: Kevin Brown; *Piano*: Daniel Clark; *Drums*: Ralph Glenmore; *Bass*: Jonathan Riesling; Women Close to Him—3 Singers and a Pianist: Marilyn Banks, Barbara Pouncie, Neisha Folkes, Debora Chase; The Man Who Came Before, a Club Manager: Dudley Williams; Two Chorus Girls—One from New Orleans, the Other from Kansas City: Patricia Dingle, April Berry. "Overture," "Prologue," "Let Jesus Come In," "Tismaswing," "An Interview," "Way Back Blues," "The Song Is You," "A Night in Tunisia," "Be Bop," "Lover Man," "Cherry Red," "Birds of Prey," "Embraceable You," "The Healing," "Performance: Bird Lives!"

Caverna Magica. 22 March 1986. Royal Danish Ballet. Music: Andreas Vollenweider. Costumes by Carol Vollet Garner. Lighting design by Timothy Hunter. Decor by Carol Vollet Garner. Assistant to Mr. Ailey: Ralph Paul Haze. First performance: Copenhagen, Royal Theater. Original cast: Mette Høennigen, Lars Damsgaard, Linda Hindberg, Torben Jeppesen, Bjarne Hecht, Claus Schroeder, and members of the Royal Danish Ballet. First U.S. performance: Kansas City, autumn 1986, Alvin Ailey American Dance Theater. First New York performance: City Center Theater, 2 December 1986, Alvin Ailey American Dance Theater. Dedicated to the memory of Ron Bundt. New York cast: April Berry, Marilyn Banks, Gary DeLoatch, Kevin Brown, Ralph Glenmore, Rodney Nugent with Adrienne Armstrong, Debora Chase, Neisha Folkes, Marey Griffith, Renee Robinson, Ruthlyn Salomons, Desire Sewer, Nasha Thomas, Christopher Huggins, Leonard Meek, Stephen Smith, Andre Tyson, Dereque Whiturs.

Witness. 22 March 1986. Royal Danish Ballet. Music: Traditional gospel, as recorded by Jessye Norman. Costumes by Kirsten Lund Nielson. Lighting design by Timothy Hunter. Decor by Douglas Grekin and Patrick Venn. Assistant to Mr. Ailey: Ralph Paul Haze. First performance: Copenhagen, Royal Theater. Original cast: Mette Høennigen. U.S. premiere: Kansas City, autumn 1986; Alvin Ailey American Dance Theater. First New York performance: City Center Theater, 2 December 1986. Program note: "My soul is a witness for my Lord." Original New York cast: Marilyn Banks.

Survivors. 13 November 1986. Alvin Ailey American Dance Theater. Music: Max Roach ("Survivors" and "Triptych"). Costumes by Toni Leslie James. Lighting design by Timothy Hunter. Decor by Douglas Grekin. Assistant to Mr. Ailey: Masazumi Chaya; Cochoreographer: Mary Barnett. Program note: "Especially for Nelson and Winnie Mandela whose determination inspires the survivors in us all." First performance: Kansas City, 13 November 1986. New York premiere: New York, City Center Theater, 9 December 1986. Original New York cast: Dudley Williams and Sharrell Mesh, with Adrienne Armstrong, Christopher Huggins, Desire Sewer, Nasha Thomas, Dereque Whiturs.

La Dea della Acqua. 29 March 1988. La Scala Opera Ballet. Music: Carmen Moore. Costumes by Randy Barcelo. Lighting design by Timothy Hunter.

Opus McShann. 4 November 1988, Kansas City. Alvin Ailey American Dance Theater. Music: Jay McShann and Walter Brown. Costumes by Randy Barcelo. Lighting design by Timothy Hunter. Decor by Randy Barcelo. Assistant to Mr. Ailey, Masazumi Chaya. First performance: 3 November 1988. New York premiere, City Center Theater, 11 December 1988. Assistant to Mr. Ailey, Masazumi Chaya. Original New York cast and order: "Overture" (The Company); "All Keys Boogie" (Carl Bailey, Kevin Brown, Deborah Chase, Raquelle Chavis, Gary DeLoatch, Neisha Folkes, Deborah Manning, Desmond Richardson, David St. Charles, Stephen Smith, Nasha Thomas); "Gee Baby Ain't I Good to You" (Sharrell Mesh-Alexander, Andre Tyson); "Doo Wah Doo" (Bailey, DeLoatch); "I Ain't Mad at You" (Marilyn Banks, Richardson, St. Charles, Smith); "Wearing the Ring" (April Berry, Bailey, Brown, DeLoatch, Richardson, Smith); "Jumpin' the Blues" (Raymond Harris, Dwight Rhoden, Dereque Whiturs, and Company); "How Long" (Dudley Williams); "Crazy Legs & Friday Strut" (Company). Choreography for "Jumpin' the Blues" by Frank Manning and Norma Miller.

Preface

1. Richard J. Powell, *Black Art and Culture in the 20th Century* (London: Thames and Hudson, 1997), 22.

Introduction

1. See Joseph Holloway, ed., *Africanisms in American Culture* (Bloomington: Indiana University Press, 1991) for essays that describe artistic traditions shared by Africans and Africans in diaspora, and Brenda Dixon Gottschild, *Digging the Africanist Presence in American Performance: Dance and Other Contexts* (Westport, CT: Greenwood Press, 1996) for a discussion of how Africanist art-making processes have been adopted by Europeans, Asians, and white Americans.

2. Paul Gilroy, *Small Acts: Thoughts on the Politics of Black Cultures* (London: Serpent's Tail, 1993), 1.

3. Ailey usually called his choreographies "ballets" to align them with the dominant mode of high modernist concert dance. See chapter 4 for a brief discussion of this strategy.

4. Muriel Topaz, "Alvin Ailey: An American Visionary," *Choreography and Dance: An International Journal* 4.1 (1996): 17.

5. Gilroy, *Small Acts*, 246.

6. Robert F. Thompson, "Dance and Culture, an Aesthetic of the Cool," *African Forum 2* (fall 1966): 88.

7. Susan Leigh Foster, "Choreographing History," in *Choreographing History*, ed. Susan Leigh Foster (Bloomington: Indiana University Press, 1995), 14.

8. Ibid.

Chapter 1: *Revelations 1962*

1. Alvin Ailey, with A. Peter Barley, *Revelations: The Autobiography of Alvin Ailey* (New York: Birch Lane Press, 1995), 98.

2. Jon Michael Spencer, *Protest and Praise: Sacred Music of Black Religion* (Minneapolis: Fortress Press, 1990), vii.

3. Arnold Shaw, *Black Popular Music in America: From the Spirituals, Minstrels, and Ragtime to Soul, Disco and Hip-Hop* (New York: Shirmer Books, 1986), 13.

4. Spencer, *Protest and Praise*, viii; John Lovell Jr., *Black Song The Forge and the Flame* (New York: Paragon House, 1972), 223.

5. Alvin Ailey, program note, Kaufmann Concert Hall YM-YWHA, 31 January 1960.

6. The *Lamp Unto My Feet* videotape is available for viewing at the New York Public Library for the Performing Arts.

7. James Truitte, interview with the author, 8 November 1994.

8. All lyrics quoted are from Hall Johnson, *I've Been 'Buked* (New York: G. Schirmer, 1946), 3–4.

9. Truitte interview, 8 November 1994.

10. James Miller, "I Wanna Be Ready" (New York: Galaxy Music Corporation, 1943), 2–3.

11. Hall Johnson, et al., *Revelations*, vocal score, 1973: 83–84. This looseleaf compilation of photocopied musical arrangements, dated 1973, is housed in the Ailey archives. Some selections include original publishers and dates.

12. Henry Louis Gates Jr., "Black Structures of Feeling," in *Figures in Black: Words, Signs, and the "Racial" Self*, ed. Henry Louis Gates, Jr. (New York: Oxford University Press, 1987), 175.

13. Hall Johnson, "Notes on the Negro Spiritual," in *Readings in Black American Music*, ed. Eileen Southern (New York: Norton, 1971), 271.

14. Houston A. Baker Jr. *Modernism and the Harlem Renaissance* (Chicago: University of Chicago Press, 1987), 22.

15. Spencer, *Protest and Praise*, 12.

16. Arthur Todd with Alvin Ailey, "Roots of the Blues," *Dance and Dancers* (November 1961): 24.

17. The many precedent works bearing this title include Helen Tamiris, "Negro Spirituals" (1928), Edna Guy, "Danced Spirituals" (1931), Hemsley Winfield, "Four Spirituals" (1932), Ted Shawn, "Negro Spirituals" (1933), Charles Williams, "Negro Spirituals" (1935), Wilson Williams, "Spiritual Suite" (1942), Janet Collins, "Negro Spirituals" (1947), and Pearl Primus, "Negro Spiritual" (1950). See John O. Perpener III, *African-American Concert Dance: The Harlem Renaissance and Beyond* (Urbana: University of Illinois Press, 2001), and Susan Manning, *Race in Motion: Modern Dance, Negro Dance* (Minneapolis: University of Minnesota Press, 2004) for more information about these early choreographies of spirituals.

18. William Moore, "Alvin Ailey (1931–1989)," *Ballet Review* (winter 1990): 15.

19. Jacqueline Quinn Latham, "A Biographical Study of the Lives and Contributions of Two Selected Contemporary Black Male Dance Artists: Arthur Mitchell and Alvin Ailey" (Ph.D. diss., Texas Women's University, 1973), 522.

20. Qtd. in John Dougherty, "From Los Angeles, Halfway Round The World In Dance," *Music Magazine* (April 1964): n.p.

21. Selma Jean Cohen, "Alvin Ailey Dance Theater," *Dance Magazine* (March 1960): 69.

22. Walter Terry, "Met Ballet Plans; Ailey, Nikolais," *New York Herald Tribune*, 7 February 1960: n.p.

23. Jill Johnston, "Mr. Ailey," *Village Voice*, 21December 1961: n.p.

24. Craig Hansen Werner, *Playing the Changes: From Afro-Modernism to the Jazz Impulse* (Urbana: University of Illinois Press, 1994), 275.

25. Toni Morrison, *Playing in the Dark: Whiteness and the Literary Imagination* (Cambridge, MA: Harvard University Press, 1992), 6.

26. Among early works, Charles Weidman's *Lynchtown* (1936) and Martha Graham's *American Document* (1938) each assumed a unique American "problem" of the Negro's place in national society. Dance historians Julia Foulkes, Ellen Graff, and Susan Manning each consider the influence of black bodies on the formation of (white) American modern dance. See Julia Foulkes, *Modern Bodies: Dance and American Modernism from Martha Graham to Alvin Ailey* (Chapel Hill: University of North Carolina Press, 2002); Ellen Graff, *Stepping Left: Dance and Politics in New York City, 1928–1942* (Durham, NC: Duke University Press, 1997); and Manning, *Modern Dance, Negro Dance*.

27. Gottschild, *Digging the Africanist Presence*, 47.

28. Louis Horst and Carroll Russell, *Modern Dance Forms, in Relation to the Other Modern Arts* (San Francisco: Impulse Publications, 1961).

29. Susan Manning has written about this topic in "Black Voices, White Bodies: The Performance of Race and Gender in How Long Brethren," *American Quarterly*, 50.1. (March 1998): 24–46.

30. Isadora Duncan, *My Life* (Garden City, NY: Garden City Publishing, 1927), 339–343.

31. De Mille program note quoted in John Martin, "De Mille Ballet Seen As Novelty," *New York Times*, 23 January 1940: 23.

32. Walter Terry, "To the Negro Dance," *New York Herald Tribune*, 28 January 1940: 10.

33. See Robert Farris Thompson, *Flash of the Spirit: African and Afro-American Art and Philosophy* (New York: Vintage Books, 1983) for a further explication of Africanist aesthetic commonalities in diaspora.

34. Morrison, *Playing in the Dark*, 14–15.

35. Perpener's excellent *African-American Concert Dance* offers an overview of the early black modern dancers who emerged in the 1930s and their techniques, repertory, and critical reception.

36. Morrison, *Playing in the Dark*, xii.

37. Werner, *Playing the Changes*, 275.

38. Peggy Phelan, *Unmarked: The Politics of Performance* (New York: Routledge, 1993), 6.

39. Lovell, *Black Song*, 226.

40. Morrison, *Playing in the Dark*, 38.

41. Gates, "Black Structures of Feeling," 175–177. Expanding on the importance of myth for black communities, Gates continues: "By forging value, by solidifying meaning, the black poet, in his or her own way, forges myth. The importance of myth, of course, is not whether it is believed, or even verifiable; the importance of myth is whether or not it is valued."

42. Phyllis W. Manchester, "Profile: Alvin Ailey," *Dancing Times*, October 1964: 10.

43. H. Johnson, "Notes on the Negro Spiritual," 272.

44. Ailey and Bailey, *Revelations*, 126.

45. Ailey, "Spirituals" file, n.d.

46. Ailey and Bailey, *Revelations*, 98.

47. Lovell, *Black Song*, 526. Johnson directed the choir for the 1930 Broadway production of Connelly's painfully stereotyped tale of Negro pathos.

48. Ailey with Todd, "Roots of the Blues," 24.

49. *Continuing Revelations*, symposium sponsored by New York Public Library, 11 May 1992.

50. W. E. Burghardt Du Bois, *The Souls of Black Folks* (New York: Dodd, Mead, 1961), 193, 197.

Chapter 2: *Early Dances*

1. Johnston, "Mr. Ailey."

2. Alvin Ailey, "Alvin Ailey," *Black Visions '89: Movements of Ten Dance Masters*, Tweed Gallery Exhibition Catalogue, 1989: 9.

3. Latham, "A Biographical Study," 446.

4. Ibid.

5. Ailey and Bailey, *Revelations*, 19; Jennifer Dunning, *Alvin Ailey: A Life In Dance* (New York: Addison-Wesley, 1996), 9.

6. Latham, "Biographical Study," 451, 458–459; Dunning, *Alvin Ailey*, 31–34.

7. Ailey and Bailey, *Revelations*, 8.

8. John Gruen, "Looking Ahead," in *The Private World of Ballet* (New York: Penguin Books, 1975), 418–419.

9. Ailey and Bailey, *Revelations*, 37.

10. Latham, "Biographical Study," 462.

11. Gruen, "Looking Ahead," 419.

12. Latham, "Biographical Study," 481–482; Dunning, *Alvin Ailey*, 61.

13. Latham, "Biographical Study," 485–486.

14. Ibid., 486–487.

15. Ibid., 488.

16. Ibid., 489.

17. Truitte interview.

18. Giora Manor, *The Gospel According to Dance: Choregraphy and the Bible from Ballet to Modern* (New York: St. Martin's Press, 1980), 150.

19. Program note, Lester Horton Dancers, *Choreo 54*, 1954.

20. Latham, "Biographical Study," 490.

21. Program notes, Lester Horton Dancers, 1954.

22. Ailey and Bailey, *Revelations*, 66.

23. Latham, "Biographical Study," 494.

24. Ross replaced choreographer George Balanchine, who had been fired by producers during the show's tryout in Philadelphia.

25. Latham, "Biographical Study," 500.

26. Brooks Atkinson, "Theatre: Truman Capote's Musical," *New York Times*, 31 December 1954: 11.

27. Latham, "Biographical Study," 582.

28. Dunning, *Alvin Ailey*, 90–93.

29. Doris Hering, "Alvin Ailey and Company, Ernest Parham and Company," *Dance Magazine*, May 1958: 65–66. John Martin, "The Dance: Review III," *New York Times*, 6 July 1958, section X, p. 11. Manchester, "Alvin Ailey and Company," 7.

30. Ailey program note, Kaufmann Concert Hall Dance Center of the 92nd Street YM-YWHA, 21 December 1958.

31. Truitte interview.

32. Ailey program note, Kaufmann Concert Hall Dance Center of the 92nd Street YM-YWHA, 21 December 1958.

33. Ibid., emphasis added.

34. Ailey program note, Kaufmann Concert Hall Dance Center of the 92nd Street YM-YWHA, 30 March 1958.

35. Truitte interview.

36. Martin, "The Dance: Review III"; Hering, "Alvin Ailey and Company," 65.

37. Carl Van Vechten, "Eloquent Alvin Ailey," *Dance 62* (1963); 28. *Ode and Homage* was performed only once more, danced in an altered version by James Truitte on 10 December 1961.

38. Anatole Chujoy, "Alvin Ailey and Company, Ernest Parham and Company, Talley Beatty, Guest Artist. YM-YWHA, N.Y., March 30," *Dance News*, May 1958: 9.

39. Manchester, "Alvin Ailey and Company," 7.

40. McKeller posed for the standing male figure representing "Romantic Art" in the rotunda at the Boston Museum of Fine Arts in 1921. Sargent also used McKeller as the model for the female figure representing "Classical Art" in the same murals. See Trevor J. Fairbrother, *John Singer Sargent* (New York: Abrams, 1994), 134–135, 141–142.

41. Robert Mapplethorpe, *Black Book* (New York: St. Martin's Press, 1986).

42. Alvin Ailey, "Alvin Ailey Talks to *Dance and Dancers*: An Interview," *Dance and Dancers*, April 1965: 32.

43. James Baldwin, "The Black Boy Looks at the White Boy" [1961], in *James Baldwin: Collected Essays*, ed. Toni Morrison (New York: Library of America, 1998), 269–270.

44. Ailey program note, Kaufmann Concert Hall Dance Center of the 92nd Street YM-YWHA, 30 March 1958.

45. Brother John Sellers (1924–1999) performed with the Ailey company for several years. Among other singers, Ella Mitchell performed the piece during the 2001 season.

46. Albert Murray, liner notes, *Revelations and Blues Suite 20th Anniversary LP*, New York: Dance Theater Foundation, 1978.

47. De Lavallade, qtd. in Ailey and Bailey, *Revelations*, 165.

48. Thompson, "Dance and Culture," 88.

49. Gilroy, *Small Acts*, 249.

50. Ralph Ellison, *Shadow and Act* (New York: Vintage Books, 1953), 78–79.

51. Henry Louis Gates Jr., *Bearing Witness: Selections from African-American Autobiography in the Twentieth Century* (New York: Pantheon, 1991), 3.

52. Harry Bernstein, "Alvin Ailey and Company," *Dance Observer*, February 1959: 24.

53. Manchester, "Alvin Ailey and Company," 7.

54. Bernstein, "Alvin Ailey and Company," 25.

55. Doris Hering, "Alvin Ailey and Company," *Dance Magazine*, February 1959: 27.

56. Ailey program note, Kaufmann Concert Hall Dance Center of the 92nd Street YM-YWHA, January 31, 1960; Terry, "Met Ballet Plans."

57. Latham, "Biographical Study," 527,

58. Cohen, "Alvin Ailey Dance Theater," 69.

59. Terry, "Met Ballet Plans."

60. Phyllis W. Manchester, "The Alvin Ailey Dance Theater," *Dance News*, March 1960: 10.

61. Ailey program note, Rebekah Harkness Foundation Dance Festival, 9 September 1962.

62. Ailey, *Creation of the World* notes, 1962.

63. Arthur Todd, "The Rebekah Harkness Foundation Dance Festival," *Ballet News*, October 1962: 122. Allen Hughes, "Dance: Alvin Ailey Is Victor over Rain," *New York Times*, 10 September 1962: n.p.

64. Ailey, *Knoxville* note, circa 1960.

65. Samuel Barber, *Knoxville: Summer of 1915* (New York: G. Schirmer, 1949), 2.

66. Ailey and Bailey, *Revelations*, 58.

67. John Percival, "Alvin Ailey Sadler's Wells," *London Times*, 2 December 1970: 13.

68. Selma Jean Cohen, "Alvin Ailey Dance Theater," *Dance Magazine*, January 1961: 60.

69. Ailey, *Knoxville* notes.

70. Phyllis W. Manchester, "Alvin Ailey Dance Theater," *Dance News*, January 1961: 10.

71. Cohen, "Alvin Ailey Dance Theater" (January 196), 60.

72. Percival, "Alvin Ailey Sadler's Wells," 13.

73. Don McDonagh, "Ailey Troupe in Brooklyn," *New York Times*, 23 April 1969: 40.

74. Latham, "Biographical Study," 538.

75. Arthur Todd, "Dance: Riches," *New York Times*, 2 July 1961: 24.

76. Ailey, *Hermit Songs* notes, circa 1961.

77. Samuel Barber, *Hermit Songs* (New York: G. Schirmer, 1954), 77–79.

78. Jack Mitchell, *Alvin Ailey American Dance Theater: Jack Mitchell Photographs* (Kansas City: Andrews and McMeel, 1993), 1–3.

79. Ailey, "Alvin Ailey Talks to *Dance and Dancers*: An Interview," 32–33.

80. "Carmen de Lavallade Stars with Ailey Dance Troupe," *New York Herald Tribune*, 11 December 1961: n.p.

81. John Martin, "Dance: Muscling In," *New York Times*, 17 December 1961: 24.

82. This act of compositional revision may be standard practice for Europeanist concert choreographers with shifting rosters of dancers, but it is absolutely essential in any communal model of African American musicality. Ailey's incorporation of this practice in his company operations aligned it explicitly with African American cultural expres-

sion, where individual interpretation overrides blank repetition or reconstruction. See chapter 4, "Break: Versioning."

83. Truitte interview; Marilyn Borde, interview with the author, 8 March 1995.

Chapter 3: *Early Company*

1. Uncatalogued Ailey notes, circa 1964.

2. Alvin Ailey et al., "Grant Proposal for Dance Theater Foundation," looseleaf notes, dated June 1965: 1–2.

3. Peter Lennon, "Not Just Hoofers," *Guardian*, 25 September 1964: n.p.

4. Ailey, "Alvin Ailey Talks to *Dance and Dancers*: An Interview," 32.

5. Ailey Looseleaf Notes, circa 1959.

6. VeVe Clark, "Katherine Dunham: Method Dancing of Memory of Difference," in *African American Genius in Modern Dance*, ed. Gerald Myers (Durham, NC: American Dance Festival, 1993), 5.

7. Pearl Primus, "Primitive African Dance (and Its Influence on the Churches of the South)," in *The Dance Encyclopedia*, ed. Anatole Chujoy (New York: A. S. Barnes, 1949), 387–389.

8. For an excellent study of early concert dancers and their accomplishments, see Perpener, *African-American Concert Dance*.

9. Ibid.

10. See Thompson, "Dance and Culture," 85–102; as well as Thompson, *Flash of the Spirit*.

11. Paul Padgette, ed., *The Dance Photography of Carl Van Vechten* (New York: Schirmer Books, 1981), 89–90.

12. Latham, "Biographical Study," 510.

13. Ibid., 507, 506.

14. Ibid., 504–505.

15. Ailey and Bailey, *Revelations*, 80.

16. Selma Jeanne Cohen, "Shirley Broughton's 5 o'Clock Dance Co.," *Dance Magazine*, April 1959: 80.

17. Qtd. in Latham, "Biographical Study," 532.

18. Qtd. in Walter Sorell, "Style, Essence, Allusion," *Dance Magazine*, August 1963: 47, 62.

19. Richard Shepard, "Theater: A Rousing 'Jerico-Jim Crow,'" *New York Times*, 13 January 1964: n.p.

20. Ailey and Bailey, *Revelations*, 88.

21. Working with Joyce Trisler, Ailey staged the dances for *La Strada* with music by Lionel Bart, Martin Charnin, and Elliott Lawrence. The show, with overall staging by Broadway musical newcomer Alan Schneider, received uniformly negative reviews. Ailey's contribution included "scurrying" dances with "an endless display of upraised black umbrellas." See William Glover, "Theater," Typescript AP report, 14 December 1969: n.p.

22. Mary Clarke, "Blues and Holy Blues: The Alvin Ailey American Dance Theatre's First Programme," *Dancing Times*, November 1964: 64.

23. H.S.H., "American Dance Co's Brilliant Show," *Times of Malaya and Straits Echo*, 3 March 1962: n.p.

24. Latham, "Biographical Study," 539–545. Dance historian Naima Prevots also interprets these events in *Dance for Export: Cultural Diplomacy and the Cold War* (Hanover, NH: Wesleyan University Press, 1998), 94–101.

25. Ailey program notes, 26 January 1962.

26. Ailey, *Been Here and Gone* file, n.d.

27. Ailey, program notes, 9 September 1962.

28. Ailey, *Been Here and Gone* file, n.d.

29. Ibid.

30. Allen Hughes, "Dance: Alvin Ailey Is Victor over Rain"; Clive Barnes, "Dancing the Blues," *The Spectator*, 16 October 1964: n.p.

31. Ailey and Bailey, *Revelations*, 105–106.

32. Qtd. in Don Oscar Becque, "Dance Conversations: The Dance as a 'Good Will' Ambassador," *Villager* (New York) 18 January 1962: n.p.

33. Akihiko Yamaki, translated by Kambayashi, 1962: n.p.; Shigeo Goda, translated by Kambayashi, 1962: n.p.

34. Sumio Kambayashi, 1962: n.p.

35. Walter Terry, "Alvin Ailey Dance Troupe: Stunning," *New York Herald Tribune*, 18 December 1965: n.p.

36. Alvin Ailey Dance Theater file, circa 1961.

37. Natalie Jaffe, "Alvin Ailey Offers Two New Dance Works," *New York Times*, 29 April 1963: n.p.

38. Ailey and Bailey, *Revelations*, 107–108.

39. John Dwyer, "Dancers Are Artistic in Festival at UB," *Buffalo Evening News*, 20 June 1964: n.p.; Samuel Singer, "Ailey Troupe Earns Cheer," *Philadelphia Inquirer*, 4 November 1963: n.p.

40. Latham, "Biographical Study," 567–568; Ailey and Bailey, *Revelations*, 109.

41. Ailey, program notes, August 1964.

42. "A Rare and Exciting Theatrical Experience," *The Herald*, 30 January 1965: n.p.

43. Ailey, program notes, London, October 1964.

44. Benny Green, "Song and Dance," *Observer Weekend Review*, 11 October 1964: n.p.; Clive Barnes, "Exciting Dancers in British Debut," *London Times*, 6 October 1964: 19; Richard Buckle, "In a Friendly Fashion," *London Sunday Times*, n.d., circa 1964: n.p.

45. Peter Williams, "Blues and All That Jazz: First View," *Dance and Dancers*, November 1964: 22.

46. Latham, "Biographical Study," 606–607, 634–640.

47. Ibid., 601.

48. In an interview, James Truitte reflected that Ailey's retirement made sense considering the company's growing profile and Ailey's steadily increasing administrative and public relations duties.

49. Ailey and Bailey, *Revelations*, 125.

50. Dunning, *Alvin Ailey: A Life in Dance*, 1996, 52.

51. Kevin K. Gaines, *Uplifting the Race: Black Leadership, Politics, and Culture in the Twentieth Century* (Chapel Hill: University of North Carolina Press, 1996), xiv.

52. Ibid., xvii–xix.

53. A. V. Coton (pseud.), "Alvin Ailey in Edinburgh," *Dancing Times*, October 1968: 12.

54. Arthur Todd, "American Negro Dance: A National Treasure," in *Ballet Annual 1962*, ed. Arnold Haskell and Mary Clarke (London: Adam and Charles Black, 1961), 92.

55. LeRoi Jones's play *Slave Ship*, which opened 13 January 1970 directed by Gilbert Moses, caused a sensation through its visceral enactment of the Middle Passage and the auction block in the New World.

56. Zita Allen, "Alvin Ailey Thrills Them at the Met," *New York Amsterdam News*, 14 July 1984: 19.

57. Richard Philp, "Twenty Years Later: the Alvin Ailey American Dance Theater," *Dance Magazine*, October 1978: 63–78.

58. In 2000, Dance Theater Foundation changed its name to become Alvin Ailey Foundation.

59. Qtd. in Latham, "Biographical Study," 610–611.

Chapter 4: *Revelations II*: 1969

1. Kathleen Cannell, "WGBH: Entrepreneur," *Christian Science Monitor*, 31 May 1969: 13.

2. Ailey, program notes, 3 February 1969.

3. Ailey's use of the term "ballet" for his work raised eyebrows among dance critics and aesthetes, in part because his work was not typically grounded in classical ballet technique. But ballet is not defined by the Oxford English Dictionary in terms of its physical technique; it is now "for the most part regarded as an artistic exhibition of skill in dancing" (2d ed., 1989). Perhaps some of the anxiety over terminology stems from a desire for an idiomatic "purity" that Ailey's dancers could never achieve.

4. Dick Hebdige, *Cut 'n' Mix: Culture, Identity and Caribbean Music* (London: Comedia, 1987), 12

5. See Richard Green, "(Up)Staging the Primitive: Pearl Primus and the 'Negro Problem' in American Dance," in *Dancing Many Drums:Excavations in African American Dance*, ed. Thomas F. DeFrantz (Madison: University of Wisconsin Press, 2002), 120.

6. Hebdige, *Cut 'n' Mix*, 11.

7. Gottschild, *Digging the Africanist Presence in American Performance*, 15.

8. Ameila Fatt, "A Dance Career: Alvin Ailey's," *Dance Magazine*, October 1966: 56.

9. "Dance Riot in Brooklyn," Ailey Company press release, 18 June 1969.

10. Richard Shepard, "Dancers Tap Brooklyn Neighbors for Funds," *New York Times*, 24 February 1969: 32.

11. Qtd. in Ellen Cohn, "'I Want to Be a Father Figure,'" *New York Times*, 13 April 1969: B35.

12. Ibid.

13. Qtd. in Stephen Smoliar, "Alvin Ailey Dances into Today's Cultural Void," *Boston after Dark,* 21 May 1969: 6.

14. Qtd. in Mary Campbell, "Ailey: More People Dig the Dance," Typescript AP report, c. 1969: n.p.

15. Qtd. in Ric Estrada, "Three Leading Negro Artists, and How They Feel about Dance in the Community," *Dance Magazine*, November 1968: 46. See also Thomas DeFrantz, "To Make Black Bodies Strange: Social Protest in Concert Dance of the Black Arts Movement," in *African American Performance: A Sourcebook*, ed. AnneMarie Bean (New York: Routledge, 1999), 83–93.

16. Clive Barnes, "A Great Lesson in Race Relations," *New York Times*, 26 December 1970: B30.

17. Abby Arthur and Ronald Maberry Johnson, *Propaganda and Aesthetics: The Literary Politics of Afro-American Magazines in the Twentieth Century* (Amherst: University of Massachusetts Press, 1979), 170.

18. Campbell, "More People Dig the Dance."

19. Hubert Saal, "Ballet in Black," *Newsweek*, 10 February 1969: 76.

Chapter 5: Touring, Touring, Touring

1. "Intense, Moving Dance Program by Ailey Group," *Daily Ledger*, 12 July 1963: n.p.

2. Frances Wessells, "Dance," *Richmond Times–Dispatch*, 11 February 1970, n.p.; Bill

Anthony, "Alvin Ailey's American Theatre Puts Dance into Soul," *PD Action*, 19 March 1971, n.p.; Lonia Efthyvoulou, "Arts Center Gives Back Stage View," *Daily Register*, 24 June 1971: n.p.; Mike Steele, "Modern Dance Hits State Milestone," *Minneapolis Tribune*, c. February 1973: n.p.

3. Qtd. in James Fisher, "Alvin Ailey at John Hancock Hall," *Boston Review of Arts*, 1 April 1971: n.p.

4. Qtd. in Arthur Todd, "Two-way Passage for Dance," *Dance Magazine*, July 1962: 41.

5. Efthyvoulou, "Arts Center Gives Back."

6. Latham, "Biographical Study," 619.

7. Noel Goodwin, "Black Octave," *Dance and Dancers*, October 1968: 23; Latham, "Biographical Study," 621.

8. The work was revived in 1999 by the Alvin Ailey Repertory Ensemble, directed by Sylvia Waters.

9. Ailey, *Quintet* file, 1968.

10. Ibid.

11. Ailey, *Quintet* notes, n.d.

12. Clive Barnes, "Ailey and Troupe in Triumph," *New York Times*, 28 January 1969: 48; Stephen Smoliar, "Ailey Troupe: Soul Works More Than Sole Work," *Boston after Dark*, 4 June 1969: n.p.

13. Lester Abelman, "Ailey Dance Troupe Box-Office Winner," *New York Daily News*, 20 December 1971: n.p.

14. Anna Kisselgoff, "Dance: Ailey Returns," *New York Times*, 19 April 1972: 37.

15. Don McDonagh, "Ailey's Dancers Crackling Again," *New York Times*, 28 April 1971: 33; Kisselgoff, "Dance: Ailey Returns," 37.

16. Qtd. in Robb Baker, "Alvin Ailey," *After Dark*, February 1974: n.p.

17. Bridget Byrne, "Ailey Dance Tranfixing," *Los Angeles Herald Examiner*, 16 July 1969: n.p.

18. Qtd. in Karen Monson, "Ailey's Goal: Dance Interest," *Los Angeles Times*, 19 July 1969: n.p.

19. While bebop did not enjoy the sweeping popularity of, say, swing music, it was, in some quarters, dance music. See Marya McQuirter, "Awkward Moves: Dance Lessons from the 1940s," in *Dancing Many Drums: Excavations in African American Dance*, ed. Thomas F. DeFrantz (Madison: University of Wisconsin Press, 2002), 82–87.

20. Marshall Stearns and Jean Stearns, *Jazz Dance: The Story of American Vernacular Dance*, 2d ed. (1964; New York: Da Capo Press, 1994).

21. Neither Cole nor Mattox have received sustained scholarly attention. See Glenn Loney, *Unsung Genius: The Passion of Dancer Choreographer Jack Cole* (New York: Franklin Watts, 1984).

22. Alvin Ailey, program note, ANTA, 25 January 1971.

23. Douglas Watt, "British Dancer Plays J. Joplin in Rock Ballet," *New York Daily News*, 26 January 1971: n.p.; Anna Kisselgoff, "Dance: No One's Sitting on His Hands," *New York Times*, 27 January 1971: 32; Marcia Siegel, "Dance: Alvin Ailey Innovates," *Boston Herald Traveler*, 6 February 1971: n.p.

24. Clive Barnes, "An Embarrassment of Riches?" *New York Times*, 20 May 1973: II, 32.

25. Clive Barnes, "The Dance: Lively and Varied Fare," *New York Times*, 9 September 1972: 12.

26. Rob Baker, "Dance at the Delacorte," *Dance Magazine*, November 1972: 60.

27. C. Barnes, "Lively and Varied Fare," 12.

28. Sam Norkin, "Dancers in the Park Fashioning a Festival," *New York Daily News*, 9 September 1972: n.p.

29. Monson, "Ailey's Goal."

30. "Ailey Troupe Saved by State Department," *New York Times*, 19 June 1970: 25.

31. "Soviets Say 'Molodtsy' to Ailey Troupe," *Dance News*, December 1970: n.p.

32. Bob Micklin, "Dance: Light Entertainment," *Newsday*, 17 November 1972: n.p.; Arlene Croce, "Standing Still," *New Yorker*, 7 January 1974: 48; William Moore, "Alvin Ailey Is Just Too Much," *The Black American*, 15.3 (1974): n.p.

33. Moore, "Ailey Is Just Too Much."

34. Croce, "Standing Still," 48.

35. Marcia Siegel, "Selling Soul" in *At the Vanishing Point* (New York: Saturday Review Press, 1972), 150–153; Croce, "Standing Still"; Bob Micklin, "Dance: Pleasing the Crowd," *Newsday*, 21 August 1974: n.p.

36. Robert Pierce, "A Choreographer of Spectacle," December 1971: n.p.

37. Qtd. in "City to Aid Ailey in Parks Program," *New York Times*, 22 February 1974: 22.

Chapter 6: Reflecting a Spectrum of Experience

1. See DeFrantz, "To Make Black Bodies Strange," 83–93.

2. Ailey's fragmentary notes on this topic indicate that he was thinking of a ballet company based in the classical ballet idiom, but resonant with African American performance practice that would encompass singers and musicians more completely than existing American ballet company practice.

3. Ailey, program notes, Brooklyn Academy of Music, 9 April 1969.

4. Carole Johnson, "Black Dance," *The Feet*, July 1971: 2.

5. For an overview of the "black dance" controversy, see Zita Allen, "The Great American 'Black Dance' Mystery," *Freedomways* 20.4 (1980: 283–291, and Thomas F. DeFrantz, "African American Dance: A Complex History," in *Dancing Many Drums: Excavations in African American Dance*, ed. Thomas F. DeFrantz (Madison: University of Wisconsin Press, 2002): 3–38.

6. See Constance Valis Hill, "Katherine Dunham's *Southland*: Protest in the Face of Repression," in *Dancing Many Drums: Excavations in African American Dance*, ed. Thomas F. DeFrantz (Madison: University of Wisconsin Press, 2002), 289–316.

7. Joseph H. Mazo, "Masekela Langage," *Women's Wear Daily*, 9 December 1977: 15.

8. Anna Kisselgoff, "Ailey Dance Theater Presents a Rousing Finale," *New York Times*, 18 August 1969: 28; Walter Terry, "Festival in Brooklyn," *Saturday Review*, 13 December 1969: 14.

9. Anna Kisselgoff, "New Ailey Work (Gymnopedies)," *New York Times*, 24 April 1970: n.p.

10. Alvin Ailey American Dance Theater program note, 18 January 1971.

11. Joseph H. Mazo, "Alvin Ailey," *Women's Wear Daily*, 20 January 1971: n.p.; Marcia B. Siegel, "Dance: 'Archipelago' Opens in NY," *Boston Herald Traveler*, 27 January 1971: n.p.

12. Siegel, "Dance, 'Archipelago' Opens in NY."

13. Frances Herridge, "Ailey Begins Season at ANTA," *New York Post*, 19 January 1971: n.p.; Mazo, "Alvin Ailey."

14. Deborah Jowitt, "Game, Set, Match," *Village Voice*, 13 May 1971: n.p.

15. Joan Pikula, "Ailey Company Opens Engagement," *Asbury Park Evening Press*, 24 June 1971: 13.

16. Norma McLain Stoop, "Of Time and Alvin Ailey," *Dance Magazine*, December 1971: 30.

17. Paul Hume, *Mass* program notes, 1972: 7, 10.

18. B.H.K., "Dance Plays Part in Kennedy Opening: Ailey Co. Featured," *Dance News*, October, 1971: n.p.

19. Jack Anderson, "Leonard Bernstein's 'Mass,'" *Dance Magazine*, August 1972: 78.

20. Jean Battey Lewis, "Dance in the Mass: Visceral Impact," *Washington Post*, 9 September 1971: n.p.

21. *Leonard Bernstein's Mass*, program booklet, 1972.

22. Lewis, "Dance in the Mass."

23. Qtd. in Jean Battey Lewis, "'Father Figure' of Dance," *Washington Post*, 3 October 1971: n.p.

24. Qtd. in Anna Kisselgoff, "Ailey Dancers to Give Mary Lou's Mass," *New York Times*, 9 December 1971: 62.

25. Marcia Siegel, "Ballet: 'Myth' by Ailey," *Boston Herald Traveler*, 22 December 1971: n.p.

26. Clive Barnes, "Playfully Seizing on a Ritual: Ailey's New 'Myth,'" *New York Times*, 16 December 1971: n.p.

27. Joseph H. Mazo and Susan Cook, *The Alvin Ailey American Dance Theater* (New York: Morrow, 1978), 9.

28. Anna Kisselgoff, "Love Is Theme," *New York Times*, 27 April 1972: 48; Marcia Siegel, "Two New Works Choreographed by Alvin Ailey for Spring," *Boston Herald Traveler*, 12 May 1972: 17.

29. Frances Herridge, "New Ailey 'Rites' at City Center," *New York Post*, 18 May 1973: n.p; Anna Kisselgoff, "Ballet: 'Hidden Rites,'" *New York Times*, 19 May 1973: 29; Bob Micklin, "Dance: Work In Progress," *Newsday*, 18 May 1973: n.p.

Chapter 7: *Other Dances*

1. Qtd. in Linda Chiavaroli, "Ailey's Dancers Have Freedom Modern Dance Companies Lack," *Rochester Democrat and Chronicle*, 8 April 1973: n.p.

2. Federico García Lorca, "The House of Bernarda Alba," in *Three Tragedies: Blood Wedding, Yerma, The House of Bernarda Alba*, trans. James Graham-Luján and Richard L. O'Connell (New York: Penguin Plays, 1941), 201.

3. Dunning, *Alvin Ailey: A Life in Dance*, 74–75.

4. George Balanchine, "Feast of Ashes," in *New Complete Stories of the Great Ballets* (Garden City, NJ: Doubleday, 1968), 150.

5. Ailey, *Feast of Ashes* file.

6. Lorca, "The House of Bernarda Alba," 150.

7. Peter Williams, "Two Looks at Harkness," *Dance and Dancers*, April 1965: 17.

8. Clive Barnes, "Harkness Ballet Presents Jack Cole's 'Requiem,'" *New York Times*, 4 November 1967: n.p.

9. Williams, "Two Looks at Harkness," 16.

10. Ailey, Blood Wedding file.

11. Clive Barnes, "Tout Paris Sees Harkness Ballet," *New York Times*, 13 March 1965: 17.

12. Ibid.

13. Cynthia Grenier, "Harkness Ballet: An Elegant Opening," *New York Herald Tribune*, 13 March 1965: n.p.

14. Ailey, *Ariadne* file.

15. Borde interview.

16. Ailey, "Alvin Ailey Talks to *Dance and Dancers*: An Interview," 32.

17. Ailey, *Macumba* file.

18. Clive Barnes, "Dance: A Paris Festival," *New York Times*, 16 June 1966: n.p.

19. Clive Barnes, "Paris Sees Dancers from U.S.," *New York Times*, International ed., 17 June 1966: n.p.

20. Wolfe Kaufman, "Harkness Eclipsed by Outdoors," *New York Herald Tribune* (Paris), 11 June 1966: n.p.

21. Clive Barnes, "Ballet in Modest but Hectic Contribution," *New York Times*, 17 September 1966: 15.

22. Walter Terry, "Dancing Incidental—And Very Brief." *World Journal Tribune*, 17 September 1966: 22.

23. See Thomas F. DeFrantz, "Ballet," in *Encyclopedia of African-American Culture and History* (New York: Macmillan Press, 1995), 236–242, and Thomas F. DeFrantz, "Ballet in Black: Louis Johnson and Vernacular Humor," in *Dancing Bodies, Living Histories: New Writings about Dance and Culture*, ed. Lisa Doolittle and Anne Flynn (Banff: Banff Centre Press, 2000), 178–195.

24. Thomas F. DeFrantz, "The Black Body in Question," *Village Voice*, 23 April 1996: 29–32.

25. Qtd. in Anna Kisselgoff, "When Ballet Dancers Stumble into Modern Dance" *New York Times*, 24 August 1975: 7.

26. Don George, *Sweet Man: The Real Duke Ellington* (New York: G. P. Putnam's Sons, 1981), 194.

27. Duke Ellington, *Music Is My Mistress* (New York: Doubleday, 1973), 201–203.

28. George, *Sweet Man*, 195–196.

29. Ellington, *Music Is My Mistress*, 202.

30. This solo appeared, in a truncated version, in the 1977 Herbert Ross film *The Turning Point*. In the film, a young, experimental choreographer is given his first opportunity to choreograph for a major ballet company obviously modeled on American Ballet Theatre. He makes an abstract, "modern" solo for the film's rising young ballerina, which he describes as "a body moving in space with music. Not to music, with music" (Arthur Laurents, screenplay, Film Company, 1977).

31. This is not to say that discreet staging of same-sex attraction or the all-male kickline of *The River* are Africanist ideas. Rather, how these compositional tools are arranged by the artists allow them valence as Africanist strategies of structure. Parody and derision are Africanist techniques of composition widely deployed in black performing arts.

32. Hubert Saal, "Dance Me a River," *Newsweek*, 6 July 1970: 86.

33. Qtd. in Stoop, "Of Time and Alvin Ailey," 31–32.

34. Clive Barnes, "Dance: Ballet Theater Opens a Six-Week Season," *New York Times*, 30 June 1971: n.p.; Harriet Johnson, "Ballet Theater Opens with 'River,'" *New York Post*, 30 June 1971: n.p.

35. Nancy Goldner, "American Ballet Theatre," *Dance News*, September 1970: 13.

36. Zelda Cameron, "Washington-Baltimore," *Dance Magazine*, March 1979: 97.

37. Qtd. in Stoop, "Of Time and Alvin Ailey," 32.

38. Barry Cunningham, "Mingus 'Up from the Dead' on Ballet," *New York Post*, 20 October 1971: 26.

39. Katharine Cunningham, "Mingus and Chain Dances," *Dance and Dancers*, February 1972: 48; Doris Hering, "Joffrey Journey," *Dance Magazine*, January 1972: 32.

40. Deborah Jowitt, "Blow Yourself Up," *Village Voice*, 21 October 1971: n.p; Cunningham, "Mingus 'Up from Dead,'" 2; Jowitt, "Blow Yourself Up."

41. Hering, "Joffrey Journey," 34.

42. Lester Abelman, "Joffrey Premieres Cool 'Mingus Dances,'" *New York Daily News*, 15 October 1971: 72; Clive Barnes, "Dance: Rather Too Much Bare Stage?" *New York Times*, 7 November 1971: n.p.

43. Brian Priestly, *Mingus: A Critical Biography* (New York: Da Capo Press, 1983), 185.

44. Clive Barnes, "Ailey's 'The Mingus Dances,'" *New York Times*, 14 October 1971: n.p.

45. Harriet Johnson, "'Lord Byron' in World Premiere," *New York Post*, 21 April 1972: n.p.

46. *Lord Byron* program notes, quoted in George Jackson, "New York Entries: Ailey," *Dance News*, June 1972: 13.

47. Anna Kisselgoff, "Ballet in 'Byron': A Tough Assignment," *New York Times*, 22 April 1972: n.p.; Jackson, "New York Entries," 13.

48. Kisselgoff, "Ballet in 'Byron'"; H. Johnson, "'Lord Byron' in World Premiere."

49. "2 World Premieres at Ballet Theater," *New York Times*, 15 June 1972: 47.

50. Patricia Barnes, "New Works, Fine Dancing," *Dance and Dancers*, April 1973: 48.

51. Qtd. in Jean Perry, "An Interracial Dance Co. Is on the Move," *Sunday News*, 24 September 1972: n.p.

52. Harold Schonberg, "Opera: A New 'Carmen,' Daring and Provocative," *New York Times*, 20 September 1972: n.p.

53. Qtd. in George Gent, "Mini-Operas Ready to Take Met Role," *New York Times*, 15 February 1973: 50.

54. George Movshon, "New York's Season," *Opera*, August 1973: 693; Harold Schonberg, "Opera: Minimet's Playful 'Four Saints,'" *New York Times*, 24 February 1973: 17.

Chapter 8: *Ailey Celebrates Ellington*

1. Qtd. in Moira Hodgson, "Ailey on Ellington," *Dance News*, April 1976: 1.

2. Most of these revivals remained in repertory a single season or two, although some works were revived again by the Alvin Ailey American Dance Theater, including Butler's *Carmina Burana* (revived again 1994), Johnson's *Lament* (revived again 1985), and McKayle's *Rainbow 'round My Shoulder* (revived again 1981).

3. Mark Tucker, "The Later Years: 1960–1974." In *The Duke Ellington Reader*, ed. Mark Tucker, (New York: Oxford University Press, 1993), 317.

4. George, *Sweet Man: The Real Duke Ellington*, 195.

5. "Ailey's Homage to the Duke," *Los Angeles Times*, 29 November 1974: n.p.

6. *Ailey Celebrates Ellington*, program dialogue, 1974.

7. Stanley Dance, "Duke Ellington 1899–1974." CD liner notes, *The Symphonic Ellington*, Santa Monica, CA: Discovery Records, 1992.

8. *Ailey Celebrates Ellington*, program dialogue, 1974.

9. Lee Winfrey, "Want a Thanksgiving Treat?" *Philadelphia Inquirer*, 28 November 1974: 6-B; John O'Connor, "TV: Holiday Specials, from Splendid to Poor," *New York Times*, 27 November 1974: 75.

10. Louis Falco (1943–93) began as a performer with the José Limón company, but established himself as a choreographer with his own company in the 1970s before achieving international celebrity for his dances for the 1980 film *Fame*. *Caravan* returned to the Ailey repertory in 2001.

11. Balanchine's work, first performed by students of the School of American Ballet, explored neoclassical movements through shifting arrangements of ballerinas and cavaliers.

12. Joseph Mazo, "Alvin Ailey's Dance Tribute to the Duke," *New York Times*, 13 April 1975: B6.

13. Qtd. in ibid.

14. *The Mooche*, program note, July 1975: 27.

15. Clive Barnes, "Dance: Spring Gala Day," *New York Times*, 17 April 1975: 47; Walter Sorell, "Alvin Ailey City Center Dance Theater April 15–May 4," *Dance News*, June 1975: 11.

16. Linda Small, "Dancing Ellington," *Dance Magazine*, November 1976: 21.

17. Bob Micklin, "Ailey 'Mooche' Misses," *Newsday*, 14 April 1975: n.p.

18. Robert Kimball, "Ailey Premieres 'Night Creature,'" *New York Post*, 23 April 1975: n.p.; Anna Kisselgoff, "Dance: 'Night Creature,'" *New York Times*, 24 April 1975: 45; Anna Kisselgoff, "Ballet: 'Night Creature' by Ailey," *New York Times*, 5 December 1980: section III, 15.

19. Clive Barnes, "Dance: Baryshnikov in Ailey's Ellington Piece," *New York Times*, 13 May 1976: 41.

20. Frances Herridge, "Reaching Height of Ailey Style," *New York Post*, 12 May 1976: n.p.

21. Jane Perlez, "The One & Only & Only One," *New York Post*, 8 May 1976: n.p.

22. Anna Kisselgoff, "Ailey, a Duke and '3 Kings,'" *New York Times*, 13 August 1976: C1.

23. Robert Kimball, "Ellington Fete Comes Up Short," *New York Post*, 16 August 1976: 14; Deborah Jowitt, "They Make Sweet Thunder," *Village Voice*, 6 September 1976: 74; Wayne Robbins, "Unsophisticated Change," *Newsday*, 11 August 1976: n.p; Amanda Smith, "A Caravan of Dances," *Dance Magazine*, August 1976: 33.

24. Qtd. in Kisselgoff, "Ailey, a Duke and '3 Kings,'" C1.

25. Hodgson, "Ailey on Ellington," 1.

26. *Ailey Celebrates Ellington*, program notes.

Chapter 9: Gender and Spectatorship

1. Ailey program, UC Riverside, 26 February 1968.

2. Olga Maynard, *Judith Jamison: Aspects of a Dancer* (Garden City, NY: Doubleday, 1982), 141.

3. *An Evening with Alvin Ailey American Dance Theater*, videotape interview, 1986.

4. Ailey program note, 4 May 1971.

5. Leon Russell, "A Song for You," in *We've Only Just Begun Plus Twenty-Four Great Wedding Songs*, ed. Tom Brown (Hialeah, FL: Columbia Pictures Publications, 1981), 24–26.

6. Bob Russell and Bobby Scott, "He Ain't Heavy, He's My Brother," in *Biggest Hits of the 1960s*, ed. Miton Okun (New York: Quadrangle, New York Times Book Company, 1974), 75–82.

7. Bob Micklin, "A Gotham Accolade for Ailey," *Newsday*, 29 January 1969: n.p.

8. Ailey and Bailey, *Revelations*, 31–42, 133–146.

9. Ibid., 146.

10. Dove danced with Merce Cunningham, Mary Anthony, Pearl Lang, and Anna Sokolow before coming to the Ailey company.

11. Elinor Rogosin, *The Dance Makers: Conversations with American Choreographers* (New York: Walker and Company, 1980), 114.

12. Anna Kisselgoff, "Dance: Ailey's 'Streams,'" *New York Times*, 4 December 1973: 55.

13. Marcia Marks, "The Alvin Ailey Dance Theater," *Dance Magazine*, February 1966: 24.

14. E. Lynn Harris, *And This Too Shall Pass* (New York: Bantam Doubleday Dell, 1996).

Chapter 10: Later Dances

1. Frantz Fanon, *The Wretched of the Earth*, trans. Constance Farrington (New York: Grove Press, 1963), 57.

2. Paul Gilroy, "Exer(or)cising Power: Black Bodies in the Black Public Sphere," in *Dance in the City*, ed. Helen Thomas (New York: St. Martin's Press, 1997), 22.

3. Gilroy, *Small Acts*, 246.

4. Paul Gilroy, *The Black Atlantic: Modernity and Double Consciousness* (Cambridge, MA: Harvard University Press, 1993), 203.

5. "Choros" premiered in Dunham's *Tropical Revue* on 19 September 1943 in New York with costumes by John Pratt and music by Vadico Gogliano.

6. Gilroy, *Small Acts*, 1.

7. Gilroy, *Black Atlantic*, 110.

8. Rogosin, *The Dance Makers*, 108–110.

9. The school officially became The Ailey School in 2001, and has been directed by Denise Jefferson since 1984.

10. Dunning, *Alvin Ailey: A Life In Dance*, 284–293.

11. Olga Maynard, *Judith Jamison: Aspects of a Dancer*, 208.

12. Dunning, *Alvin Ailey*, 284–293.

13. Mazo and Cook, *The Alvin Ailey American Dance Theater*, 9, 17.

14. *Revelations: The Friends of Alvin Ailey*, newsletter (spring 1978): 1.

15. Jamison left the Ailey company in 1977. During her absence, she created the role of Potiphar's Wife in John Neumeier's *Joesphslegende* for the Vienna State Opera, and in 1978 appeared in Maurice Béjart's updated version of *Le Spectre de la Rose* with the Ballet of the Twentieth Century.

16. *Passage* program note, Alvin Ailey American Dance Theater, 6 May 1978: 34.

17. Frances Herridge, "Jamison's Glad to Be Back Where She Belongs," *New York Post*, 28 April 1978: n.p.

18. Maynard, *Aspects of a Dancer*, 184.

19. Herridge, "Jamison's Glad."

20. *Passage* program note, 34.

21. Marilyn Hunt, "Pennsylvania Ballet," *Dance Magazine*, September 1978: 42.

22. Peter Rosenwald, "Classical and American Dance at Its Best," *Wall Street Journal*, 18 May 1978: n.p.

23. Margery Mina, "Dance: Alvin Ailey American Dance Theater," *The Aquarian*, 28 June 1978: 11; Clive Barnes, "Highflying Alvin Ailey in Opening," *New York Post*, 4 May 1978: 37.

24. Anna Kisselgoff, "Dance: Ailey Opens with 2 Premieres," *New York Times*, 5 May 1978: C3.

25. Qtd. in Ken Sandler, "Alvin Ailey Company Draws the World," *Newsday*, 26 November 1978: n.p.

26. Dunning, *Alvin Ailey*, 318.

27. Mary Campbell, "Dance," AP Typescript Feature, 3 May 1979: n.p.

28. Ailey, program note, 5 May 1979.

29. Charles Mingus, *Beneath the Underdog* (New York: Penguin, 1971).

30. Anna Kisselgoff, "Dance: New 'Fire Sermon' Keeps Ailey Fans Guessing," *New York Times*, 5 May 1979: 14.

31. Ailey, program note, 29 November 1979.

32. Dunning, *Alvin Ailey*, 322.

33. Jennifer Dunning, "Dance: Ailey Homage to Joyce Trisler," *New York Times*, 3 December 1979: C14; Dunning, *Alvin Ailey*, 324.

34. Peter Rosenwald, "Alvin Ailey's Company Stages Its Spring Season," *Wall Street Journal*, 16 May 1980: n.p.

35. Maynard, *Aspects of a Dancer*, 205, 213.

36. Ailey and Bailey, *Revelations*, 136–137.

37. *New York Times*, 8 March 1980.

38. Dunning, *Alvin Ailey*, 330–342; Maynard, *Aspects of a Dancer*, 222–225; Ailey and Bailey, *Revelations*, 133–146.

39. Ailey and Bailey, *Revelations*, 146.

40. Julinda Lewis Williams, "Ailey's New Phases: Jazz in Motion," *Black American*, December 1980: n.p.

41. Joseph Mazo, "Voodoo and Vaudeville," *Women's Wear Daily*, 7 December 1981: n.p.

42. Anna Kisselgoff, "Dance: Festive Works at Alvin Ailey Gala," *New York Times*, 5 December 1981: 13.

43. Diana Maychick, "Ailey Casts New 'Spell' For Godunov and Jamison," *New York Post*, 25 November 1981: n.p.; Kisselgoff, "Festive Works," 13.

44. Tobi Tobias, "Ode to a Fisherman," *New York*, 21 December 1981: 74–75.

45. Norma McLain Stoop, "AAADT City Center, N.Y., Dec. 3, 1981," *Dance Magazine*, March 1982: 98.

46. Tobias, "Ode to a Fisherman," 75; Stoop, "AAADT City Center," 98.

47. Kisselgoff, "Festive Works," 13.

48. Ailey, program note, 11 December 1981.

49. Ibid.

50. Anna Kisselgoff, "Dance: Premiere of Ailey 'Landscape,'" *New York Times*, 13 December 1981: B18.

51. Anita Finkel, "AAADT, New York City Center, Dec 2–20, 1981," *Ballet News*, March 1982: 30; Clive Barnes, "Ailey's New Freedom in 'Landscape,'" *New York Post*, 14 December 1981: n.p.

52. C. Barnes, "Ailey's New Freedom"; Linda Winer, "A Lovely 'Landscape,'" *New York Daily News*, December 1981: 52.

53. Kisselgoff, "Premiere of Ailey 'Landscape,'" B18.

54. Anna Kisselgoff, "Dance: Ailey 'Satyriade' and 3 Duets in 'Waves,'" *New York Times*, 6 December 1982: C15.

55. Burt Supree, "Satyrs in Squaresville," *Village Voice*, 14 December 1982: 118.

56. Clive Barnes, "Alvin Ailey Makes a 'Fantasia' Out of Ravel's 'Satyriade,'" *New York Post*, 6 December 1982: n.p.; Kisselgoff, "Ailey 'Satyriade,'" C15; Tobi Tobias, "Mixed Feelings," *New York*, 20 December 1982: n.p.

57. E. J. Dionne, "New Alvin Ailey Dance Shakes Paris," *New York Times*, 16 April 1983: n.p.

58. Ailey, program note, 10 July 1984.

59. The Ailey company enjoyed a season at the Met 9–21 July 1984.

60. Qtd. in Dionne, "New Alvin Ailey Dance Shakes Paris."

61. Julinda Lewis, "Alvin Ailey American Dance Theater at the Metropolitan Opera House July 9–21, 1984," *Dance Magazine*, November 1984: 20.

62. Rob Baker, "'Isba': Exotic and Mysterious," *New York Daily News*, 5 December 1983: n.p.

63. Marilyn Tucker, "Ailey's Mix of Message and Fun," *San Francisco Chronicle*, 13 February 1984: n.p.; Rob Baker, "Morrison, Ailey-style," *New York Daily News*, 17 July 1984: n.p.; Clive Barnes, "Ailey's French Connection," *New York Post*, 12 July 1984: n.p.

64. Freda Pitt, "Italy," *Ballet News*, November 1983: 38.

65. Ibid.

66. Anna Kisselgoff, "Dance: 2 New York Premieres by Alvin Ailey," *New York Times*, 5 December 1983: C12.

67. Clive Barnes, "Ailey Premiere Is Neatly Danced," *New York Post*, 6 December 1983: n.p.

68. Robert Greskovic, "Reports: New York," *Ballet News*, April 1984: 34.

69. Kisselgoff, "2 New York Premieres," C12.

70. Baker, "'Isba': Exotic and Mysterious."

71. Janice Berman, "For Bird, from Ailey," *Newsday*, 1 December 1985: n.p.

72. Harry Haskell "Ailey Excited, Nervous about 'Bird' Debut," *Kansas City Star*, 23 September 1984: n.p.

73. Anna Kisselgoff, "Dance: Ailey Tribute to Charlie Parker," *New York Times*, 6 December 1985: C4; Joseph Mazo, " 'For Bird—With Love': Flights of Dramatic Fancy," *The Record*, 6 December 1985: 8.

74. Qtd. in Maya Wallach, "Gary DeLoatch Brings the Street to the Stage," *New York City Tribune*, 16 December 1988: n.p.

75. Qtd. in Berman, "For Bird, from Ailey."

76. Dunning, *Alvin Ailey*, 371–372.

77. Erik Aschengreen, "Show, Drama, and a Splash of Soul," trans. Marianne Bork, *Berlingske Tidende*, 24 March 1986: n.p.

78. Clive Barnes, "Big Daddy Ailey: The Joys of Living," *New York Post*, 4 December 1986: 32.

79. Tullia Limarzi, "2 Premieres, 1 Revival at Ailey Gala," *Staten Island Advance*, 5 December 1986: n.p.

80. Dunning, *Alvin Ailey*, 369.

81. Ailey, program note, 9 December 1986.

82. Janice Berman, "Choreographer's Memories Fueled 'Survivors,' " *Newsday*, 18 December 1986: n.p.

83. Anna Kisselgoff, "Dance: 'Survivors,' Tribute to Mandelas," *New York Times*, 11 December 1986: C19.

Chapter 11: Concluding Moves

1. Patrick Pacheco, "The Book of Revelations: Alvin Ailey at the Precipice," *New York Daily News Magazine*, 4 December 1988: 12.

2. Several dance critics continue to hound Ailey's memory as if there may be something to be gained by this process. In 2001, Joan Acocella opined, "Alvin Ailey, who founded the troupe in 1958, is honored today as a great American choreographer, but the truth is that he created one great piece, the 1960 'Revelations' (and it is very great, on a par with the best of Balanchine and Graham), and never again made anything half as interesting." Clearly, Acocella is not among those "honoring" Ailey as a great American choreographer. Could this fact be a source of her discomfort? Or might it be the fact of the Ailey company's success that some critics find irksome? Researchers will be hard pressed to find African American critical writing that disparages Ailey's choreographic output or the company's method wholesale. Why, then, do some (white) dance critics feel perennially compelled to express their anxiety about performances that apparently mean so little to them? See Joan Acocella, "The Spirit Moves," *The New Yorker*, 17 December 2001: 99.

3. Qtd. in Sandler, "Alvin Ailey Company Draws the World."

4. Ibid.

5. Qtd. in Dionne, "New Alvin Ailey Dance Shakes Paris."

6. Qtd. in Phyllis Stewart, "Ailey . . . Magic in the Dance." *Long Island Press*, 17 August 1975: 3.

7. Qtd. in Gruen, "Looking Ahead," 423.

8. Works in this vein made by artists who worked with the Alvin Ailey American Dance Theater include Donald Byrd's "Enactments in Time of Plague" (1988), Garth Fagan's "The Disenfranchised" section of *Griot New York* (1991), and Bill T. Jones's "D-Man in the Water" (1989).

9. Ellen Cohn, "Alvin Ailey, Arsonist," *New York Times*, 29 April 1973: 33.

10. Zita Allen, "An American Dilemma: Alvin Ailey's Hard Times," *Village Voice*, 2 June 2, 1980: 30.

11. Peter Rosenwald, "Alvin Ailey: Dancing On a Tightrope," *New York*, 9 May 1977: 56.

12. Sarita Allen, Interview with the author, 25 January 1997, Dallas, TX.

13. Suzanne Merry, "AAADT (City Center, May 2–20, 1979)," *Dance Magazine*, August 1979: 20.

14. Richard Philp, introduction to *Alvin Ailey American Dance Theater: Jack Mitchell Photographs* (Kansas City: Andrews and McMeel, 1993), viii.

15. Qtd. in Pacheco, "The Book of Revelations," 11.

16. Qtd. in Phyllis Stewart, "Ailey . . . Magic in the Dance," 3.

17. Marcia Siegel, "Going for Another Score," *New York*, 8 January 1979: 73.

18. Camille Hardy, "Recession-Proof Dance Leadership," *Dance Magazine*, October 1992: 52.

19. Kisselgoff, "Dance: Festive Works at Alvin Ailey Gala," 13.

20. David Vaughan, "Alvin Ailey: Revelations, and More Revelations," *Dance Magazine*, February, 1975: 38.

21. Jonathan Probber, "Alvin Ailey and Kansas City: The Attraction Is Mutual," *New York Times*, 30 November 1986: B6.

22. Vaughan, "Alvin Ailey: Revelations, and More Revelations," 40.

23. Jennifer Dunning, "The Life and Times of an American Classic," *New York Times*, 3 December 1995: B1.

24. Damon Wright, "Black Integrity, Black Chic," *Soho Weekly News*, November 1978: n.p.; Dunning, "Life and Times," B1.

25. Qtd. in Dunning, "Life and Times," B1.

26. Qtd. in "*Dance Magazine* Awards 1975: Alvin Ailey, Cynthia Gregory, Arthur Mitchell," *Dance Magazine*, July 1975: 67.

27. Dunning, *Alvin Ailey: A Life in Dance*, 410–414.

28. Qtd. in Ken Sandler, "Black Is Still an Issue," *Soho Weekly News*, 30 November 1978: 26.

29. Qtd. in Sandler, "Alvin Ailey Company Draws the World."

30. Qtd. in Jennifer Dunning, "Ailey's Troupe Explores Its Roots," *New York Times*, 27 November 1983: n.p.

Books and Journals

Adamczyk, Alicia J. *Black Dance: An Annotated Bibliography*. New York: Garland Press, 1989.

Ailey, Alvin. "Alvin Ailey." *Black Visions '89: Movements of Ten Dance Masters*. Tweed Gallery Exhibition Catalogue, 1989: 8–9.

Ailey, Alvin, with A. Peter Bailey. *Revelations: The Autobiography of Alvin Ailey*. New York: Birch Lane Press, 1995.

Ailey, Alvin, et al. "To Hear Another Language." *Callaloo: An Afro-American and African Journal of Arts and Letters* 12.3 (summer 1989): 431–452.

Allen, Zita. *Alvin Ailey American Dance Theater: 25 Years*. New York: Dance Theater Foundation, 1983.

Baker, Houston A., Jr. *Modernism and the Harlem Renaissance*. Chicago: University of Chicago Press, 1987.

Balanchine, George. "Feast of Ashes." In *New Complete Stories of the Great Ballets*. Garden City, NY: Doubleday, 1968: 150.

Baldwin, James. "The Black Boy Looks at the White Boy" [1961]. In *James Baldwin: Collected Essays*, ed. Toni Morrison. New York: Library of America, 1998. 269–295.

Barber, Beverly Hillsman. "Pearl Primus: Rebuilding America's Cultural Infrastructure." In *African American Genius in Modern Dance*, ed. Gerald Myers. Durham, NC: American Dance Festival, 1993. 9–11.

Barber, Samuel. *Hermit Songs*. New York, G. Schirmer, 1954.

———. *Knoxville: Summer of 1915*. New York: G. Schirmer, 1949.

Clark, VeVe. "Katherine Dunham: Method Dancing of Memory of Difference." In *African American Genius in Modern Dance*, ed. Gerald Myers. Durham, NC: American Dance Festival, 1993. 5–8.

De Lavallade, Carmen. "Alvin Ailey." In *Revelations: The Autobiography of Alvin Ailey*, by Alvin Ailey with A. Peter Bailey. New York: Birch Lane Press, 1995. 164–166.

DeFrantz, Thomas F. "African American Dance: A Complex History." In *Dancing Many Drums: Excavations in African American Dance*, ed. Thomas F. DeFrantz. Madison: University of Wisconsin Press, 2002. 3–38.

———. "Ballet." In *Encyclopedia of African-American Culture and History*. New York: Macmillan, 1995. 236–242.

———. "Ballet in Black: Louis Johnson and Vernacular Humor." In *Dancing Bodies, Living Histories: New Writings about Dance and Culture*, ed. Lisa Doolittle and Anne Flynn. Banff: Banff Centre Press, 2000. 178–195.

———. "Foreword: Black Bodies Dancing Black Culture—Black Atlantic Transformations." In *Embodying Liberation: the Black Body in American Dance*, ed. Dorothea Fischer-Hornung and Alison D. Goeller. Hamburg: Lit Verlag, 2001 Forecaast 4. 11–16.

———. "Simmering Passivity: The Black Male Body in Concert Dance." In *Moving Words: New Directions in Dance Criticism*, ed. Gay Morris. New York: Routledge, 1996. 107–121

———. "Stoned Soul Picnic: Alvin Ailey and the Struggle to Define Official Black Culture." In *Soul: Black Power, Politics, and Pleasure*, ed. Monique Guillory and Richard C. Green. New York: New York University Press, 1998. 216–227.

———. "To Make Black Bodies Strange: Social Protest in Concert Dance of the Black Arts Movement." In *African American Performance: A Sourcebook*, ed. Annemarie Bean. New York: Routledge, 1999. 83–93.

Du Bois, W. E. Burghardt. *The Souls of Black Folks*. New York: Dodd, Mead, 1961.

Duncan, Isadora. *My Life*. Garden City, NY: Garden City Publishing Company, 1927.

Dunning, Jennifer. *Alvin Ailey: A Life in Dance*. New York: Addison-Wesley, 1996.

———. "Amazing Truth." *Choreography and Dance*. Vol. 4, part 1. 1996: 47–54.

Ellison, Ralph. *Shadow and Act*. New York: Vintage Books, 1953.

Ellington, Duke. *Music Is My Mistress*. New York: Doubleday, 1973.

Emery, Lynne Fauley. *Black Dance in the United States from 1619 to 1970*. 2d ed. 1972; Pennington, NJ: Princeton Book Company, 1988.

Fairbrother, Trevor J. *John Singer Sargent*. New York: Abrams, 1994.

Fanon, Frantz. *The Wretched of the Earth*. Trans. Constance Farrington. New York: Grove Press, 1963.

Foster, Susan Leigh. "Choreographing History." In *Choreographing History*, ed. Susan Leigh Foster. Bloomington: Indiana University Press, 1995: 3–21.

Foulkes, Julia. *Modern Bodies: Dance and American Modernism from Martha Graham to Alvin Ailey*. Chapel Hill: University of North Carolina Press, 2002.

Gaines, Kevin K. *Uplifting the Race: Black Leadership, Politics, and Culture in the Twentieth Century*. Chapel Hill: University of North Carolina Press, 1996.

García Lorca, Federico. "The House of Bernarda Alba." In *Three Tragedies: Blood Wedding, Yerma, The House of Bernarda Alba*. Trans. James Graham-Luján and Richard L. O'Connell. New York: Penguin Plays, 1941. 149–201.

Gates, Henry Louis Jr., ed. *Bearing Witness: Selections from African-American Autobiography in the Twentieth Century*. New York: Pantheon, 1991.

———. "Black Structures of Feeling." In *Figures in Black: Words, Signs, and the "Racial" Self*, ed. Henry Louis Gates Jr. New York: Oxford University Press, 1987. 167–296.

George, Don. *Sweet Man: The Real Duke Ellington*. New York: G. P. Putnam's Sons, 1981.

Gilroy, Paul. *The Black Atlantic: Modernity and Double Consciousness*. Cambridge, MA: Harvard University Press, 1993.

———. "Exer(or)cising Power. Black Bodies in the Black Public Sphere." In *Dance in the City*, ed. Helen Thomas. New York: St. Martin's Press, 1997. 21–34.

———. *Small Acts: Thoughts on the Politics of Black Cultures*. London: Serpent's Tail, 1993.

Gottschild, Brenda Dixon. *Digging the Africanist Presence in American Performance: Dance and Other Contexts*. Westport, CT: Greenwood Press, 1996.

Graff, Ellen. *Stepping Left: Dance and Politics in New York City, 1928–1942*. Durham, NC: Duke University Press, 1997.

Green, Richard C. "(Up)Staging the Primitive: Pearl Primus and 'the Negro Problem' in American Dance." In *Dancing Many Drums: Excavations in African American Dance*, ed. Thomas F. DeFrantz. Madison: University of Wisconsin Press, 2002. 105–139.

Gruen, John. "Looking Ahead." In *The Private World of Ballet*. New York: Penguin Books, 1975. 417–451.

Harris, E. Lynn. *And This Too Shall Pass*. New York: Bantam Doubleday Dell, 1996.

Hebdige, Dick. *Cut 'n' Mix: Culture, Identity and Caribbean Music*. London: Comedia, 1987.

Hill, Constance Valis. "Katherine Dunham's *Southland*: Protest in the Face of Repression." In *Dancing Many Drums: Excavations in African American Dance*, ed. Thomas F. DeFrantz. Madison: University of Wisconsin Press, 2002. 289–316.

Hodgson, Moira, and Thomas Victor. "Alvin Ailey City Center Dance Theater." In *Quintet: Five American Dance Companies*. New York: Morrow, 1976. 48–83.

Holloway, Joseph, ed. *Africanisms in American Culture*. Bloomington: Indiana University Press, 1991.

Horst, Louis, and Carroll Russell. Modern *Dance Forms, in Relation to the Other Modern Arts*. San Francisco: Impulse Publications, 1961.

Jamison, Judith, with Howard Kaplan. *Dancing Spirit: An Autobiography*. New York: Doubleday, 1993.

Johnson, Abby Arthur, and Ronald Maberry Johnson. *Propaganda and Aesthetics: The Literary Politics of Afro-American Magazines in the Twentieth Century*. Amherst: University of Massachusetts Press, 1979.

Johnson, Hall. *I've Been 'Buked*. New York: G. Schirmer, 1946.

———. "Notes on the Negro Spiritual." In *Readings in Black American Music*, ed. Eileen Southern. New York: Norton, 1971. 268–275.

Jones, LeRoi. *Blues People: The Negro Experience in White America and the Music That Developed from It*. New York: Morrow, 1963.

Latham, Jacqueline Quinn. "A Biographical Study of the Lives and Contributions of Two Selected Contemporary Black Male Dance Artists: Arthur Mitchell and Alvin Ailey." Ph.D. diss., Texas Women's University, 1973.

Loney, Glenn. *Unsung Genius the Passion of Dancer Choreographer Jack Cole*. New York: Franklin Watts, 1984.

Long, Richard. *The Black Tradition in American Dance*. New York: Rizzoli International, 1989.

Lorca, Federico García. "The House of Bernarda Alba." In *Three Tragedies: Blood Wedding, Yerma, the House of Bernarda Alba*, translated by James Graham-Luján and Richard L. O'Connell. New York: Penquin Plays, 1941.

Lovell, John, Jr. *Black Song: The Forge and the Flame*. New York: Paragon House, 1972.

Manning, Susan. "Black Voices, White Bodies: The Performance of Race and Gender in How Long Brethren." *American Quarterly* 50.1 (March 1998): 24–46.

———. *Race in Motion: Modern Dance, Negro Dance*. Minneapolis: University of Minnesota Press, 2004.

Manor, Giora. *The Gospel According to Dance: Choregraphy and the Bible from Ballet to Modern*. New York: St. Martin's Press, 1980.

Mapplethorpe, Robert. *Black Book*. New York: St. Martin's Press, 1986.

Maynard, Olga. *Judith Jamison: Aspects of a Dancer*. Garden City, NY: Doubleday, 1982.

Mazo, Joseph H., and Susan Cook. *The Alvin Ailey American Dance Theater*. New York: Morrow, 1978.

McDonagh, Don. "Alvin Ailey." In *The Complete Guide to Modern Dance*. Garden City, NY: Doubleday, 1976. 125–132.

McQuirter, Marya. "Awkward Moves: Dance Lessons from the 1940s." In *Dancing Many Drums: Excavations in African American Dance*, ed. Thomas F. DeFrantz. Madison: University of Wisconsin Press, 2002. 81–104.

Miller, James. "I Wanna Be Ready." New York: Galaxy Music Corporation, 1943.

Mingus, Charles. *Beneath the Underdog*. New York: Penguin, 1971.

Mitchell, Jack. *Alvin Ailey American Dance Theater: Jack Mitchell Photographs*. Kansas City: Andrews and McMeel, 1993.

Morrison, Toni. *Playing in the Dark: Whiteness and the Literary Imagination*. Cambridge, MA: Harvard University Press, 1992.

Murray, Albert. Liner notes. *Revelations and Blues Suite 20th Anniversary LP*. New York: Dance Theater Foundation, 1978.

Padgette, Paul, ed. *The Dance Photography of Carl Van Vechten.* New York: Schirmer Books, 1981.

Perpener, John O., III. *African American Concert Dance: The Harlem Renaissance and Beyond.* Urbana: University of Illinois Press, 2001.

Phelan, Peggy. *Unmarked: The Politics of Performance.* New York: Routledge, 1992.

Philp, Richard. Introduction to *Alvin Ailey American Dance Theater: Jack Mitchell Photographs.* Kansas City: Andrews and McMeel, 1993. vii–xii.

Powell, Richard J. *Black Art and Culture in the 20th Century.* London: Thames and Hudson Ltd., 1997.

Prevots, Naima. *Dance for Export: Cultural Diplomacy and the Cold War.* Hanover, NH: Wesleyan University Press, 1998.

Priestly, Brian. *Mingus: A Critical Biography.* New York: Da Capo Press, 1983.

Primus, Pearl. "Primitive African Dance (and Its Influence on the Churches of the South)." In *The Dance Encyclopedia*, ed. Anatole Chujoy. New York: A. S. Barnes, 1949. 387–389.

Rogosin, Elinor. *The Dance Makers: Conversations with American Choreographers.* New York: Walker and Company, 1980. 102–117.

Russell, Bob, and Bobby Scott. "He Ain't Heavy, He's My Brother." In *Biggest Hits of the 1960s*, ed. Miton Okun. New York: Quadrangle, New York Times Book Company, 1974. 75–82.

Russell, Leon. "A Song for You." In *We've Only Just Begun Plus Twenty-Four Great Wedding Songs*, ed. Tom Brown. Hialeah, FL: Columbia Pictures Publications, 1981. 24–26.

Shaw, Arnold. *Black Popular Music in America: From the Spirituals, Minstrels, and Ragtime to Soul, Disco and Hip-Hop.* New York: Schirmer Books, 1986.

Siegel, Marcia B. "Black Dance: A New Separatism." In *At the Vanishing Point.* New York: Saturday Review Press, 1972. 137–173.

———. "Revelations." In *The Shapes of Change: Images of American Dance.* Berkeley: University of California Press, 1979. 289–295.

———. "Selling Soul." In *At the Vanishing Point.* New York: Saturday Review Press, 1972.

Spencer, Jon Michael. *Protest and Praise: Sacred Music of Black Religion.* Minneapolis: Fortress Press, 1990.

Stearns, Marshall, and Jean Stearns. *Jazz Dance: The Story of American Vernacular Dance.* New York: Schirmer Books, [1964] 1979.

Thompson, Robert Farris. "Dance and Culture, an Aesthetic of the Cool." *African Forum* 2 (fall 1966): 85–102.

———. *Flash of the Spirit: African and Afro-American Art and Philosophy.* New York: Vintage Books, 1983.

Todd, Arthur. "American Negro Dance: A National Treasure." In *Ballet Annual 1962*, ed. Arnold Haskell and Mary Clarke. London: Adam and Charles Black, 1961. 92–105.

Topaz, Muriel, ed. "Alvin Ailey: An American Visionary." *Choreography and Dance: An International Journal* 4.1 (1996): ____.

Tucker, Mark. "The Late Years: 1960–1974." In *The Duke Ellington Reader*, ed. Mark Tucker. New York: Oxford University Press, 1993.

Warren, Larry. *Lester Horton: Modern Dance Pioneer.* Pennington, NJ: Dance Horizons, 1977.

Washington, Ernest L., ed. "Alvin Ailey: The Man and His Contributions." *Talking Drums! The Journal of Black Dance* 1.4 (May 1990): ____.

Werner, Craig Hansen. *Playing the Changes: From Afro-Modernism to the Jazz Impulse.* Urbana: University of Illinois Press, 1994.

Periodicals

Abelman, Lester. "Ailey Dance Troupe Box-Office Winner." *New York Daily News*, 20 December 1971: n.p.

———. "Joffrey Premieres Cool 'Mingus Dances.'" *New York Daily News*, 15 October 1971: 72.

Acocella, Joan. "The Spirit Moves." *The New Yorker*, 17 December 2001: 99–101.

"Ailey Troupe Saved by State Department." *New York Times*, 19 June 1970: 25.

"Ailey's Homage to the Duke." *Los Angeles Times*, 29 November 1974: n.p.

"Alvin Ailey Arrested at Student Housing." *New York Times*, 8 March 1980: 25.

"The City: Alvin Ailey Arrested at Student House." *New York Times*, 30 March 1980: 25.

Ailey, Alvin. "Alvin Ailey Talks to *Dance and Dancers*: An Interview." *Dance and Dancers*, April 1965: 32–33.

———. Alvin Ailey with Arthur Todd. "Roots of the Blues." *Dance and Dancers*, November 1961: 24–25.

Allen, Zita. "Alvin Ailey Thrills Them at the Met." *New York Amsterdam News*, 14 July 1984: 19.

———. "An American Dilemma: Alvin Ailey's Hard Times." *Village Voice*, 2 June 1980: 29–31.

———. "The Great American 'Black Dance' Mystery." *Freedomways* 20.4 (1980) 283–291.

Anderson, Jack. "Leonard Bernstein's 'Mass.' *Dance Magazine*, August 1972: 78.

Anthony, Bill. "Alvin Ailey's American Theatre Puts Dance into Soul." *PD Action*, 19 March 1971, n.p.

Aschengreen, Erik. "Show, Drama, and a Splash of Soul." Trans. Marianne Bork. *Berlingske Tidende*, 24 March 1986: n.p.

Atkinson, Brooks. "Theatre: Truman Capote's Musical." *New York Times*, 31 December 1954: 11.

Baker, Rob. "Alvin Ailey." *After Dark*, February 1974: n.p.

———. "Dance at the Delacorte." *Dance Magazine*, November 1972: 59–63.

———. " 'Isba': Exotic and Mysterious." *New York Daily News*, 5 December 1983: n.p.

———. "Morrison, Ailey-style." *New York Daily News*, 17 July 1984: n.p.

Barnes, Clive. "Ailey and Troupe in Triumph." *New York Times*, 28 January 1969: 48.

———. "Ailey Premiere Is Neatly Danced." *New York Post*, 6 December 1983: n.p.

———. "Ailey's French Connection." *New York Post*, 12 July 1984: n.p.

———. "Ailey's New Freedom in 'Landscape.'" *New York Post*, 14 December 1981: n.p.

———. "Ailey's 'The Mingus Dances.'" *New York Times*, 14 October 1971: 54.

———. "Alvin Ailey Makes a 'Fantasia' Out of Ravel's 'Satyriade.'" *New York Post*, 6 December 1982: n.p.

———. "Ballet in Modest but Hectic Contribution." *New York Times*, 17 September 1966: 15.

———. "Big Daddy Ailey: The Joys of Living." *New York Post*, 4 December 1986: 31–32.

———. "Dance: A Paris Festival." *New York Times*, 16 June 1966: n.p.

———. "Dance: Ballet Theater Opens a Six-Week Season." *New York Times*, 30 June 1971:

———. "Dance: Baryshnikov in Ailey's Ellington Piece." *New York Times*, 13 May 1976: 41.

———. "The Dance: Lively and Varied Fare." *New York Times*, 9 September 1972: 12.

————. "Dance: Rather Too Much Bare Stage?" *New York Times*, 7 November 1971.

————. "Dance: Spring Gala Day." *New York Times*, 17 April 1975: 47.

————. "Dancing the Blues." *The Spectator*, 16 October 1964: n.p.

————. "An Embarrassment of Riches?" *New York Times*, 20 May 1973: II, 32.

————. "Exciting Dancers in British Debut." *London Times*, 6 October 1964: 19.

————. "A Great Lesson in Race Relations." *New York Times*, 26 December 1970: B30.

————. "Harkness Ballet Presents Jack Cole's 'Requiem.'" *New York Times*, 4 November 1967: ___.

————. "Highflying Alvin Ailey in Opening." *New York Post*, 4 May 1978: 37.

————. "Paris Sees Dancers from U.S." *New York Times*, International. 17 June 1966: n.p.

————. "Playfully Seizing on a Ritual: Ailey's New 'Myth.'" *New York Times*, 16 December 1971: ____.

————. "Tout Paris Sees Harkness Ballet." *New York Times*, 13 March 1965: 17.

Barnes, Patricia. "New Works, Fine Dancing." *Dance and Dancers*, April 1973: 48–52.

Becque, Don Oscar. "Dance Conversations: The Dance as a 'Good Will' Ambassador": n.p. *Villager* (New York), 18 January 1962: n.p.

Berman, Janice. "Choreographer's Memories Fueled 'Survivors.'" *Newsday*, 18 December 1986: n.p.

————. "For Bird, from Ailey." *Newsday*, 1 December 1985: n.p.

Bernstein, Harry. "Alvin Ailey and Company." *Dance Observer*, February 1959: 24–25.

B. H. K. "Dance Plays Part in Kennedy Opening: Ailey Co. Featured." *Dance News*, October 1971: n.p.

Buckle, Richard. "In a Friendly Fashion." *London Sunday Times*, 1964.

Byrne, Bridget. "Alvin Ailey Dance Tranfixing." *Los Angeles Herald Examiner*, 16 July 1969: n.p.

Cameron, Zelda. "Washington-Baltimore." *Dance Magazine*, March 1979: 97–99.

Campbell, Mary. "Ailey: More People Dig the Dance." Typescript AP Report, Ailey Archives, 1969, n.p.

————. "Dance." Typescript AP Report, Ailey Archives, 3 May 1979: n.p.

Cannell, Kathleen. "WGBH: Entrepreneur." *Christian Science Monitor*, 31 May 1969: n.p.

"Carmen de Lavallade Stars with Ailey Dance Troupe." *New York Herald Tribune*, 11 December 1961: n.p.

Chiavaroli, Linda. "Ailey's Dancers Have Freedom Modern Dance Companies Lack." *Rochester Democrat and Chronicle*, 8 April 1973: n.p.

Chujoy, Anatole. "Alvin Ailey and Company, Ernest Parham and Company, Talley Beatty, guest artist. YM-YWHA, N.Y., March 30." *Dance News*, May 1958: 9.

"City to Aid Ailey in Parks Program." *New York Times*, 22 February 1974: 22.

Clarke, Mary. "Blues and Holy Blues: The Alvin Ailey American Dance Theatre's First Programme." *Dancing Times*, November 1964: 64–65.

Cohen, Selma Jeanne. "Alvin Ailey Dance Theater." *Dance Magazine*, March 1960: 69.

————. "Shirley Broughton's 5 o'Clock Dance Co." *Dance Magazine*, April 1959: 64, 80.

————. "Alvin Ailey Dance Theater." *Dance Magazine*, January 1961: 60–61.

Cohn, Ellen. "Alvin Ailey, Arsonist." *New York Times Magazine*, 29 April 1973: 20–33.

————. " 'I Want to Be a Father Figure.'" *New York Times*, 13 April 1969: B35.

Coton, A. V. (pseud.) "Alvin Ailey in Edinburgh." *Dancing Times*, October 1968: 12.

Croce, Arlene. "Standing Still." *New Yorker*, 7 January 1974: 47.

Cunningham, Barry. "Mingus 'Up from the Dead' on Ballet." *New York Post*, 20 October 1971: 2, 27.

Cunningham, Katharine. "Mingus and Chain Dances." *Dance and Dancers*, February 1972: 48–50.

"*Dance Magazine* Awards 1975: Alvin Ailey, Cynthia Gregory, Arthur Mitchell." *Dance Magazine*, July 1975: 66–69.

DeFrantz, Thomas F. "The Black Body in Question: Scarce on Ballet Stages, African Americans Nevertheless Pace American Dance." *Village Voice*, 23 April 1996: 29–32.

Dionne, E. J. "New Alvin Ailey Dance Shakes Paris." *New York Times*, 16 April 1983: n.p.

Dougherty, John. "From Los Angeles, Halfway Round the World in Dance." *Music Magazine*, April 1964: n.p.

Dunning, Jennifer. "Ailey's Troupe Explores Its Roots." *New York Times*, 27 November 1983: n.p.

———— "Dance: Ailey Homage to Joyce Trisler." *New York Times*, 3 December 1979: C14.

————. "The Life and Times of an American Classic." *New York Times*, 3 December 1995: B1.

Dwyer, John. "Dancers Are Artistic in Festival at UB." *Buffalo Evening News*, 20 June 1964: n.p.

Efthyvoulou, Lonia. "Arts Center Gives Back Stage View." *Daily Register* (Redbank, NJ), 24 June 1971: n.p.

Estrada, Ric. "Three Leading Negro Artists, and How They Feel about Dance in the Community." *Dance Magazine*, November 1968: 46.

Fatt, Amelia. "A Dance Career: Alvin Ailey's." *Dance Magazine*, October 1966: 52–59.

Finkel, Anita. "AAADT, New York City Center, Dec 2–20, 1981." *Ballet News*, March 1982: 30–31.

Fisher, James. "Alvin Alley at John Hancock Hall." *Boston Review of Arts*, 1 April 1971: n.p.

Gent, George. "Mini-Operas Ready to Take Met Role." *New York Times*, 15 February 1973: 50.

Glover, William. "Theater." Typescript AP Report, 14 December 1969: n.p.

Goda, Shigeo. "Fiery Sense of Protest." *Daily Sports*, 23 April, 1962.

Goldner, Nancy. "American Ballet Theatre." *Dance News*, September 1970: 11–13, 15.

Goodwin, Noel. "Black Octave." *Dance and Dancers*, October 1968: 23–30.

Green, Benny. "Song and Dance." *Observer Weekend Review*, 11 October 1964: n.p.

Grenier, Cynthia. "Harkness Ballet: An Elegant Opening." *New York Herald Tribune*, 13 March 1965: n.p.

Greskovic, Robert. "Reports: New York." *Ballet News*, April 1984: 33–34.

H.S.H. "American Dance Co's Brilliant Show." *Times of Malaya and Straits Echo*, 13 March 1962: n.p.

Hardy, Camille. "Recession-Proof Dance Leadership." *Dance Magazine*, October 1992: 48–52.

Haskell, Harry. "Ailey Excited, Nervous about 'Bird' Debut." *Kansas City Star*, 23 September 1984: n.p.

Hering, Doris. "Alvin Ailey and Company." *Dance Magazine*, February 1959: 27.

————."Alvin Ailey and Company, Ernest Parham and Company." *Dance Magazine*, May 1958: 65–66.

————. "Joffrey Journey." *Dance Magazine*, January 1972: 31–36.

Herridge, Frances. "Ailey Begins Season at ANTA." *New York Post*, 19 January 1971: n.p.

————. "Jamison's Glad to Be Back Where She Belongs." *New York Post*, 28 April 1978: n.p.

————. "New Ailey 'Rites' at City Center." *New York Post*, 18 May 1973: n.p.

————. "Reaching Height of Ailey Style." *New York Post*, 12 May 1976: n.p.

Hodgson, Moira. "Ailey on Ellington." *Dance News*, April 1976: 1–2.

Hughes, Allen. "Dance: Alvin Ailey Is Victor over Rain." *New York Times*, 10 September 1962: n.p.

Hunt, Marilyn. "Pennsylvania Ballet." *Dance Magazine*, September 1978: 39–43.

"Intense, Moving Dance Program by Ailey Group." *Daily Ledger* (Fairfield, IA), 12 July 1963: n.p.

Jackson, George. "New York Entries: Ailey." *Dance News*, June 1972: 13.

Jaffe, Natalie. "Alvin Ailey Offers Two New Dance Works." *New York Times*, 29 April 1963: n.p.

Johnson, Carole. "Black Dance." *The Feet*, July 1971: 2.

Johnson, Harriett. "Ballet Theater Opens with 'River.'" *New York Post*, 30 June 1971: n.p.

————. "'Lord Byron' in World Premiere." *New York Post*, 21 April 1972: n.p.

Johnston, Jill. "Mr. Ailey." *Village Voice*, 21 December 1961: n.p.

Jowitt, Deborah "Blow Yourself Up." *Village Voice*, 21 October 1971: n.p.

————. "Game, Set, Match." *Village Voice*, 13 May 1971: n.p.

————. "They Make Sweet Thunder." *Village Voice*, 6 September 1976: n.p.

Kambayashi, Sumio. "Carmen de Lavallade — Alvin Ailey American Dance Company Review Excerpts Compiled by the Press and Program Office of Tokyo American Cultural Center." Photocopy Typescript, Alvin Ailey Archives, 1962.

Kaufman, Wolfe. "Harkness Eclipsed by Outdoors." *New York Herald Tribune* (Paris), 11–12 June 1966: n.p.

Kimball, Robert. "Ailey Premieres 'Night Creature.'" *New York Post*, 23 April 1975: n.p.

————. "Ellington Fete Comes Up Short." *New York Post*, 16 August 1976: n.p.

Kisselgoff, Anna. "Ailey, a Duke and '3 Kings'." *New York Times*, 13 August 1976: C1, C10.

————. "Ailey Dance Theater Presents a Rousing Finale." *New York Times*, 18 August 1969: 28.

————. "Ailey Dancers to Give Mary Lou's Mass." *New York Times*, 9 December 1971: 62.

————. "Ballet: 'Hidden Rites.'" *New York Times*, 19 May 1973: 29.

————. "Ballet in 'Byron': A Tough Assignment." *New York Times*, 22 April 1972: n.p.

————. "Dance: 'Night Creature' by Ailey.'" *New York Times*, 5 Decmber 1980: III, 15.

————. "Dance: Ailey Opens with 2 Premieres." *New York Times*, 5 May 1978: C3.

————. "Dance: Ailey Returns." *New York Times*, 19 April 1972: 37.

————. "Dance: Ailey 'Satyriade' and 3 Duets in 'Waves.'" *New York Times*, 6 December 1982: III 15.

————. "Dance: Ailey Tribute to Charlie Parker." *New York Times*, 6 December 1985: C4.

————. "Dance: Ailey's 'Streams.'" *New York Times*, 4 December 1973: 55.

————. "Dance: Festive Works at Alvin Ailey Gala." *New York Times*, 5 December 1981: 13.

————. "Dance: New 'Fire Sermon' Keeps Ailey Fans Guessing." *New York Times*, 5 May 1979: 14.

————. "Dance: 'Night Creature.'" *New York Times*, 24 April 1975: 45.

————. "Dance: No One's Sitting on His Hands." *New York Times*, 27 January 1971: 32.

————. "Dance: Premiere of Ailey 'Landscape.'" *New York Times*, 13 December 1981: B18.

————. "Dance: 'Survivors,' Tribute to Mandelas." *New York Times*, 11 December 1986: C19.

————. "Dance: 2 New York Premieres by Alvin Ailey." *New York Times*, 5 December 1983: C12.

———. "Love Is Theme." *New York Times*, 27 April 1972: 48.

———. "New Ailey Work (Gymnopedies)." *New York Times,* 24 April 1970: n.p.

———. "When Ballet Dancers Stumble into Modern Dance." *New York Times*, 24 August 1975: 1, 7.

Lennon, Peter. "Not Just Hoofers." *Guardian*, 25 September 1964, n.p.

Lewis, Jean Battey. "Dance in the Mass: Visceral Impact." *Washington Post*, 9 September 1971: n.p.

———. " 'Father Figure' of Dance." *Washington Post*, 3 October 1971: n.p.

Lewis, Julinda. "Alvin Ailey American Dance Theater at the Metropolitan Opera House July 9–21, 1984." *Dance Magazine*, November 1984: 20.

Limarzi, Tullia. "2 Premieres, 1 Revival at Ailey Gala." *Staten Island Advance*, 5 December 1986: n.p.

Manchester, Phyllis Winifred. "Alvin Ailey and Company." *Dance News*, February, 1959: 7.

———. "The Alvin Ailey Dance Theatre." *Dance News*, March 1960: 10.

———. "Alvin Ailey Dance Theater." *Dance News*, January 1961: 10–11.

———. "Profile: Alvin Ailey." *Dancing Times*, October 1964: 10–11.

Marks, Marcia. "The Alvin Ailey Dance Theater." *Dance Magazine,* February 1966: 24–25.

Martin, John. "Dance: Muscling In." *New York Times*, 17 December 1961: x24.

———. "The Dance: Review III." *New York Times*, 6 July 1958: X 11.

——— "De Mille Ballet Seen As Novelty." *New York Times,* 23 January 1940: 23.

Maychick, Diana. "Ailey Casts New 'Spell' for Godunov and Jamison." *New York Post*, 25 November 1981: n.p.

Mazo, Joseph. "Alvin Ailey." *Women's Wear Daily*, 20 January 1971: n.p.

———. "Alvin Ailey's Dance Tribute to the Duke." *New York Times*, 13 April 1975: B6.

———. "'For Bird—With Love': Flights of Dramatic Fancy." *The Record*, 6 December 1985: 8.

———. " 'Masekela Langage.' " *Women's Wear Daily*, 9 December 1977: 15.

———. "Voodoo and Vaudeville." *Women's Wear Daily*, 7 December 1981: n.p.

McDonagh, Don. "Ailey Troupe in Brooklyn." *New York Times*, 23 April 1969: 40.

———. "Ailey's Dancers Crackling Again." *New York Times*, 28 April 1971: 33.

Merry, Suzanne. "AAADT (City Center, May 2–20, 1979)." *Dance Magazine*, August 1979: 19, 22–23.

Micklin, Bob. "Ailey 'Mooche' Misses." *Newsday*, 14 April 1975: n.p.

———. "Dance: Light Entertainment." *Newsday*, 17 November 1972: n.p.

———. "Dance: Pleasing the Crowd." *Newsday*, 21 August 1974: n.p.

———. "Dance: Work In Progress." *Newsday*, 18 May 1973: n.p.

———. "A Gotham Accolade for Ailey." *Newsday*, 29 January 1969: n.p.

Mina, Margery. "Dance: Alvin Ailey American Dance Theater." *The Aquarian*. Westbury, NY. 28 June 1978: 11.

Monson, Karen. "Ailey's Goal: Dance Interest." *Los Angeles Times*, 19 July 1969: n.p.

Moore, William. "Alvin Ailey (1931–1989)." *Ballet Review* (winter 1990): 12–17.

———"Alvin Ailey Is Just Too Much." *The Black American* 15.3 (1974): n.p.

Movshon, George. "New York's Season." *Opera*, August 1973: n.p.

Norkin, Sam. "Dancers in the Park Fashioning a Festival." *New York Daily News*, 9 September 1972: n.p.

O'Connor, John. "TV: Holiday Specials, from Splendid to Poor." *New York Times,* 27 November 1974: 75.

Pacheco, Patrick. "The Book of Revelations: Alvin Ailey at the Precipice." *New York Daily News Magazine*, 4 December 1988: 11.

Percival, John. "Alvin Ailey Sadler's Wells." *London Times*, 2 December 1970: 13.

Perlez, Jane. "The One & Only & Only One." *New York Post*, 8 May 1976: n.p.

Perry, Jean. "An Interracial Dance Co. Is On the Move." *Sunday News*, 24 September 1972: n.p.

Philp, Richard. "Twenty Years Later: The Alvin Ailey American Dance Theater." *Dance Magazine*, October 1978: 63–78.

Pierce, Robert. "A Choreographer of Spectacle." Ailey Archives. December 1971: n.d.

Pikula, Joan. "Ailey Company Opens Engagement." *Asbury Park Evening Press*, 24 June 1971: 13.

Pitt, Freda. "Italy." *Ballet News*, November 1983: 38–39.

Probber, Jonathan. "Alvin Ailey and Kansas City: The Attraction Is Mutual." *New York Times*, 30 November 1986: B6.

"A Rare and Exciting Theatrical Experience." *The Herald*, 30 January 1965: n.p.

Robbins, Wayne. "Unsophisticated Change." *Newsday*, 11 August 1976: n.p.

Rosenwald, Peter. "Alvin Ailey: Dancing on a Tightrope." *New York*, 9 May 1977: 54.

———. "Alvin Ailey: Dancing on a Tightrope." *USIS News Feature*, 23 June 1977: n.p.

———. "Alvin Ailey's Company Stages Its Spring Season." *Wall Street Journal*, 16 May 1980: n.p.

———. "Classical and American Dance at Its Best." *Wall Street Journal*, 18 May 1978: n.p.

Saal, Hubert. "Ballet in Black." *Newsweek*, 10 February 1969: 76.

———. "Dance Me a River." *Newsweek*, 6 July 1970: n.p.

Sandler, Ken. "Alvin Ailey Company Draws the World." *Newsday*, 26 November 1978: n.p.

———."Black Is Still an Issue." *Soho Weekly News*, 30 November 1978: 26.

Schonberg, Harold. "Opera: A New 'Carmen,' Daring and Provocative." *New York Times*, 20 September 1972: n.p.

———. "Opera: Minimet's Playful 'Four Saints.'" *New York Times*, 24 February 1973: 17.

Shepard, Richard. "Dancers Tap Brooklyn Neighbors for Funds." *New York Times*, 24 February 1969: 32.

———. "Theater: A Rousing 'Jerico-Jim Crow.'" *New York Times*, 13 January 1964: n.p.

Siegel, Marcia B. "Ballet: 'Myth' by Ailey." *Boston Herald Traveler*, 22 December 1971: n.p.

———. "Dance: Alvin Ailey Innovates." *Boston Herald Traveler*, 6 February 1971: n.p.

———. "Dance: 'Archipelago' Opens in NY." *Boston Herald Traveler*, 27 January 1971: n.p.

———. "Going for Another Score." *New York*, 8 January 1979: 73.

———. "Two New Works Choreographed by Alvin Ailey for Spring." *Boston Herald Traveler*, 12 May 1972: n.p.

Singer, Samuel. "Ailey Troupe Earns Cheer." *Philadelphia Inquirer*, 4 November 1963: n.p.

Small, Linda. "Dancing Ellington." *Dance Magazine*, November 1976: 20–21, 26, 28, 30–31.

Smith, Amanda. "A Caravan of Dances." *Dance Magazine*, August 1976: 33–34.

Smoliar, Stephen. "Ailey Troupe: Soul Works More Than Sole Work." *Boston after Dark*, 4 June 1969: n.p.

———. "Alvin Ailey Dances into Today's Cultural Void." *Boston after Dark*, 21 May 1969: 6.

Sorell, Walter. "Alvin Ailey City Center Dance Theater April 15–May 4." *Dance News*, June 1975: 5, 11.

———. "Style, Essence, Allusion." *Dance Magazine*, August 1963: 47, 62.

"Soviets Say 'Molodtsy' to Ailey Troupe." *Dance News*, December 1970: n.p.

Steele, Mike. "Modern Dance Hits State Milestone." *Minneapolis Tribune*, February circa 1973: n.p.

Stewart, Phyllis. "Ailey . . . Magic in the Dance." *Long Island Press*, 17 August 1975: 1–3.

Stoop, Norma McLain. "AAADT City Center, N.Y., Dec. 3, 1981." *Dance Magazine*, March 1982: 98–102.

———. "Of Time and Alvin Ailey." *Dance Magazine*, December 1971: 28–32.

Supree, Burt. "Satyrs in Squaresville." *Village Voice*, 14 December 1982: 118.

Terry, Walter. "Ailey, Butler, Horton." *New York Herald Tribune*, 28 November 1960: n.p.

———. "Alvin Ailey Dance Troupe: Stunning." *New York Herald Tribune*, 18 December 1965: n.p.

———. "Dancing Incidental—And Very Brief." *World Journal Tribune*, 17 September, 1966, 22.

———. "Festival in Brooklyn." *Saturday Review,* 13 December 1969: 49.

———. "Met Ballet Plans: Ailey, Nikolais." *New York Herald Tribune*, 7 February 1960: n.p.

———. "To The Negro Dance." *New York Herald Tribune*, 28 January 1940: 10.

———. "Two Negro Dance Leaders." *Saturday Review*, 10 February 1968: n.p.

Tobias, Tobi. "Mixed Feelings." *New York*, 20 December 1982: n.p.

———. "Ode to a Fisherman." *New York*, 21 December 1981: 74–75.

Todd, Arthur. "Dance: Riches." *New York Times,* 2 July 1961: 24.

———. "Two-way Passage for Dance." *Dance Magazine*, July 1962: 39–41.

———. "The Rebekah Harkness Foundation Dance Festival." *Ballet News*, October 1962: 122.

Tucker, Marilyn. "Ailey's Mix of Message and Fun." *San Francisco Chronicle*, 13 February 1984: n.p.

"2 World Premieres at Ballet Theater." *New York Times*, 15 June 1972: 47.

Van Vechten, Carl. "Eloquent Alvin Ailey." *Dance* 62 (1963): 26–28.

Vaughan, David. "Alvin Ailey: Revelations, and More Revelations." *Dance Magazine*, February 1975: 38–41.

Wallach, Maya. "Gary DeLoatch Brings the Street to the Stage." *New York City Tribune*, 16 December 1988: n.p.

Watt, Douglas. "British Dancer Plays J. Joplin in Rock Ballet." *New York Daily News*, 26 January 1971: n.p.

Wessells, Frances. "Dance." *Richmond Times-Dispatch*, 11 February 1970: n.p.

Williams, Julinda Lewis. "Ailey's New Phases: Jazz in Motion." *Black American* (1980?): n.p.

Williams, Peter. "Blues and All That Jazz: First View." *Dance and Dancers*, November 1964: 20–23.

———. "Two Looks at Harkness." *Dance and Dancers*, April 1965: 14–18.

Williams, Peter, and Noel Goodwin. "More Ailey Revelations." *Dance and Dancers*, August 1973: 29–34.

Wilson, Arthur. "Special Tribute to Alvin Ailey and the Alvin Ailey American Dance Theater on Its 30th Anniversary: A Million Roses Celebrating Champions." *Attitude* (winter 1989): 37–76.

Winer, Linda. "A Lovely 'Landscape.'" *New York Daily News*, December 1981: 52.

Winfrey, Lee. "Want a Thanksgiving Treat?" *Philadelphia Inquirer*, 28 November 1974: n.p.

Wright, Damon. "Black Integrity, Black Chic." *Soho Weekly News,* November 1978: n.p.

Yamaki, Akihiko. "Impressive with Negro 'Blood.'" *Hochi Shumbun*, 21 April 1962.

Programs and Videography

All programs are housed in the archives of the Alvin Ailey American Dance Theater, 211 West 61st Street, New York, New York. All rehearsal and archival performance videotapes are housed in the archives of the Alvin Ailey American Dance Theater, or at the Dance Collection of the Library and Museum of the Performing Arts at Lincoln Center in New York. The following videotaped performances of Ailey's choreography were professionally produced and are available commercially or at the Dance Collection of the Library and Museum of the Performing Arts at Lincoln Center.

Ailey Dances. Videotape. Produced by James Lipton Productions and ABC Video Enterprises. Directed by Tim Kiley. 1982. Includes *Night Creature*, *Cry*, *The Lark Ascending*, and *Revelations*.

The Alvin Ailey American Dance Theater: Steps Ahead. Producer and director: Thomas Grimm; coproducer: Margaret Selby; host: Judith Jamison. Includes *For Bird—With Love*. Telecast on Thirteen/WNET's Great Performances: Dance in America series 8 February 1991.

Alvin Ailey: Memories and Visions. Produced by Ellis Haizlip and Alonzo Brown Jr. for WNET/13, 1974. Directed by Stan Lathan. Includes excerpts from *Blues Suite*, *The Lark Ascending*, *Mary Lou's Mass*, *Cry*, *Love Songs*, *Hidden Rites*, and *Revelations*.

Americans All. Documentary. Narrator: Melba Tolliver. 1974.

An Evening with Alvin Ailey American Dance Theater. Produced and directed by Thomas Grimm, 1986. Includes *Cry* and *Revelations*.

Going Home: Alvin Ailey Remembered. A production of WNET/Thirteen. Producers: Steven Weinstock, Kevin Cosgrove, and Andrew Carl Wilk; director: Andrew Carl Wilk. 1989.

In the Company of Alvin Ailey. Telecast on WNET-TV's *Skyline* series. Producer: Alonzo F. Brown Jr.; director: Jon Merdin; host: Harry Belafonte. Interview with Ailey, 1978.

Jazz City. Italian television production with excerpts from *Cry*, *Blues Suite*, *Survivors*, *For Bird—With Love*, *Night Creature*, and *Revelations*. 1988.

Like It Is. Telecast on January 30, 1971 by WABC-TV. Producer Charles Hobson; director: Dan Fanelli. Panel discussion by Katherine Dunham, Eleo Pomare, Carole Johnson, Alvin Ailey, and program host Gil Noble.

On Being Black. Producer: Luther James; director: Kirk Browning. Includes *Revelations*. Telecast on WGBH-TV in May 1969.

Profile: Alvin Ailey. Produced by ARC Videodance as part of the television series *Eye on Dance*. Producers: Celia Ipiotis and Jeff Bush; video director: Richard Sheridan; program director: Celia Ipiotis. Telecast 7 October 1989.

Revelations. Producer Pamela Ilott; director Martin Carr. Telecast on *Lamp Unto My Feet*, WCBS-TV, New York, 4 March 1962.

Riedaiglia. Associate producer: Marian Horosko; narrator: John Beal. Telecast by WNET/13, New York, 6 June 1971 on its series *Fanfare*.

Rocka My Soul. Made-for-television documentary on the Alvin Ailey American Dance Theater. Producer/director: Gordon Kelly; interviewer: Yvonne Barkley. Includes excerpts of *Blues Suite* and *Revelations*. 1967.

Three by Three. Directed by Patricia Birch. Includes excerpts of *Blues Suite* and *Revelations*. Telecast on WNET/Channel 13, 18 October 1985.

A Tribute to Alvin Ailey. Coproduced by Danmarks Radio and RM Arts; Producer/director: Thomas Grimm, 1990. Includes *For Bird—With Love*, *Witness*, and *Memoria*.

The Turning Point. Director: Herbert Ross. Screenplay by Arthur Laurents. Twentieth-Century Fox Studios. Includes "Vortex" from *The River.* 1977.

Miscellany

All miscellany may be found in the archives of the Alvin Ailey American Dance Theater, 211 West 61st Street, New York, New York, or at the Kansas City Mid-Atlantic Black Archives, 2033 Vine Street, Kansas City, Missouri.

Ailey, Alvin, et al. "Grant Proposal for Dance Theater Foundation." Looseleaf notes, dated June 1965.

"Alvin Ailey American Dance Theater." United States State Department Documents. N.d.

"Alvin Ailey Memories and Visions." *WNET* Press release. May 1974.

"Company Itinerary." Tunisia tour. 22 July–2 August 1970.

Continuing Revelations. Symposium sponsored by New York Public Library, May 1993.

Dance, Stanley. "Duke Ellington 1899–1974." CD liner notes, *The Symphonic Ellington.* Santa Monica, CA: Discovery Records, 1992.

"Dance Riot in Brooklyn." Ailey Company press release, 18 June 1969.

Johnson, Hall, et al. *Revelations.* Vocal score. Looseleaf compilation of photocopied musical arrangements, dated 1973. Some selections include original publishers and dates.

National Endowment for the Arts. *Annual Report* 1970.

Revelations: The Friends of Alvin Ailey. In-house newsletter, spring 1978.

"Reviews Excerpted by the Press and Program Office of Tokyo American Cultural Center," by Shigeo Goda, Sumio Kambayashi, and Akihiko Yamaki. Translated by Sumio Kambayashi, 1962.

"Tentative Outline Proposal to Foundations for a Development Grant." June 1965.

Interviews

Interview with Sarita Allen. 25 January 1997, Dallas, TX.

Interview with Marilyn Borde. 8 March 1995, New York.

Interview with Carole Johnson. 20 January 1995, Philadelphia.

Interview with Stanley Perryman. 18 January 1996, Seattle.

Interview with James Truitte. 8 November 1994, Cincinnati.

Interview with Dudley Williams. 16 May 1997, New York.